THE MODERN REPUBLICAN PARTY IN FLORIDA

PETER DUNBAR AND MIKE HARIDOPOLOS

UNIVERSITY PRESS OF FLORIDA

Gainesville Tallahassee Tampa Boca Raton
Pensacola Orlando Miami Jacksonville Ft. Myers Sarasota

This book may be available in an electronic edition.

24 23 22 21 20 19   6 5 4 3 2 1

Library of Congress Control Number: 2019932365
ISBN 978-0-8130-6612-7

The University Press of Florida is the scholarly publishing agency for the State University System of Florida, comprising Florida A&M University, Florida Atlantic University, Florida Gulf Coast University, Florida International University, Florida State University, New College of Florida, University of Central Florida, University of Florida, University of North Florida, University of South Florida, and University of West Florida.

University Press of Florida
2046 NE Waldo Road
Suite 2100
Gainesville, FL 32609
http://upress.ufl.edu

CONTENTS

1

FOUNDATION OF FLORIDA'S POLITICAL HISTORY

FLORIDA HAS A LONG and varied political history. Today, we know Florida as the third-most-populous state in the Union, growing at a rate of nearly one thousand residents each day, and as Florida's population has grown and its voter demographics have changed, its political influence on the national scene also has grown.[1] For more than a century, its state governmental infrastructure—both legislative and executive—was controlled by Democrats, but by the beginning of the twenty-first century, the infrastructure of governance was solidly in the control of Republicans. What was once an unquestioned state for the Democrats in all respects for the better part of the twentieth century is now considered the bellwether state in presidential elections. What was considered part of the Democratic "Solid South" in state politics has now become a Republican stronghold, and Florida was the first southern state to make this transition into the modern era.[2] In historical terms, this political transformation has occurred in a relatively short span of time, and to understand the shift in party dominance from the Democrats to the Republicans, the context of Florida's political and social history provides relevant insights on how and why it occurred.[3]

"Because of its history," writes Matthew Corrigan in his book about Republican Governor Jeb Bush, "a conservative political tradition collides with an ever-changing diverse population in the state of Florida to produce a unique political makeup."[4]

Population translates to people, and the people who assembled under the Republican banner in the last half of the twentieth century to usher in the two-party era in Florida politics were not just the marquee names who captured victories in the race for governor or won seats to represent Florida in Washington, D.C. They included the individuals who volunteered as part of the Republican Party organization; they joined the clubs that carried the Republican banner; they were candidates who offered themselves for local city and county offices; and they were the men and women who came to the Florida House and Senate to serve as part-time citizen legislators.

In less than a half century, Republicans transformed the political landscape and ushered in a new era with new leaders; they created a new structure for governance; and they championed a political dogma that changed long-standing government policies. They organized; they created an ever-expanding network of people; they built an organization that grew and matured from within; and they invited disenchanted voters from the traditional Democratic ranks to join them as the Republicans assumed the reins of power in the state capital. It was a political transformation that was, in many ways, unique, and from its early beginnings, it was a transformation that was both unlikely and unforeseen.

Few in Florida's early history contemplated such enviable population growth, nor was there an expectation that the state would find itself in a political transition that ushered its voters into the epicenter of the nation's politics. Initially, Florida was not a part of the Founding colonists' efforts that culminated in the creation of the United States; and the European explorers who first explored Florida's coast near the end of the fifteenth century were the Spanish. Juan Ponce de León gave Florida its name in 1513, and the Spanish established the first permanent European settlement at St. Augustine, where they fortified it by constructing the Castillo de San Marcos, an elaborate and imposing fort that the British were never able to conquer with military force.[5] Despite its early settlement by the Spanish, however, Florida remained a political chess piece in the interplay between the two nations for nearly two centuries.

When the French and Indian War ended in 1763, the British gained possession of the Castillo de San Marcos and all of Florida, but this occurred in a negotiated settlement. British rule and influence in Florida were short-lived, however. Twenty years later, when the Treaty of Paris ended the American Revolution, the British Crown surrendered most of its North American possessions; the thirteen colonies became the United States; Spain regained control of the Florida Territory; and almost seven decades would pass before Florida joined the other colonies as a part of the United States.[6] In the interim before statehood, the Florida Territory became a pawn in three wars and an occasional passing reference in the political events and personalities of its neighbors to the north.

Territorial Political Roots

The state became an arcane footnote in the political struggles of the new nation in 1804, when Aaron Burr fled to the South and sailed down the St. Johns River while corresponding with the Spanish governor of Florida after killing Founding Father Alexander Hamilton in a duel.[7] Three years later, Burr was arrested for treason and accused of planning to form an empire out of the territories around the Gulf of Mexico, including Texas and Florida; the plan was never realized.[8]

Florida remained in undisturbed Spanish control and on the political fringe of the new nation until the War of 1812. Yet there was interest in Florida, and even before the U.S. Congress declared war against the British, President James Madison and his secretary of state, James Monroe, considered plans to seize territorial Florida from Spanish control. A government secret agent, General George Mathews, was dispatched to the Florida-Georgia border by the Madison administration with instructions to promote an attack into Florida by armed frontiersmen, and as the war against the British began, many of the southern activists in the region also saw the conflict as an opportunity for territorial expansion into Florida.[9] Fearing that the British might seize Florida if the United States failed to act quickly, the frontiersmen, covertly supported by the U.S. military, seized the important port of Fernandina and besieged the Spanish fortifications at St. Augustine.

However, when the Spanish minister in Washington complained and the Congress also took notice, President Madison, fully preoccupied with the British aggression, quietly reversed course and ordered the withdrawal of American military forces from the territory, and Florida once again became an irrelevant afterthought in the nation's politics.

These initial border skirmishes helped to convince Spain that Florida was not defensible in the long term, however; and Spain's weakness grew more apparent in 1817 and 1818, when President James Monroe sent Andrew Jackson to Georgia to secure its border with Florida.[10] Spain had failed to prevent Indians in Florida from conducting raids on Georgia settlements, and Florida had become an inviting refuge for runaway slaves from the adjacent southern states. After his arrival, Jackson not only defeated the Indians in the First Seminole War but also attacked Pensacola and overthrew the Spanish governor.[11] While some in Monroe's administration urged censure of Jackson, Secretary of State John Quincy Adams used the events to pressure Spain to cede the Florida Territory to the United States.[12]

Faced with its declining strength in the Americas and uprisings among its other South American possessions, Spain acquiesced to Adams's pressure, and as part of the Adams-Onis Treaty in 1819, the United States acquired territorial Florida from Spain for $5 million.[13] No money actually changed hands under the terms of the treaty because the United States simply assumed the debts owed by the Spanish government to American citizens.[14] The terms of the Adams-Onis Treaty were ratified by the U.S. Congress in 1821, and when the first territorial government for Florida was put into place, it was headed by the hero of the Battle of New Orleans and future U.S. President Andrew Jackson.[15] Jackson became the first of three future U.S. presidents to find temporary assignment in Florida, where their roles enhanced their individual political résumés, but none left behind a meaningful legacy for the state's political future.

From 1835 to 1842, territorial Florida was immersed in the Second Seminole War. The Indian Removal Act of 1830 and the Treaty of Payne's Landing in 1832 required the Indians to evacuate Florida by 1835. When many Seminoles retreated into the tropical swamps of south Florida instead of relocating, it brought the second future president of the country, Zachary

Taylor, to the state. Taylor was tasked to lead the federal troops in Florida to enforce the terms of the Indian Removal Act. Colonel Taylor's troops spent seven years fighting under his command, and during that period the wilderness Territory of Florida was explored and mapped; roads and forts were built; tens of thousands of American citizens were employed in military and civilian capacities; and the Armed Forces Act of 1842 encouraged the permanent settlement of Florida.[16]

The Armed Forces Act allotted 160 acres to each homesteader able to defend it and reside on the acreage for at least five years, and under these provisions of the act, the promotion of Florida began. With the incentives to relocate to the territory, the ever-changing population demographics that would lead to the state's unique political makeup began to take root.

The Blueprints of Governance and the Capitol

The U.S. Congress enacted the Territorial Act in 1838, and the act called for the selection of delegates to begin work on Florida's first constitution and to provide for the design of the political structure to govern the territory's growing population. From December 3, 1838, until January 11, 1839, delegates met and deliberated in the city of Saint Joseph, near present-day Port St. Joe in Gulf County, to complete their task.[17] The new constitution from the convention of delegates provided for a governor to head the executive branch, a legislative branch that consisted of a Senate and a General Assembly, and a judicial branch with several levels of courts; the governmental structure was not unlike that of present-day Florida.

The constitution authorized the governor to serve a single four-year term, and it provided that the governor was ineligible for reelection—deliberate constitutional features that were preserved in Florida with only a brief intermission until 1968. From the outset, the governor's selection coincided with the election of the nation's president, but a change in 1964 in the statewide election to the off-years from presidential elections reversed the political fortunes of the time and contributed to a permanent change in the state's political landscape.[18]

The legislative branch created by the delegates in 1839 remains structurally the same in the modern era, with two bodies—a Senate and House of Representatives—but the political considerations for the geographical composition of individual districts in each chamber are different in the modern era.[19] The state's initial constitution left to the Legislature the political considerations for the district configurations and district boundary lines, and these political considerations remained a legislative prerogative in the constitution of 1885.[20] It was not until 1967 that the districts in both legislative bodies were required to be apportioned on population groupings of substantially equal size and without regard to other political factors that had been previously considered.[21] This mandate, too, reversed political fortunes and brought permanent changes to the political landscape in Florida's capital city.

Tallahassee was established as the territorial capital in 1823.[22] It was considered an attractive area centrally located between the main population centers of the time, Pensacola and St. Augustine, and for the first few years, government business in the capital was conducted in three log cabins.[23] The first Capitol Building to house the governmental functions in Tallahassee was constructed in 1826 on the highland area where the modern Capitol complex is situated. The core of the current complex, called the Old Capitol, was not built until 1902, more than fifty years after statehood, and today's modern Capitol Building—now occupied by a Republican administration and Republican majorities in both Houses of the Legislature—was not completed until 1977.[24]

On March 3, 1845, during his final day in office, President John Tyler signed the legislation that admitted Florida into the Union as the nation's twenty-seventh state.[25] Florida, a slave state, was accompanied into the Union by Iowa, a free state, maintaining the era's national balance of power between slave and free states.[26] After gaining statehood status, the internal infrastructure improvements continued, and in Brevard County, for example, the Army Corps of Engineers dug the Haulover Canal to connect the Indian River to Mosquito Lagoon and built a sixty-five-foot wooden lighthouse at Cape Canaveral.[27] In 1849, the state finalized construction of the Hernandez-Capron Trail connecting St. Augustine to Fort Pierce, and more than a century later, the Interstate 95 corridor followed the same alignment.[28]

As Florida made the transition from territorial status to statehood, its population continued to grow. From roughly 35,000 residents in 1830, the number of permanent Floridians increased to more than 140,000 by 1860, and the population mix among the citizenry in the new state was divided approximately fifty-fifty between white and nonwhite residents.[29]

Statehood and the Civil War

In partisan political terms, the Democratic Party dominated Florida from the time of statehood in 1845 until well past the middle of the twentieth century, interrupted only by the political upheaval of the Reconstruction era following the Civil War. When the nation's two-party system first emerged in the 1790s, the Federalists were centered chiefly in the North, whereas Democratic-Republicans, inspired by Thomas Jefferson's agrarian, political philosophy, dominated the South. As the Missouri Compromise allowed the admission of more new states and made slavery an increasingly controversial political issue, southern states rallied around the Democratic Party to defend their "peculiar institution" of slavery.[30] It was no surprise that Florida, whose first permanent American settlers were southerners crossing the border from Georgia and Alabama, adopted the political views of the other southern states, becoming part of the Democratic "Solid South." Following the election of Abraham Lincoln in 1860, stark political differences between the North and South plunged the nation into civil war, and the conflict became the catalyst for political change.

On November 26, 1860, Florida governor Madison S. Perry called up the General Assembly to consider seceding from the Union. In January 1861, the General Assembly convened in Tallahassee to consider the governor's call, and January 10, 1861, following the lead of South Carolina and Mississippi, the delegates voted 62 to 7 in favor of secession.[31] Even before the war's first shots rang out at Fort Sumter in South Carolina, federal troops stationed in Florida retreated to Fort Pickens on Santa Rosa Island. For over a year after the hostilities began, Union forces held fast against the Confederate siege of Fort Pickens until the attacking forces were called off to join the main Confederate army. Fort Pickens, like St. Augustine, remained in Union hands for the duration of the Civil War.[32]

Few Civil War battles were actually fought in Florida, and Tallahassee was the only state capital east of the Mississippi River never captured by advancing Union armies before hostilities ended in 1865. Over the war's duration, more than fifteen thousand Floridians fought for the Confederacy. Although this was a small number compared with the numbers of soldiers from the other Confederate states, Florida contributed a greater percentage of its able-bodied population than any of the other southern states. Perhaps Florida's most significant contribution to the Confederate cause consisted of raw materials and supplies, such as beef, pork, fish, fruit, molasses, and salt.[33] By war's end, one-third of the Floridians who fought for the Confederacy had died in the fighting, and many of the others returned home ill or injured.

A minority of Florida residents, particularly those in the coastal towns whose livelihoods depended on northern trade, remained loyal to the Union throughout the Civil War, but by the war's end most Floridians were relieved by the return of peace regardless of who had won. On May 10, 1865, Union troops occupied Tallahassee and raised the American flag over the state Capitol, and Florida resumed its place in the Union under the national Republican administration of President Andrew Johnson.[34]

Republicans and the Reconstruction Era

With President Johnson appointing a new Florida governor in the summer of 1865, Republicans made their first appearance in the state and assumed control of the state's governmental institutions. With the arrival of the Republicans, the Reconstruction era in Florida and in the South began. These postwar years of Reconstruction served as the only break in the dominance of the Democratic Party rule in Florida that otherwise lasted well over a century. During the break from Democrat dominance, however, Florida Republicans oversaw the state's contribution to the political changes that revised the U.S. Constitution in three meaningful ways and redefined the foundations of political governance.

These Reconstruction-era Republican initiatives began in the U.S. Congress, and they were subsequently ratified by the requisite number of states, including Florida.[35] The initiatives abolished slavery under the provisions of the Thirteenth Amendment to the nation's Constitution; guaranteed equal protection under the law for all citizens under the mandate of the Fourteenth Amendment to the Constitution; and secured the right to vote for African Americans with the ratification of the Fifteenth Amendment to the Constitution. Each of the amendments had its societal impact, and none had more impact on the eventual realignment of political power in Florida than the Fourteenth Amendment. Nearly a century after its ratification, the equal protection clause of the Fourteenth Amendment became the basis for population-based districts in state legislative bodies across the country, and the implementation of this "one-person, one-vote" principle in Florida became a significant contributing factor to the Republican reemergence long after their reign during the Reconstruction era had ended.[36]

Most southerners viewed the Reconstruction era as the rule of "carpetbaggers" from the North and "scalawags" from the South. Northern carpetbaggers flocked to the South for various reasons. Some were Civil War veterans who had fought for the Union in the South. Others were politicians, businessmen, and abolitionists who saw southern Reconstruction as an opportunity for self-promotion, investment, or social and economic renewal.[37] The carpetbaggers united with the scalawags, who were native to the South and partial to the Union cause, and together they joined with newly enfranchised blacks to solidify Republican dominance during the Reconstruction era. It was a political coalition that held no kinship with the political leaders who had preceded it or with the political leaders who followed.

End of the Era, Return of Democratic Dominance,
and a New Constitution

The dominance of the Republican coalition during Reconstruction was short-lived. In the 1876 presidential election, Samuel J. Tilden, a New York

Democrat, won 51 percent of the national popular vote, while Rutherford B. Hayes, an Ohio Republican, won only 48 percent of the vote. Tilden also led in the undisputed electoral votes by a 19-vote margin, 184 to 165, but 20 electoral votes from the South, including Florida's 4 electoral votes, remained in dispute.[38] It was the first time, but certainly not the last, that the state's electoral votes held the nation's presidency in doubt. In addition to Florida, the other disputed electoral votes were from Louisiana and South Carolina, and among the charges questioning the validity of the popular vote in these states were accusations of fraud, intimidation, and corruption.[39] Unlike the presidential race in 2000, there were no "hanging chads" in 1876, but the Florida Supreme Court did order a recount of the votes, and the recount favored a disputed victory for Republican Rutherford B. Hayes.[40]

Congress appointed a fifteen-member Electoral Commission to ultimately resolve the dispute in all of the states, and after the commission's deliberations, the recount in Florida was agreed to, and all 20 electoral votes from the three states—and consequentially the presidency—were awarded to Hayes.[41] In return, Hayes pledged to end the era of Reconstruction, and fulfilling his pledge after assuming office, Hayes ordered the withdrawal of the federal troops from all the southern states including Florida. With the withdrawal of the troops, political power in the southern states returned almost immediately to the Democrats, leaving a bitter and lasting Republican legacy from the era with the new political leadership.[42]

The Republican carpetbaggers and scalawags who came to power following the Civil War were seen as plunderers and con artists by native Floridians, according to political science professor Matthew Corrigan, and "for a century these feelings would make it difficult for the Republican Party to be an accepted political party in the state."[43] As a result, the ensuing decades saw the contests for political power in Florida take place among factions in the Democratic Party, and there were no meaningful Republican voices to be heard in the state's political arena.

In the 1880s and 1890s, farmers throughout the southeastern and midwestern United States coalesced to form the Populist reform movement. In

Florida, this Populist movement represented an alliance between discontented farmers and progressive blacks unhappy with the status quo, but it included no nexus to the Republican Party, and it did not directly challenge the Democratic establishment. The splinter movement experienced only limited success under the Democratic banner, and only a few Florida politicians, among them Governor Napoleon Bonaparte Broward, incorporated the Populist notions into their political platforms, and the administration of Governor Broward was a "stormy one."[44]

Broward championed farmers, labor, and small businesses; he worked to drain the Everglades; and he became an advocate for an eight-hour workday.[45] Most other state Democratic leaders, however, were alarmed by the participation of black citizens in Florida politics, and the Legislature responded to their participation with the passage of the so-called Jim Crow laws. The Jim Crow initiatives included literacy tests, poll taxes, multiple ballots, and segregated education that effectively brought an end to the Populist movement.[46] Though the most oppressive of these laws were repealed by the Legislature in the 1930s, the resulting social structure they created remained in place in Florida and in most of the South until the 1960s.

As the vestiges of Reconstruction began to disappear, Florida voters approved a new state constitution 1885, and while it preserved the three branches of government of its predecessor, the power of the executive branch of state government was diluted and shared among the offices of seven statewide elected executives—the governor, secretary of state, attorney general, comptroller, superintendent of public instruction, commissioner of agriculture, and treasurer and insurance commissioner—sitting as the Florida cabinet.[47] The governor remained limited to a single term in office, but there were no limits on the terms of service of the other members of the cabinet, leaving the state's chief executive one of the nation's weakest when compared to other states.[48] The effect was to keep the keys of power in the grip of the Legislature rather than the executive branch.[49] In time, this vestige from the post-Reconstruction era and the Democrat majority status in the Legislature presented unique challenges for Florida Republicans when their voices began to reemerge in the modern political era.

A New Surge in Population

During the post–Reconstruction era and the return to Democratic dominance in state affairs, Florida began to experience renewed growth, as well as
other economic changes. Between 1877 and 1897, the miles of rail tracks in
the state increased more than sixfold, from 485 miles to 3,149 miles, and in
the process the rail corridors provided the catalyst for a new spurt of population growth.[50] Henry Flagler led other major industrialists from the North
to Florida in search of new opportunities for development. Flagler, who
helped to found and form Standard Oil in the mid-1860s, opened hotels
in St. Augustine, Jacksonville, Ormond Beach, Palm Beach, and eventually
Miami.[51] To transport his tourists to these hotels, Flagler purchased an existing railroad in northeast Florida, extended it southward, and renamed it the
Florida East Coast Railway.[52] By 1912, Flagler's railroad reached Key West
and had established Florida as a principal tourist destination for wealthy
Americans from other parts of the country.[53]

On the state's west coast, Henry Plant spurred the development of the
Tampa Bay region in a similar fashion when he formed the South Florida
Railroad.[54] Plant's railroad established lines from Jacksonville in northeast
Florida to the Gulf of Mexico by way of Live Oak to Tampa via Kissimmee.[55] In time, beachside resorts and population centers emerged around
the new infrastructure of both rail corridors; the new residents from other
parts of the country settling there brought a different political perspective
with them; and it was around these emerging coastal hubs where small pockets of Republicanism began to take root as the new century arrived.

In 1898, during the civil war between Spain and its colony in Cuba, the
USS *Maine* mysteriously exploded in Havana Harbor. Following the sinking
of the *Maine*, the United States entered the conflict, and Florida became the
training ground for American forces preparing to embark for Cuba. Once
more, the influx of military personnel became a catalyst to spur growth in
the state. The U.S. military established camps in Tampa, Jacksonville, Fernandina, Pensacola, Lakeland, and, at the insistence of Henry Flagler, in the
infant town of Miami. Tampa received more than sixty thousand federal
troops during the conflict, and among these troops were the Rough Rid-

ers, led by yet another future U.S. president, Lieutenant Colonel Theodore Roosevelt.[56]

By the turn of the twentieth century, Florida's population stood at over a half-million people, and the automobile was also becoming a viable form of transportation for Americans, spurring roadways and related infrastructure construction. Entrepreneur Carl Fisher, a wealthy automobile enthusiast and founder of the Indianapolis Motor Speedway, created the "Dixie Highway," a network of north-south roadways from the Midwest to Miami.[57] In 1915, Fisher led a cavalcade of fifteen cars with great fanfare across the United States into Miami to feature the new mode of travel.[58] That same year, the Legislature created the State Road Department, predecessor of the Florida Department of Transportation, to organize the construction of the state's highway system, and more pathways into Florida began to emerge.[59] The transportation alternatives not only expanded the opportunities for Florida's existing industries that found markets in other states but also paved the way for two other phenomena that would forever shape Florida's future—the Great Florida Land Boom and tourism.

The Great Florida Land Boom began in 1920 after the end of World War I, and improved social and working conditions throughout the country enabled many Americans to visit Florida and relocate to the state as permanent residents. In only five years, from 1920 to 1925, Florida's population increased by more than one-third. Land speculation ran rampant, with even former Democratic presidential candidate William Jennings Bryan promoting Florida real estate.[60] In 1923, the state Legislature adopted the "homestead exemption" protections for residents and proposed a constitutional amendment, approved by the voters the following year, that prohibited a state income tax.[61] These initiatives, too, fueled the frenzy.

By 1925, as the speculation of the Great Florida Land Boom reached its height, the price of Florida real estate had grown unsustainably high; it discouraged the influx of new buyers; and the state's real estate market began to collapse. Mother Nature contributed to the collapse as well. After a severe winter in 1925, a powerful hurricane the following September tore through Miami and created a storm surge that reached thirty miles inland to Lake Okeechobee; in the process, it swallowed entire residential neighborhoods.

By the end of 1926, three years before the Great Depression enveloped the entire country, Florida's vibrant economic prosperity came to a virtual halt.[62] But there would be future growth spurts, and with the growth came new voters and changing demographics in the voter base.[63]

Despite both boom and bust in the early decades of the twentieth century, the Democratic Party continued to control Florida politics and elect its anointed candidates. Only once, in 1916, did the Democrats lose their grip on state politics and a firm hand on the governor's office. In that year, Sidney Catts, a boisterous Protestant preacher, narrowly lost in the Democratic primary and opted to run for governor as a third-party candidate on a platform opposing Catholics, corporations, and alcohol. Catts won the three-way election; he served four years as the only third-party governor in Florida's political history; and he was the first to crack the wall of solid Democratic dominance.[64]

The state also left the Democratic "Solid South" in the 1928 presidential election when its six electoral votes were delivered to Republican Herbert Hoover. In the same election year, William J. Howey, the Republican candidate for governor, managed to capture 39 percent of the vote total against Democrat Doyle Carlton. Although Carlton won the election comfortably, because Howey's percentage of the popular vote exceeded 30 percent of the vote total, the Republican Party achieved formal legal recognition under Florida's election code. The threshold vote total entitled the Republicans to official status as a political party, and it allowed Republicans the right to participate in the primary election process. In theory, Florida had become a two-party state in the eyes of the law; in actuality, however, Florida Republicans could not claim true two-party status for nearly four more decades.[65]

New Floridians and Changing Demographics

Florida's economy stagnated from the end of the Great Land Boom until the start of World War II, when Florida again stepped up to help with America's war efforts during the 1940s.[66] The U.S. military established massive training camps and flight schools throughout the state—in all, more than two hundred different facilities to support the nation's war efforts.[67] At Eglin

Field in Okaloosa County, Jimmy Doolittle and his pilots trained for their thirty-second raid over Tokyo; future members of the famous Black Sheep Squadron earned their wings in Jacksonville and Miami; soldiers trained in camps scattered throughout Florida for the battlefields in Europe; and U.S. Marines practiced amphibious landings along the coastline to prepare for assaults on islands in the Pacific.[68]

More than 250,000 Floridians served in the American armed forces during World War II, and Florida's ranchers and farmers supplied food to military personnel stationed at the many army and navy bases located across the state. In total, almost 2.2 million service and support personnel were stationed in Florida during various times throughout the war.[69] As with the nation's war efforts in earlier generations, the mobilization during World War II brought renewed growth to Florida and vibrancies back to the state's economy.[70] The expanded military presence in Florida during World War II also brought with it other ancillary benefits. It was a catalyst to accelerate the construction of roads and other infrastructure. It introduced thousands of new Americans to the state's beaches, its mild climate, and its welcoming coastal environment. And these factors, too, contributed to the return of Florida's postwar economic prosperity.

By the mid-1950s, air-conditioning became available to middle-class households, making the hot days of the summer months more tolerable.[71] The environment that had been attracting wealthy Americans since the turn of the century in the winter months now became available year-round for all Floridians.[72] The other timely innovations that promoted comfort for the state's residents were technologies for effective mosquito control. These new control technologies were in widespread use by the end of the 1940s, and the control efforts were enhanced and assisted by the military and its use of the pesticide DDT.[73] Use of the pesticide made it possible to control saltwater mosquitos and other pests, and it made possible year-round living on Florida's barrier islands.[74]

To accentuate the advantages of Florida living, Democrat Millard Caldwell, the state's post–World War II governor, promoted the creation of the Florida Department of Commerce. Caldwell also traveled the country, especially in the northern states, to market relocation to Florida and to attract new businesses and residents to the state.[75] His marketing travels promoted Florida's warm climate, its low taxes, and the state's right-to-work laws, which helped to cement Florida's initial pro-business credentials. By 1960, through a variety of factors, the state was once again experiencing rapid growth, and nearly two-thirds of the state's current residents had been born outside of Florida.[76]

At the beginning of the twentieth century, Florida was the nation's thirty-third-most-populous state, with slightly more than 500,000 residents. Only 20 percent of these residents lived in urban or suburban centers of population, and the majority of Floridians made their homes in the northern part of the state, many of them in rural communities.[77] By midcentury these population demographics and geographical living patterns had changed, however. As David R. Colburn and Susan A. MacManus described the transition that followed the end of the Second World War: "In less than an average life span today, Florida became by 2010 the most populous state in the region and the fourth-most-populous in the nation, a haven for seniors and foreign residents that boasts a dynamic multiracial and multiethnic culture. Most Floridians now reside closer to the Caribbean than they do to Georgia and, for most of them, their image of themselves and their state has changed dramatically to reflect the new geographic orientation."[78]

Amid these changing demographics, the improved infrastructure, the influx of new Florida residents, the immigration of refugees from Communist Cuba, and an improved economic environment, the modern Republican Party found fertile ground and began to plant its roots in the state's new and growing multiethnic population.

2

FOUNDATIONS OF EMERGING
REPUBLICANISM

EARNING OFFICIAL STATUS as a political party in 1928 along with the legal standing to conduct primary elections in Florida became the cornerstone for Republicans to build on their efforts to bring meaningful two-party status to the state's political landscape. It was to be two more decades of effort and organization before small pockets of Republican voters became noticeable majorities in a few Florida communities, and it took two additional decades before Republican officeholders were meaningful contributors to the governance process in the state's capital, but the process had begun in earnest. Once they had established their initial presence at the ballot box, Republican Party loyalists began to build an organization and voter support that enabled their candidates to take advantage of the schisms appearing in the ranks of the Democrats. Republicans were also beneficiaries of the legislative redistricting mandates from the U.S. Supreme Court.

In less than a decade following the end of World War II, Florida became the first southern state to enter the modern era of two-party politics—first in election campaigns for the nation's presidency and then in campaigns for control of the offices in the state capital.[1]

The Modern Era

The modern political era in Florida began midcentury, when the recognizable trends toward two-party politics manifested themselves in 1948, and five Florida counties actually delivered a majority of their votes for Republican Thomas Dewey in that year's presidential election.[2] Bigger breakthroughs followed within a decade after the first inroads had been made for Dewey. During the 1950s in both presidential elections, Florida voters delivered the state's electoral votes for the Republican nominee, and Florida sent its first Republican members to the U.S. Congress in the post-Reconstruction era.[3] In the 1960s, a Republican captured the governor's office for the first time; a Florida Republican was elected to the U.S. Senate for the first time; and, by the end of the 1960s, both Houses of the Florida Legislature had meaningful Republican minorities.[4]

The 1970s were in some ways a holding pattern for Republicans in terms of political gains at the state level. With a single exception, however, Florida's electoral votes continued to be counted for the Republican nominee in presidential elections; more of the party's candidates were elected to seats in the U.S. Congress; and Florida sent another Republican to Washington, D.C., as an elected member of the U.S. Senate.[5] During the 1980s, voters elected the Republican Party's second governor; gains in the Florida Senate pushed the Republicans closer to the majority in the upper chamber; and Republican Party candidates made the first inroads into the statewide-elected offices on the Florida cabinet.[6] Florida's transition into this new modern era of two-party politics came relatively quickly, and it brought the state into "a place of national prominence [in] less than a lifetime."[7]

Among the contributing factors during these decades of progress by Republicans were the increases and changes in the state's population; the periodic infighting between the candidates from the majority Democratic Party; and the intervention of the federal courts into the apportionment of legislative districts that had been previously considered a "political question" and outside the scope of the courts' jurisdiction. Initially, the "political question" was a legal mystery to most voters, but in time, legislative apportionment and each of the other factors provided opportunities for the expanded Republican presence in the state's political arena.[8] Each of the factors helped to usher in the new era of two-party politics in Florida.

Growth and Demographic Changes

Florida's history has been marked by spurts of rapid population growth by those relocating from other places to make Florida their home, and the impacts of these growth spurts contributed to the realignment of the partisan voting patterns in the state.[9]

In 1900, the state's population hovered slightly above 528,000 people, and the population in Florida increased by approximately 30 percent in each subsequent decade. By 1910, it had grown to 752,619; and by 1920, the population was nearing one million permanent residents.[10] During the 1920s, fueled by the Great Land Boom, Florida experienced a major boost in population, growing to 1,468,211 residents by 1930. By 1940, the state's population had reached 1,897,414 people, and the growth spurred by the in-migration of the military personnel and those supporting the war industries during World War II brought the state's population to 2.7 million residents by the presidential election year of 1952. In 1960, 4,951,560 permanent residents called the state home, and Florida had become the tenth-most-populous state in the country.[11]

During the first half of the century, there was another demographic phenomenon of note: the shift of the population centers from north Florida to the central and southern parts of the Florida peninsula along the rail corridors initially opened by Henry Flagler and Henry B. Plant. In 1900, two-thirds of the state's population lived in north Florida, and only 5 percent of the population called south Florida home. By 1950, the living patterns had reversed, and almost two-thirds of the state's residents lived in central and south Florida, leaving only one-third of the state's population in north Florida.[12] With this geographical population shift and the corresponding growth in raw numbers came the winds for political change.

In the context of these changes, political science professor V. O. Key in 1949 noted that there was a lack of structure and political organization in the dominant Democratic Party. Key also observed that Florida was a "political curiosity" because, unlike other one-party states, its one-party rule was maintained by a Democratic Party with little central organization, relying instead on factions led by individual Democratic politicians. "Florida is not only unbossed, it is unled," Key concluded. "Anything can happen in elections, and does."[13]

Key also noted three reasons for Florida's unusual political structure and why he predicted that it would progress differently from the rest of the South. According to Key, these were "a rapidly growing nonnative population, a highly diversified economy, [and] a highly urbanized population."[14] Amid these unusual demographics and the lack of cohesiveness within the Democratic majority, a path began to emerge for Republicans to become relevant players in Florida politics. In part, the recurring fractures in the solidarity of the Democratic Party were a significant contributing factor to the emerging pathway.

"Alongside the tremendous demographic changes that persisted throughout the 1950s," wrote political scientist David Colburn in 2007 in his book about the state's changing political landscape, "the civil rights developments and massive resistance of that era redefined Florida and its politics. These dramatic developments splintered the state Democratic Party, helped pave the way for the emergence of the Republican Party in Florida, and made the state a centerpiece in the battle between the two parties for state and national dominance."[15]

Cracks in the Democratic Party Wall

While Republicans struggled for a toehold in Florida politics as the twentieth century passed its halfway mark, the previously unchallenged and strong foothold of the majority-party Democrats began to show signs of fracturing. The growing factions began with philosophical differences between rural Democratic loyalists and those Democrats who were clustering in the growing urban and suburban centers.[16] Geographically, the split was perceived generally to be between north and south. Philosophically, the split was between those who were self-proclaimed conservatives and those whom the conservative Democrats considered to have liberal leanings more aligned with Democrats from other parts of the country.[17]

As consistent growth accentuated the changing population demographics, the philosophical differences in the Democratic Party between the factions became more pronounced in the state's political arena. As Florida Republicans began to make their voices heard in the national presidential elections, the differences in philosophy between conservative and liberal Democrats at the state level became more pronounced. Little regard was given, however, to how the infighting between the Democrats during the primary might affect the outcome of contests with Republicans in the general election. In the initial years of the modern era, the differences in the Democratic primaries didn't seem to matter.[18]

In 1950, the Democratic primary race for a seat in U.S. Senate garnered notoriety statewide as the opposing campaign rhetoric focused on the liberal and conservative philosophies of the candidates. The primary election featured challenger George Smathers, claiming the conservative mantle for the Democrats, and the incumbent, U.S. Senator Claude Pepper. Pepper, who had served as a member of the Senate since 1936, ran defending his record as a "New Dealer" on a liberal platform forged during the presidency of Franklin Roosevelt. Smathers counterattacked the Pepper legacy based on Pepper's ties to the nation's labor unions; Pepper's continued support for more federal spending; and Smathers's claim that Pepper was soft on communism, using campaign ads that labeled the incumbent senator "Red Pepper."[19] Capitalizing on his conservative claims with Florida voters, Smathers won the bitter Democratic contest. The divisive primary battle with Pepper had no carryover effect in the general election, however, and Smathers comfortably defeated his Republican opposition in the general election to become the state's new U.S. senator.[20]

Four years later, the "liberal/conservative" schism among the Democrats surfaced again—this time in the battle for the Democratic nomination in the special election for governor between Charley Johns and LeRoy Collins. As the Senate president in 1953, Johns was next in the line of succession when Governor Daniel McCarty died in office that year because Florida had no lieutenant governor, and Johns assumed the governorship until the special election could be held the following year.[21] In the 1954 Democratic primary election, Collins stepped forward to challenge Johns and his philosophical following, and the debate of contrasts within the Democratic Party was renewed.

Charley Johns was born in Starke in rural north Florida and claimed the "conservative" label during the campaign. He initially had been elected to the House of Representatives in 1935, but after one term, he moved on to the state Senate, where he served until 1966 with the exception of the short period when he served as the state's acting governor.[22] His "conservative" political views on segregation, legislative apportionment, and other policies followed those attributed to traditional Democrats from the "Solid South," and these became the planks in his campaign platform in 1954.

"Johns epitomized everything conservative about Southern Democrats," wrote author and political science professor Matthew T. Corrigan. "He was from a small rural county and a strong supporter of segregation."[23]

Collins's background and his philosophy were different. He was born in Tallahassee, and his views contrasted sharply with those of Johns. He attended New York's Eastman School of Business; he received his law degree from Cumberland University; and he was elected to the Florida House in 1936 at the age of twenty-five and to the Florida Senate in 1940.[24] He resigned from the Legislature to serve in the U.S. Navy during World War II, and he was reelected to the state Senate when he returned from his naval service in 1946. Collins was known for his work in the areas of women's rights and labor, and for his commitment to strengthen and modernize Florida's school system.[25] In the Democratic primary election, LeRoy Collins was the clear philosophical alternative to Charley Johns.

The two candidates went after each other hard in the primary, with Johns framing Collins as a lawyer serving the needs of big corporations, and with Collins framing Johns as governing by "cronyism" among his like-minded colleagues. Collins led the business progressive faction of the Democratic Party into the primary election and urged Floridians to build a new state based firmly on an urban, diversified economy, and his approach presented a distinct contrast to the rural alliances of Johns.[26]

Johns and his rural allies from the Legislature became known as the "Pork Chop Gang," a name brilliantly coined by *Tampa Tribune* editor James Clendinen. The segregationist views of Johns and his followers were much different from those of Collins, a "southern moderate," and his followers.[27] The two candidates contrasted on issues of policy—notably fair legislative apportionment, race, and civil rights—offering Democratic voters a clear philosophical choice in the primary election. When the primary concluded, Collins and his policy positions prevailed, and he went on to face Republican J. Tom Watson in the general election. Watson was not a meaningful factor in the 1954 general election, and LeRoy Collins easily won the governor's chair despite the deeply divisive primary battle that he had fought with Johns.

The liberal-conservative divide in the Smathers-Pepper primary race and the Johns-Collins campaign did not resurface in the elections of either 1956 or 1960. In 1956 Collins repeated his success, winning renomination without significant Democratic infighting and then besting Republican William A. Washburn in the general election, amassing more than 73 percent of the popular vote.[28] In 1960, no Democratic candidate for governor stepped forward to claim the "moderate/liberal" label. Farris Bryant won the nomination from among a field of six other self-proclaimed conservative Democrats that included Jacksonville Mayor Haydon Burns, and Bryant comfortably defeated the Republican nominee, George C. Peterson, in the 1960 November general election.[29]

After two statewide election cycles of relative calm, however, the schism in the Democratic ranks returned in the bitter primary election contests between Haydon Burns and Robert King High that were held in 1964 and 1966. In the primary battles between Burns and High, the political wounds cut deep into Democratic solidarity, and the resulting political damage did not heal before the 1966 November general elections.[30] The schism that remained became part of the foundation of the Republican reemergence in the modern era, but it was preceded by a change in the timing of statewide elections for governor and members of the cabinet that was also significant.

Stepping onto the National Stage

While the philosophical split among Democratic factions festered in the races for statewide office, another political phenomenon materialized among the Florida voters. With the sole exception of the 1928 presidential election, when Florida's electoral votes went to Republican Herbert Hoover, the state had been a consistent part of the Democratic "Solid South" from the end of the Reconstruction era to well into the twentieth century.[31] By midcentury, however, the political landscape in national elections took on a different complexion.

Even as the catalyst of the Second World War and the growing population began to alter the makeup of Florida's electorate, like the Democratic presidential candidates before him, Franklin Roosevelt enjoyed strong electoral support among Florida voters through the war years. Roosevelt captured 72 percent of the vote in Florida in the 1932 presidential election; 76 percent of the popular vote in 1936; 74 percent of the vote in 1940; and 70 percent of the vote in 1944. With the end of the war, however, the traditional support for Democratic presidential nominees started to wane. Florida voters began to abandon their role as part of the Democratic "Solid South," and voters' allegiances in national elections shifted to support the Republican Party's nominee for the presidency.

Harry Truman was able to continue the long-running Democratic trend in the 1948 presidential election, winning the popular vote among Floridians, but 16 percent of the vote that year went to "Dixiecrat" candidate Strom Thurmond, and voters in sufficient numbers defected to Republican Thomas Dewey to give him a third of the state's popular vote total.[32] Contributing to Dewey's statewide total were votes from the counties of Pinellas, Sarasota, Palm Beach, Broward, and Orange, where he won outright. Dewey's victories in these counties provided the first evidence of the growing Republican strength, and the potential of Republican voters in what was to become known as the "urban horseshoe" became a relevant part of the emerging era in Florida politics.

In the 1952 presidential election, even more Floridians left the Democratic fold.[33] Voters in the state overwhelming gave their support to Republican and World War II hero Dwight Eisenhower over the Democrat nominee, Illinois Governor Adlai Stevenson, putting the state's electoral votes in the Republican column.[34] In 1956, President Eisenhower repeated the feat, winning among Florida voters by a margin of 57 percent to 43 percent, and Florida was in the Republican column in consecutive presidential elections for the first time since Reconstruction.[35] This offered clear validation that registered Democrats were willing to cross over and vote for a Republican, at least in the national elections.

Despite Eisenhower's success, Florida Republicans had initial difficulty transferring the Republican president's appeal to their state and local candidates. While Eisenhower won comfortably among the Florida voters in the fall of 1952, Democrat Dan McCarty rolled up a three-to-one victory over Republican Harry Swan in the race for governor.[36] When Eisenhower captured the state in his reelection campaign in 1956, the traditional pattern in state elections repeated itself, and Democrat LeRoy Collins comfortably defeated Republican William Washburne in the race for governor by a similar margin of almost three to one.[37]

In 1960, Richard Nixon carried the state in the presidential race against John Kennedy, but again the Republican popular vote lagged in the statewide elections, and Democrat Farris Bryant handily bested Republican George C. Peterson in the race for governor, capturing nearly 60 percent of the popular vote. Notable in the 1960 state gubernatorial race was that the final margin between the Democrats and Republicans had narrowed perceptibly. Notable, too, were the vote totals from the horseshoe counties of Pinellas, Sarasota, Manatee, Orange, Osceola, Brevard, Martin, Palm Beach, and Broward.[38] Like the results in presidential election for Republican Thomas Dewey in 1948, a majority of the total popular vote in each of these counties went to the losing Republican gubernatorial candidate George Peterson.[39]

Phantom "Coattails"

Despite their continued success in statewide races, the concern among Democratic leaders was that the tendency of voters to turn to the Republican candidate in the presidential race might create "coattails" down the ticket in the state races.[40] Said differently, a popular Republican presidential candidate might have a tendency to attract voters to other Republican candidates farther down on the ballot, and a Democratic nominee for governor might lose to a Republican because of the presidential "coattails."[41]

With the intent of eliminating this potential threat, the logical answer for the Democrats was to move Florida's statewide races to the off-year when the presidential race did not appear on the ballot.[42] The Democratic-controlled Legislature approved the initiative for the change and moved the statewide races to the off-years beginning in 1966. To implement the shift in Florida's statewide elections, the term of the governor elected in 1964 was truncated after only two years, but the governor elected in 1964 was permitted to run again in 1966 for a full four-year term as the state's chief executive.[43]

In the fall of 1964, Democratic presidential candidate Lyndon Johnson won a slim victory over the Republican nominee, Barry Goldwater, but no coattails materialized in the state race for governor. Continuing the historic trend, the Democratic gubernatorial candidate, Haydon Burns, captured 56 percent of the popular vote and defeated the Republican nominee, Charles Holley, but the margin between the two parties in the gubernatorial race continued to narrow from its historical trend.[44]

The race for governor was the premier event of the elections in 1966. There was no longer the shadow of a national campaign for the presidency to occupy voters' attention, but the schism among Democrats in their primary elections had returned. Governor Burns had won the 1964 Democratic nomination in a hotly contested primary that included six hopefuls, and he ultimately bested Miami Mayor Robert King High in a bitter runoff election. Within the Democratic Party, Burns, from Jacksonville, had been considered the conservative choice; while High, from Miami, was considered the liberal alternative among the party's voters.[45] Two years later, in 1966, the rivalry between Burns and High renewed itself in the Democratic primary election, but in 1966, High derailed Burns's reelection plans for a full four-year term.[46] Robert King High came away the victor after a primary campaign full of more bitter and vicious exchanges between the candidates, and the Democratic discord, not coattails, breathed viability into the general election campaign for the Republicans and their candidate for governor, Claude Kirk.[47]

In his analysis of the 1966 general election, David Halberstam wrote: "Kirk himself was the beneficiary of a . . . violent campaign which tore at every nerve in Florida's political fabric, urban-rural, North-South, liberal-conservative, leaving in the wake of High's eventual victory a party which was in shambles, a victor more severely wounded than he realized."[48]

"By the time Democratic candidates Burns and High were finished with their campaigns for the party nomination," remembered Democratic gubernatorial candidate Fred Karl in 1964, "there was so much animosity that reconciliation was impossible. Burns, the loser, was so bitter that he didn't feel bound by party loyalty, and to say he was unwilling to support High was an understatement."[49]

The traditional Democratic solidarity in the races for governor finally broke apart when Burns and large numbers of his supporter failed to reconcile and support High in the general election; and those who fashioned themselves conservative Democrats rallied under the banner of "Demo-Kirks" and campaigned for the Republican Claude Kirk.[50] In November, with the support of disgruntled Democrats, support from a growing Republican Party organization, and increasing numbers of registered Republican voters, Claude Kirk was elected governor. In the process, he became Florida's first statewide-elected Republican official since the close of the Reconstruction era nearly a century earlier.[51]

The irony of the switch to off-year elections in 1966 had backfired on the Democrats, and it became part of the momentum that made Republicans relevant players in the modern era of Florida politics. But the 1966 elections had other far-reaching consequences, and these consequences, too, marked 1966 and the early months of 1967 as historical bellwether times for the state's emerging Republican Party network.

Swann v. Adams

One of the Republican legacies of the Reconstruction era that followed the nation's Civil War was the adoption of the equal protection clause of the Fourteenth Amendment to the U.S. Constitution. Nearly a century after it became part of the country's Constitution, Charles Baker, the Republican mayor from Millington in Shelby County, Tennessee, began legal proceedings in federal court under the equal protection clause, asking that his state's legislative districts be apportioned equally by population based upon a one-person, one-vote formula. Mayor Baker's case made its way through the federal courts and into the U.S. Supreme Court, where, in 1962, the Supreme Court rendered its landmark ruling on legislative apportionment. In their opinion, the Supreme Court justices rejected arguments that legislative districting was a "political question" and determined that if "discrimination is sufficiently shown, the right to relief under the equal protection clause is not diminished by the fact that the discrimination relates to political rights."[52]

The consequences that followed the Supreme Court's decision in *Baker v. Carr* forever changed the fundamental makeup of state legislative bodies across America. The effect of the Court's ruling was to prospectively mandate that all legislative districts be apportioned on a legal standard of "one-person, one-vote" and that boundaries for legislative districts be based upon equal groupings of the state's population.[53] Once the U.S. Supreme Court had issued its landmark reapportionment opinion in *Baker v. Carr,* it became only a matter of time before its mandate was extended to Florida.

In the final years of the Pork Chop era, both Houses of Florida's Legislature were badly malapportioned, with 18 percent of the state's population electing a majority of the Florida Senate, and 17.6 percent of the state's population electing a majority of the members serving in the Florida House of Representatives.[54] In raw political terms, the major metropolitan areas and the fast-growing suburban hubs throughout Florida were grossly underrepresented, particularly in the urban horseshoe, and it was in these geographical settings where Republicanism had begun to reveal its presence in the presidential elections.[55] Yet, the malapportionment of state legislative districts prior to the decision in *Baker v. Carr* muted voices from these emerging urban and suburban population hubs in the state Capitol, including the emerging voices of Republicans.

Florida's malapportioned legislative seats were also part of what divided the conservative wing of the Democratic Party from the progressive urban/ suburban factions of the party because the existing malapportioned districts left control of both legislative bodies with the rural county legislators of the Pork Chop Gang.[56] In 1962, voters in Dade County led by named plaintiff Richard Swann followed the lead of Mayor Baker in Tennessee and filed their own challenge to the malapportioned districts in Florida under the equal protection clause of the Fourteenth Amendment.[57] Two years later, in June 1964, in the case of *Swann v. Adams*, the U.S. Supreme Court agreed with the Dade County voters and determined that the state's efforts to comply with the one-person, one-vote standard articulated in *Baker v. Carr* had not been met by the Florida Legislature.[58]

Following the Supreme Court's decision, the Legislature tried again in June 1965 to properly reapportion itself, but again the redistricting plan failed to meet the requirements of the new standard in the eyes of the U.S. Supreme Court.[59] In March 1966, the Legislature returned to Tallahassee for a special session and a third attempt to create House and Senate districts that could pass constitutional muster under the Supreme Court's mandate.[60] But like each prior attempt, the new districting plans for a 117-member House and a 48-member Senate were rejected by the U.S. Supreme Court on January 9, 1967.[61]

The results that ensued from the Supreme Court's final rejection of Florida's legislative districts in its 1967 decision were to invalidate all of the legislative elections that had occurred in November 1966.[62] The members of the House of Representatives and Florida Senate who were elected in the fall of 1966 never arrived in the state capital to take part in the regular session of the Legislature that convened on April 4, 1967.[63] It was instead the members from the newly reapportioned legislature districts that were selected in special elections on March 28, 1967, who assembled to engage in policy debates and interact with the state's newly elected Republican governor.[64]

A Reapportioned Legislature

After the three unsuccessful efforts by the members of the Florida Legislature in 1965 and 1966 to reapportion its two chambers, the U.S. District

Court for the Southern District of Florida determined that the judicial apportionment of Florida's legislative districts, both Senate and House, was required.[65] Evaluating the options available, the federal court ultimately entered an order that made sweeping changes in the population groupings for the districts of both Houses.

The principal architect of the 1967 judicial apportionment plan ultimately approved by the federal court was University of Florida political science professor Manning Dauer. Using whole counties and multimember districts as building blocks, the Dauer plan apportioned Florida's population into legislative districts for both the Senate and the House that effectively implemented the mandate that the U.S. Supreme Court had articulated in *Baker v. Carr*.[66] In the process, Dauer's configuration for new legislative districts offered the potential for new voices from the urban and suburban population centers in Florida, and among these new potential voices were Republicans in meaningful numbers.

On February 8, 1967, the federal court accepted Dauer's configuration for the new districts and directed that "the Legislature of Florida shall be reconstituted and reapportioned as set forth in the plan of apportionment in this Court's order . . . providing for 48 Senate districts and 119 House of Representative districts."[67] The order of the Court also directed that special elections be held for the new legislative seats prior to the convening date of the regular legislative session on April 4, 1967, and while each decennial census would prompt other reapportionment battles, when the election cycle ordered by the Court in 1967 was complete, the composition of the Florida Legislature seated on April 4 was radically different from those that preceded it.[68]

The voter groupings in the Dauer plan varied in size, and some voters had the opportunity to vote for more than one member of the House and the Senate. In the House, only three districts were single-member districts, and in the Senate, only five districts were represented by a single senator. All of the remaining districts in both Houses of the Legislature were nested into multimember groupings where candidates ran at-large among the same group of voters, and in many of the urban and suburban areas, these groupings were sizable. Examples of the large multimember districts in the Dauer plan included those anchored by both Hillsborough and Duval Counties, where eleven House members campaigned among the same group of voters; Pinellas County, where nine House members and four senators were elected at large by the same voters; in the Orange-Seminole County grouping, eight House members were elected from the same population base; the Broward County grouping also included eight House members; and in Dade County, twenty-two members of the House of Representatives and nine members of the Florida Senate ran in districts comprised of the same population base.[69]

While the Dauer districting plan created compliance with the "one person, one vote" standard articulated in *Baker v. Carr*, a collateral effect of the new multimember districting scheme was to dilute some of the voices of minority voting blocs in the urban and suburban areas of the state and limit participation by certain elements of the population. The phenomenon became apparent when the newly apportioned Legislature was seated in 1967—there were no African Americans in either House; only two women were seated in the 119-member Florida House; and only one woman was elected to the 48-member Florida Senate. From the state's Hispanic population, only three legislators were elected—two were seated in the House and one in the Senate. Republican voters were impacted, too, particularly in the multimember districts anchored by Dade and Hillsborough Counties, where no Republicans were among the thirty-three members elected to the House of Representatives from those districts.[70] These perceived discriminatory flaws in the multimember districting scheme were presented in a court filing by Dade County Supervisor of Elections Claude Brown, but they were not considered by the district court, and the political debate over the use of multimember districts in Florida was deferred to future decennial apportionments.[71]

Despite flaws in the plan, the impact of the new districts changed the people and the politics of the Florida Legislature. Voices of the Pork Chop Gang from rural Florida towns and communities like Starke (Charley Johns), Cedar Key (Randolph Hodges), Monticello (Scott Dilworth Clarke), Callahan (Harry Stratton), Wildwood (E. C. Rowell), Bonifay (H. B. Douglas), Quincy (Dewey Johnson), Irvine (L. K. Edwards), Jasper (J. Braham

Black), Bushnell (J. C. Getzen), Marianna (John Rawls), and Umatilla (J. Edwin Baker) no longer controlled the legislative agenda.[72] The population centers—Miami, Fort Lauderdale, West Palm Beach, Tampa, St. Petersburg, Orlando, Sarasota, and other cities in the state's urban regions—now elected a majority of the policymakers in both Houses; and among the policymakers were the new and relevant voices of the Republican minority, including legislative leaders like Don Reed, Mary Grizzle, Bill James, Jim Tillman, Bill Young, Warren Henderson, and Ken Plante.[73]

In her book *Making Modern Florida*, Mary E. Adkins summarized the end of the Pork Chop era this way:

> No one could deny that the elections of the mid-1960s, especially the two most recent ones, had put a new and very different face on Florida's legislature. In contrast to the 1963 legislature, the last in which the Pork Choppers held firm control, the new crop had less than half as many ranchers and farmers, more attorneys, 50 percent more real estate workers and nearly 50 percent more insurance and banking professionals. It had barely half as many hunters and fishermen, and more than twice the number of tennis, golf, and handball enthusiasts. The new legislature even included a few surfers. The new legislature still spent time outside, but in a way that did not directly extract resource from Florida soil. The new legislators, of course, reflected the new urban distribution of Florida's population.[74]

A "New Game" in the Capitol and Voices of a New Foundation

Less than two decades after delivering the state's electoral votes for the Republican presidential candidate in the fall of 1952, Republican standard-bearers arrived in the state Capitol as members of the Legislature in sufficient numbers to impact the policies being made in the state capital. With the exception of Representative Sam Campbell from DeFuniak Springs in rural Walton County in the Florida Panhandle and Senators Tom Slade, John J. Fisher, and William T. Stockton Jr. from the northeast corner of the state around Jacksonville, all the other fifty-six Republican members of the Legislature were from urban and suburban counties in central Florida and along the east and west coasts of the state.[75] Changing living patterns; growing Republican organizations in the new urban areas; a fortuitous change to Florida's statewide elections; a bitter primary campaign among the Democratic gubernatorial contenders; and the reapportionment mandate from the U.S. Supreme Court under the equal protection clause of the Fourteenth Amendment had all contributed to the timing.

In the span of a matter of months, Republicans had captured the governor's office; twenty of the forty-eight new seats in the Florida Senate had been won by Republicans; and in the House of Representatives, thirty-nine of 119 seats were now occupied by members of the Republican minority.[76] Their numbers in the House totaled exactly one-third of that body, and their total was enough to sustain a veto by the new Republican governor. It was enough to provide a powerful voice for the new Republican minority, and it allowed the Republican policymakers to "exert tremendous influence" in Florida's Capitol.[77]

"[Reapportionment] reinvented what we had for a legislature," remembered former Republican State Senator Tom Slade, reflecting on the events of the time.[78]

When the regular session of the Legislature convened in April 1967, between the new governor and the new Republican presence in the Legislature, a foundation for the modern Republican Party in Florida became a political reality and was set firmly in place. In the contemporary words of longtime Clerk of the Florida House of Representatives Allen Morris, "It's a new kind of ball game in Tallahassee."[79]

The "new kind of ball game" did not just play out in Tallahassee, however. Capturing the governor's office in November 1966 and establishing a relevant role in the new Legislature energized Republicans around the state. Local party organizations became meaningful; Republican clubs—men's and women's—sprang up and flourished as regular gatherings for the party faithful; and groups of Young Republicans organized around the new ideological spectrum and mobilized to support candidates for office, both locally and at the state level.[80]

It was a network that began at the precinct level; it was a network where young enthusiasts could progress to prominent places in the political process; it was an organization willing to expand the consistent party message; and it was a long-term commitment to political change.[81] While headlines about the Republican emergence focused on the party's successes at the ballot box, there was more to the story. It was the story of a growing network of people—those with a shared philosophy and committed to rebalancing the political spectrum. While some sought the limelight of political office, others were content to volunteer their time and donate their money to further the objectives of the emerging alternative to nearly a century of Democratic political dominance.[82]

Through the individuals that were infused with the motivation to be involved and drawn to an alternative approach different from the state's traditional solid Democratic dogma, the modern era of two-party politics in Florida was almost at once a permanent part of the new political landscape. The Republican voice in the emerging two-party reality was particularly prominent in the urban horseshoe, or what was to become known in Republican Party parlance as the "golden horseshoe," and it was in the urbanizing communities of the horseshoe where the first local roots for the party were planted.[83]

3

PLANTING LOCAL
REPUBLICAN ROOTS

IN A STUDY of the changing state electorate in the 1970s, political science professor Paul Cohen noted that many of the growing numbers of Republican voters were not native to Florida, and that "90 percent of the state's Republicans were born outside the state."[1] Despite growing numbers, however, the Republicans arriving in Florida in the early decades of the century came with a lack of loyalty to any local politicians and were met with the absence of a formal Republican Party organization. For these new arrivals and others seeking an alternative to the Democratic dominance in the state's political arena, the challenge became one of creating an organization and a support network around which their loyalty could be cultivated and their candidates could be recruited.

Whereas Democrats paid little attention to their own central party organization as the middle of the twentieth century approached, Republicans had a much different focus, and party activists began to organize their network in local communities where the influx of new voters was concentrated. Roots for this new Republican network were planted initially in Florida's urban horseshoe.[2]

Beginnings in the Horseshoe

Those moving into Florida from northern and midwestern states tended to be younger white-collar workers, middle-income retirees, and those with military backgrounds who stayed or returned to Florida after their time in the service. Especially following World War II, many of these new residents tended to settle in a geographical pattern that was to become known as the urban horseshoe. The geography of the horseshoe initially extended from the southeast coast of Florida in Broward County north to Daytona Beach in Volusia County; across central Florida along the I-4 corridor through the counties adjacent to urban and suburban Orlando; and then to Pinellas County and the Tampa Bay area on the west coast. From Pinellas County, it initially extended south to Manatee and Sarasota Counties.[3] As it grew and matured over time, the horseshoe extended its reach farther south into Miami-Dade County on the east coast and south to Charlotte, Lee, and Collier Counties on the Florida Gulf coast.[4]

Florida voters differed from those in most other states because so many residents were newly arrived and tended to see themselves as a resident of a region first and as a state resident second.[5] To begin organizing, focus was on regional geography, particularly the geography of the horseshoe, where it became the priority for the emerging Republican Party. The first efforts began in the 1940s with Republican C. C. Spades, and his focus was in the urban counties that were the terminus of the big migration from the Midwest and North. The first limited successes from Spades's organizational efforts came in the 1948 presidential race, when Republican Thomas Dewey carried Pinellas, Sarasota, Palm Beach, Broward, and Orange Counties in the general election.[6]

Following on the initial strides by Spades, others began efforts of their own to build local party structures and recruit local and legislative candidates to carry the Republican banner. Eisenhower benefited from the same Florida county organizations that brought the party its initial breakthroughs in Dewey's election, and these counties in the horseshoe emerged as the foundation for Florida Republicans in statewide elections. Over time, each of the horseshoe counties became fertile ground for cultivating interest and Republican support for candidates in local races and in seats for the state's legislative bodies, and many of the Republican Party's first successes came in Florida's central West Coast region.[7]

The ICY Machine

At the local level in Pinellas County and in the surrounding Tampa Bay area, the key turning point for Republicans came with the rise of a savvy young lawyer named William Cramer. It was Cramer who was "the real builder of the Republican Party" in Pinellas County—the first local stronghold for the party in Florida.[8] His work played a fundamental role in the inauguration of Republican organizations throughout the urban horseshoe following C. C. Spades's initial efforts. With the help of his aide and confidant Jack Insco and a young Republican turned budding politician, C. W. "Bill" Young, Cramer is credited with building a local party framework that consistently recruited and elected Republican candidates. Through the political organization started by Insco, Cramer, and Young that became known as the "ICY Machine," Pinellas Republicans earned success both in local elections and in elections that sent Republicans to the House and Senate as members of the state Legislature. At the beginning it was a daunting task: when the three began to organize, the statewide voter registration was nearly fourteen to one in favor of the Democrats, yet despite the disproportionate numbers, the efforts of the ICY Machine proved productive.[9]

Cramer, a graduate of Harvard Law School and the "C" at the heart of the ICY Machine, grew up in St. Petersburg and returned to Pinellas County after his graduation in 1948 where he began working to create a network of support for Republican Party candidates. The initial success of the new network followed two years later in 1950, when Cramer was elected to the Florida House of Representatives, where he served a single term. In 1952, he made an initial bid for a seat in the U.S. House of Representatives but narrowly lost. Two years later, in his second attempt, Cramer was successful and became the first Republican to be seated in the U.S. Congress from Florida.[10] Bill Cramer held a seat in Congress for sixteen years while simultaneously helping to build the Pinellas County Republican organization for the benefit of others who followed.[11]

Jack Insco, the "I" in the ICY Machine, was an aide to Congressman Cramer, and it is Insco who is credited with possessing the unique political organizational skills that over time designed and built the foundation of the Republican network in Pinellas County. He recruited the precinct captains; he promoted membership in the Republican clubs among the faithful; and he organized the internal party structure. From within the organization, the Republican Party in Pinellas County recruited candidates for local office and for seats in the state Legislature; the network of party loyalist supported their campaigns; and party volunteers mobilized Republican voter turnout.[12]

The "Y" in the ICY Machine was Charles William Young, better known as C. W. "Bill" Young. He was born in Harmarville, Pennsylvania, in 1930 and at the age of fifteen moved to Pinellas County, where he later joined the Cramer team. As he matured, Young became a major political force in Republican politics for more than fifty years. He joined the Army National Guard in 1948 and served until 1957; he became an active organizer of the county's Young Republicans; and in 1960, he began to make his own imprint on Florida politics when he was elected to the Democrat-dominated Florida Senate. He was the Senate's lone Republican when first elected and by default became the chamber's first Republican minority leader.[13]

Bill Young continued as the Republican leader when the reapportioned legislative districts brought meaningful Republican numbers to the Senate in the spring of 1967, and Young did not relinquish the role until he was elected to fill the U.S. congressional seat vacated by Bill Cramer in 1970.[14] In Congress, Bill Young became known as an expert on military issues; he chaired the powerful House Appropriations Committee from 1999 to 2005; and he served as a member of Congress until his passing in 2013.[15] Through his long and distinguished career, C. W. "Bill" Young remained an important force in the growth of Republican politics in Florida.

The ICY Machine organized by Cramer, Insco, and Young was not just the first of its kind; it was also the most sophisticated of the early efforts in the horseshoe. Once it began to show its muscle, others began to implement similar local Republican Party organizations in ways that Democrats had shown no interest in emulating.[16] Among the more memorable incentives that Insco and the ICY Machine initiated for the team of Republican grassroots workers and organizers in both Pinellas and Pasco Counties was affectionately known as the annual "Turkey Trot."[17]

"Insco would load up a truck with hams and turkeys, and the Republican committeemen and committeewomen would get hams and turkeys for Thanksgiving," remembered former Republican House Leader Ron Richmond, "and we called it the 'Turkey Trot.'"[18]

The precinct committeemen and committeewomen in Pinellas County played an important and effective part in the new organization, and none was more effective than precinct captain Marion Keith in the large Clearwater condominium community known as On Top of the World. Under her supervision, designated captains for each building in the complex were recruited to support the party's candidates in both primary and general elections, and under Keith's watchful eye, every door was canvassed before Election Day on behalf of the ICY Machine's Republican slate of candidates.[19]

Marion Keith and the reputation of Republican solidarity at On Top of the World grew, and over time, it extended beyond the candidates for state and local office in Pinellas County.[20] During national campaigns for the White House, it brought three United States presidents into the condominium complex as Keith's guest—Gerald Ford in 1980, Ronald Reagan in 1984, and George H. W. Bush in 1992—where they each showcased their messages for the local Republican residents in the community.[21]

The influence of the ICY organization grew and solidified as others came to prominence in this first generation of Pinellas Republicans. Notable among the others who stepped forward in the 1960s and early 1970s were local officials like Pinellas County Commissioner Charles E. "Chuck" Rainey, St. Petersburg Mayor Herman Goldner, Sixth Circuit State Attorney James T. "Jimmy" Russell, Russell's successor, Bernie McCabe, and longtime Pinellas County Tax Collector Sanford Jasper.[22] The early generation of Republicans also included long-serving legislative officeholders like Mary Grizzle, John Ware, Henry Sayler, John "Jack" Savage, Ed Whitson, Dennis MacDonald, Roger Wilson, Curt Kiser, Betty Easley, Richard Deeb, Harold Wilson, Ron Richmond, Dorothy Sample, and Tom Woodruff.[23]

Sandra Mortham with President George H. W. Bush after his speech at the condominium community On Top of the World. Mortham family collection.

Immediate Dividends from the Horseshoe

Parts of the structure and organization from the ICY Machine were exported and replicated in other parts of Florida. Following the elections in 1966, William Murfin, the new chairman of the state Republican Party, spearheaded the effort to cultivate similar political roots around the urban horseshoe to those planted in Pinellas County. Murfin, who was an East Coast party leader at the time of Claude Kirk's election in 1966, was a strong ally of the ICY Machine, and he shared the Machine's dedication to building a grassroots organization for Republicans capable of electing both statewide and legislative candidates to office.[24] Under Murfin's leadership, "[party] people were trained, candidate seminars were held, and voter registration drives were conducted all in preparation for 1968. Meanwhile, the Democrats did little or nothing"[25]

Murfin's network initially brought together an eclectic group of person-

Left to right: House Republican Leader Don Reed, Congressman Bill Cramer, Republican Party Chairman Bill Murfin, and Governor Claude Kirk with Richard and Pat Nixon at the 1968 Republican National Convention in Miami. Photo courtesy of the State Archives of Florida.

alities, and the most visible early successes manifested themselves in the state legislative races.[26] The excitement and energy around Kirk's success in the November 1966 fall elections, followed by the court-ordered special legislative elections less than five months later, created the opportunity to establish a sustainable Republican beachhead. It was around these special legislative elections in 1967 that local pockets of energized Republicans began to plant the taproots for the party in other parts of Florida.

From the ICY Machine's organization in Pinellas County following Kirk's election, three new Republicans from Pinellas County—Henry Saylor, Richard Deeb, and Harold Wilson—joined Bill Young in the Florida Senate, and five new Republican members from Pinellas County—Ed Whitson, A. S. "Jim" Robinson, Don Stafford, William Fleece, and Jack Murphy—joined veteran Republicans Mary Grizzle, Jack Savage, Ray Osborne, and Charles E. "Chuck" Rainey in the Florida House.[27]

From Sarasota County, Republican State Senator Warren Henderson was joined by new Republican House members Granville Crabtree, Kent McKinley, and future House Republican Leader James K. "Jim" Tillman. From Orange and Osceola Counties in central Florida, two new Republicans—Robert Elrod and future Senate Republican Leader Ken Plante—took seats in the Florida Senate, and in the lower chamber, the delegation from Orange and Seminole Counties included six new Republicans—Robert Shadley, David Lindsey, William Gorman, Jan Fortune, E. Pope "Sandy" Bassett, and William Gibson—who all joined veteran John Ducker in the Florida House of Representatives.[28]

Along the urban coastal communities of the horseshoe on the lower East Coast, Broward County also sent solid Republican delegations to both the House and Senate, and notable among the new members of the Florida Senate were Charles Weber, Jack Bell, Chet Stolzenburg, and future Senate Republican Leader David Lane. In the House, the new Broward representatives included Republicans Joel Gustafson, George Caldwell, James Eddy, Art Rude, Richard Bird, Hank Prominski, Charles King, and Joe Martinez. The Republican legislative delegation from Palm Beach and Martin Counties included State Senator and future U.S. Congressman L. A. "Skip" Bafalis; and in the House, returning Republican Leader Donald H. "Don" Reed Jr. was joined by local party activist and future House Republican Leader William G. "Bill" James, Jack Poorbaugh, Joseph Humphreys, Robert Rust, and Robert DeYoung.[29]

Farther up the East Coast of the horseshoe from St. Lucie, Indian River, and Brevard Counties, five new Republicans—Chuck Nergard, Bill Pfeiffer, Charles Davis, Bill Powell, and Cliff McNulty—were elected to the House, and Elizabeth J. "Beth" Johnson and C. S. "Cliff" Reuter joined the Republican caucus in the Senate as new members of the upper chamber.[30] From the fringes of the northern loop of the horseshoe, Ralph Clayton and Dennis J. Patrick O'Grady were elected to the Florida Senate representing Citrus, Hernando, Lake Sumter, and Volusia Counties.[31]

In the short span of the three election cycles that followed, this cadre of new Republican standard-bearers emerging from the horseshoe counties established a permanent beachhead for Florida Republicans in the state capital.

Republican Leaders from the Horseshoe

In the years and decades that followed as the Republican Party progressed toward the majority control of state government, the urban and suburban areas of the horseshoe remained the foundation for the party's growth and expansion. From the various parts of the region, the voters in the horseshoe provided the party with statewide officeholders as well as leaders in the state Legislature.[32]

Most of the party's initial successful statewide officeholders were residents of communities in the horseshoe. U.S. Senators Ed Gurney, Paula Hawkins, and Mel Martinez were from Orange County, Senator Connie Mack III was from the southwest leg of the horseshoe, and Senator Marco Rubio was from Miami-Dade County. The horseshoe counties were home to Florida's first Republican governors—Claude Kirk from Palm Beach County, Bob Martinez from Hillsborough County, Jeb Bush from Miami-Dade County, Charlie Crist from Pinellas County, Rick Scott from Collier County, and Ron DeSantis, who was raised in Dunedin in Pinellas County before settling in northeast Florida. It was home, too, for all but one of the lieutenant governors who served with them—Ray Osborne from Pinellas County with Claude Kirk, Bobby Brantley from Seminole County with Bob Martinez, Frank Brogan from Martin County and Toni Jennings from Orange County with Jeb Bush, Jeff Kottkamp from Lee County with Charlie Crist, Carlos Lopez-Cantera from Miami-Dade County with Rick Scott, and Jeanette Nuñez from Miami-Dade County with Ron DeSantis.

Joining the Florida cabinet from horseshoe counties as the Republicans expanded their influence into the state's executive branch of government were Secretaries of State Sandra Mortham from Pinellas County and Katherine Harris from Sarasota County.[33] The state's first Republican treasurer, Tom Gallagher, was from Miami-Dade County; the state's first Republican commissioner of education, Frank Brogan, was from Martin County; the first two Republican commissioners of agriculture, Charles Bronson from Osceola County and Adam Putnam from Polk County, were from horseshoe counties.[34] The first four Republican attorneys general—Charlie Crist from Pinellas County, Bill McCollum from Orange County, Pam

Bondi from Hillsborough County, and Ashley Moody from Hillsborough County—were from horseshoe counties; and the first two Republican chief financial officers—Tom Gallagher from Miami-Dade County and Jeff Atwater from Palm Beach County—were also residents of the horseshoe.[35]

In the three decades that followed the party's emergence during the Eisenhower presidential elections, horseshoe voters sent Florida Republicans to the U.S. Congress, too. William Cramer was the first to break the mold, and he was later succeeded by his protégé C. W. "Bill" Young from the Pinellas ICY Machine. From other parts of the horseshoe voting bloc, Republican congressional candidates further diminished the solid, historical Democratic hold on Florida's seats in the U.S. Congress. These new Republicans included Ed Gurney, Lou Frey, and John Mica from Orange County; William McCollum from Seminole County; J. Herbert Burke, Edward J. Stack, and Clay Shaw from Broward County; Skip Bafalis and Tom Lewis from Palm Beach County; Richard Kelly from Pasco County; Andy Ireland from Polk County; Connie Mack III and Porter J. Goss from Florida's Southwest Coast; and Michael Bilirakis from Tarpon Springs in Pinellas County.[36]

In the state House of Representatives following Don Reed from Palm Beach County, all of the subsequent Republican minority leaders were selected from districts representing communities in the horseshoe.[37] In sequence, Reed was followed by Jim Tillman from Sarasota County, Bill James from Palm Beach County, Curt Kiser from Pinellas County, Ronald R. "Ron" Richmond from Pasco County, R. Dale Patchett from Indian River County, James Lombard from Sarasota County, Sandra Mortham from Pinellas County, and Daniel Webster from Orange County. Webster had the unique distinction of being the last of the Republican minority leaders and the first Republican Speaker of the Florida House.[38]

Florida Senate districts in the horseshoe produced leaders for that chamber, too. Following Bill Young from Pinellas County, the next nine Senate Republican leaders also represented urban/suburban districts in the horseshoe.[39] Those who followed in sequence after Young included Warren Henderson from Sarasota County, David Lane from Broward County, John Ware from Pinellas County, Ken Plante from Orange County, Jim Scott

Meeting of Florida Republican leaders at Ed Gurney's home. *Left to right, standing:* Republican Party Chairman Duke Crittenden, House Republican Leader Don Reed, House Republican Leader Pro Tempore Ray Osborne, Senate Republican Leader Bill Young, and Congressman Herb Burke. *Left to right, seated:* U.S. Congressman Bill Cramer, Governor Claude Kirk, and U.S. Senator Ed Gurney. Photo courtesy of the State Archives of Florida.

from Broward County, Clark Maxwell from Brevard County, Dick Langley from Lake County, Toni Jennings from Orange County, and William G. "Doc" Myers from Martin County.[40] Ironically, the final Republican minority leader and first Republican Senate president, Ander Crenshaw, was not from a horseshoe district but represented the Jacksonville area in northeast Florida.[41]

The influence of the urban horseshoe continued after Republicans assumed majority status in both Houses of the legislature. Nine of the eleven

Republican Senate presidents who followed Ander Crenshaw—Jim Scott from Broward County, Toni Jennings from Orange County, John McKay from Manatee County, Tom Lee from Hillsborough County, Ken Pruitt from St. Lucie County, Jeff Atwater from Palm Beach County, Mike Haridopolos from Brevard County, Joe Negron from Martin County, and Bill Galvano from Manatee County—were residents of the horseshoe.[42] In the Florida House of Representatives following Dan Webster, eight of the next eleven Republican House Speakers—Tom Feeney from Orange County, Johnnie Byrd from Hillsborough County, Marco Rubio from Miami-Dade County, Dean Cannon from Orange County, Will Weatherford from Pasco County, Steve Crisafulli from Brevard County, Richard Corcoran from Pasco County, and Jose Oliva from Miami-Dade County—also called the horseshoe home.[43]

Roots beyond the Horseshoe—Northeast and North

The first inroads for the Republican Party beyond the horseshoe came in the legislative delegations from northeast Florida. While the bulk of the Republican members of the Legislature were elected from the central and the coastal arcs of the horseshoe, Duval County was also on the forefront of the Republican revolution that accompanied Claude Kirk's 1966 election victory. From northeast Florida, no Republicans were initially sent to the House in the aftermath of the 1966–67 elections, but three of the five senators elected from the multicounty district anchored by Duval County were Republicans—John J. Fisher, William T. Stockton Jr., and Tom Slade.[44] New Republican members in the Duval delegation to the House of Representatives followed two years later with the election of Representatives J. Wertz Nease and Earl Dixon in 1968.[45]

Particularly significant among these initial Republican officeholders from northeast Florida was Tom Slade. Slade served in the upper chamber until 1970 before leaving public office, but he remained an active presence in Republican Party politics for four more decades. In addition to his work in the Duval County Republican Party organization, Slade also mobilized the northeast region of Florida in 1986 for Bob Martinez in his successful gubernatorial campaign, and he later assumed chairmanship of the state party during the final Republican push to take majority control of the state's governmental institutions that culminated during the 1990s.

Tom Slade was only the first of several prominent Republicans to emerge from Jacksonville as the party's influence grew in northeast Florida. Over the next decade, other leaders included Ander Crenshaw, who was first elected to the state House of Representatives in 1972 and then to the Senate in 1986.[46] In his capacity as the Senate Republican leader, it was Crenshaw who eventually led Republicans from the minority to the majority, serving as the last Republican minority leader and the first Republican Senate president in 1993.[47] Other legislative leaders from northeast Florida included Representatives Bill Bankhead and Fred Tygart from Duval County, who were elected in 1978; Representative James E. "Jim" King, who came to the House of Representatives from Jacksonville in 1986; Representatives Steven R. "Steve" Wise and Joseph "Joe" Arnall, who were elected in 1988; and Representative James B. "Jim" Fuller, who arrived in 1992, each beginning his service while the Republicans were still the minority party in the Florida House.[48]

Tygart left the House in 1982 to take a seat as a circuit judge, but Bankhead, King, Wise, Arnall, and Fuller served until control in both Houses passed from the Democrats to the Republicans. Bill Bankhead, elected to the Senate in 1982, was part of the caucus that selected Crenshaw as the first Republican Senate president. Jim King, Steve Wise, Joe Arnall, and Jim Fuller were all part of the House caucus that picked Dan Webster to become the first Republican Speaker, and King was named by Speaker Webster as the body's first Republican majority leader. In a special election in 1999, Jim King was elected to the Florida Senate, and in 2002, he became the fifth Republican to serve as that body's president. Steve Wise followed King to the Senate in 2001 and was part of the caucus that designated King as the body's presiding officer.[49]

Over the ensuing decades, the Republican grassroots planted in Duval County spread south to Clay, St. Johns, and Putnam Counties. Republican Chance Irvine was elected to the House in 1984 from Clay County, and she was succeeded by John Thrasher in 1992.[50] During his tenure of public service, Thrasher became one of the party's most influential leaders. He was one of the Republicans who spanned the bridge from minority status into the majority of the House of Representatives, serving as the first Republican chairman of the powerful House Rules Committee and as the second Republican House Speaker.[51] Later elected to the Florida Senate, where he chaired the Senate Rules Committee, Thrasher also served as an interim chairman of the State Republican Party.

In time the Republican influence at the top of the horseshoe also pushed north into Hernando and Citrus Counties on the West Coast and into Marion County in central Florida. In the elections of 1988, George Albright came to the Florida House from Marion County and was part of the Republican caucus that selected the first Republican Speaker.[52] Albright was followed in succession by Hugh H. Gibson III and Larry Cretul, and in 2012, Cretul rose to become the seventh Republican Speaker in the modern era.[53]

Republican Ginny Brown-Waite from Hernando County came to the Florida Senate in 1992 to serve as a member of the new majority for a decade before concluding her public service as a member of the U.S. Congress.[54] In the same election, Jeff Stabins from Spring Hill came to the state House from Hernando County and became part of the Republican caucus that elected the first Republican Speaker.[55] The Republican conversion in Citrus County began with Paul Hawkes in 1990, and Hawkes was followed in 1996 by Nancy Argenziano.[56] Argenziano's victory in 1996 gave Republicans their sixty-first member of the Florida House, and with her victory, Republicans claimed the majority in the body for the first time since Reconstruction.[57]

Roots beyond the Horseshoe—The Panhandle

To the northwest, Republican presence in the Florida Panhandle was sporadic in the first two decades of the party's resurgence. Sam Campbell from Walton County was part of the Republican House caucus from 1967 to 1968 but declined to return for another term. Representative Tom Tobiassen from Pensacola came to the House in 1968 as a Republican and was also part of the party's caucus during the Kirk administration, but Tobiassen switched his party allegiance to the Democrats in 1982 and left the Republican fold.[58]

There were more sporadic successes from the Panhandle in 1986, when voters from Escambia and Santa Rosa Counties elected Republican Tom Banjanin to the House, and the voters from Okaloosa and Walton Counties elected Republican State Representative Robert Hardin.[59] After serving three terms as a member of the House, Hardin was elected to the Senate in 1992, where he became part of the caucus that selected Crenshaw as the first Republican presiding officer. In 1992, Banjanin's public service brought him home to Escambia County as a member of the county commission, where he helped to build the party at the local level.

A more dominant Republican presence in the Panhandle did not manifest itself until after the turn of the century, but the change did come. A shifting political climate, accelerated growth and development in the region's coastal areas, the presence of the U.S. military, and an increasing population of retired military personnel all led to realignment with Republican policies and philosophy that was more compatible with the new population. In time, the Panhandle region produced Republican leaders of its own.[60] In 1994, retired General Robert Milligan from Panama City successfully defeated incumbent Gerald Lewis to become Florida's first Republican comptroller.[61] In 2004, Republican Representative Allan Bense from Bay County was selected as Speaker of the Florida House, and in 2012, Senator Don Gaetz from Okaloosa County was picked by his Republican colleagues to be the Senate president.[62]

Roots beyond the Horseshoe—Southeast

Looking south on Florida's East Coast to Miami-Dade County, the Republican Party faced a different dilemma. As the party began to plant its roots, Miami and its surrounding urban population had large numbers of Republican voters, but it also had far more Democratic voters. In the initial Dauer judicial apportionment plan imposed by order of the federal court, all legislative seats in Dade County were at-large seats and were contested county-wide.[63] The practical effect of the Dauer plan was to dilute the Republican vote in the Democratic majority with no meaningful opportunity for the minority Republicans to elect a candidate. The districting plan adopted by the Legislature in 1972 divided the county into districts, but the geographical groupings in the House consisted of five or six seats with candidates running at large within a single geographical area.[64] The effect of the legislative multimember districts approved in 1972 was to preserve the dilution of Republican voters in geographical groupings with dominant Democratic majorities in a fashion similar to the districting configurations of the Dauer plan.[65]

The first Republican to overcome the disadvantages of the Democratic multimember districting plan in south Florida was John Malloy from Miami, who was elected in 1972, but Malloy served only a single two-year term and did not return to political prominence.[66] In a 1974 special election, Tom Gallagher narrowly won a seat in the House of Representatives and became the second Republican member to serve from Miami-Dade County. Unlike Malloy, Gallagher became a continuing Republican anchor in the Democratic stronghold for more than a decade, successfully retaining his seat in the House until 1986, when he opted to make his first bid for statewide office in the Republican gubernatorial primary won by Bob Martinez. By the time Gallagher departed, other Republicans had stepped up to follow him into the Legislature.[67]

In the 1982 decennial reapportionment, legislative districts changed from large, multimember districts in the urban areas to single-member districts throughout Florida for both the state Senate and the House of Representatives.[68] The effect of the new districting scheme was to diminish the dilution of minority voters that had been a consequence of the previous two districting plans, and the 1982 district configurations opened new opportunities for minority candidates in the urban and suburban areas.[69] This was true both for African American voters in counties like Pinellas, Orange, and Broward where Republicans had dominated; and it was equally true for the large minority bloc of Republican voters in Miami-Dade County, many of them Cuban Americans.[70]

When the new districting scheme took effect during the 1982 election cycle, Republican voters immediately made their presence known in Miami-

Dade County, sending Roberto Casas, Humberto Cortina, and Ileana Ros-Lehtinen to the Florida House of Representatives. With their arrival, Tom Gallagher was no longer Miami's lone Republican.[71] In addition to Gallagher, both Casas and Ros-Lehtinen began long careers as Republican officeholders with their elections to the Florida Legislature. After serving two terms in the House, Ros-Lehtinen was elected to the Florida Senate in 1986; and she won a seat in the U.S. Congress in 1989, blazing a path for other Republicans and others of Cuban American heritage.[72] Casas, too, followed his House service with ten years as a member of the Florida Senate. He was part of the caucus that selected the first Republican Senate president; and in 1996, Casas was selected by his colleagues to serve as the president pro tempore of the Senate during the presidency of Toni Jennings.[73]

State Representative Tom Gallagher confers with Miami-Dade County colleagues on the floor of the House chambers. *Left to right:* Representatives Luis Morse, Roberto Casas, Ileana Ros-Lehtinen, Gallagher, and Arnhilda Gonzalez-Quevedo. Photo by Don Dughi; courtesy of the State Archives of Florida.

In 1984, the single-member districts saw more new faces from Miami-Dade County appear in the state capital. Javier Souto, Rodolfo "Rudy" Garcia Jr., Arnhilda Gonzalez-Quevedo, and Alberto "Al" Gutman won elections and joined the other Miami-Dade Republicans in the House of Representatives.[74] The elections of 1986 brought two more Republicans—Luis Morse and Lincoln Diaz-Balart—into the House Republican caucus; and in 1988, these Dade County Republicans were joined by Lincoln's brother Mario Diaz-Balart, Nilo Juri, Luis Rojas, Carlos Valdez, and Bruce Hoffmann.[75] Rojas, Morse, and Valdez were all still serving when the Republicans ascended to the majority in the House.

Initially, there were no Republican opportunities in Miami-Dade County, but as the 1980s progressed, the influence of Republican standard-bearers in the county spread. Javier Souto moved from the House to the state Senate and later returned home to become a long-serving member of the Miami-Dade County Commission. Brothers Lincoln and Mario Diaz-Balart along with Al Gutman moved on to seats in the Florida Senate; and as state senators, both Gutman and Lincoln Diaz-Balart took part in the selection of the first Republican Senate president.[76] The Diaz-Balart brothers—Lincoln in 1992 and Mario in 2002—like Ros-Lehtinen before them, were both subsequently elected as members of the U.S. Congress following their public service in the state Legislature.[77]

Roots beyond the Horseshoe—Southwest

In the less-populated lower Southwest Coast of Florida, Hugh Paul Nuckolls from Fort Myers was the first to break up the Democrat's solid hold of the region's districts in the state House of Representatives, winning a seat in the House in 1972 and continuing his service for a decade.[78] Naples Republican Mary Ellen Hawkins followed Nuckolls to the state House in 1974, winning a seat from Collier County. Hawkins served as a member of the Florida House for two decades, and as a ranking Republican member of the powerful Appropriations Committee, she became one of the Republican caucus's leading experts on the state's budget.[79] Frederic H. "Fred" Burrall from Charlotte County was also elected to the House of Representatives in 1974, and during

Burrall's ten-year tenure he rose in the caucus to become the Republican leader pro tempore from 1978 to 1982.[80]

In the election cycles that followed, Burt Saunders, Dudley Goodlette, Mike Davis, Garrett Richter, Tom Grady, Kathleen Passidomo, Matt Hudson, Byron Donalds, and Bob Rommel kept Collier County in the House Republican caucus, and Richter and Passidomo each continued their service in the Florida Senate. From districts representing Charlotte County, the Republican tradition started by Fred Burrall was continued by Greg Gay, David L. "Dave" Thomas, Lindsay Harrington, David Bitner, Michael J. Grant, Jerry Paul, Paige Kreegel, and Kenneth L. "Ken" Roberson; and from Lee County the tradition that had begun with Paul Nuckolls was continued by Fred Dudley, Tim Ireland, Ralph Livingston, Bruce Kyle, Jeff Kottkamp, Gary Aubuchon, Carole Green, Nicholas R. "Nick" Thompson, Trudi Williams, Matt Caldwell, Dane Eagle, Heather Fitzenhagen, and Spencer Roach.[81]

For those building the grassroots of the Republican Party, the state legislative seats, the races for statewide office, and seats in the U.S. Congress were focal points. The legislative seats created energy and excitement and captured the imagination of local party regulars. The Legislature was also important because it controlled the redistricting process, and the state party looked to the legislative branch Republicans as the best source of viable statewide and congressional candidates, but the legislative seats and the seats in the U.S. Congress were not the only successes from the horseshoe.[82]

Expanding the Local Roots

Republicans also had ballot-box success at the local level. Party candidates captured early control of county commission majorities in places like Pinellas, Sarasota, Brevard, Broward, Collier, and Pasco Counties, and legislators who began locally as county commissioners included Warren Henderson and Ray Pilon from Sarasota County, John W. "Jack" Bell and J. W. "Bill" Stevens from Broward County; C. S. "Cliff" Reuter, Clark Maxwell, and Thad Altman in Brevard County; Doc Myers in Martin County; Ginny Brown-Waite from Hernando County; Gustavo "Gus" Barreiro from Miami-Dade County; Burt Saunders from Collier County; Don Brown from

Walton County; Ray Sansom from Okaloosa County; Travis Cummings from Clay County; Neil Combee from Polk County; Elizabeth Porter from Columbia County; Cyndi Stevenson from St. Johns County; Jayer Williamson from Santa Rosa County; Pat Patterson from Volusia County; Ken Sorensen from Monroe County; and future House Speaker Larry Cretul and Charlie Stone from Marion County.[83] Steve Seibert began on the Pinellas County Commission and later joined the administration of Jeb Bush as the secretary of the Department of Community Affairs, and like other county leaders, Seibert helped to broaden the Republican base and cultivate the party's roots at both the state and local level.[84]

In the early years of the new era and as the Republican Party matured, city mayors, city commissioners, and members of town councils from the urban and suburban areas emerged to become part of the party's local grassroots. They cultivated local support among Republicans, and for many, it was a platform to higher office. These local Republican leaders included mayors like Herman Goldner in St. Petersburg; Harry Dale in Sanford; Don Slesnick in Coral Gables; Charles LeCher in Clearwater; Gerald S. "Jerry" Rehm and Tom Anderson in Dunedin; Thomas F. "Tom" Lewis in North Palm Beach; Clay Shaw in Fort Lauderdale; Bill Stevens in Oakland Park; J. J. "Toby" Holland in Palmetto; Tim Deratany in Indialantic; Jerry Maygarden in Pensacola; Allen Trovillion in Winter Park; Hugh Gibson and David Mealor from Lake Mary; Frank Attkisson in Kissimmee; Dennis Baxley in Belleview; Dorothy Hukill in Port Orange; Aaron Bean in Fernandina Beach; Julio Robaina in South Miami; Fred Costello in Ormond Beach; Dan Raulerson in Plant City; Robert Cortes in Longwood; Mel Ponder in Destin; and Kathleen Peters from South Pasadena.[85]

There were also the city commissioners and town council members who helped build the Republican base like David Clark from North Palm Beach; Seth McKeel from Lakeland; Lee Constantine from Altamonte Springs; Frank Stone from Casselberry; James C. "Jim" Hill Jr. from Jupiter; Rene Garcia, Esteban Bovo, and Eduardo Gonzalez from Hialeah; Marco Rubio from West Miami; Bill Posey from Rockledge; Charles W. "Charlie" Clary from Destin; Lindsey Harrington from Punta Gorda; Carol Hanson and Bill Hager from Boca Raton; William "Bill" Andrews from Delray

Beach; William L. "Bill" Proctor from St. Augustine; Rich Glorioso from Plant City; Carl Littlefield from Dade City; Ed Hooper and Karen Seel from Clearwater; Peter Nehr from Tarpon Springs; Sandra Mortham from Largo; Nan LeFils and Heather Fiorentino from New Port Richey; Kimberly Mitchell from West Palm Beach; Lois Benson from Pensacola; Clay Ford from Gulf Breeze; Daniel "Danny" Burgess Jr. from Zephyrhills; Jim Boyd from Palmetto; Shawn Harrison from Tampa; and Don Davis, Dan Davis, Dick Kravitz, Mike Hogan, and Lake Ray from Jacksonville.[86]

There were other local officials, too. Among them were Hillsborough County Supervisor of Elections Jim Sebesta; Clerk of the Circuit Court from Seminole County Maryanne Morse; Lake County School Board Chairman Richard "Dick" Langley; Clay County School Board Chairman John Thrasher; county school board members Stan Mayfield from Indian River; Kurt Kelly from Marion County; Stan Jordon from Duval County; Charles Van Zant from Clay County; Nancy Detert from Sarasota County; Larry Metz from Lake County; and Janet Adkins from Nassau County.[87] Included, too, were Okaloosa County School Superintendent Don Gaetz; Palm Beach County Sheriff William Heidtman; Pinellas County Sheriff Everett S. Rice; Alachua County Sheriff Steve Oelrich; Monroe County Sheriff Allison DeFoor; Martin County Sheriff Robert Crowder; Stuart City Attorney Tom Warner; Miami-Dade Assistant State Attorney Gaston Cantens; Hernando County Aviation Authority board member David Russell; and Canaveral Port Authority board member Tom Goodson.[88]

The work that began with local Republican officials was continued by several of the members of the House Representatives who took part in the historic election of the first Republican Speaker of the Florida House and those who followed. They included Charlie Sembler from Sebastian, who became the Indian River tax collector after his service in the House; Jim Fuller, who continued his public service as the Duval clerk of court after his service in the House; Ken Pruitt, who capped his service in the Legislature as the president of the Florida Senate and then returned to St. Lucie County to become the property appraiser; Carlos Lopez-Cantera, who concluded his service as the majority leader of the Florida House and returned to Miami-Dade to become property appraiser before continuing his public service as Florida's lieutenant governor; and George Albright, who returned to Marion County to be the county tax collector after serving six terms in the Florida House.[89] Mike Fasano served two terms in the Florida Senate before returning home to be the Pasco County tax collector; Mike Bennett followed his service in the Florida Senate as the supervisor of elections in Manatee County; and Carey Baker followed his service in the House and Senate as the property appraiser in Lake County.[90]

After fourteen years of legislative service, Rich Crotty returned to Orange County to continue his public service first as the elected property appraiser and then as the Orange County mayor.[91] Others who began in the Legislature and returned home to continue service on county commissions included Charles E. "Chuck" Rainey, John Morroni, and Kathleen Peters from Pinellas County; Tom Banjanin from Escambia County; Gustavo Barreiro and Javier Souto from Miami-Dade County; Sandra Murman, Rhonda Storms, and Victor Crist from Hillsborough County; and Lee Constantine from Seminole County.[92]

Left to right: State Representatives Curt Kiser, Peter Dunbar, and Betty Easley seated with Pinellas County precinct committeewoman Marion Keith at a Clearwater Women's Republican Club luncheon. Dunbar family collection.

There were those who never sought or found the limelight of public office who were important parts of the Republican network, too. Like Marion Keith in her Clearwater condominium community, they devoted their time, effort, and resources to the party and its candidates. For most, their time was spent behind the scenes in support of the Republican Party's candidates; they helped to implement campaign strategies; they sponsored events; they wrote checks and raised campaign funds; they provided a fabric of consistency for the local efforts of the party; and they were important contributors to the emergence of the Republican Party in the modern era.

In the early years and as the era matured, at the apex of the horseshoe in Seminole and Orange Counties, they included Fred Streetman, Larry Johnson, Jim Stelling, Mack McClendon, Oscar Juarez, Genean Hawkins McKinnon, and Jeanie Austin.[93] In Broward and Palm Beach Counties, contributors included Broward Republican Chairman Gray Boylston, Peggy Benedict, Jeanne Hanson, Dr. Zack Zachariah, Anita Mitchell, Bobbie James, Ed Pozzuoli, Monroe "Al" Coogler, Bill Sklar, and Nancy Brinker in their roles with the Republican Jewish Federation, long-serving National Republican committeeman Peter Feaman, and Jean Pipes, who helped with the initial organization of the Florida Federation of Republican Women.[94]

From Miami-Dade County, Alex Courtelis, Jorge Mas, Carlos Salman, Harry Davant, Julio Rebull, Mary Ellen Miller, George Warren, Rodney Barreto, Sylvester Lukis, Armando Codina, and Al Cardenas, who, in time, became the party's longest-serving Republican state committeeman, were among the early mainstays of the Republican network.[95] Farther up the East Coast, they included Charlie Kane and Sherri Plymale from Martin County; Vernon Smit, Mike Brown, Don Cuozzo, Donna Calabrese, and Hal Roberts from St. Lucie County; from Brevard County, Jim and Cynthia Handley and Dr. Max King; and from Polk County, Doc Dockery and David Hart.[96]

From the West Coast along the urban horseshoe, they included Tony Battaglia, Gus Stavros, Dick Beard, Al Hoffman, Mel Sembler, Brent Sembler, Harry Jennings, Laird Lile, Tina Matte, Noel LeCher, Jack Hebert, David Dunbar, Jean Friday, Ed Armstrong III, Alan Bomstein, and long-serving Pinellas County Republican Party Chairman Ray Aden.[97] From Jacksonville and northeast Florida, they included Bill Taylor, Mike Hightower, Tom Pettway, Marty Fiorentino, Phil Leary, and Lanny and Susie Wiles; and in north central Florida and the Florida Panhandle, they included Richard Coates, Quincee Messersmith, Mary Bebout, Tommy Thomas, and Charlie Hilton.[98]

Once these local officials and local party volunteers planted the Republican roots in the communities around the horseshoe, it spawned an organization that brought structure to the party; the emerging structure supported the party's successful candidates who were recruited from among its midst; and the initial grassroots of the party expanded to the other parts of Florida, where voters were discontent with the dogma and dominance of the Democrats.

4

ORGANIZING TO SPREAD
THE INFLUENCE

THE OFFICEHOLDERS WHO CARRIED the Republican Party banner in the decades following Bill Cramer's election to the U.S. Congress in 1954 are readily identifiable in the publications that chronicle Florida's political history, but there were many others who made their service possible who are not as readily remembered.[1] They built the party's infrastructure; they organized the Republican volunteers and party loyalists; they recruited an ever-expanding network of young staff members; and they articulated and spread the party's philosophical doctrine among the state's voters.[2] Many began as local party officials, club members, campaign volunteers, legislative aides, and as members of the state Republican Party staff; and as they progressed to new and different roles, the influence of the party expanded with them.

The efforts of the Republican Party and its leadership were not without conflict and disagreement, but at its core, the focus and commitment of Republican Party loyalists and volunteers to the continuity of the organization's structure were different from the attention that Florida Democrats gave to the structure of their party.[3] It was a difference that remained a factor as the two-party era matured, and it was accentuated in the aftermath of the 2016 elections with the revelation that the Democratic Party still had no formal county organization in twelve of Florida's sixty-seven counties.[4]

Organizing the Party Faithful

When the Republicans emerged at the beginning of the modern political era, the Democratic Party was essentially without meaningful organization at either the state or local level.[5] Democrats lacked party discipline; their party candidates failed to fly a consistent philosophical banner; and Democrats divided their messages between the conservative, rural wing and the urban, liberal wing of the party.[6] The Democratic primary contests between LeRoy Collins and Charley Johns and between Haydon Burns and Robert King High were manifestations of the differences, and the contrasts extended into the Legislature, where philosophical differences between those from the Pork Chop era and the new Democrats from urban and suburban districts were present as well.[7] The reality for the Democrats was that there was no meaningful or consistent party structure, which, for Republicans, represented an opportunity.[8] "Democratic nominees, taking the general elections for granted, gave no thought to party organization," wrote political author Martin Dyckman in his 2010 book about the era, "an indifference the Republicans would exploit."[9]

Despite times of conflict and disruption within the Republican Party on how it would be led, party leaders made the effort to exploit the opportunity offered by the Democrats and alter the direction of Florida politics. The objective was to create a fully integrated political network, and Republicans made that their mission.[10] They organized a party structure at the state and local level; they supported the creation of Republican clubs; they defined the philosophy and the contrasts with the opposition party for their membership; they extended the welcome mat to those voters who were potential converts and discontented with the dogma of the Democrats; and they provided the manpower and resources for the campaigns of Republican Party candidates.

"Building the party began locally and then expanded with help from Republicans in the Legislature," remembered former Party Chairman Al Cardenas. "It was a brick-by-brick local effort that made the foundation possible."[11]

Beginning with Jack Insco and the ICY Machine in Pinellas County and Bill Murfin, who chaired the state Republican Party following Claude Kirk's election in 1966, the Republican efforts to organize the party structure began at the local level and continued at a steady pace.[12] The formal party organization consisted of local county committeemen and committeewomen in individual voting precincts; and these individuals selected the chairperson of the Republican executive committee in each county. There were state committeemen and committeewomen from each county, too; and these individuals elected the chairperson of the state Republican Party to oversee the staff and to implement the organization's statewide goals and objectives.[13]

As the modern political era progressed, Republicans became better organized and more disciplined than their Democratic counterparts.[14] The party organization helped to institutionalize modern campaign techniques, deploy effective direct-mail strategies, and effect winning campaigns with smaller campaign coffers than their Democratic opponents.[15] The structure the Republicans built provided continuity, a meaningful network of volunteer supporters, and, when fully matured, a state party office with paid staffers with which Republican partisans could align and use to cultivate the campaigns of their candidates.[16] From the local county executive committees around the horseshoe, some of the men and women who began as party officials made their way to Tallahassee to take seats in the Florida Senate and the state House of Representatives, and others won seats in the U.S. Congress. Florida's first Republican woman U.S. senator, Paula Hawkins, served twenty-four years as the state's national Republican committeewoman, and Florida's third Republican governor, Jeb Bush, began his Florida political career as the chairman of the Republican Executive Committee in Miami-Dade County.[17]

Before serving in the Florida Senate, William T. Stockton Jr. was the Republican state committeeman from Duval County; David Lane was a Republican precinct committeeman from Broward County before his service in the Senate; Cliff Reuter was the chairman of the Brevard County Republican Party before he was elected to the Senate;[18] David H. "Dave" McClain[19] and James "Jim" Sebesta served on the Hillsborough County Republican executive committee before they were elected to the Senate;[20] Charles H.

"Charlie" Bronson and Howard Futch chaired the Brevard County Republican executive committee before they came to the Senate;[21] and both Al Gutman and Javier Souto preceded their Senate service as members of the Republican executive committee in Miami-Dade County.[22]

Among the local party officials winning seats in the state House of Representatives from central Florida were E. Pope "Sandy" Bassett, Bobby Brantley, Tom Feeney, Bob Brooks, and Jason Brodeur from the Seminole County Republican executive committee; Chance Irvine from the Clay County Republican executive committee; Debbie Mayfield from the Indian River County Republican executive committee; Randy Ball from the Brevard County Republican executive committee; Earl Ziebarth from the Volusia County Republican executive committee; Kurt Kelly from the Marion County executive committee;[23] John Mica, Tom Drage, David Simmons, and Jim Kallinger from the Republican executive committee in Orange County; John Quinones and Mike Horner from the Osceola County Republican executive committee; Larry Metz and H. Marlene O'Toole from the Lake County Republican executive committee; and Dennis Ross from Republican executive committee in Polk County.[24]

On the West Coast, future State Representatives James C. "Jim" Frishe, Frank Farkas, Leslie Waters, Larry Crow, Peter Dunbar, R. Z. Safley, Gus Bilirakis, and Kim Berfield all served as precinct committee representatives on the Pinellas County Republican executive committee; Mike Fasano was the Republican state committeeman from Pasco County; Blaise Ingoglia was from the Hernando County Republican executive committee; Ted Ewing, Mark Ogles, and Donna Clarke served on the Sarasota County Republican executive committee; Jerry Paul was a member of the Republican executive committee in Charlotte County; Tim Ireland, Gary Aubuchon, Dane Eagle, and Ray Rodrigues were members of the Lee County Republican executive committee; and David Bitner served on the Charlotte County Republican executive committee before his election to the Florida House.[25]

On the lower East Coast, Representative Gayle Harrell served as a member of the Martin County Republican executive committee; Carlos Valdes, Jorge Rodriguez-Chomat, and Erik Fresen were members of the Miami-Dade County Republican executive committee before their elections to the Legislature; Manny Diaz Jr. was the Republican state committeeman from Miami-Dade County before his election to the Legislature; MaryLynn Magar was the Republican state committeewoman from Martin County before her election to the House; and Randy Avon was a member of the Republican executive committee in Broward County before his election to the Florida House.[26]

In addition to the local Republican executive committees, the state party structure was also an important cog in the emerging network of the Republican organization, and in many circumstances, it was the most visible arm of the party. As a matter of custom when Florida had a sitting Republican governor, party leaders considered the governor to be the head of the Republican Party, and with rare exception, party officials deferred to the governor's choice to chair the state Republican Party, beginning with Claude Kirk.[27]

The State Party Chairs

Bill Murfin was Kirk's initial choice to be chairman of the state party, and in the late 1960s, Murfin boldly predicted, "The South holds the future for Republicans."[28] During his tenure as party chairman, Murfin managed the campaign efforts through the 1968 elections that saw Florida Republicans deliver the state for Richard Nixon in the presidential election and send Ed Gurney to Washington, D.C., as Florida's first elected Republican U.S. senator.[29] Following the 1968 elections, Murfin left Florida for Washington, D.C., and joined the Nixon administration at the Small Business Administration, leaving a temporary organizational and grassroots vacuum at the party.[30]

Kirk's choice to replace Murfin was Duke Crittenden, but his legacy did not resemble Murfin's, and from the beginning, Crittenden found himself in the middle of an intraparty struggle between the Claude Kirk and Bill Cramer forces inside the party organization.[31] After the losses by both Cramer and Kirk in the 1970 general election, Crittenden was voted out as chairman by party officials and was replaced by Cramer ally Tommy Thomas from Panama City.[32]

The change in chairmanship highlighted the tension between the allies

Right to left: Republican Party Chair Tommy Thomas, U.S. Congressman Bill Cramer, and House Republican Leader Curt Kiser. Photo courtesy of the Florida Historic Capitol Museum.

of the ICY Machine and those loyal to Claude Kirk during the early years of the modern era, but despite the internal struggles, the commitment to organizing the party faithful continued under Thomas's leadership.[33] Republicans did not abandon the party structure or settle into a mentality of indifference. Beginning with Tommy Thomas and over the next three decades, each of the Republican Party state chairs could look back at their tenure and find successes in the Republican efforts during their time as the party's leader.

While Thomas served as the party chairman, the organization continued to mature; Republicans carried the state for Richard Nixon in the 1972 presidential election;[34] the Republican presence in the Florida Legislature remained stable; and Republican Paula Hawkins became the first woman from either political party to win a statewide election when she defeated Gerald Lewis for a seat on the Florida Public Service Commission in 1972.[35] After leaving his role as head of the state party, Thomas signed on to serve as the state chairman in Florida for both of Ronald Reagan's successful presidential campaigns.[36]

William M. "Bill" Taylor of Jacksonville Beach succeeded Thomas as the party chairman after the 1974 elections and headed the Republican Party's efforts through the elections of 1980. During Taylor's early tenure, Florida Republicans suffered through the aftermath of Watergate; Republican membership in the Florida Legislature fell to its lowest level of the modern era; and the state electoral votes returned to the Democratic column in the 1976 presidential race between Jimmy Carter and Gerald Ford.[37] But despite the setbacks, by the time Taylor left his post as the party chairman after the 1980 elections, the number of Republicans in the state Legislature was once again on the rise; Florida was back in the Republican column in the presidential election with Ronald Reagan's victory; Florida voters had elected Republican Paula Hawkins to the U.S. Senate; and Bill McCollum, Clay Shaw, and Skip Bafalis were new Republican faces in Florida's delegation to the U.S. Congress.

Former State Senator Henry Sayler from Pinellas County followed Taylor as the Republican Party chair 1980. When he assumed the role, the party was more than sixty thousand dollars in debt, but within a matter of months, he had raised more than six hundred thousand dollars to stabilize the treasury.[38] Sayler managed the Republican Party's efforts in the campaigns of 1982 and 1984. In 1982, three new Republicans—Michael Bilirakis from Tarpon Springs, Tom Lewis from North Palm Beach, and Connie Mack III from Fort Myers—joined the Florida congressional delegation; Congressman Andy Ireland from Polk County switched from the Democratic to the Republican Party and was successfully reelected; Republican membership in the state House of Representatives reached its highest number to date; and Florida's electoral votes in the presidential election remained in the Republican column when Ronald Reagan was reelected to his second term in the White House.[39]

Jeanie Austin followed Henry Sayler after the 1984 elections, and Austin was the first woman to chair the Florida Republican Party. During her tenure, Republican voter registration climbed from 36 percent to 42 percent of the state's voting population; after a twenty-year hiatus, Bob Martinez became the state's second Republican governor; Florida voters sent Republican Connie Mack III to the U.S. Senate to replace retiring Democratic Senator Lawton Chiles;[40] the 1988 elections delivered the state's electoral votes to George H. W. Bush in the presidential election; and Republicans made their first inroads into the posts on the Florida cabinet.[41] Austin's success in Florida earned her an invitation to cochair the Republican National

Leaders at a Republican unity gathering on the steps of the Florida Historic Capitol. *Right to left, front:* Republican Party Chair Jeanie Austin, Ambassador Mel Sembler, Tom Slade. *Left to right, rear:* Art Teele, Representative Jeff Stabins, Senator Ander Crenshaw, Representative Sandra Mortham, Representative Stan Bainter, Ken Conner, Senator Jim Scott, and Secretary of Commerce Jeb Bush. Green family collection.

Committee with Lee Atwater from South Carolina, and in 1989 she vacated her position as state party chair to assume her new role with the National Committee.

When Bob Martinez came to Tallahassee to assume his seat as Florida's new governor, his initial choice to replace Austin as chair of the Republican Party was former State Senator Van Poole, and Poole and his staff managed the state party's efforts through the elections of 1992. In 1990, although Martinez's reelection bid was not successful, there were other important Republican strides. Republicans held on to the two cabinet posts—secretary of state and treasurer and insurance commissioner—that had been won in special elections two years earlier; and the new faces in the state's congressional delegation included Republicans Craig T. James from Volusia County, Cliff Stearns from Gainesville, and Ileana Ros-Lehtinen from Miami-Dade County.[42] In the 1992 elections, Republicans under Poole's leadership captured one-half of the seats in the forty-member state Senate; Florida's electoral votes went to the Republican presidential ticket; and four more new Florida Republicans were elected to the U.S. Congress—Tillie Fowler from Duval County, John Mica from Orange County, Charles Canady from Polk County, and Dan Miller from Manatee County.[43]

Poole relinquished the reins of the state Republican Party to Tom Slade in 1993, and Slade's tenure marked the institutionalization of modern campaign techniques and some of the most sophisticated refinements to the Republican Party's campaign operations.[44] Under his supervision, the party "exercised discipline, outreach, and ingenuity in ways that had not been seen in Republican circles previously."[45] Slade's assembled staff directed campaigns, raised money, promoted greater diversity in candidate recruitment, brought focus to the Republican ideology, and the party's efforts paid tangible dividends for Republicans.[46] During Slade's tenure as chairman, Republican candidates captured a majority of the seats in both Houses of the state Legislature—the Senate in 1994 and the House in 1996; and in 1998, Florida voters elected Jeb Bush as the state's third Republican governor of the modern era.[47] The same 1998 elections saw the party's candidates capture a majority of the seats on the Florida cabinet, and Republicans assumed

Left to right: Sally Bradshaw, Ann Herberger, and Tom Slade discuss strategy during the 1998 Jeb Bush gubernatorial campaign. Green family collection.

majority control of Florida's executive branch of state government for the first time in the modern era.[48]

Tom Slade left his post at the state party following the 1998 elections, and Governor Bush's choice to replace Slade as chairman was Miami attorney and Republican Party Vice Chairman Al Cardenas.[49] Cardenas continued the structure and continuity that Slade had put in place, and in the fall elections of 2000, the Republican Party claimed fifteen of the state's twenty-five seats in the U.S. Congress; Republicans maintained the majority in the Florida House under the leadership of Speaker Tom Feeney; they retained their majority status in the Florida Senate under President John McKay;[50] and George W. Bush won a narrow and controversial victory in the presidential election over Democrat Al Gore.[51]

At the conclusion of Cardenas's term, Governor Bush expressed no preference for his successor and left the decision to Republican Party officials to select the new chair from within their ranks. At the state Republican Party convention in 2003, Carole Jean Jordan from Indian River County came away the winner in a three-person contest to become the second woman to head the party's statewide organization.[52] During Jordan's tenure, the party successes continued. In 2004, Florida voters elected Republican Mel Martinez to the U.S. Senate and retained fifteen of the state's twenty-five seats in the U.S. Congress in the Republican column.[53] The state's electoral votes went to the Bush-Cheney ticket in the presidential election, and the Republican Party maintained its control of both Houses of the Legislature under Speaker Allan Bense and Senate President Tom Lee.[54]

In the election that followed in 2006, Charlie Crist was elected to the governor's office as a Republican,[55] and Crist's hand-picked choice to replace Jordan as the head of the state party was Jim Greer.[56] It proved a bad choice for Florida Republicans. During Greer's tenure, the work of Slade, Cardenas, and Jordan began to unravel in controversy.[57] Allegations of corruption and the theft of party funds ultimately resulted in Greer's indictment on six felony charges for funneling money from Republican Party coffers into a consulting company that he controlled, and the theft and mismanagement promptly led to Greer's removal.[58]

In the wake of the growing controversy and subsequent indictments, Republican legislative leaders Mike Haridopolos and Dean Cannon turned to state Republican Senator John Thrasher to rehabilitate the floundering state party organization. Thrasher was equal to the task, and by the fall elections of 2010, Thrasher had accomplished his objectives to stabilize and revitalize the Republican organization, and the chairmanship and leadership of the state Republican Party was passed to former State Representative Dave Bitner.[59]

Charlie Crist left the Republican Party to seek a seat in the U.S. Senate as an independent in 2010, but under the party structure stabilized by Thrasher and headed by Bitner, Republican Marco Rubio defeated Crist in the fall elections. In addition to Rubio's victory in the U.S. Senate race, Republicans claimed the governor's office with Rick Scott's victory over Democrat Alex Sink; all of the state cabinet posts were won by the Republican candidates; seventeen of Florida's twenty-five seats in the U.S. Congress went to the party's candidates; and Republicans continued to control both Houses of the Legislature under Senate president Mike Haridopolos and House Speaker Dean Cannon with supermajorities for the first time.[60]

Despite the embarrassing setbacks brought on by Crist's selection of Jim Greer, from the early years of Murfin, Crittenden, Thomas, and Taylor through Thrasher's stabilizing hands, the state Republican Party remained the central support structure that enhanced the role of local Republican executive committees.[61] The state party also encouraged the organization of other components of the Republican infrastructure that took on a social character and fostered small-group gatherings that complemented the Republican Party's formal business structure.

Federation of Republican Women

As the numbers of Republican voters grew in Florida, it was local Republican clubs that provided the venues for small-group gatherings, and at the gatherings, there were opportunities for members to meet candidates, recruit new supporters for the Republican cause, and socialize among their fellow party faithful.[62] These social forums included Young Republican Clubs, clubs for college Republicans, community clubs, and clubs sanctioned by the National and Florida Federations of Republican Women.

The network of sanctioned Republican women's clubs was considered the nation's largest grassroots political organization, and in Florida, the Republican women's clubs were the first to make a meaningful impact within the party's organizational structure.[63] Four years before Florida voters sent the first Republican to the U.S. Congress, the Florida Federation of Republican Women received their authorizing charter from the national organization, and with the charter, the women's clubs began to organize. As Republicans approached majority status in both Houses of the Florida Legislature and as the twentieth century came to a close, the Florida Federation of Republican Women had more than fifty affiliated women's clubs throughout the state.[64] From the grassroots of the club memberships and the local county party executive committees, Republican women stepped into the political arena in increasing numbers to become successful candidates for office and expand their voices into the modern era of Florida's two-party politics.

Like the formal party organization itself, early leaders in the Florida Federation of Republican Women came to prominence from the counties in the urban horseshoe. From the ICY organization and Pinellas County, Mary Grizzle, Betty Easley, Sandra Mortham, and Dorothy Sample were among those who emerged from the Federation clubs to have long and active careers as elected Republican officials. From Lake County, Anna Cowin preceded her service in the Florida Senate by serving as the president of the Leesburg Federated Republican Women's Club. Senator Kelli Stargel was president of the Republican Women's Club of Lakeland, and Representative Colleen Burton was a member of the Lakeland Republican Club before their elections to the Legislature. Rachel Burgin was a member of the Plant City Women's Republican Club before she was elected to the Florida House.[65] From Orange and Seminole Counties in central Florida, Paula Hawkins and Toni Jennings became two of the party's highest-ranking public officeholders—Hawkins as a member of the U.S. Senate and Jennings as president of the Florida Senate and later as Florida's lieutenant governor.[66] Other women's clubs contributed and produced leaders, too.

From Palm Beach County, Federation activists included Roberta "Bobbie" James, whose husband, Bill James, became the Republican leader of the Florida House in 1974, and Carol Hanson, who served as a council member and vice mayor of Boca Raton before coming to the Florida House, where she served for seven terms.[67] State Representative Sharon Merchant had club affiliations with the Federated Republican Club of Palm Beach and the Young Republican Club of Palm Beach County, and during her tenure in the Florida House, Merchant took part in the selection of Florida's first Republican House Speaker.[68] Debbie Sanderson from Broward County rose from the presidency of the East Broward Women's Republican Club to serve eight terms as a member of the Florida House and then as a member of the Florida Senate.[69] Faye Culp was president of the Hillsborough Women's Republican Club before she came to the Florida House to serve six terms.[70] Like Merchant, both Sanderson and Culp were part of the House Republican caucus that elected the first Republican Speaker.[71] Farther to the south from the Riviera Republican Women's Club in Dade County, club member Ileana Ros-Lehtinen was elected to the Florida House in 1982 and became the first Hispanic woman to serve in the Florida Legislature.[72]

In the upper east region of the urban horseshoe, Beth Johnson from the Cocoa Beach Women's Republican Club in Brevard County was one of the new senators who came to the Legislature in the initial Republican surge during the 1966–67 elections.[73] Jane Robinson from the Titusville Women's Republican Club followed Johnson from Brevard County when she was elected to the House in 1970, where she subsequently served three terms. Marilyn B. Evans-Jones from Brevard County served as a director of the National Federation of Republican Women, and she came to the Capitol in 1976 to serve ten years as a member of the state House of Representatives and in 1997 was an appointee on the Constitutional Revision Commission.[74] Representative Dixie Sansom came to the Florida House from Brevard County as a member of the club of the Federated Republican Women of South Brevard Beaches.[75] Carole Jean Jordan from Vero Beach began as a member of the Republican Women of Indian River Club; she rose in the party ranks to become the chair of the state Republican Party in 2003; and she followed her service at the state party as the elected property appraiser in Indian River County.[76] Debbie Mayfield was also a member of the Republican Women of Indian River Club, and she came to the state Capitol to serve first as a four-term member of the House of Representatives and then as a member of the Florida Senate.[77]

Frances L. "Chance" Irvine, from the Federated Republican Women's Club of Clay County, was a state committeewoman and chairperson of the county Republican Party.[78] In 1984, she became the first Republican to be elected to the state House of Representatives from Clay County, and she served four terms as a member of that chamber. Jennifer Carroll was also a member of the Federated Republican Women's Club of Clay County and the Clay County Republican Executive Committee before her service in the Florida House; and in 2010, Carroll was elected as Florida's lieutenant governor on the ticket with Governor Rick Scott.[79]

From the western leg of the urban horseshoe, Peggy Simone came from the Manatee County Republican Club to the Legislature and served four terms in the House of Representatives.[80] Lisa Carlton was a member of the Sarasota Republican Executive Committee and came to Tallahassee to serve two terms in the Florida House of Representatives and ten years in the Florida Senate, where she capped her legislative career as a member of the Legislative Budget Commission and the chairperson of the powerful Senate Fiscal Policy & Calendar Committee.[81] Like Marilyn Evans-Jones, Carlton also was appointed to serve as a member of the Constitutional Revision Commission in the 2017.

Senator Nancy Detert followed her term as president of the Republican Women's Club of Sarasota with service in both Houses of the Florida Legislature before returning home to serve on the Sarasota County Commission.[82] Carole Green from Charlotte County was affiliated with the Republican Women Federated and served three terms in the Florida House before joining the administration of Governor Jeb Bush as the secretary of the Department of Elder Affairs.[83] Ginny Brown-Waite from Spring Hill and the West Hernando Republican Club was elected first to the Hernando County Commission and then as a member of the Florida Senate in 1992; she concluded her public service as a member of the U.S. Congress.[84]

The social and political settings offered by the Federated Republican Women's Clubs were one of the important focal points for the party organization. Club members opened their homes for coffee hours and provided other resources for Republican candidates; in the early years, members hand-addressed campaign mail pieces when no preprinted labels were available; they helped to compile voter lists for neighborhood canvassing before the lists were available electronically; and from across the horseshoe, successful candidates came from within their ranks.[85]

"In large measure," reflected Sandy Mortham on her successful 1994 statewide campaign, "I still attribute my win in the Secretary of State's race in large measure to the Florida Federation of Republican Women and their president, Carole Jean Jordan."

The women's clubs were important contributors to the Republican Party network as it was being assembled, but they were not the only social and political venues where Republican loyalists gathered. The affiliated local Republican clubs and the Young Republican Clubs provided similar opportunities to the party network.

Young Republicans and the Local Republican Clubs

Members of the local Republican clubs and the Young Republican Clubs, the "YRs," also combined social gatherings with a variety of campaign activities. The clubs offered camaraderie among like-minded contemporaries, and in the case of the YRs, "they breathed youthful energy into the party organization."[86] From their ranks came more volunteers and supporters; from the club memberships came more individual candidates willing to step into the political arena; and from the young volunteers came many of the initial campaign technicians and staffers who helped contribute to the party's growing success.[87] The clubs provided the volunteers to erect yard signs, the membership support to populate campaign rallies, and the manpower for door-to-door canvassing of residential neighborhoods to distribute campaign literature and seek support for the Republican Party's slate of candidates.[88]

"Without the energy and support of the Young Republicans and the Republican women," remembered former State Representative and former Lieutenant Governor Bobby Brantley, "I don't think I would have ever won an election."[89]

Like the affiliated women's clubs, the YR Clubs and the other local Republican clubs were particularly prevalent in the urban horseshoe counties. In central Florida, the cadres of young Republicans were organized in the Orange County Young Republican Club, the Seminole County Young Republican Club, and the South Brevard Young Republican Club. In Pinellas County, the Republican clubs affiliated with the ICY Machine's organization were the Greater Pinellas Young Republican Club, the North Pinellas Republican Club, and the St. Petersburg Young Republican Club. In south Florida, YRs gathered as members of the Broward County Young Republican Club, the Hollywood Young Republican Club, the South Florida Young Republican Club, the Dade County Young Republican Club, the Biscayne Bay Young Republican Club, and the Young Republicans for Freedom. There were also active Young Republican Clubs in Lee, Palm Beach, Indian River, Charlotte, and Sarasota Counties; and from the active memberships of these YR Clubs came not only the volunteers and the workers for campaigns but also future legislators, members of the U.S. Congress, and future statewide officeholders.

From the West Coast of horseshoe counties, Bill Young from Pinellas County was one of the first YRs to seek public office, and before his election to the Florida Senate, he was a member of the St. Petersburg Young Republican Club. As part of the YRs, Young also served as the state chairman of the Florida Young Republicans and as the national YR committeeman from Florida.[90] From the central Florida counties in the horseshoe, among the first YRs to prominently step forward and begin careers of public service were Lou Frey from Orange County, who also served as state YR chairman, and Dennis Patrick O'Grady from Citrus County.[91] Active in building a central Florida party organization through the region's Young Republicans, Frey won a seat in the U.S. Congress in 1968, and O'Grady joined the Republicans in the state Senate in 1967 as one of the youngest members of the chamber during his tenure of service.[92]

Following the lead of Young, Frey, and O'Grady, YRs from Republican clubs throughout Florida found their way into public service. From Young's region, several of the leaders from the clubs in Pinellas County became elected leaders in Florida government. Before their election to the House of Representatives, both Dennis MacDonald and Dennis Jones served as the president of the St. Petersburg YRs.[93] Jones served eleven terms in the Florida House; he was part of the caucus that elected the first Republican House Speaker; he rose to become the body's Speaker pro tempore in 1998; and he concluded his public service as a member of the Florida Senate.[94] Future House Republican Leader Ron Richmond was president of the West Pasco Republican Club before his election to the Legislature, and Jack Latvala was president of the North Pinellas Republican Club before his election to the Florida Senate.[95]

The general memberships of the YR clubs were productive venues for candidate recruitment, too.[96] State Representatives Roger Wilson, Richard Price, Laurent "Larry" Belanger, George Hiebner, Tom Woodruff, and Larry Crow were all active members of the St. Petersburg Young Republican Club before their elections.[97] Richard Corcoran and Chris Sprowls were members of the Pasco County Young Republican Club, and among those who earned their initial party credentials in the Greater Pinellas County Young Republican Club were Charles LeCher, Curt Kiser, and Peter Dunbar.[98] Sprowls was elected to the Florida House after his YR activities and garnered the pledges

Congressman Lou Frey and Representative Marilyn Evans-Jones were both early activists in the network, Frey as a Young Republican and Evans-Jones as a director of the National Federation of Republican Women. Photo courtesy of the Florida Historic Capitol Museum.

to become the body's Speaker; during his participation with the YRs, LeCher was elected the mayor of Clearwater; Kiser was initially elected to the Florida House as a YR, continued his service in the Florida Senate, and was a part of the caucus that selected the first Republican Senate president; and Dunbar spent ten years in the Florida House before joining the senior staff of Republican Governor Bob Martinez.[99]

Like Frey and O'Grady from the central Florida counties, the Orange County Young Republican Club produced other successful candidates for public office. John Ducker, Bill Sublette, Fred Hagen, Bruce McEwan, and David Simmons each served as the club president before their elections to the Legislature.[100] Both Bobby Brantley and Carl Selph served as president of the Seminole Young Republican Club before beginning their public careers; and future House Majority Leader Adam Hasner was a YR club president before his election to the House.[101] Maryanne Morse was a founding member of the Seminole County Young Republican Club in the early 1970s; she became the secretary of the Republican Party of Florida in 1980 before becoming the state's national Republican committeewoman; and in 1988, she was elected to be the clerk of the court for Seminole County, where she served for nearly three decades.[102]

Others who began their political careers from the clubs in central Florida include State Representatives Eugene C. "Gene" Mooney, William D. "Bill" Gorman, Lewis Earle, John Mica, Rich Crotty, Lawrence R. "Larry" Kirkwood, Tom Drage, and future Senate President Andy Gardner. All began as members of the Orange County Young Republican Club.[103] Representative Chris Dorworth was a member of the Seminole Republican Club before his election; Senator Clark Maxwell and Representative William E. "Bill" Powell were members of the South Brevard YRs before their elections; Representative Charles Davis was a member of the Indian River YRs; Pat Patterson was from the West Volusia Republican Club; and State Senator Bill Bankhead was a Young Republican from Ponte Vedra in St. Johns County before coming to the Legislature.[104]

From the horseshoe counties in southwest Florida, Representative and future State Senator Bob Johnson had his roots in the Sarasota County Young Republican Club; Representative Greg Gay had his roots in the Charlotte County YRs; Representative Ralph Livingston was a member of the Cape Coral Republican Club; Representative Mark Flanagan was from the Manatee County YRs; and Representative Jeff Kottkamp was a member of the Sanibel-Captiva Republican Club.[105]

In southeast Florida, the Republican club memberships produced still more candidates for public office. Representative Tom Warner was a member of the Jupiter-Tequesta Republican Club before his election to the Florida House; Russell Sykes, Frank Messersmith, and James C. "Jim" Hill Jr. were all YRs in Palm Beach County before their elections.[106] Robert J. "Bob" Shelly was president of the Pompano Beach Republican Club before he came to the Legislature; State Senator George Williamson was from the Fort Lauderdale Republican Club; Representative Daniel Bass was a member of the Broward County Young Republican Club; and Van Poole was a member of the Hollywood Young Republican Club as he began a career that took him first to the Legislature as a member of both the House and Senate and then to the administration of Bob Martinez before becoming chairman of the state Republican Party.[107]

From Miami-Dade County, Mario Diaz-Balart was the president of the South Florida Young Republicans before beginning a public career that took him to the Florida Legislature as member of both the House and the Senate and then to the U.S. Congress.[108] Roberto Casas and Manuel "Manny" Prieguez were members of the Young Republicans for Freedom; Bruce Hoffmann and Carlos Lacasas were members of the Biscayne Bay Young Republicans; Al Gutman and Scott McPherson were members of the Dade County YRs; and Manny Diaz Jr. served as president of the Hialeah–Miami Lakes Republican Club.[109] All later became elected Republican members of the Florida House of Representatives, and Casas, Gutman, and Diaz continued their public service as members of the Florida Senate.[110]

For several of the Young Republicans, their careers as elected officials did not end in the Legislature. After three terms in the state House of Representatives, Bobby Brantley was picked to be Bob Martinez's running mate and was subsequently elected lieutenant governor.[111] Jeff Kottkamp was elected as Florida's lieutenant governor on the ticket with Charlie Crist following his service in the House.[112] After two terms in the state House, John Mica won a seat in the U.S. Congress; and after his service in the Florida Legislature, Rich Crotty returned to Orange County to serve as the county property appraiser and Orange County mayor.[113] Van Poole, Al Cardenas, and Dave Bitner rose from the ranks of the Young Republicans and made their way into the formal party structure to chair the state Republican Party.

Overall, the component pieces of the party organization proved important to the Republican success. The state and local committeemen and committeewomen, the active Republican women, the local Republican clubs, and the youthful energy of the YRs all became part of the growing Republican fabric. The structure, both official and social, helped the Republican Party mature into an organization that was not dependent on the personalities of individual candidates. Each part of the structure contributed to a broader political philosophy, and as the components of the organization matured, each became part of a base of support for Republican candidates that the Democrats had not been able to duplicate.[114] As the era of two-party politics emerged, Republicans simply became better at fielding candidates and running campaigns.[115]

Practical Politics and Support Personnel

From the perspective of the Republican Party's growing organization, there was more to winning campaigns than simply recruiting good candidates.[116] Recruitment was only a starting point, and the business of successful campaigns required planning, organization, and execution. Campaigns required voter-outreach techniques, campaign messages and materials, and by necessity, a budget and funding for the budget.[117]

"Viewed from the outside over a long time," wrote veteran capital reporter Bill Cotterell in the aftermath of the 2016 elections, "the difference between the parties seems to be in the operating methods, as much as beliefs. The Republicans put their heads down, charge straight ahead and win elections."[118]

To provide the guidance for these operating methods and techniques and to gather the needed financial assets, the Republican Party organization recruited and trained a staff knowledgeable in campaign techniques to craft and implement plans for their candidates. In Florida, it began with the state party chairmen, who turned to the ranks of the Young Republicans and other volunteers eager to learn the "science" of campaigns and support the party's campaign efforts.[119] The Republican organization learned from the initial techniques employed by Jack Insco and the ICY Machine, and it looked to the National Republican Party, which offered campaign schools and experienced campaign officials like Robert E. Lee, who came to Florida to run Claude Kirk's campaign in 1966.[120] In time, other Republican consultants were recruited to Florida, too—among them Randy Enwright, Rich Heffley, David Johnson, Sally Bradshaw, Mike Harrell, Brewser Brown, Todd Reid, Meredith O'Rourke, Melissa Stone, Slater Bayliss, Jennifer and Greg Ungru, and Kirk Pepper—and unlike their Democratic counterparts who were recruited to Florida campaigns and left when the elections were over, the Republican consultants tended to remain in the Florida political network; in the process, the expertise of the Republican infrastructure continued to expand.[121]

Beginning in an era of low-budget campaigns and before the internet and social media, successful Republican elections in the horseshoe relied heavily on direct mail, telephone banks, and canvassing door-to-door, which remains a viable and effective technique.[122] Later, the process was refined to include paid field staff and campaign advisors, but in the early years, the Republican efforts were grassroots in the truest sense. Often there were only enough financial resources for local and legislative candidates to deliver one direct mailing to voter households. For early campaigns, "postal workers" for the direct-mail efforts consisted of volunteers who stuffed envelopes, organized the mail pieces in postal trays by zip code, and stacked the trays in a candidate's living room for transport to the post office in time for the mail to arrive just prior to Election Day.[123] Sometimes the pieces were positive, and sometimes the pieces were "brown cows" that scrutinized the record of a Democratic opponent.[124]

When the Republicans began their final push toward a majority in the Houses of the Florida Legislature and control of the Florida cabinet in the 1990s, the relationship between the Republican Party staff and its public officials was more sophisticated and more closely coordinated.[125] For the young staff contingent that stepped forward, it was also an opportunity. Many who came forward were from college campuses, and others came from roles as first-time campaign volunteers. They stayed involved in the political system for years; they grew into new roles as they gained experience; and many assumed key positions in the party's hierarchy as the Republican tide continued to rise among Florida voters.[126]

"Campaigns were the springboard for up-and-comers," remembered Stephen Shiver, who was one of the young staffers taking advantage of the opportunity, "and the up-and-comers were like an ever-expanding network that just continued to build on itself."[127]

As the process matured and volunteers and employees gained experience, the Republican Party produced skilled consultants, campaign managers, and a field staff to support candidates running on the Republican ticket.[128] Often overlooked by the media coverage during elections, these political staffers and consultants became an important part of the Republican Party base and essential to the success of its candidates. They staffed and managed the campaigns; they coordinated fund-raising and campaign logistics; they helped to organize the efforts of local volunteers; and they implemented campaign techniques that included the use of direct mail, telephone calling plans, and voter-turnout strategies.[129] When the election cycle and the campaigns concluded, some of these key staff members joined the new leaders they helped to elect in state government positions and converted their service into policymaking roles. Others on staff remained with the Republican Party for extended periods, and still others took their skills with them to the private sector. From the private sector, they raised and contributed campaign funds, and periodically they returned to active participation in campaigns as managers, consultants, and finance directors for other Republican candidates.[130]

Notable early examples included Herb Harmon, Jack Latvala, Rocky Pennington, Marian Johnson, Lanny Wiless and Amy Baker, who began as Republican Party staffers during the chairmanships of Bill Taylor and Henry Sayler. Following her tenure at the party, Amy Baker joined the successful gubernatorial campaign of Bob Martinez and, after the election, joined the new administration as a member of the governor's senior staff.[131] After their time with the party, Harmon, Latvala, and Pennington migrated to the private sector to create one of the state's earliest and most successful Republican political consulting and direct-mail businesses, distributing more than ten million pieces of direct mail during George H. W. Bush's 1992 presidential campaign.[132] From the private sector, Pennington remained affiliated with the state party and managed state Senate campaigns as the Republicans edged toward the majority in the upper chamber.[133]

After her tenure with the state Republican Party, Johnson worked for the party's presidential nominees before joining Associated Industries of Florida as their political director and as a vice president at the Florida Chamber and executive director of the Florida Chamber's Political Institute.[134] Latvala eventually entered the political arena in his own right, serving fifteen years as a member of the Florida Senate in two different sequences, rising in the upper chamber to be first the Senate majority leader and then the chairman of the powerful Senate Appropriations Committee.[135] Wiles took his experience into national Republican politics, and he was part of the campaigns for four different Republican presidents beginning with Ronald Reagan.[136]

As the sophistication and staff at the state party offices grew, there were others like Jon Johnson who followed the early examples of Harmon, Latvala, and Pennington. Johnson began at the state party offices as a college student during Jeanie Austin's chairmanship, working first on phones and in opposition research and then in campaign fieldwork before joining the Martinez administration as chief of staff at the Department of Professional Regulation. After his service at the Department, Johnson made his way into the private sector, where he remained an important part of the Republican fund-raising network.[137]

During the sequential chairmanships of Tom Slade and Al Cardenas, the party organization brought in another team of staff members to direct campaigns, raise funds, and expand the Republican influence.[138] After their tenures at the party, many of these young staff members also took their talents beyond the Bush Building Republican Party headquarters to other roles. Among them were Randy Enwright, John Wehrung, David Johnson, Rich Heffley, Gene McGee, Brewser Brown, Shelley Green, Dane Eagle, Brecht Heuchan, Greg Turbeville, Frank Terraferma, Joel Springer, Stephen Shiver, Jamie Wilson, Portia Palmer, and David Rivera.[139]

Randy Enwright started in partisan politics as an intern with the Missouri Republican Party; he rose to become the party's political director; and after successfully managing the 1988 primary campaigns in Missouri and in the Iowa caucuses for President George H. W. Bush, he joined the staff

State Republican Party staff on a break at the 1996 GOP National Convention in San Diego. *Right to left:* Shelley Green, Todd Schnick, Debbie Mortham, Travis Blanton, and Paula Nelson. Green family collection.

of the National Republican Party in Washington. Enwright was recruited to Florida by Tom Slade in 1995, and he served as the state party's executive director until 2000. During his tenure, Republicans completed their transition to the majority in both Houses of the Legislature; they took over majority control of the executive branch cabinet; and voters elected Florida's third Republican governor.[140]

Enwright continued as a Republican consultant in the private sector after leaving his staff role at the party; he recruited Kirk Pepper and Greg Ungru to Florida from the National Republican Committee during the 2006 election cycle; and he became a permanent fixture in the Florida political arena as Republicans continued their rise to dominance.[141] John Wehrung also remained in the political arena to work in both legislative and statewide campaigns after he left the party staff; David Johnson did as well, and in addition to his stint as the state party's executive director, his campaign acumen took him to Republican campaigns for governor and the U.S. Senate in other parts of the country, too.[142] Shelley Green came to the party out of college to be Slade's executive assistant; her work in the network continued in the private sector after her time on the party staff; and she remained an active contributor working with Richard Coates, who served first as the state party's general counsel and then as an independent legal advisor in the Republican network.[143]

Rich Heffley and Gene McGee provided key consulting services at the state party for the Republican candidates that captured majority membership in the Florida House, and after their time at the party, both Heffley and McGee departed for new roles in the Republican network.[144] Heffley became the chief of staff for Sandra Mortham during her term as Florida's secretary of state, and he continued as a Republican strategist for a continuous series of Republican legislative leaders after entering the private sector. Gene McGee was also a member of Mortham's senior staff, and he, too, continued as an advisor and consultant for Senate President Jim King and other Republican leaders after his public service.[145] Brewser Brown was the state party's communications director during Slade's chairmanship, and Brown transitioned into the executive branch of state government to become first the chief of staff for Frank Brogan at the Department of Education and then Brogan's chief of staff in the lieutenant governor's office.[146] Six years after his stint with the state party, Dane Eagle came to Tallahassee as a member of the Florida House.[147]

Other party staffers spent time in the formal policy process with the legislators whom they helped to elect. Brecht Heuchan joined the staff of the first Republican Speaker, Dan Webster; Greg Turbeville served on the staff of Florida's second Republican Speaker, John Thrasher; and Frank Terraferma, who began as a young campaign volunteer and was recruited to the party staff by Heffley, served on the staff of House Speaker Allan Bense.[148] Al Cardenas brought Jamie Wilson to the party staff as the executive director during his tenure as party chairman, and Cardenas assigned minority outreach programs for the Republicans to new staff members Portia Palmer and David Rivera. All three transitioned to long careers in the political arena.[149] Joel Springer interrupted his employment at the state party to join the Senate staff of John McKay during his presidency; Geoffrey Becker served as political director of the state party between service in the House Majority Office and a tenure on the staff of Governor Rick Scott; and Stephen Shiver spent two stints on the state party staff between his roles in campaigns and service in the Legislature.[150]

Shiver's path took him first from the Republican Party to Frank Brogan's successful campaign for commissioner of education; next he was the chief of executive assistant to House Speaker Tom Feeney; and he returned

State Republican Party staff members with Speaker Feeney at a fund-raising event in Yankee Stadium. *Left to right, standing:* Chip Case, Kim Stone Kirtley, Tom Feeney, Stephen Shiver; *kneeling:* John Law and Frank Terraferma. Shiver family collection.

to the party as executive director during Carole Jean Jordan's time as the state Republican Party chair before he entered the private sector.[151] During his tenure as executive director, Shiver brought others to the party staff, among them Andy Palmer and Sarah Busk. Busk began as aide to the party chair; she was appointed as an alternate delegate to the 2004 Republican National Convention; she served as a consultant to Governor Scott's Inaugural Committee; and she transitioned into a successful private-sector career with Shiver at the lobbying offices of former Republican Party Chairman Al Cardenas.[152] Like Shiver, Andy Palmer spent two separate stints on the state party staff, initially serving as the director of political affairs and then as executive director for Chair Carole Jean Jordan following Shiver. Palmer served as the director of Republican House campaigns for Speaker-designate Dean Cannon in 2010; and he returned to the party as its executive director under Dave Bitner's chairmanship before making a successful entry to the private sector.[153] Kirk Pepper transitioned from the state party to the House Speaker's office during Cannon's speakership before he, too, entered the private sector.[154]

There were other individuals who were part of the network, too. Some began as young campaign volunteers like Mat Bahl, Derek Whitis, Charlie Dudley, Brian Jogerst, and Chris Finkbeiner.[155] Others began with the Republican Party staff and transitioned into legislative roles; notable among them were Travis Blanton, Sarah Bascom, Kim McGlynn, Christina Johnson, Steve Madden, Cameron Yarbrough, and Katherine Becker.[156] Like those who preceded them and the others who followed, these individuals were typical of the many new faces who entered the political process and choose to remain involved, serving as consultants and advisors and espousing the party philosophy as the Republican network in Florida continued to expand.

Platform Planks and Political Philosophy

Like the approaches to their organizational structure, Florida's Democratic and Republican Parties were different in their approaches to party dogma and philosophy. Republican ideology was consistently defined from the outset of the modern era, with its candidates embracing the party's emphasis on low taxes, limited government, economic development, environmental protection, social stability, and traditional cultural values. In contrast, when the reality of two-party politics began to emerge, Democrats were still in the midst of an internal battle between their "conservative" and "liberal" wings, with candidates running their own campaigns outside the party structure.[157] Former Democratic Governor Millard Caldwell described his party's approach this way: "The dominant [Democratic] party in Florida prepares no gubernatorial platform and the determination of the objectives to be followed during the succeeding four years is largely left to the candidate. The Legislature, by custom, has adopted the practice of treating the successful candidate's platform as the public mandate."[158]

In the statewide races and in the Legislature, the intraparty Democratic platform struggles were over issues of race, environmental sensitivity, education, and whether control of the reins of state government were to remain with the northern and rural elements of the Democratic Party led by members of the Pork Chop Gang or pass to Democratic leaders for the urban population centers.[159] Republicans had no Pork Chop Gang or rural elements to speak of, and their political base found its home in the changing demographics of the urban horseshoe and the constituencies found there. From the beginning, Republicans made the effort to define their political ideology with an agenda that highlighted the differences between the parties "and articulated a philosophy attuned to what the public was looking for."[160] While the Democrats tended to rely on the personalities of their individual candidates, Republicans "had a united philosophical messaging" toward their political ideology.[161]

The bookends between the Republican emergence and Republican dominance were the administrations of Claude Kirk and Jeb Bush, and the basic party ideology that began with Kirk remained remarkably consistent as Republicans moved toward the majority that culminated with the election of Bush.[162] Between the bookends, many of the campaign platform planks became part of the state's modern public policy—public policy not possible during the Democratic Pork Chop era and not possible without the Republicans.[163] Beginning with their initial statewide success at the ballot box—the election of Claude Kirk—the Republican political philosophy focused on themes that included modernizing state government and making it more responsive, protecting the state's environment, improving public education, and creating a friendly environment for businesses and employers.[164] At times, the objectives advocated by Republicans aligned with those of the Democrats, and the successes were notable.[165] At other times, the political philosophies clashed and put the parties at odds with each other, giving voters the opportunity to see the differences and choose between candidates with contrasting philosophies.

Many of the new voters relocating to Florida and the urban horseshoe tended to be Republicans, and the wave of newcomers served to reinforce one consistency among the state's voters—that "Floridians have shown a persistent dislike of liberal, free-spending candidates at the state level."[166] That made taxes an issue, too; and beginning with the campaign of Claude Kirk, limitation on state taxes and limitations on state spending became prominent campaign themes that remained a part of the Republican dogma as the modern two-party era matured.[167]

The tax increases advocated by Robert King High in his race against Claude Kirk in 1966 became the first significant policy confrontation between the two parties. Following Kirk's defeat in 1970, the battle renewed itself between Republicans in the Legislature and the new Democratic Governor Reubin Askew over Askew's initiative to enact Florida's corporate income tax.[168] During Governor Martinez's first months in office, the bipartisan attempt to preserve the repeal of the sales tax exemptions enacted during the last year of Bob Graham's tenure as governor fractured along partisan lines in a matter of weeks after the Legislature adjourned. The partisan confrontation over taxes during the Martinez years continued when Democrats in the Legislature pushed to increase Florida's gas tax, and Republican legislators and their governor opposed the efforts. The gas tax battle continued through the balance of Martinez's term and consumed partisan energy through two regular and two special legislative sessions before it was resolved.[169]

Florida's next Republican governor, Jeb Bush, campaigned on themes similar to his Republican predecessors. He committed to provide tax relief, protect the environment, improve public schools, and reform the social services for children, elders, and the disabled.[170] During Bush's tenure, the governor and his legislative allies gave consistent attention to tax cuts; and the theme remained a Republican mantra through the two terms of Governor Rick Scott.[171]

Beginning with Florida's first Republican governor, there were other planks in the platform, too. Kirk's "white paper" campaign topics offered reforms centered around (1) modernizing the state's government; (2) protecting the state's environment; and (3) criminal justice initiatives highlighted by his "War on Crime."[172] The basic themes from the 1966 campaign remained with Kirk during his term in office; and variations of the themes renewed themselves during the administrations of Bob Martinez, Jeb Bush, and Rick Scott.

During the interim between Republican governors, Republican legislators shouldered the advocacy for these party policy themes.[173] Some of the objectives were compatible with the philosophy of the urban Democrats, and initiatives to reform and modernize state government passed the Legislature with bipartisan support at the beginning of the modern era. Notable examples included the state's new constitution and the reorganization of Florida's executive branch of state government that followed its passage by the voters. These were initiatives that would not have been possible without the unified votes of the Republicans in the House of Representatives led by Don Reed.[174]

Republican legislators also carried forward variations of the environmental themes that Kirk had featured in his campaign white papers.[175] Some of the environmental innovations included legislation sponsored by Senate Republican Leader Bill Young that imposed environmental cleanup obligations on shippers that spilled pollutants into Florida harbors.[176] Florida's first laws to protect the state's sensitive natural wetlands originated as a Republican initiative; the House sponsor of the legislation to reclaim lands mined for phosphate was a Republican; and the first initiative creating protections for Florida's saltwater environment in the estuaries and the fisheries found below the mean high-water line was sponsored by a Republican.[177]

During the administration of Governor Bob Martinez, the basic themes of government reform, environmental protection, and "tough-on-crime" remained prominent in the Republican dogma. Arriving in Tallahassee, Martinez faced a deteriorating prison system with severe overcrowding, poor food service, and inadequate medical care that left the state with indiscriminate releases from it prisons.[178] Four weeks after he assumed office, Martinez stepped forward with solutions that included procedures to eliminate the indiscriminate releases; criteria for longer and stiffer sentences for violent offenders and career criminals; and a program to rebuild the state's prison system.[179] In a one-day special session, the foundation for all three parts of the governor's program was approved with bipartisan support in the Legislature.[180] As his administration progressed, the environmental initiatives during Martinez's tenure included the Preservation 2000 land preservation program cosponsored by Representative Safley in the House; it included the initial funding for the restoration of the Kissimmee River Basin; and it also included his successful efforts to block offshore oil exploration in the coastal waters of the Gulf of Mexico.[181]

The basic Republican doctrine renewed itself again during the administration of Jeb Bush. Bush continued the Martinez preservation initiative for environmentally sensitive lands, and Republican Senator Jack Latvala sponsored the program's renewal in the Legislature, renaming the program Florida Forever.[182] New criminal justice initiatives during the Bush administration included "10–20–Life" for criminals using firearms in the commission of a felony and mandatory minimum sentences for convicted felons. Government-reform initiatives advocated by Bush further modernized the agencies and departments of state government; brought new technologies into the system to improve agency services and department accountability; and streamlined the structure of the state's executive branch.[183]

Beyond the basic themes espoused by Florida Republicans during the early years of the modern era, national Republican policies had an impact as well. The demographic diversity of new Hispanic residents and the policies of the Nixon and Reagan administrations toward communism, particularly toward Communist Cuba, brought large numbers of Cuban Americans into the Republican camp.[184]

"The Cuban Americans in Miami-Dade came en masse to the Republican fold after President Kennedy left people on the beach at the Bay of Pigs," recalled former Republican State Representative Jim Brodie from Miami.[185]

The anti-Castro policies that were embraced by the Republican dogma at the national level were important to the Cuban American community centered in south Florida, and their allegiance to the Republican Party was another important building block in the party's foundation during the closing decades of the twentieth century.[186]

In contrast to the Republicans, Democrats entered the modern era with divided priorities among the liberal and conservative factions of their party; there was an inconsistency in the advocacy of policies by their candidates from different parts of the state with different perspectives; and Democrat campaigns relied more on the loyalty of voters to individual candidates than to a consistent party philosophy.[187] For Republicans, their basic party ideological spectrum provided consistent messaging from one election to the next and from one candidate to the next, and the consistency helped to create a home for like-minded voters who identified with the Republican messages.[188]

The Conversion of the Believers

The documented population spurts brought new numbers of Republican voters to Florida from other parts of the country, but the momentum for two-party competition came from others who were already residents of the state, too. Change in party registration and Democratic voters willing to cast their ballots for Republican candidates came from those who were discontented with their initial alignment as Democrats and disillusioned with the national Democratic Party.[189] They included voters who identified more readily with the consistent Republican dogma and voters who found the policy messages of Republican candidates more attractive than those of their Democratic counterparts.[190] Some of the conversions were immediate, while other changes happened over a generation or more; Republicans enthusiastically welcomed the converts.

Notable among the immediate converts in the early years of the modern era was Claude Kirk, who surfaced initially in the political arena heading

"Democrats for Nixon" in 1960; but by 1964, he had changed parties and was the Republican Party's nominee for the U.S. Senate; and two years later, he became the party's first successful statewide candidate.[191] Bob Martinez, Florida's second Republican governor, was also a Democrat when his public service began.[192] State Senator and later Chairman of the state Republican Party Tom Slade and early Senate Republican Leader John Ware also began their public carriers as Democrats, but both returned to the Florida Legislature after court-ordered reapportionment in 1967 as members of the new Republican minority.[193]

Jim Smith began his career in public service when he was elected Florida's attorney general in 1978 as a Democrat, and he became another high-visibility convert less than a decade later. He ran unsuccessfully in the Democratic primary for governor in 1986 as the conservative choice but lost to Steve Pajic, who was more identified with the liberal wing of the Democratic Party.[194] After the election cycle, Smith joined the new administration of Bob Martinez; switched his allegiance to the Republican Party; and returned to the Florida cabinet as secretary of state when Martinez appointed him to fill the vacancy created by the resignation of Democrat George Firestone, in the process becoming the first Republican member of the Florida cabinet in the modern era.

Andy Ireland from Winter Haven was elected to the U.S. Congress as a Democrat four times beginning in 1976 but switched parties in 1984 and returned to the Congress for five more terms as a Republican.[195] Bill Grant from Madison came to the Florida Senate as a Democrat in 1982 and was subsequently elected to the U.S. Congress in 1986, but like Ireland, Grant switched parties in 1989 and completed his service in Congress as a Republican.[196]

Jerry Thomas served in the Florida Legislature for twelve years—two terms in the House and eight years in the Senate—rising to preside over the upper chamber as Senate president from 1970 until 1972 as a Democrat. After his tenure in the Legislature, Thomas left the Democratic Party; became a Republican convert; ran unsuccessfully as the Republican nominee for governor in 1974; and concluded his career of public service as the undersecretary of the treasury during the presidency of Republican Gerald Ford.[197]

Like Thomas, Charles Canady came to the Florida House as a Democrat in 1984 but changed his party affiliation to Republican in 1989.[198] In 1992, Canady continued his public service as a four-term Republican member of the U.S. Congress before returning to serve as the general counsel in the office of Governor Jeb Bush and later as a justice on the Florida Supreme Court.[199]

Other converts from the legislative arena included Representative Jerry Melvin, who came to the House of Representatives in 1968 and served five terms as Democrat, but he returned to the House in 1994 to serve eight more years as a Republican, where he was part of the caucus that selected the first Republican Speaker.[200] Dexter Lehtinen was elected to the Florida House as a Democrat but joined his wife, Ileana Ros-Lehtinen, on the other side of the aisle five years later and concluded his service in the Florida Senate as a Republican. State Senator W. D. Childers was elected in 1970, and like Jerry Thomas, he rose to become Senate president as a Democrat, but in 1995, Childers switched parties and served six more years in the Senate as a Republican. George Kirkpatrick came to the Florida Senate in 1980 and served eighteen years as a member of the Democratic caucus, but he, too, switched parties and concluded his final two years in the Senate as a member of the Republican caucus.[201] Harry C. Goode Jr. came from one of Brevard County's founding families and was elected mayor of Melbourne in 1979. In 1986, Goode came to the Florida House as Democrat and served seven terms—the first six as a Democrat before switching parties and completing his final term as a Republican.[202]

Malcolm Beard served fourteen years as the Democratic sheriff of Hillsborough County; he came to the Florida Legislature as a Democrat in 1978, but in 1985 he switched his party affiliation and concluded his legislative career as a Republican member of the Florida Senate.[203] Charlie Dean was also a Democrat when he was elected as sheriff of Citrus County, but after serving in that capacity for sixteen years, he concluded his public service in the mature era of the two-party system as a Republican member of the Florida Legislature, serving from 2002 to 2007 in the House of Representatives and from 2007 to 2016 as a member of the Florida Senate.[204]

Other conversions happened within families with a tradition of public service, and some took place over a generation or more. Lisa Carlton's great-granduncle served as the governor of Florida; her grandfather was the Hardee County tax assessor; her uncle served as a member of the Florida Senate; her cousin served in the Florida House; and her father served as a member of the Sarasota County Commission—all were Democrats.[205] Different from those of earlier family generations, however, Lisa Carlton chose the Republican Party. She began her public service as an administrative assistant for Representative Jim Lombard when he was the Republican leader of the Florida House. In 1994, Carlton was elected to the House of Representatives as a Republican; she continued her fourteen-year legislative career as a member of the Republican caucus in the Florida Senate; and in 2006, she was designated as the president pro tempore of the body by her Republican colleagues.[206]

Toni Jennings became one of the most prominent Republican women of the modern era. She began as a Young Republican and campaign vol-

Left to right: Senators Jeff Atwater, Mike Bennett, Lisa Carlton, and Carey Baker being sworn in at legislative organizational session. Photo by Caroline Ferguson; courtesy of the State Archives of Florida.

unteer, and she was elected to the Florida House of Representatives at the age of twenty-seven and to the Florida Senate four years later. In the Senate, Jennings was selected twice to serve as leader of the Republican caucus; she served an unprecedented two terms as the chamber's presiding officer; and she concluded her public service during the second term of Jeb Bush as Florida's lieutenant governor. Her father, Jack Jennings, had preceded Toni in public service; he was a prominent local Democrat and chairman of the Orange County school board. When she registered to vote for the first time at twenty-one as a Republican, Toni Jennings remembered Orange County Supervisor of Elections Dixie Barber asking her, "Does your daddy know you're doing this?"[207]

Napoleon Bonaparte Broward served as the governor of Florida between 1905 and 1909 as a Populist Democrat. Four generations later, his great-grandson Jeff Atwater was elected to the Florida Legislature as a Republican—first as a member of the House and later as member of the upper chamber, where he became the Senate president. After his tenure in the Legislature, Atwater continued his public service as the state's chief financial officer and part of the Republican majority on the Florida cabinet.[208]

Democrat Bill Chappell served as a member of the Florida House; presided over the House as its Speaker in 1961; and concluded his public service as a Democrat member of the U.S. Congress. A generation later, his stepson, Charles McBurney, was elected to the Florida House as Republican, where he served nine years as a member of the Republican majority.[209] Steve Crisafulli became the tenth Republican Speaker of the Florida House in 2014, but in early generations of the family, his cousin Doyle Carlton served as Florida's Democratic governor and his uncle Vassar Carlton was elected to the Florida Supreme Court as a Democrat in the era when justices were chosen in partisan elections.[210]

Greg Evers had a sixteen-year career in the Florida Legislature as a Republican, serving in both the House and Senate, but in prior generations of his family, three of Evers's cousins were also members of the Florida House of Representatives and were elected to the body as Democrats.[211] Another of Evers's cousins, Durell Peaden, came to the Florida House of Representative as Democrat but concluded his service in the Florida Senate as a Republican. John Mica was elected on the Republican ticket to the Florida House in 1976 and in 1992, and on the Republican ticket to the U.S. Congress.[212] His older brother Dan had preceded him as a member of Congress, but Dan Mica served as a Democrat.

John R. Broxson from Santa Rosa County served in the Florida House and the Florida Senate in the 1960s as a Democrat, but in 2010, his brother Douglas V. "Doug" Broxson came to the Florida Legislature from Santa Rosa County as a Republican, where he, too, served as a member of both chambers. Republican Representative Jim Boyd from Manatee County was preceded by his uncle Wilbur Boyd, who served in the Florida House and then the Senate from 1959 to 1972 as a Democrat.[213] The service of Republican Brad Drake from Walton in the Florida House was preceded by the legislative service in three different decades by his grandfather J. Troy Peacock, who served as a Democratic member of the House, and by his cousin Pat Thomas, who was the last Democrat to serve as the president of the Florida Senate before control passed to the Republicans.[214]

Democrat Randolph Hodges from Cedar Key served as Senate president during the era of the Pork Chop Gang, and his son Gene Hodges served as Democrat member of the House of Representative for nine terms.[215] Randolph Hodges's granddaughter and Gene's niece Dana Young continued the family's tradition of public service in the Florida Legislature, but her service was as a member of the Republican majority—serving first as a member and majority leader in the House of Representatives and later as a member of the Republican majority in the Florida Senate representing the citizens of Hillsborough County.[216] Young was a Democrat through her college years and was interning in the U.S. Congress when she attended President Reagan's State of the Union address in 1985. "He was inspiring," she recalled, "and it was clear to me that I was more like Reagan and less like the Democrats on the national scene." It became the catalyst for a switch to the Republican Party before beginning a political career of her own.[217]

Sandra L. "Sandy" Murman came from Tampa to the Florida House of Representatives as a Democrat in 1996 but switched parties prior to her re-election in 1998 and served three more terms as a member of the Republican caucus.[218] In her final House term, Murman was designated as Speaker pro tempore, and after her legislative service, she returned to Hillsborough County to serve as a Republican member of the county commission.[219] Joe Negron from Stuart also entered the political arena as a Democrat, but Negron lost in his initial bid for a seat in the Florida House in a 1989 special election.[220] He returned to the political arena in 2000 as a Republican to win a seat in the state House of Representatives, where he served three terms; and in 2009, voters elected him to the Florida Senate, where he was chosen by his colleagues to serve as the Senate's president for the 2016–18 term.[221]

Lacy Mahon Jr. served in the Florida House from Duval County for two terms in the 1950s as a Democrat, but in 2000, his son Mark Mahon came to the Florida House from Jacksonville and served eight years as a member of the Republican majority.[222] Representative David Troxler came to the House from Duval County in 1988 as a Republican, but his father had previously served as a Democratic House member from Marion County in 1943.[223] Representative Holly Raschein's great-grandfather also served as a Democrat member of the Florida House, but Raschein came to the House of Representatives from Monroe County as a Republican three generations later.[224]

Ron Schultz was elected property appraiser in Pinellas County in 1976 as a Democrat and served in that capacity for twelve years. Schultz switched parties, became a Republican, and served for five years as the property appraiser in Citrus County; he concluded his public service as a Republican member of the Florida House of Representatives.[225]

Ben Hill Griffin Jr. from Frostproof was also from the Pork Chop era, serving in the Florida House from 1956 until 1963 and in the Florida Senate from 1965 until 1968. Three of Senator Griffin's grandchildren—J. D. Alexander, Baxter Troutman, and Katherine Harris—entered public service in a new generation, and all three were elected as Republicans. Alexander served as a member of the Florida House from 1998 to 2002 and as a member of the Florida Senate from 2002 to 2012; Baxter Troutman was elected to the Florida House of Representatives in 2002 and served four terms; and Katherine Harris came to the Florida Senate in 1994, was elected Florida's secretary of state in 1998, and concluded her career in public service as a Republican member of the U.S. Congress.[226]

Not all the conversions went one way, however. A few officials who started under the Republican banner declined to continue building the network and switched parties midcareer to become Democrats. Earl Dixon from Jacksonville began in the state House as a Republican, but he changed his party affiliation and served two more terms as a Democrat before fading from the political scene. Tom Tobiassen was elected to the Florida House in 1968 as a Republican and continued his service as a Republican in the Senate before returning to the House and serving five terms as a Democrat.[227] The public service and party allegiance of James A. "Jim" Glisson was similar to that of Dixon and Tobiassen. Glisson came to the Legislature in 1968, where he served two terms in the House of Representatives and four years in the Senate as a Republican; but in 1977, he switched parties and concluded his public service in the Florida Senate as a Democrat.[228]

Perhaps the most notable of the converts from the Republican ranks to the Democrat Party was the Republican Party's fourth governor in the modern era, Charlie Crist. After nearly two decades as a Republican officeholder, Crist left the party to run as an independent for the U.S. Senate in an unsuccessful campaign against the former Republican House Speaker Marco Rubio. In 2014, Crist attempted to return to Florida's governor's office as a Democrat, but he was unsuccessful yet again, losing to the Republican incumbent governor, Rick Scott.[229] In 2016, Crist was finally able to resurrect his career as a Democrat when he was successfully elected to the U.S. Congress.[230]

Despite these periodic defections from the growing Republican Party fold, the prevailing tendency was overwhelmingly in the other direction. According to the director of the Florida Chamber Political Institute, Marian Johnson, the most switches between Florida's major political parties occurred between September 2015 and March 2016, and the net gain for the Republican Party totaled 54,585 new registered voters.[231] From the outset, those switching their allegiance to the Republican Party were a welcome and important part of the growing foundation for Republicans in the modern era.

A growing base of new voters; a commitment by party regulars to build the Republican organization; and the consistent messaging of Republican dogma that endured through the decades of growth, all contributed to make two-party politics a reality in Florida. In time, the new reality created a transition for Republicans from the loyal opposition to the new governing majority.

The emerging new reality also contributed to another significant shift, this one among those providing financial support to candidates in the Florida political arena. Political donors who had continued to focus support for the majority party Democrat candidates in the early decades of the new era began to rebalance their traditional giving policies and allocated support for Republicans as well.[232] Included among those from the business community making an early conversion in their allocation of financial resources and providing support for Republican were Steve Wilkerson, Ron Book, Robert Coker, Buddy Gridley, and Charlotte Audie.[233]

5

A STATEWIDE
TWO-PARTY REALITY

THE MOST VISIBLE EVIDENCE of the transition from Democratic dominance to a competitive two-party state for most observers was measured, at least in part, by the outcomes of the races for Florida's statewide offices. When Republicans became viable competitors in the modern two-party environment, there were seven executive branch agencies that were headed by statewide elected officers—the governor, secretary of state, commissioner of education, commissioner of agriculture, comptroller, attorney general, and the treasurer and insurance commissioner—collectively, they formed the Florida cabinet.[1] Each position was held by a Democrat when the era began, but in time, Republicans occupied them all.

The Governors—Claude Kirk

The elections of 1966 were a landmark for Republicans throughout the South and especially in Florida. It was a year that saw a wave of Republicans from the South elected to Congress as Republican membership grew by forty-seven seats in the U.S. House of Representatives and grew by three seats in the U.S. Senate.[2] Florida Republicans also enjoyed their first statewide success in 1966, when Claude Kirk captured the governor's office, and it was the Republican Party's first opportunity to hold a seat on the Florida cabinet.

Claude R. Kirk Jr. was born in San Bernardino, California, in 1926; he enlisted in the Marines in 1943, serving as a second lieutenant during World War II; he attended the University of Alabama law school after the war, where he earned a law degree; and while enrolled, he was called back to serve in the Korean War. After moving to Florida, Kirk found business success in Jacksonville, where he cofounded the American Heritage Life Insurance Company with Ashley Verlander and the Davis brothers before turning his attention to the political arena.[3]

Kirk's first notable foray into politics was in 1960, when he headed the "Democrats for Nixon" campaign in Florida, but he reregistered as a Republican before beginning a political career of his own. In 1964, Kirk entered the partisan political arena in a statewide run for the seat in the U.S. Senate occupied by incumbent Democrat Spessard Holland, but in the general election he lost decisively to Holland.[4] Two years later, in his second statewide attempt, Kirk captured the Republican nomination for governor without major opposition, in part because "no political observer at the beginning of 1966 gave any Republican the slightest chance of unseating the incumbent."[5] Kirk had expected to face incumbent Governor Haydon Burns in the November general election, but after a bitter primary, Democrats nominated Miami Mayor Robert King High as their choice for governor, sending Governor Burns to the sidelines.

Although Burns did not win his party's nomination, he still impacted the general election by successfully defining High as a south Florida liberal during the primary campaign. Once High entered the campaign against Kirk in the aftermath of the primary fight, the Miami mayor remained weak among the voters in the conservative regions of central and north Florida, and the key strategy of Kirk's campaign centered on winning those conservative Democratic votes.[6]

Kirk's path to the governor's mansion was not without intraparty resistance from the emerging Republican base, however. After High's unexpected victory in the primary, Congressman Bill Cramer, who had initially declined to run against the assumed winner Burns, began to rethink his decision, seeing a path to victory for himself over the liberal Miami mayor. Cramer's advisors approached Kirk and asked that he make a public announcement about a "health problem" that required him to leave the race, allowing Cramer to be installed as the Republican Party nominee.[7] For his part, Kirk never considered bowing out, and he went on to defeat High and win the governor's mansion, but Kirk's refusal to acquiesce to Cramer's overture had consequences. The schism between the two prominent Republicans enabled early cracks to form in the emerging party base, and the repercussions manifested themselves four years later; but in the fall of 1966, focus remained on the opportunity to elect a Republican to the governor's office.

Burns's unexpected primary loss paved the way for fund-raising and conservative support to open up for Kirk, even turning some Republican heads at the national level, which facilitated bringing veteran Republican campaign manager Robert E. Lee to the Kirk team.[8] Following High's victory in the primary and the arrival of Lee, Kirk sent a team to meet with Burns in Tallahassee that included his new campaign manager, young campaign volunteer, and future Senate Republican Leader Ken Plante, and former professional baseball player and former American Heritage Insurance associate Bunny Mick.[9] Once Kirk's envoys were seated at their Tallahassee meeting, recalled Plante, Burns leaned forward and spoke directly at Lee about his bitter dislike for Robert King High.

"Mr. Lee, this chair is worth a million dollars a year to the man who sits in it, and that son of bitch cost me four million dollars," Burns said of High. "What do I have to do to keep him out of it?"[10]

Burns basically answered his own question.

Following his meeting with Kirk's envoys, Burns began quietly turning his political and fund-raising operatives over to the Republican nominee. With these new resources, Kirk was transformed from a political unknown to a viable contender with the help of other well-connected Republicans and his new alliance with conservative Democrats. Notable among these individuals were House Republican Leader Don Reed, Republican State Senator Skip Bafalis, and Democratic State Representative and "Pork Chopper" E. C. Rowell. Rowell joined with Burns to open doors traditionally aligned with conservative Florida Democrats, and Reed was constantly providing key contracts and new potential contributors to Lee for Kirk to cultivate.[11] Reed and Bafalis both traveled continuously with Kirk throughout the campaign and coached him on specific issues and details about the inner workings of Tallahassee.[12]

One of the innovative campaign techniques employed to mobilize former Burns supporters began shortly after the primary, and it originated with Lloyd C. Hagaman.[13] A Democrat and supporter of Burns in the primary, Hagaman coined the campaign theme of "Be a Demo-Kirk, Support Claude R. Kirk." He printed thousands of signs to create the Demo-Kirk identity and traveled to every county in Florida distributing the signs and recruiting other sympathetic Democrats to the Kirk campaign. Hagaman's efforts became a unifying theme for conservative Democrats unwilling to support High.[14]

In time, the coaching by Reed and Bafalis turned campaign rhetoric and generalities into the Kirk "white papers," which were released in the month preceding the general election.[15] The white papers showed a serious side of the campaign and provided a remarkably accurate preview of the Kirk administration. In them can be found the origins of the "War on Crime" and suggestions for a statewide law enforcement agency.[16] There were sharp criticisms of the dredge-and-fill operations in the state's coastal estuaries and recommendations for a new surface water management program.[17] There were platform planks for modernizing the structure of Florida's state government, and they included Kirk's recurring "no new taxes" mantra.[18] The combination of new resources, support from conservative Burns Democrats, and credible campaign messages left Kirk and the Republicans optimistic as Election Day approached.[19]

On the weekend before the election, James Clendinen of the *Tampa Tribune* "predicted a Democratic triumph by a margin of as much as 100,000 votes." But Clendinen had badly miscalculated the mood of Florida voters. After their votes were counted on Election Day, the reverse proved true. Kirk won by 152,957 votes, capturing the popular vote outright in fifty-six of Florida's sixty-seven counties.[20]

Despite the 1966 Election Day success, many of the opportunities it offered were squandered during Kirk's four-year term. The aftermath of Cramer's attempt to replace Kirk created a rift between the two Republican leaders that never fully healed. In 1968, Kirk compounded the intraparty friction when he abandoned his fellow delegates at the Republican National Convention, voting to nominate Nelson Rockefeller as the party's presidential nominee while others in the Florida delegation threw their support to Richard Nixon.[21] Republicans in the Legislature had been unwavering in their support for Kirk during the first two years of his administration, but in 1969, Kirk turned his back on his Republican legislative allies, embarrassing them publicly by vetoing a legislative pay raise sponsored by House Republican Leader Don Reed. It was an initiative that Kirk had previously told Reed in private he would accept.[22]

When asked by Republican Senator Tom Slade what he should tell his colleagues about the switch on the pay raise, Kirk replied succinctly: "Tell them I lied."[23]

The rift widened further as the 1970 elections approached. In an attempt to shore up eroding Republican support in the ICY stronghold of Pinellas County, Kirk appointed State Representative Ray Osborne from St. Petersburg to be his lieutenant governor, skipping over his friend and political ally Skip Bafalis.[24] The choice of Osborne failed on two accounts. On one hand, Bafalis felt betrayed and opted to run in the 1970 Republican primary against Kirk,[25] and on the other hand, it failed to shore up support among the West Coast Republicans. Instead, Cramer and the ICY Machine remained upset with Kirk; the Machine recruited Jack Eckerd to oppose the governor in the Republican primary; and former Party Chairman Bill Murfin returned to Florida to oppose Kirk and manage the Eckerd campaign.[26] In retaliation, Kirk and his allies recruited G. Harrold Carswell to run in the 1970 Republican primary and oppose Cramer in the race to replace retiring U.S. Senator Spessard Holland.[27]

By 1970, the schism among the party factions was in full bloom and could not be healed, leaving Kirk and Cramer in a battle on many fronts over the leadership of the Florida Republican Party. Both Kirk and Cramer won their primary elections, but when the dust from the general election cleared, both Kirk and Cramer had lost—Kirk to Democrat Reubin Askew and Cramer to Democrat Lawton Chiles. The deep intraparty rift between

Florida's first lieutenant governor, Ray Osborne, greeting Izzy and Murray Stewart at the governor's mansion reception flanked by Erika Kirk (*right*) and Osborne's executive assistant R. Z. Safley (*left*). Safley family collection.

Kirk and Cramer had other ripples of consequence, too. The losses at the top of the ticket in 1970 left Republican legislators without a Republican chief executive, which diminished their voices in policymaking; and it also diminished the effectiveness and delayed the establishment of the state Republican Party organization that ultimately became important to the viability of a competitive two-party system.[28] It was to be almost two decades before these rifts were fully healed.

Even without a governor from their party, however, Republican legislators remained in sufficient numbers in both the House and the Senate to be consistently relevant in periodic bipartisan coalitions with the urban Democrats, who did not adhere to the policies of the rural conservative wing of their party.[29] The Legislature also became fertile ground for the Republican Party's cultivation of its new leaders. The elections in 1970, 1972, and 1974 brought several members of the party's next generation to prominence, among them Van Poole and Chester Clem, who later became chairmen of the state Republican Party. The same elections saw the arrival of future Senate Republican Leaders Richard Langley, Clark Maxwell, and Ander Crenshaw to the Legislature; and they also brought future Republican Leaders Curt Kiser and Ron Richmond and future Republican Leaders Pro Tempore Lewis Earle and Fred Burrall to the Florida House.[30]

Unexpected Legacy

In a variety of ways, many of the background players from the Kirk years did not simply fade away but instead became part of an unexpected legacy that contributed to the growing Republican influence in the state. Despite the infighting among Republicans and the disappointment of the 1970 general election defeats by headliners at the top of the ticket, there was more to the legacies of these headliners than their defeats. Other individuals who came forward to staff the administration's agencies and the Republican legislative offices persevered and continued to support the growing foundation of the party. Many from the era, most of them young, remained in the process and began careers of their own that brought them to prominence as Republicans. They remained enthused and remained committed to the Republican cause, some as elected officials; some as personnel within the governmental structure; some as fund-raisers; and others simply as supporters of the Republican emergence.[31]

Among those who remained, State Senator Bill Young became U.S. Congressman Bill Young, rising to chair the powerful House Appropriations Committee and serving as a senior Republican leader for nearly four decades.[32] Skip Bafalis resurrected his career after his primary loss to Kirk, and he also became a member of the U.S. Congress.[33] Ken Plante, who began as a campaign volunteer in 1966, rose to become the Republican leader of the Florida Senate in 1976, and Plante concluded his public service three decades later as the legislative affairs director for Florida's third Republican governor, Jeb Bush. State Senator Tom Slade became a Republican organizer in northeast Florida after his legislative career; and in 1986, he was a key supporter in the campaign that brought Bob Martinez to Tallahassee as Florida's second Republican governor.[34] In the Florida House, Jim Tillman and Bill James, who both had come to the Legislature during the 1966–67

Republican surge following Kirk's election, continued their service and became House Republican leaders.[35]

From the administration, Wade Hopping, Kirk's director of legislative affairs, served briefly as a member of the Florida Supreme Court and followed his public service with a long and distinguished career as a lawyer and lobbyist, never abandoning his Republican credentials. Kirk administration staff attorney Wilbur Brewton followed a similar path to Hopping as an influential Tallahassee Republican-credentialed, lawyer-lobbyist.[36] Nora Herron from the governor's staff transitioned to the House Republican office under Republican Leaders Curt Kiser and Ron Richmond before joining the private sector of the political network for more than four decades.[37] Gene Mooney, a young Kirk staffer at the State Road Department, left the administration to win a seat in the Florida House of Representatives in 1970; and Mooney was joined two years later in the House by Curt Kiser, who had served as a member of Kirk's legal staff.[38] In the same 1972 elections, former Pinellas legislative delegation attorney Ron Richmond was also elected to the Florida House, and both Kiser and Richmond followed Tillman and James to become House Republican leaders.

R. Z. "Sandy" Safley served as the executive assistant to Lieutenant Governor Ray Osborne during the final two years of the Kirk administration, and his involvement in Republican politics continued as well.[39] Safley managed the successful congressional campaign of Republican Richard Kelly; worked in the campaigns of Pinellas Republicans for nearly three decades; and later came to the Florida House of Representative as a member to serve five terms.[40] Jim Bax served first as the director of the Division of Economic Opportunity and then as secretary of the Department of Health and Rehabilitative Services in the Kirk administration.[41] After leaving the department, Bax remained an active Republican from the private sector as both a fund-raiser and supporter for more than four decades, and he returned to public service briefly as chairman of the board of the state-sponsored Florida Residential Property and Casualty Joint Underwriting Association.[42] Nathaniel Reed served as the chair of the Air and Water Pollution Control Board during the Kirk administration and was retained briefly in that role by Governor Askew.[43] Reed left Florida to join the Republican administration of Richard Nixon as an undersecretary at the U.S. Interior Department, and later returned to Florida where, for more than a generation, he was the definitive Republican voice for the protection of Florida's environmental treasures.[44]

From Don Reed's House Republican staff, Jon Shebel returned to the private sector to build Associated Industries of Florida into one of the state's preeminent business trade organizations in the capital city. While the Florida Chamber, the Florida Truckers Association, and other trade and business associations stayed the course with support for the Democrats in the early years of the era, Shebel became one of the first to enter the private sector as a prominent and successful advocate with a focus on the new and emerging Republicans. In 1967, Peter Dunbar was hired as the first director of the House Republican Office by Leader Reed; in 1972, he was recruited to be the Pasco County attorney after Republicans captured a majority of the county commission; he returned to the Florida House in 1978 as a member; and in 1988, he joined the staff of Florida's second Republican governor as general counsel and director of legislative affairs. Before joining the private sector, Doug Bruce took his experience on Reed's House staff to the Florida Senate, where he became the staff director of the Senate Republican Office during Ken Plante's tenure as Republican leader; and Marie Robinson, who remained with the House Republican Office to become its staff director, later continued her public service as the inspector general at the Florida Department of Revenue.[45]

There were others throughout Florida who became energized during the Kirk years by accepting appointments to positions on boards and agencies and filling vacancies in local elected offices.[46] In any given year, the Florida governor makes about a thousand such appointments, and the first Republican administration provided opportunities for many who had not previously been invited to participate during the years of Democratic dominance.[47] They, too, became part of the unexpected legacies that contributed to the new foundation of the emerging Republican network.

Paula Hawkins—Another Republican First

Kirk's split with his own allies and his conflict with the ICY Machine and Cramer over who would lead Florida's Republican Party doomed his bid for reelection. Democrats Reubin Askew and Bob Graham followed in succession as Florida governors, and a Republican did not occupy that office again for sixteen years, but that did not stop the Republican Party from making other strides in pursuit of statewide offices. The first Republican statewide success after the 1970 elections was a seat on the Florida Public Service Commission.[48]

An elected body in Florida until 1978, the Public Service Commission maintained jurisdiction over the state's regulated utilities, which consisted of the investor-owned electrical power companies, private telephone service providers, commercial trucking, and the state's privately owned water and sewer companies. During its era of elected membership, the commission was often considered too friendly with the companies it regulated, and following a decision by the commission to permit the new corporate profits tax ushered in by Askew and the Democratic-controlled legislature to be a direct dollar-for-dollar pass-through to the consumer, the perceived anti-consumer decision became a key election issue in 1972.[49]

Incumbent Democrat Commissioner Jess Yarborough, who had supported the commission's pass-through of the tax, drew opposition to his reelection in the primary from fellow Democrat Gerald Lewis, but the Republicans also seized on the political opportunity. At the urging of Bill Young and other Republican leaders, the party recruited its Republican National Committeewoman Paula Hawkins to enter the race as well. Hawkins, an Orange County housewife and activist in the Federation of Republican Women, stepped into the race, campaigning as an advocate for the consumer; it was a theme that resonated with voters. Gerald Lewis successfully defeated Yarborough in the Democrat primary but lost his bid for a seat on the commission to Hawkins by 32,059 votes in the November general election.[50]

With her victory, Paula Hawkins became the first woman of either political party to be elected to a statewide office in Florida, and it was not to be the only "first" in her political career. In 1974, she was an unsuccessful candidate in the race for the Republican nomination to the U.S. Senate, but in 1976, she was reelected to the Public Service Commission despite Jimmy Carter's victory over Gerald Ford in the presidential race at the top of the ticket.[51] Once again, Hawkins broke new ground for the Republicans by becoming the first member of the party in the modern era to be successfully reelected in a statewide campaign.[52]

In 1978, Hawkins made another unsuccessful attempt at statewide office as the lieutenant governor running mate with Jack Eckerd when the Repub-

Paula Hawkins at her new desk at the Florida Public Service Commission. Photo courtesy of the Florida Historic Capitol Museum.

lican ticket lost to Democrats Bob Graham and Wayne Mixon in the general election. In 1980, Hawkins tried again to win a seat in the U.S. Senate, and in her second attempt, she succeeded by defeating the Democratic nominee Bill Gunter, thus accomplishing two more "firsts."[53] With her victory, Paula Hawkins became the first Florida woman to be elected to the U.S. Senate and only the fifth woman from the South.[54] Hawkins also became the first woman in the country ever elected to a full term in the U.S. Senate without the benefit of a family connection.[55]

Despite her several "firsts" as a Republican woman, Hawkins lost her reelection bid for the U.S. Senate seat to Bob Graham in 1986, and she returned to her home in the urban horseshoe community of Winter Park when her term in the Senate concluded. For Republicans, the disappointment of Hawkins's defeat in 1986 was overshadowed by another statewide election victory in the race for governor.

The Governors—Bob Martinez

It had been two decades since Claude Kirk's election before another Republican occupied the Florida governor's mansion, but in the wake of Paula Hawkins's loss to Bob Graham, another Republican emerged to continue to build the party's presence as state's chief executive. Like Kirk, Florida's second Republican governor also began as a Democrat.

When Claude Kirk was elected to office in 1966, Bob Martinez was a registered Democrat, and he had just left the classroom as a teacher to assume the position of executive director of the Hillsborough County Classroom Teachers Association.[56] In 1979, he was elected mayor of Tampa in a nonpartisan race, and after his reelection as mayor in 1983, Martinez set his sights on a possible race for governor. In a private memorandum from his longtime friend and political advisor Mac Stipanovich, the merits of campaigning as a Democrat and as a Republican were set out for Bob Martinez to consider.[57]

"Philosophically, I believe that [your] attitudes and record are more comparable with the Republican Party than the Democratic Party," Stipanovich wrote. "And you cannot run well unless you feel comfortable. As unprofessional as this sounds, I believe you must listen to your heart. If you 'feel' more comfortable with Republicanism as you understand it, then we should follow the program described below."[58]

The program described by Stipanovich consisted of a series of conferences with Florida Republican leaders followed by a meeting at the White House with President Ronald Reagan. When the conferences and meetings suggested by Stipanovich had concluded and a week after his session with President Reagan, Bob Martinez reregistered as a Republican. In doing so, he became part of what former White House speechwriter and author Peggy Noonan described as "the quiet realignment of the eighties," and Martinez began to consider his run for governor as a Republican.[59] In the year that followed, he continued to meet with Republican leaders around Florida; he was invited to be a featured speaker at the Republican National Convention on behalf of American mayors; and on March 1, 1985, Bob Martinez became the first prominent Republican to enter the race for governor.[60]

In the fall of 1985, Martinez was joined in the Republican primary race by former Congressman Lou Frey, State Representative Tom Gallagher, and former state Republican Party Chairman Chester Clem. Martinez began the Republican primary race as the front-runner and never faded. He garnered slightly more than 40 percent of the vote in the initial four-way primary election, and in the runoff primary against second-place finisher Lou Frey, the race was never close. Martinez captured 66 percent of the vote, comfortably earning the Republican nomination and the right to meet the Democrat nominee in the November general election.[61] In the general election, Martinez faced off against State Representative Steve Pajic, who won the hotly contested Democratic runoff primary over former attorney general Jim Smith with 50.6 percent of the votes.[62] Smith was considered the more conservative of the two Democrat contenders, and as they had twenty years before in the race between Burns and High, Democratic primary voters selected the more liberal alternative in Pajic to carry the party's banner into the November general election.[63]

Coming off of a comfortable victory in the primary runoff, Martinez began the race against Pajic with a small lead in the public opinion polls. Although the race was close and often within the margin of error, the Republican network was again energized by the viable opportunity to elect a governor from their own party. As the campaign entered its final weeks, campaign manager Mac Stipanovich directed the media advertising for Martinez to emphasize the message that had been delivered by Smith during the Democratic primary—that Pajic was the "liberal" choice in the race.[64] In the October 24 televised debate between the two candidates, Martinez reinforced the message, and in the process, he solidified his position as the front-runner. Stipanovich recalled that internal polling by Martinez pollster David Hill showed Pajic dropping 9 points in the two days following the debate.[65]

Through Election Day, Martinez never relinquished his grip on the lead that had materialized; and two weeks after the debate, Florida voters elected Bob Martinez their fortieth governor—the second Republican chief executive in 110 years. The remaining statewide cabinet posts on the ballot—the state comptroller, secretary of state, attorney general, commissioner of agriculture, commissioner of education, and the treasurer and insurance commissioner—all remained in Democratic hands as they had for more than a century, but 1986 harkened more winds of change.[66]

Like the election of Claude Kirk twenty years earlier, the election of Bob Martinez presented another opportunity for Florida Republicans to build a solid foundation and to continue the state's political realignment. The Martinez victory began a renewed march toward Republican control of the state's political infrastructure; but unlike Kirk, Martinez began to immediately consolidate the party foundation that had fractured during the four-way Republican primary, and the political differences were quickly healed.[67]

After the election, Martinez welcomed Republican primary opponent Tom Gallagher and his running mate, Betty Easley, to his administration—Gallagher as the secretary of the Department of Business Regulation and Easley as a senior member of the governor's office staff. Jim Smith, who had been defeated by Pajic in the Democratic primary runoff, switched parties to become a Republican, and he too, joined the Martinez administration as a senior staff advisor.[68] During the new Martinez administration, future governor Jeb Bush came to statewide prominence for the first time by accepting the post of the Department of Commerce secretary; and during the

Tom Gallagher with his running mate, Betty Easley, during the 1986 gubernatorial campaign. Photo courtesy of the Florida Historic Capitol Museum.

course of the administration, Bob Martinez asked others to serve; in the process, his appointees continued the quiet realignment in Florida's political landscape.

The Republican numbers in the Florida Legislature grew greater as well. When Martinez began his preparations to run for governor in 1984, Republicans occupied 37 of the 120 seats in the House of Representatives and 10 of the 40 seats in the Florida Senate.[69] After his election in 1986,

Republican members in the House had increased to 45 of that 120-member body and increased in the Senate to 15 of that 40-member body.[70] The legislative gains, combined with the support of a chief executive from their own party, once again elevated the Republican minorities in both legislative chambers to a more meaningful policy role with their ability to sustain a gubernatorial veto.

For Martinez at the beginning of his term, the only elected Republican allies in the Capitol were the Republican members of the Legislature. When his term concluded in 1990, his Republican allies in the House had increased their numbers to forty-six; in the Senate their numbers had increased to seventeen, four short of a majority in the upper chamber; and there were new Republican allies in the executive branch that included two elected members of the Florida cabinet.[71] Despite these Republican gains, however, a second Martinez term was always in doubt.

The reelection campaign of an incumbent begins on his or her first day in office, and so it was for Bob Martinez. The events that materialized during his days in office became the barometer for the governor's image and the legacy that became his record. For Governor Martinez, the events brought both success and disappointment. There was the vision of his Preservation 2000 environmental initiative; the successful implementation of Florida's growth management laws; the modernization of the state's prison system; the mobilization of resources against the use of illegal drugs; and the successful fight to halt offshore oil exploration adjacent to the Florida coastline. But then too, there were the highly visible battles over the "services tax" and gas tax increases for transportation funding; the controversial abortion debate; and the recurring criticism from Democratic legislative leaders.[72]

By the spring of 1990, the formal race for governor and Martinez's bid for reelection had been under way for more than a year. Two Democratic contenders, Congressman Bill Nelson and State Senator George Stuart had sparred with each other for months seeking the right to face Martinez in the fall, and Nelson had become the front-runner. But even with a clear fund-raising lead and support from many key Democratic leaders, his campaign and his image among Florida voters had begun to erode in a matchup against Martinez.

A feature article in *Florida Trend* critical of the Nelson campaign reinforced the "empty suit" theme that had been coined by Mac Stipanovich almost a year earlier, and that characterization of Nelson appeared to stick in the minds of the public. As April 1 approached, public opinion polls showed that voters favored Martinez and that the governor was running ahead of both Democratic contenders.[73] The earlier assumption by the pundits that Martinez's vulnerability made him a certain loser was proving a flawed theory.

Quietly, behind the scenes, key Democrat strategists led by Jim Krog began to urge Lawton Chiles to reconsider his earlier decision not to run and enter the race against Martinez.[74] After a series of meetings, Chiles agreed to do so, and with the emergence of Lawton Chiles, Martinez's favorable poll numbers reversed themselves. Following Chiles's announcement that he too was a candidate for governor, the April 25 public opinion poll conducted by the *New York Times* regional newspapers showed him with an immediate 28 percentage point lead over Martinez.[75] The work of Governor Martinez's own pollster, David Hill, on April 28 showed a similar margin. Within weeks the Stuart campaign folded, and in the fall primary, Lawton Chiles handily defeated Bill Nelson, garnering 69.5 percent of the vote to become the designated standard-bearer for the Democratic Party.[76]

In the September primary, Martinez defeated four relatively unknown opponents by capturing 69 percent of the vote and entered the general election fray with a nearly solid Republican constituency behind him.[77] The initial postprimary polls showed that Martinez had narrowed the initial margin and that Chiles and Martinez were in a virtual dead heat. On September 20, Mason Dixon Opinion Research pegged the candidates with 45 percent each and 10 percent of the electorate undecided. The Florida Opinion Poll by the *New York Times* regional newspapers on October 13 showed the race 42 percent for Chiles, 40 percent for Martinez, and 18 percent still undecided.[78]

"In relative terms," observed Charles Holmes of the *Palm Beach Post* in late October, "Governor Martinez's campaign comeback is remarkable. He trailed Mr. Chiles, the popular former U.S. Senator, by 28 percentage points in a poll last April. Now the race is dead even."

But as the final ten days of the campaign ticked away, Chiles gradually pulled away. By election evening, he posted a comfortable margin of victory over Martinez, capturing almost 57 percent of the popular vote.[79] Democratic voters had remained loyal to their nominee, and the Republicans were unable to stem the tide.

The cumulative impact of a unified Democratic Party, widespread support from the print media, and other elements from Florida's political establishment were more than Martinez could overcome. Martinez carried only sixteen of Florida's sixty-seven counties, none within the primary readership of the daily newspapers that had opposed him.[80]

"Chiles, the political icon with a homespun manner," observed Bill Cornwell and Morris Kennedy of the *Tampa Tribune* the morning after the election, "may have been the only person who could have pulled it off."[81]

"There is no parallel in American politics for the recovery like the one the Governor has achieved," said Martinez pollster David Hill at a meeting at the beginning of the race, "but the history of Republicans in the Sunbelt states should not be forgotten. The history in those states, including Florida, is that Republicans get elected, but they don't get reelected."[82]

In the final analysis, the history for Republicans had repeated itself in Florida in 1990, but the foundation for the Republican future had been even more firmly laid during Bob Martinez's tenure as governor.[83]

Continuing Legacy

In addition to the new Republican members of the Florida cabinet and increased numbers in the Legislature, there were others from the administration who remained in the process as well. Many of the staff and appointees assembled during the Martinez administration and during his two statewide campaigns remained, like those from the Kirk years, and continued to build the party's presence and influence. Many of the Republican House and Senate members who supported Martinez and sponsored his initiatives were reelected and continued on the path that led toward Republican majorities in both the House of Representatives and the Florida Senate.

Early in the administration, former State Senator Van Poole left his post as a department secretary to assume the chairmanship of the state Republican Party, and Poole oversaw the Republican campaign efforts in 1988, when the first two Republicans were successfully elected to the Florida cabinet. Both cabinet members, Jim Smith and Tom Gallagher, came from posts in the Martinez administration. Tom Slade, who worked as the campaign coordinator for northeast Florida in both of the governor's elections, succeeded Poole as the chairman of the Republican Party, and during his tenure, Republicans continued their rise to majority party status in the Florida Legislature.

During Martinez's final year in office, the Florida Senate included fifteen Republicans, and the body was governed by a coalition of Republicans and conservative Democrats.[84] Two years later, in 1992, Republicans captured exactly one-half of the seats in the forty-member Senate and claimed an equal voice in the chamber's deliberations.[85] In 1994, Republicans captured a majority of the seats in the Florida Senate, and Jim Scott, one of Martinez's strongest supporters in the state Senate, assumed the Senate presidency.[86] State Representative Dan Webster, who had been a key ally in the final transportation funding initiative advocated by Governor Martinez in 1990, led Republican candidates to a one-vote majority in the Florida House of Representatives in 1996. With the majority, Webster became the Speaker of the House—the first from the Republican Party to preside over the House in 122 years.[87]

The staff members and appointees from the administration who made their way into the permanent political fabric also became part of the continuing Republican legacy. After a short period on the governor's staff, Betty Easley was appointed to the Public Service Commission, and in 1990, she was joined on the commission by House Republican Leader Pro Tempore Frank Messersmith.[88] Amy Baker was part of the senior staff during all four years of the Martinez administration. After the 1990 campaign, she joined the staff at the Department of Community Affairs; and she served as a staff director for the first Republican Senate president, Ander Crenshaw, in 1994. Baker continued her public service at the Department of Children and Family Services before joining the Appropriations Committee staff of the Florida House, and she followed her service in the House as the state's coordinator of the Office of Economic and Demographic Research—the state's chief financial prognosticator.[89]

Steve McNamara, who served as the secretary of the Department of Business Regulation during the latter part of the Martinez administration, returned to public service as the chief of staff for House Speaker John Thrasher; his service continued later as the chief of staff for Senate President Mike Haridopolos; and McNamara concluded his public service as one of the chiefs of staff for Governor Rick Scott before returning to his teaching post at Florida State University.[90] Allison DeFoor had been a judge, the Monroe County sheriff, and the chairman of the Monroe County Republican Party when he was asked to join the ticket with Martinez in 1990. Although unsuccessful in the campaign, it transitioned DeFoor from a regional player in south Florida into a position of statewide influence as the senior environmental advisor for Florida's next Republican governor, Jeb Bush.[91] Tom Pelham served as the secretary of the Department of Community Affairs during the Martinez administration and oversaw the final implementation of Florida's comprehensive growth management program. Like DeFoor, Pelham returned to the administration of Jeb Bush to serve a second time as the department secretary.[92]

As Republicans emerged and voters supported party candidates in ever-increasing numbers during the modern era, Florida businesses, trade associations, and the lobbyists that represented them had lagged behind the trend and continued to pragmatically support the eroding Democratic majority. Jon Shebel, Wade Hopping, and Wilbur Brewton were three of the early few to break from the historical trend when they entered the private sector following the Kirk years, but others leaving the Martinez administration joined the transition that Shebel and the others had begun. Deputy Director of Operations Carol Dover entered the private sector as head of the Florida Outdoor Advertising Association and later assumed the presidency of the Florida Restaurant and Lodging Association. The director of the Governor's Crime and Law Enforcement Commission, Deborah Huey, transitioned from her role in the administration to become the director of legislative affairs of the Florida Dental Association; and Jon Johnson from the Department of Professional Regulation became part of the government affairs team at the Florida Medical Association.[93]

Others became independent advocate-lobbyists for a variety of business interests, and notable among them were Mac Stipanovich, Brian Ballard, Jim Magill, Will McKinley, Paul Bradshaw, Brian Jogerst, Alison Dudley, and Hayden Dempsey. Stipanovich managed both of the governor's campaigns, served as his first chief of staff, and for decades following the Martinez administration, he was a frequent and articulate Republican pundit, as well as a prominent and successful lobbyist.[94] Brian Ballard began with Martinez as a campaign aide in 1986; he joined the administration to become director of operations after the election; and later he became Martinez's chief of staff before making a successful transition into the private sector to become one of the state's premier business lobbyists.[95] Like Ballard, Jim Magill began as a young staff member in the first Martinez gubernatorial campaign; he joined the governor's senior staff after the election, serving first in the press office and then as director of scheduling. After his service with Martinez, Magill joined the staff of Republican Leader Jim Lombard before spending time at the state Republican Party to staff campaign efforts—first for the state House and then for the state Senate during the election cycle when Republicans captured a majority of the seats in the Florida Senate. Magill joined Stipanovich in the private sector after his tenure at the state party but returned briefly to the staff of Governor Jeb Bush, where he served as the director of legislative affairs during Bush's second term.[96]

Will McKinley began as a legislative intern in the Florida Senate in the office of State Senator Van Poole and then was part of the campaign staff in Poole's unsuccessful race for the U.S. Senate. He served as an assistant secretary at both the Department of Business Regulation and the Department Professional Regulation during the Martinez administration, and he was tapped by Chairman Van Poole to be the state Republican Party's executive director before he, too, entered the private sector.[97] Paul Bradshaw served as a senior attorney in the Martinez budget office and later as the governor's chief cabinet aide; and in 1998, Bradshaw joined the campaign team of Florida's next Republican governor, serving as a senior policy advisor to the Bush campaign before he, too, transitioned to the private sector as a successful capital lobbyist.[98]

Brian Jogerst began as a legislative aide for Lieutenant Governor Bobby

Governor Bob Martinez (*right*) with his chief of staff, Brian Ballard. Ballard family collection.

Brantley and joined Brantley in the Martinez administration before work-ing for Senate Republican Leader Dick Langley and Senate President John MacKay.[99] Alison Dudley also began as a legislative aide before joining the Martinez administration in the legislative affairs office; like Jogerst, she en-tered the private sector as a lobbyist after her public service. Mike Gomez and Cathy Quick were part of the governor's legislative affairs staff, and both continued long careers in state government—Gomez at the Depart-ment of State and the Department of Revenue and Quick at the Depart-ment of Agriculture.[100] Hayden Dempsey joined the Martinez staff late in the administration as a young intern, and as Magill did, Dempsey became a part of the next Republican administration, joining Governor Bush after his election as the governor's legislative affairs director and deputy general counsel. Dempsey returned to offices in the Capitol a third time during the administration of Governor Rick Scott to serve as the new chief executive's legislative affairs director.[101]

There was more to the political legacy of Governor Martinez than the members of the staff from his administration who stayed behind and stayed involved. There were also the hundreds of men and women who accepted appointments to boards and commissions; there were volunteers who came to the campaign and stayed involved to work for others; there were the Republican leaders in the Legislature who continued the march toward majority status; and for the first time, there were Republicans on Florida's cabinet. If the unexpected legacy from the Kirk administration was a catalyst that contributed to an expanding Republican base, the legacy from the Martinez administration solidified the foundation upon which the Republican Party's majority status was ultimately built.

The Cabinet

Before Martinez assumed office in Tallahassee, there were no statewide elected Republicans serving in the Florida cabinet, and Democrats held majorities in both Houses of the Legislature.[102] All of that began to change following the election of Bob Martinez, and it gave credibility to conclusions shared by Mac Stipanovich during a return visit to the Florida governor's mansion in 2011. While Governor Martinez and members of his administration gathered as guests of Governor Rick Scott to celebrate the twenty-fifth anniversary of his election, Stipanovich opined that the legacy left by Martinez was one of the catalysts that permanently changed Florida's political landscape.

"Every Republican who's been in the mansion since 1986," Stipanovich told the gathering, "went through a hole in the wall that Bob Martinez put there. He was Hispanic in a state that never elected a Hispanic to statewide office. . . . He championed growth management, created the Florida Forever land-buying program, and little by little, Republicans kept gaining in power in the Legislature, completing their takeover of both Houses in 1996."[103]

It was not just the Republicans who occupied the governor's mansion and those who came to the Legislature who benefited from the Republican efforts during the Martinez years. A century of exclusive Democrat dominance in the Florida cabinet began to crumble as well, and it was a dominance that influenced large portions of the state's governmental institutions under its collegial structure.[104] Because the authority of Florida's executive branch was apportioned among the governor and the independent members of the cabinet who were elected statewide, the structure was considered unique among the fifty states, and without support from members of the cabinet, the role of the governor is tempered significantly.[105] Overcoming a solid Democratic cabinet was a challenge for Claude Kirk during his entire term in office, and the same circumstances faced Florida's second Republican governor following his election.

When Bob Martinez assumed his role as the chairman of the Florida cabinet, he was joined by six other cabinet members—Secretary of State George Firestone, Treasurer and Insurance Commissioner Bill Gunter, Comptroller Gerald Lewis, Commissioner of Education Betty Castor, Commissioner of Agriculture Doyle Conner, and Attorney General Bob Butterworth—and all were Democrats.[106]

In time, these six elected cabinet posts became three.[107] In 1998, the Florida Constitution Revision Commission presented a revision to the voters that reduced the cabinet membership to three, and Florida voters approved the change in November 1998 to become effective in January 2003.[108] The revision converted the secretary of state and the commissioner of education to officials appointed by the governor. It combined the Office of the Comptroller and the position of state treasurer and insurance commissioner into the Florida Department of Financial Services, and the head of the new department became the state's chief financial officer. When the reorganization was complete, the chief financial officer joined the commissioner of agriculture and the attorney general as the third member of the Florida cabinet.[109]

During the Republican emergence, however, all six cabinet posts were statewide elected positions, and to wrest control of the executive branch of state government from the hands of the Democrats, Republicans faced the challenge that included all six offices that made up the Florida cabinet. During the term of Governor Martinez, the shift from Democrat to Republican control of the cabinet began.

Secretaries of State and State Treasurers

The first crack in the solid, uninterrupted Democratic control of the Florida cabinet began in 1987, with George Firestone's resignation as the secretary of state. Martinez was able to temporarily fill the vacancy created by Firestone's resignation. The governor's choice to be Florida's secretary of state was newly registered Republican Jim Smith. It began Smith's second stint on the cabinet where he had previously served as the state's Democratic attorney general, and in the process, Jim Smith became the first Republican in the modern era to sit as a member of the Florida cabinet.[110]

The tenure of Smith's appointment continued until a special election in the fall of 1988, when voters chose him over Democratic State Senator George Stuart Jr. to complete the balance of Firestone's unexpired term. The party's successes in the 1988 general election marked the first time that a Republican had been successfully elected to the cabinet, and Smith's race

Governor Bob Martinez flanked by the first Republican members of the Florida cabinet: State Treasurer Tom Gallagher and Secretary of Jim Smith (*from left*) and Secretary of Commerce Jeb Bush (*right*). Photo by Don Dughi; courtesy of the State Archives of Florida.

was not the only contest where a post previously held by the Democrats moved into the Republican column. In the same election, Tom Gallagher also won a seat on the cabinet as the state's treasurer and insurance commissioner.[111] Gallagher had joined the Martinez administration two years earlier as the secretary of the Department of Professional Regulation, but he resigned that post to challenge Democratic State Senator Ken Jenne to fill the vacancy created by Bill Gunter when he left the cabinet to run for the U.S. Senate. Following the 1988 elections, Gallagher joined Smith and Martinez on the cabinet, leaving the four remaining posts in the hands of incumbent Democrats.

Once the partisan shift began on the Florida cabinet, it was only a matter of time before the new Republican presence on the cabinet became the dominant presence. A Democrat never returned to the secretary of state's office while it remained an elective office, and Smith was followed in sequence by former House Republican Leader Sandra Mortham, who defeated Democratic State Representative Ron Saunders in 1994, and former Republican State Senator Katherine Harris, who beat Democrat Karen Gievers in 1998 before the office was converted to a position appointed by the governor.[112]

Gallagher was also reelected in 1990 and held the treasurer's post until 1994, when he tried again unsuccessfully to win the Republican nomination for governor. Bill Nelson returned the treasurer's office to the Democratic Party by turning back Republican Tim Ireland by a narrow margin in the 1994 elections, and Nelson served as the state treasurer until 2000, when he resigned to run for the U.S. Senate. Gallagher returned to the office in 2000 by beating Democratic State Representative John Cosgrove, and Gallagher remained the state's treasurer and insurance commissioner until the office was merged with the comptroller's office to create the cabinet post of chief financial officer in 2002.[113]

Legacies from a Republican Cabinet

Like the legacies created by Republican governors, the new Republican cabinet officers had a similar impact on the Republican political network. Young staff members who came to the cabinet offices and then continued careers in government and in the private sector also contributed to the network's expansion. From the secretary of state's office in addition to Rich Heffley and Gene McGee, the staffers who moved on to other roles of policy influence included Paul Mitchell, Marc Dunbar, Sonya Deen, Emmett "Bucky" Mitchell, David Rancourt, Clay Roberts, and Kelly Horton. From Tom Gallagher's office as treasurer and later as the state's chief financial officer, staff members included Colleen Castille, Eva Armstrong, Mark Casteel, Karen Chandler, Doug Darling, Robert Reyes, Rick Mahler, and Quincee Messersmith. Each continued with successful careers that kept them active and involved—some in other positions of public service, some from within the formal Republican Party structure, and others in the private sector supporting party candidates and influencing the governmental political process for private sector businesses.

Castille began as a senior cabinet aide for Gallagher, and after her service with Gallagher, she joined the new administration of Jeb Bush, serving initially as the governor's chief cabinet aide, later as the secretary of the Department of Community Affairs, and concluding her public service as the secretary of the Department of Environmental Protection.[114] Armstrong also joined the Bush administration, serving as the director of the Division of State Lands; and during her tenure as the director, Armstrong oversaw the state's acquisition of more than 1.1 million acres of conservation lands under the Preservation 2000 and Florida Forever programs.[115] Rancourt joined the Bush administration as well, serving first as part of the Bush transition team and then as the governor's deputy chief of staff.[116]

Paul Mitchell began his tenure on the staff of Tom Gallagher in the state treasurer's office in 1989, and he transitioned to the Department of State after Sandra Mortham's election in 1994. He rejoined Gallagher as his chief of staff at the Department of Education, and he concluded his service as the chief of staff in the newly created post of chief financial officer under Gallagher.[117] Clay Roberts began on staff in the Legislature as the Republicans came into the majority; he joined the secretary of state's staff and served as the director of the Division of Elections under Katherine Harris; he bowed out of partisan politics after his service at the Department of State, when he accepted a judgeship on the First District Court of Appeals.[118] In addition to her role on Gallagher's senior staff, Karen Chandler served as the communications director for three Republican Senate presidents.[119] Mark Casteel also served on the staff of a Republican Senate president before his time as the general counsel in Gallagher's office.[120]

Doug Darling began on the staff of Republican Comptroller Bob Milligan; he continued as a member of the senior staff for the chief financial officer during Gallagher's tenure; and he held positions at both the Department of Education and the Department of Environmental Protection before concluding his public service as the deputy chief of staff and director of cabinet affairs for Governor Rick Scott.[121] Rick Mahler began as a young legislative aide and transitioned to the senior staff of Chief Financial Officer Tom Gallagher after his legislative service. Mahler rose to become Gallagher's chief of staff after Paul Mitchell entered the private sector; he returned briefly to the Legislature, where he served as a joint committee staff director; and Mahler followed Mitchell into the political network of the private sector after his second round of legislative service.[122] Quincee Messersmith's experience from Gallagher's office later accompanied her to a role as an elected member of the Wakulla County Commission.[123]

After his time at the Department of State, Bucky Mitchell served in the general counsel's office at the Department of Education; and he transitioned to legislative staff in the Florida House of Representatives before taking his election law expertise to the private sector.[124] Marc Dunbar returned to the private sector after his service with Secretary Mortham, but he volunteered as part of the Republican Party's legal team following the 2000 presidential election; he was a legal advisor to Governor Rick Scott's reelection campaign; and he continued public service as a Scott appointee to the Northwest Florida Water Management District governing board. Kelly Horton, Gene McGee, Sonya Deen, and Robert Reyes all continued to be active after their cabinet service, too, combining political fund-raising and campaign consulting with their private sector activities.[125]

Commissioners of Education and Comptrollers

Republicans held on to both the secretary of state's office and the office of the treasurer and insurance commissioner despite Bob Martinez's defeat by Lawton Chiles in the fall elections of 1990, but the remaining cabinet posts—commissioner of education, comptroller, commissioner of agriculture, and attorney general—remained in Democratic hands. As the elections of 1994 approached, Republicans once again mounted campaigns for these statewide posts on the cabinet, and as the elections approached, state Republican Party Chairman Tom Slade had a single-minded commitment to the Republican cause and focused on two of the remaining offices held by the Democrats. His two key recruits in the cause were Frank Brogan and Robert "Bob" Milligan.[126]

Brogan began his career as a fifth-grade schoolteacher and was eventually elected to serve two terms as the superintendent of schools in Martin County before being recruited by Slade to enter the statewide political arena as the Republican candidate to head the Florida Department of Education. Brogan's Democratic opponent was former State Representative Douglas L. "Tim" Jamerson, who had been appointed earlier in the year by Governor Lawton Chiles to fill the remaining months in the term of Betty Castor, who had resigned to become the president of the University of South Florida.[127] The position of commissioner of education was created in 1870, but no Republican had ever occupied the office. When Frank Brogan beat Jamerson in 1994, he became the third Republican to be elected to the Florida cabinet; the first Republican in 124 years to head the state's Department of Education; and, at age forty-one, the youngest person in the state's history to occupy the office.[128]

The office of state comptroller was created in 1845, and it, too, transitioned into Republican hands in 1994. Slade's recruit to carry the Republican banner for the post in 1994 was retired U.S. Marine Corps Lieutenant General Robert "Bob" Milligan from Panama City in Bay County. In the fall elections, Milligan garnered 51 percent of the popular vote to best incumbent Democrat Gerald Lewis and join Brogan as one of the two new Republican members of the cabinet.[129] Four years later, in 1998, Milligan was successfully reelected to the post, gathering 61 percent of the vote in his second statewide run against Democrat Newall Jerome Daughtrey.[130] Bob Milligan completed two full terms in office, and the office of the comptroller was not to be occupied again by a Democrat before the post was combined with the treasurer and insurance commissioner to create the state's new chief financial officer.

As with the office of comptroller, there was never to be an elected Democratic commissioner of education again before the position became an appointed office in 2003. Brogan did not seek a second term and instead accepted Jeb Bush's invitation to be his running mate in his successful gubernatorial campaign in 1998. The Democrats attempted to retake the commissioner of education post that Brogan left with former House Speaker Peter Rudy Wallace as their nominee, but Tom Gallagher defeated Wallace to keep the post in the Republican column. Two years later, Gallagher also left the office when he was elected to the post of state treasurer and insurance commissioner for a second time, and Gallagher was succeeded at the Department of Education by Republican Charlie Crist, who defeated Democrat George Sheldon to become the state's final elected commissioner of education.[131]

The Governors—Jeb Bush

Following his election in 1986, Governor Bob Martinez brought Jeb Bush to Tallahassee to serve in his administration as the secretary of the Florida Department of Commerce, and four years after Martinez's reelection defeat, Bush stepped forward in 1994 as the Republican challenger to the reelection bid of Lawton Chiles.[132] Bush won the nomination in a seven-way Republican primary, but he was unsuccessful in his attempt to beat the incumbent Democrat, narrowly losing to Chiles by 63,940 votes in an election where more than 5.2 million votes were cast.[133] In its historical context at the time, the Bush/Chiles election contest was the closest race for governor between the two major parties in Florida's history, and the defeat did not deter a second attempt by Bush.[134]

In 1998, Jeb Bush made his second run for the office, and this time, the results at the ballot box were different. The race pitted Bush and his running mate, Frank Brogan, against Governor Buddy MacKay, who had ascended to the governor's office after the untimely death of Governor Chiles earlier in the year, and MacKay's running mate was State Senator Rick Dantzler.

Bush began his second race for governor a full year before the election, and unlike 1994, he faced no opposition for the nomination in the primary and had virtually unanimous support from the Republican constituency going into the general election.[135] The themes of the Bush campaign in 1998 embraced similar messages as prior Republican gubernatorial nominees, and like Kirk and Martinez, the Bush platform included planks of environmental protection, reduced taxes, modern and more efficient government, safe neighborhoods, and a world-class education system.[136]

From the outset, early polling showed the Bush-Brogan ticket with a substantial lead over the Democratic ticket, and the margin remained basically unchanged throughout the duration of the campaign.[137] When the votes were tabulated on Election Day, the results turned a close and disappointing loss from 1994 into an overwhelming victory in 1998.[138] The Bush-Brogan ticket captured 55 percent of the statewide popular vote, and Jeb Bush returned to the Capitol in Tallahassee to become Florida's third Republican governor of the modern era.[139] Unlike his predecessor Republicans, when Jeb Bush arrived in the governor's office he was joined on the Florida cabinet by a Republican comptroller, Republican commissioner of education, and a Republican secretary of state.[140] Collectively with the new governor, these statewide elected Republicans made up a majority of the cabinet for the first time.

By 1998, Republicans had also become the majority in both Houses of the Legislature, and with the control of the state's governmental institutions, changes in policy that prior Republican governors were not able to achieve were now possible for Jeb Bush.[141] As the new century dawned, Bush brought a new "star quality" to the Florida Republican Party and the changes in policy advocated by Republicans began to materialize.[142] New criminal justice initiatives were enacted by a Legislature controlled by Republican majorities; the commitment to protect the state's environment was renewed; state taxes were reduced and sales tax holidays enacted; and reforms in the state's education system brought innovations and new choices to Florida's students.[143]

During the first term of Jeb Bush, there were no "political stumbles" by the governor; there were no internal schisms among Republican Party leaders; and opposition voices from the Democratic minority in the Legislature provided little traction for opposing political points of view. By 2002, Jeb Bush was the prohibitive favorite to be reelected to a second term, and no Republican stepped forward to challenge his reelection in the primary. After narrowly winning a three-way Democratic primary, attorney Bill McBride was the Democrats' choice to challenge Bush's reelection, but the general election race was never close.[144] Bush was able to translate his knowledge of the demographic trends and voting patterns of the state into effective campaign strategies, and he capitalized on both the growing number of Hispanic voters and the high turnout rates in the conservative, rural counties that were often ignored by other campaigns.[145]

When the results from the November general election were tabulated, Bush had won the popular vote in fifty-three of Florida's sixty-seven counties; he had outdistanced his Democratic opponent by more than 650,000 votes; and he had amassed 56 percent of the total statewide popular vote.[146] It was an overwhelming victory, and in the process, Jeb Bush became the first Florida Republican governor to be successfully reelected. The 2002 elections also saw the consolidation of the Florida cabinet from six to three elected members, and the authority of the governor during Bush's second term was enhanced significantly by the change.

With the reelection of Governor Bush, the Republican base in the state was strengthened further. During his tenure in office, Bush became a catalyst that contributed to the conversion of the balance of the Florida cabinet from Democratic hands to Republican officeholders, and the Republican margins in the Legislature were increased and solidified. What had been a one-vote majority in the Florida House two years before Bush arrived in the Capitol had become a twenty-four-vote supermajority during his final year in office. In the Florida Senate, Republicans had a three-vote margin before Bush arrived, and the margin had more than doubled by the final year of his term.[147]

During the eight years of his administration, Jeb Bush set a high standard in the number of women, Hispanics, and African Americans he appointed to positions in his administration; and through his policy successes, he emerged as the most effective and influential of Florida's modern-era governors. Catalysts for the successes came through a combination of structural changes that consolidated the Florida cabinet and the enhanced accumulation of authority in the office of the state's chief executive.[148] Bush also had consistent support from a Legislature that aligned with his policies—something that his Democratic predecessors had rarely experienced; and Bush brought what he described as "high-voltage energy" to his role in the governor's office in pursuit of his objectives.[149]

After his second term came to a close, other Republicans followed Jeb Bush in sequence as the state's chief executive, and for more than two decades after voters elected the Chiles/MacKay ticket in 1994, no Democrat was again able to occupy Florida's governor's mansion. The influence of Florida's first two-term Republican governor also remained during the administrations of his successors. Policies seeking state tax reductions, tax credits and incentives to bring new businesses to Florida, and reforms to expand education choices for Florida's students remained priorities; and the influence and political standing of Jeb Bush among Florida voters continued to contribute to the Republican Party's successes in the elections that followed.[150]

Expanding Legacy

As had been the case with other Republican officeholders, there were staff members and gubernatorial appointees whom Jeb Bush brought into his administration who remained in the process and helped to expand the fabric of Republican influence. Among those who continued in prominent roles in the political network, either in the private sector or in public service, were Sally Bradshaw, Anitere Flores, Carlos Muniz, Ashley Ross, David Hart, Slater Bayliss, Karen Unger, Mark Kaplan, Ann Herberger, Chris Clark, Mandy Clark, Alan Levine, Chris Dudley, Brett Doster, Jason Gonzalez, Brad Thomas, Patricia Levesque, Carol Gormley, Brandi Brown, Brian Jablonski, and Jason Unger.

Sally Bradshaw came to Florida from the National Republican Committee staff and worked at both the state party and in the House Republican Office before joining Jeb Bush to direct his campaign for governor. As Bush's first chief of staff, Bradshaw helped to build the foundation for his first successful term as chief executive. Anitere Flores began as an education policy advisor for Governor Bush and continued her career in public service first as a member of the Florida House and then as a member of the state Senate.[151] Carlos Muniz served as a deputy general counsel for Governor Bush; joined the senior staff of Republican House Speaker Larry Cretul; later served as deputy attorney general and chief of staff for Republican attorney general Pam Bondi; after the 2016 elections, he was tapped to join the administration of President Trump at the U.S. Department of Education; and in 2019, Governor Ron DeSantis named Muniz to the Florida Supreme Court.[152] Carol Gormley, a highly regarded health-care policy expert, served as a deputy chief of staff for Governor Bush. She followed her tenure in the governor's office as a senior health-care policy advisor in both the Florida House and Florida Senate; and in 2018, she was named as the chief of staff for the House of Representatives by Speaker Jose Oliva.[153] Brandi Brown was the director of external affairs for Governor Bush; she served as deputy chief of staff at the Agency for Health Care Administration; and she became the chief executive officer of the Florida Chamber Foundation before joining the Foundation for Excellence in Education in 2018.[154] Mandy Clark also joined the Foundation for Excellence in Education as its national director of development.

Karen Unger began as a district aide to U.S. Congressman Clay Shaw. She was an early Bush supporter during his first campaign and headed his 2002 reelection; she served as one of governor's chiefs of staff; and she later served as president of the University of Florida Alumni Association.[155] Mark Kaplan also served as chief staff for Bush; he was an appointee to the State Board of Education; and he later became the governmental affairs vice president for the University of Florida.[156] Brett Doster began as a campaign aide in the governor's first statewide campaign; he returned to the campaign team in 1998 and served as the Florida political director for the Bush-Cheney presidential ticket in 2000; and from these initial campaigns, Doster built one of the state's premier political consulting firms.[157]

Brian Yablonski served as deputy chief of staff and director of policy for Governor Bush, and, after entering the private sector, he served eight years as a member of Florida's Fish and Wildlife Commission.[158] Ashley Ross began in the Bush legislative affairs office; spent time in state Senate campaigns with the state Republican Party; and returned to a policy role as the deputy chief of staff for Republican Senate President Joe Negron. Slater Bayliss began his career with the Republican Governors' Association; he came to Florida to work in the 1998 Bush campaign and became part of the Bush administration as an economic development policy advisor. After joining the offices of former Party Chairman Al Cardenas in the private sector, Bayliss was appointed to serve on the board of the Florida Sports Foundation, where he was joined by Jason Unger; he served as chairman of Florida Sports Charitable Foundation; and he was a special advisor to the Inaugural Committee of Governor Rick Scott.[159] Chris Clark also began on the staff of Governor Bush; remained in the process and later became chief of staff for Senate President Don Gaetz; and, after entering the private sector, served as part of the transition team for Governor Ron DeSantis.[160]

David Hart began as a college Young Republican; worked in the presidential campaign of George H. W. Bush and the gubernatorial campaigns for Jeb Bush; and, after serving in the administration of Governor Bush, transitioned into a successful career in the private sector as a governmental affairs advisor. After his tenure as the general counsel in the Executive Office of the Governor, Jason Gonzalez returned to the private sector, where he continued to provide counsel to other Republican governors; after his time as the chief of staff for Lieutenant Governor Brogan, Chris Dudley took his Republican credentials to the private sector, joining the lobbying offices of Paul Bradshaw; and Brad Thomas, who had worked in the House of Representatives before joining the staff of Governor Bush as a policy advisor, left the partisan political arena when he accepted an appointment to the First District Court of Appeals.[161]

Part of the Bush legacy could also be found in the Foundation for Florida's Future, which he founded in 1995 before he was elected as Florida's chief executive.[162] The Foundation was created as a non-profit, nonpartisan organization and was designed to support and advocate for the education reforms championed by Bush and other Republicans. After he concluded his time as governor, the foundation remained active with its mission objectives, and the foundation retained affiliations with many who campaigned for Bush or were part of his staff during his two terms as governor.[163]

The directorship of the foundation was eventually assumed by Bush's deputy chief of staff for education policy, Patricia Levesque. Levesque had served as a policy advisor for three Republican Speakers before joining Bush as his education policy advisor.[164] Mat Bahl was also a member of the foundation's staff between his service with House Speakers Dean Cannon and Richard Corcoran.[165] The foundation board of trustees included Colleen Castille, who served as the secretary of Environmental Protection during the Bush administration; former Republican House Speaker Tom Feeney; former Senate President and Lieutenant Governor Toni Jennings; former Bush general counsel Raquel "Rocky" Rodriguez; former Republican State Representative Trey Treviesa; and Alan Levine, who served the governor as a senior health and human services advisor. The Foundation Board also included prominent Republican fund-raisers Zachariah P. Zachariah and Al Hoffman.[166]

Commissioners of Agriculture

After the 1998 elections brought Governor Bush to the Capitol, only three Democrats remained as members of the six-member Florida cabinet—Attorney General Bob Butterworth, state Treasurer and Insurance Commissioner Bill Nelson, and Commissioner of Agriculture Bob Crawford; but the shift of the cabinet seats to the Republican column continued shortly after the arrival of the new governor.

Like Governor Martinez's appointment of Jim Smith as the first Republican secretary of state, Jeb Bush brought the first Republican commissioner of agriculture to the cabinet with the appointment of State Senator Charles H. "Charlie" Bronson. The vacancy in the commissioner's post was created by the resignation of Commissioner Bob Crawford, who left the office to become the head of the Florida Citrus Commission, and it was an opportunity for Governor Bush to extend Republican influence into the state's agricultural business sector.[167]

Charlie Bronson was a fifth-generation cattle rancher who entered poli-

Florida's last seven-member cabinet (*left to right*): Comptroller Robert Milligan, Secretary of State Katherine Harris, Agriculture Commissioner Charles Bronson, Attorney General Bob Butterworth, Governor Jeb Bush, Education Commissioner Charlie Crist, and Treasurer Tom Gallagher. Photo courtesy of the State Archives of Florida.

tics through the Republican Party structure, beginning first as the Republican state committeeman from Brevard County in 1988 and then as the chairman of the Brevard County Republican Party in 1992.[168] In 1994, Bronson was elected to the Florida Senate, and he served as a member of the Republican majority in the Senate until Bush appointed him to the cabinet in May 2001.[169] When Bronson was seated as a member of the cabinet, there began what was to be an uninterrupted Republican presence in the commissioner's office.

Combining his experience in the party network and his agricultural heritage, Bronson was subsequently elected to two full four-year terms as the commissioner of agriculture, first by defeating Democrat David Nelson with more than 57 percent of the popular vote in 2002 and then by besting Democrat Eric Copeland in 2006 by a similar margin.[170]

At the conclusion of his second full term, Bronson retired from public office and was succeeded by Republican Adam Putnam, another fifth-generation member of a Florida agricultural family.

Putnam began his political career in 1996 as a twenty-one-year-old member of the Florida House of Representatives from Polk County, and he served two terms in the state House.[171] In 2000, Putnam's public service took him to the U.S. Congress, where he served five terms as a member of the U.S. House of Representatives before returning to Florida to seek the agriculture commissioner's post. Following the 2010 general election, Putnam took his seat on the Florida cabinet after turning back Democrat Scott Maddox by a comfortable 17-point margin to become Florida's second Republican commissioner.[172] Four years later, in 2014, like Bronson before him, Putnam repeated the feat, beating Democrat Thad Hamilton by a similar 17-point margin for a second four-year term as the commissioner of agriculture.[173]

In 2018, as Adam Putnam's tenure came to a close, four-term State Representative Matt Caldwell won the Republican nomination to succeed Putnam, but in the general election his efforts fell short by the narrowest of margins. In what proved to be the closest statewide contest of an election cycle where more than eight million votes were cast, Caldwell lost by fewer than 6,000 votes, and the commissioner's post on the Florida cabinet returned to Democratic hands.[174]

Attorneys General

As 2000 ushered in the new century and the members of the Florida cabinet still numbered six plus the governor, six of the seven offices were held by Republicans. The only remaining cabinet office occupied by a Democrat was that of attorney general, and it was held by Bob Butterworth. What had once been a solid bastion for the Democrats had been ceded almost completely to the Republicans, and in the next election, the attorney general's post, which had been held by a Democrat since Reconstruction, became the last cabinet office to move into the Republican column.

Democrat Bob Butterworth was elected as the state's attorney general in 1986, and he served until in 2002, when he filed to run for the Florida Senate against Republican State Representative Jeff Atwater.[175] Butterworth lost the Senate bid, and, in the process, continued the up-and-coming career of Atwater; Butterworth's departure from the cabinet left vacant the only post held by a Democrat going into the elections of 2002. It was an opportunity for Republicans, and once again the Republican Party made the most of a vacancy left by a departing Democratic officeholder. In the fall elections with no incumbent attorney general, the vacancy was filled by Republican Charlie Crist, who bested Democratic State Senator Buddy Dyer by capturing 53.4 percent of the general election popular vote.[176]

When Crist won the attorney general's post in 2002, the previously adopted amendment to the state constitution consolidating the cabinet to the governor and three other statewide offices also took effect, leaving the executive branch with four statewide elected officials. With the consolidation of the cabinet combined with the results from the 2002 elections, all of the seats on the new four-member cabinet were held by Republicans. Jeb Bush was reelected to his second term as Florida's governor; Charlie Bronson was elected to his first full term as the commissioner of agriculture; Tom Gallagher became the state's first chief financial officer; and Charlie Crist was seated as the state's new Republican attorney general after defeating Buddy Dyer.[177]

With Republicans occupying all four seats on the newly reorganized cabinet, what had been tangible evidence of the Democratic dominance in the Florida Capitol for more than a century had completely evaporated from the executive branch of government after the elections in 2002.[178] In 2006, after a single four-year term, Crist left the attorney general's post to run for governor, and Republican Congressman Bill McCollum stepped forward to carry the party's nomination into the general election. McCollum had little difficulty holding the post for the Republicans, capturing 52.7 percent of the vote on Election Day and beating Democratic State Senator Skip Campbell to keep a Republican in the attorney general's office.[179]

Four years later, McCollum also stepped down to run for governor. In a closely contested Republican primary election between Tampa attorney Pam Bondi, Lieutenant Governor Jeff Kottkamp, and former State Rep-

Attorney General Pam Bondi (*center*) on the Senate podium with President Mike Haridopolos and Stephanie Haridopolos following passage of the anti-opiate initiative during the final day of the 2012 legislative session. Photo courtesy of the Florida Senate.

resentative Holly Benson, Bondi won the right to carry the Republican banner into the general election against State Senator Dan Gelber.[180] Once again the contest between the political parties was not close, and Republican Bondi captured 54.8 percent of the vote to turn back Gelber's effort to win the post.[181] In 2014, Bondi captured 55.1 percent of the vote in the race against former Democrat State Representative George Sheldon to win a second term as Florida's attorney general and continue what had become Republican solidarity on the cabinet.[182]

In the fall elections of 2018, Floridians picked Republican Ashley Moody as Pam Bondi's successor, and for the fifth consecutive election cycle, a Republican was seated as the state's attorney general.[183]

Chief Financial Officers

In 2002, the chief financial officer's post combined the offices of the state comptroller and the treasurer and insurance commissioner, and the new cabinet post appeared on the ballot to be contested in a partisan battle for the first time. In reality, it was no contest at all. Incumbent Treasurer and Insurance Commissioner Tom Gallagher qualified to seek the new post and was designated as the Republican Party nominee without primary opposition. From the Democrat side, no one bothered to step forward and contest the race, and Tom Gallagher was elected without opposition as the state's first chief financial officer.[184] Gallagher served a single term, and in 2006, he vacated the post in an unsuccessful attempt to seek the Republican nomination for governor.

Senate President Tom Lee captured the Republican nomination in the effort to succeed Gallagher in the September primary election, but in the general election, Lee lost to Democrat Alex Sink, returning a single cabinet post to Democratic hands following the elections in 2006.[185] Four years

Transfer of the gavel on the Senate podium between outgoing Senate President and new Chief Financial Officer Jeff Atwater (*right*) and incoming Senate President Mike Haridopolos (*left*). Photo courtesy of the Florida Senate.

later, after a single term like Gallagher, Sink opted to seek the governor's office and vacated the CFO's office, leaving the post to be filled by a new face during the 2010 election cycle. Senate President Jeff Atwater was designated as the Republican nominee without primary opposition and handily defeated Democrat Loranne Ausley in the November general election, capturing 57.3 percent of the popular vote and returning the post to the Republican column.[186]

With Atwater's victory, all of the seats on the Florida cabinet were again occupied by Republicans. In 2014, Jeff Atwater was successfully reelected to a second term as the state's chief financial officer, capturing 58.9 percent of the popular vote and defeating Democrat William Rankin.[187] In the process, Atwater's victory preserved the Republican solidarity on the cabinet for another four years, but he did not complete his term. In 2017, he resigned midyear to accept a post at Florida Atlantic University, and Governor Rick Scott selected Public Service Commissioner and former State Representative Jimmy Patronis to fill the vacancy left by Atwater. In the fall elections of 2018, Patronis retained the post by besting former Democratic State Senator Jeremy Ring by accumulating 51.89 percent of the popular vote.[188]

With the Patronis victory, the only cabinet office occupied by a Democrat was the commissioner of agriculture's post, and the results of the 2018 elections left the Democratic minority in the Legislature as the only other voice of loyal opposition in the state Capitol as the third decade of the twenty-first century approached.[189]

The Governors—Charlie Crist

The statewide successes brought new vibrancy to the Republican Party's primary elections, particularly in the races to be the Republican gubernatorial nominee. When Jeb Bush reached the end of his second term, a four-way primary included two of the Republican Party's sitting cabinet officers, Attorney General Charlie Crist and Chief Financial Officer Tom Gallagher.[190] Charlie Crist won the nomination and, with his running mate, Jeff Kottkamp, easily turned back the Democratic ticket of Jim Davis and Darryl Jones by a margin of more than 7 percent of the popular vote in the 2006 general election.[191] In the process, Charlie Crist became Florida's fourth Republican chief executive, but Crist's legacy would be different from those of his Republican predecessors.

Governor Crist served a single term, but unlike prior Republican governors, he chose not to seek a second. He came to the office with a record that had embraced the conservative Republican dogma in his prior posts, but unlike his predecessors, he abandoned the core Republican doctrine before leaving the governor's office.[192] Instead of contributing to the continued growth of the Republican network during his time as governor, Crist's legacy was marred by the scandal created by his choice of Jim Greer as the state Republican Party chairman; and as Crist left the governor's office to pursue a seat in the U.S. Senate, he abandoned his Republican credentials altogether, embracing first the role as an independent and then becoming a registered Democrat.[193]

Crist's departure from the Republican Party did little for his continued political ambitions. His pursuit of higher office as an independent proved fruitless in 2010, when he lost his bid for a seat in the U.S. Senate to Republican Marco Rubio, and he fared no better as a Democrat in 2014, when he tried to return to the governor's office and was turned back by the Republican incumbent Rick Scott.[194] In 2016, Crist was finally able to resurrect his checkered political career in a successful bid for a seat in the U.S. Congress as a Democrat.[195]

While Crist reinvented himself as a Democrat and abandoned the Republican fold, there were those who joined his Republican administration in prominent roles and then stayed the course as part of the Republican network. They included individuals who returned as senior staff for other Republican officeholders; others who became activists and consultants in the private sector; and still others who became public officials under the party banner. Prominent among those who served during the Crist administration and continued in the political arena included George Lemieux, Dane Eagle, Eric Eikenberg, Erin Isaac, Jim Rimes, Kathy Mears, and Shane Strum.[196]

George Lemieux served as chief of staff for Crist and accepted an appointment to the U.S. Senate before returning to the private sector.[197] Dane

Eagle served in the administration as a young aide and returned to Tallahassee as a Republican member of the Florida House of Representatives, where he became House majority leader during the 2018–20 legislative term. Eric Eikenberg began his political career on the staff of Congressman Clay Shaw; he joined the Crist administration as chief of staff; and he later became the head of the influential Everglades Foundation.[198] Jim Rimes and Erin Isaac continued in the Florida political arena as prominent campaign advisors for Republican candidates and campaigns.[199] Kathy Mears began her public service in the Florida Legislature, and after her tenure on Crist's staff, she returned to the Florida House, where her public service continued.[200] Shane Strum followed Eikenberg as chief of staff at the end of Crist's term and then entered the private sector before returning to the governor's office as Ron DeSantis's first chief of staff.[201]

The Governors—Rick Scott

When Charlie Crist left the governor's office to run for the U.S. Senate in 2010, two viable Republican candidates—political novice and former health-care executive Rick Scott and Attorney General and political veteran Bill McCollum—faced off in the primary election seeking the nomination to be Florida's next governor. Rick Scott was an outsider to Republican politics; he was opposed by most of the Republican establishment, and he was considered a long shot when the primary campaign began; but, campaigning as an outsider and drawing on his own personal resources, he proved a formidable contender.[202] In the close and hotly contested race between the two Republicans, Scott won a narrow victory, besting McCollum by 36,369 in the primary and earning the right to face Democrat Alex Sink in the November 2010 general election.[203]

Alex Sink had successfully carried the Democratic banner four years earlier and had been the only Democrat to interrupt the Republican dominance on the cabinet when she won the race to succeed Tom Gallagher as Florida's chief financial officer in 2006. In the 2010 Democratic gubernatorial primary, Sink captured the nomination with more than 76 percent of the vote, and with her previous statewide success and overwhelming victory in the primary, she was considered an early favorite to beat Scott in the November general election.[204]

Despite entering the race as an outsider and a political newcomer to the Republican establishment, Scott was able to effectively consolidate his support among the Republican Party base following the primary.[205] His campaign platform embraced variations of the basic Republican tenets to which party loyalists had adhered since Claude Kirk, and his message emphasized the basic Republican Party dogma of less government, lower taxes, job creation, and cultivating a friendlier environment for businesses.[206] He also adopted a variation on the public safety theme, calling for stronger laws on illegal immigration.[207] As the campaign unfolded under the stewardship of Susie Wiles, Scott spent almost $75 million of his own personal fortune during the primary and general elections, and the self-funding efforts and the support from the Republican base proved enough.[208]

In a close race marked by negative character attacks by both campaigns, Rick Scott bested Sink by 61,550 votes, and with the victory, Scott followed Jeb Bush and Charlie Crist as Florida's third consecutive Republican governor.[209] It proved to be the narrowest victory margin of any Florida governor's race, but unlike the previous close race in 1994 between Jeb Bush and Lawton Chiles, the victory in 2010 went to the Republican.[210]

The new governor did not have the same "star quality" as Jeb Bush, and his relationship with the Legislature was at times turbulent, but unlike Charlie Crist, he did not stray from his campaign themes and the basic Republican dogma.[211] To underscore his conservative approach to governance, Scott opted to forego his state salary; he sold off the state aircraft used by other Florida governors; and he opted to travel on his personal jet at his own expense.[212] Through his first term, Governor Scott focused consistently on bringing down the state's unemployment rate; he regularly made trips to recruit new businesses to Florida; and he annually recommended to the Legislature cuts in the state's corporate income tax and other tax levies. Successes accumulated during Scott's first term, but as the 2014 elections neared, the negative images from the first campaign remained, and Scott appeared vulnerable in his bid for reelection.[213] In the Republican primary, however, Scott drew only token opposition and was

Left to right: Speaker Dean Cannon, Governor Rick Scott, Senate President Mike Haridopolos, and Senate President Pro Tempore Mike Bennett on the podium of the House chambers as Governor Scott prepares to deliver his first state-of-the-state address. Photo courtesy of the State Archives of Florida.

easily renominated for a second term, garnering more than 87 percent of the vote in the primary.[214]

In the Democratic primary, two candidates vied for the nomination to challenge Scott in the November election—state Senate Democratic Leader Nan Rich and Scott's predecessor and newly registered Democrat Charlie Crist. Ultimately, the primary race was not close, and Crist captured slightly more than 74 percent of the vote to win the Democratic nomination.[215] In a general election not unlike the race four years earlier, the election was expensive; it featured bitter attack ads from both sides; and it was decided by a margin of less than 2 percent.[216] When the rigors of the campaign concluded, election night totals showed that Rick Scott had been reelected to a second term as Florida's chief executive by a margin of 64,145 votes; and for Republicans, it represented the fifth successive race for governor that had been won by their party's nominee.[217]

While Scott was not initially embraced by the Republican establishment, his atypical approach represented a timely renewal of the outsider status that had contributed to the emergence of a two-party political system in Florida more than a generation earlier.[218] His messages were consistent with Republican Party dogma; during his tenure as the titular head of the party, Republicans maintained control of the Florida cabinet; Republican numbers in the Florida Legislature remained stable with significant majorities; and two years after his reelection, Florida voters provided the winning margin to another unconventional Republican outsider, delivering the state's twenty-nine electoral votes to Donald Trump in the 2016 presidential campaign.[219]

Continuing Legacy

As did his predecessors, Governor Scott created a pool of young Republican activists who served in the administration and began to migrate into a Republican network as it continued to grow. Among the staffers emerging from the Scott administration creating parts of the new legacy were Melissa Stone, Brad Piepenbrink, Jackie Schutz Zeckman, Jesse Panuccio, Chris and Brittany Finkbeiner, Monica and Dan Russell, Jennifer Ungru, Tim Cerio, Will Spicola, and Jeff Woodburn.[220] Melissa Stone managed Scott's successful reelection campaign and served as the governor's chief of staff before returning to the private sector as a Republican campaign consultant. Chris Finkbeiner came from the staff of Senate President Mike Haridopolos to serve as a deputy chief of staff during the governor's first term; and he joined Sellers as the deputy campaign manager during Scott's reelection bid before entering the private sector. Chris's wife, Brittany Finkbeiner, came from the Florida Senate staff to serve as legal counsel at the Department of Economic Opportunity and the Department of Business and Professional Regulation before she, too, entered private practice.

Brad Piepenbrink and Jeff Woodburn also began as legislative staff; both transitioned to the senior staff of Governor Scott during his second term; and Piepenbrink rose to become the chief of staff as the governor's second term concluded.[221] Jackie Schutz Zeckman served as a campaign advisor in each of the governor's campaigns; she was named communications director in the governor's office in 2014; and she became one of Scott's chiefs of staff before returning to the private sector.[222] Will Spicola began as a member of the legal staff at the Department of Business and Professional Regulation and joined the governor's office as general counsel after Scott's reelection. Both Woodburn and Spicola transitioned from the governor's office to assume roles with the Constitutional Revision Commission (CRC) in 2017—Woodburn as the commission's executive director and Spicola as the CRC's general counsel.[223] Tim Cerio also served as the governor's general counsel and was Spicola's predecessor in that role, and he was appointed by Scott to Florida's Constitutional Revision Commission following his tenure.

Jennifer Ungru moved to Florida while working for the Republican National Committee and transitioned from that role to the Majority Office of the Florida House before joining the Scott gubernatorial campaign in 2010. Following the election, she served as a deputy chief of staff for Governor Scott and later as chief of staff at the Agency for Health Care Administration before leaving the public sector and continuing her involvement in the Republican network from the private sector. Monica Russell served as the communications director during Scott's first term; left the office to perform the same duties during the campaign; and returned to the governor's office as the director of cabinet affairs before entering the private sector. Her husband, Dan Russell, also served in the administration as general counsel at the Florida Lottery before he returned to private practice.[224] Jesse Panuccio was another who served the administration as the governor's general counsel and as the secretary of the Department of Economic Opportunity. After his service with Governor Scott, Panuccio left Florida to continue his public service in the administration of the new Republican president Donald Trump.[225]

Beyond those in the governor's office and the departments of his administration, there were also appointments to boards and agencies in all regions of the state from the water management districts to the judicial nominating commission, and from professional boards and agencies to appointments to the Constitutional Revision Commission. These new faces, too, became part of the Republican Party's expanding political network.

The Governors—Ron DeSantis

As Governor Scott concluded his second term in office, two Republican officeholders stepped forward to seek the party's nomination for governor and continue the uninterrupted Republican dominance of the state's chief executive office into a third decade. The primary contest was between three-term Congressman Ron DeSantis and former Congressman and two-term Commissioner of Agriculture Adam Putnam. Putnam had run successfully twice in statewide races in his bids for the commissioner of agriculture post, and he was favored by the state's Republican establishment and was considered the front-runner as the race began, but that would change as the campaigned progressed.[226]

DeSantis grew up in Dunedin on Florida's West Coast; received his undergraduate degree at Yale and his law degree from Harvard; and after service in the U.S. Navy, returned to the Northeast Coast of Florida, where his career in public office began with a successful run for an open congressional seat in 2012. In Congress, his record was distinctly conservative, and he became a close ally and defender of President Trump after the president's election in 2016. As the primary campaign unfolded, DeSantis remained true to what he described as "his conservative ideology in the tradition of Ronald Reagan."[227] His platform was not unlike his Republican predecessors, and it stressed low taxes, a business-friendly environment, keeping citizens safe, and protecting Florida's environment.[228] As the third week of June came to a close, the president publicly endorsed DeSantis and followed the endorsement by attending a campaign rally for DeSantis in Tampa; with the endorsement of President Trump, the early lead for Putnam reversed itself, and DeSantis never trailed again, ultimately capturing the Republican nomination with 56.5 percent of the vote.[229]

Following the primary, DeSantis named House Speaker Pro Tempore Jeanette Nuñez as his running mate; Susie Wiles was brought on to direct the campaign just as she had been for President Trump and in Rick Scott's first gubernatorial race; and Florida Republicans prepared for the general election against the Democrat nominee, Andrew Gillum, and his running mate, Chris King.[230]

Left to right: Governor Ron DeSantis with Speaker Jose Oliva and Senate President Bill Galvano at a January 8, 2019, inaugural luncheon. Seated in the background (*left to right*) are Attorney General Ashley Moody, First Lady Casey DeSantis, and Lieutenant Governor Jeanette Nuñez. Photo courtesy of the Florida Senate.

The dynamics of the campaign featured nominees that represented clear contrasts in the political spectrum—Gillum on the liberal left and DeSantis on the conservative right.[231] The political debate between national Democrats and President Trump bled over into the campaign, and the debate brought large infusions of out-of-state campaign funds into Florida as the campaign pushed into its final weeks.[232] At the heart of the contrast in messaging, Democrats promised to change Florida's political landscape while DeSantis promised "to helm a mostly steady ship" and "was underestimated most every step of the way."[233] Virtually every poll through Election Day— thirty-four of thirty-six polls—showed DeSantis and Nuñez running behind their Democratic opponents, but on Election Day, their projections proved to be flawed when voters delivered the winning margin to the Republican ticket.[234] With more than 8.2 million votes cast—a record turnout for midterm elections in Florida—the Republican network turned out more of its supporters, and DeSantis edged Gillum by a margin of slightly more than 32,000 votes.[235]

Gillum had initially conceded defeat on election night but then withdrew his concession with a demand that every vote be counted.[236] In the days following the election, Democrats mounted a series of challenges during the state's mandatory recount period, and the campaign director, Susie Wiles, turned to Jennifer Ungru to assemble a team of seasoned recount veterans to protect the narrow Election Day victory.[237] The team members included State Senator Lizbeth Benacquisto, Representative Chris Sprowls, Representative Paul Renner, former Representatives Miguel De Grandy and Peter Dunbar, former Republican Party Executive Director Mike Grissom, communications expert Erin Isaac, Tim Baker with the DeSantis campaign team, and a legal team supervised by Marc Dunbar in Tallahassee and Ed Pozzuoli in southeast Florida.[238]

Meeting in the 2018 "recount situation room" are (*right to left*) Jennifer Ungru, Erin Isaac, Marc Dunbar, Tim Baker, and Mike Grissom. Edenfield family collection.

Under the supervision of Ungru in a Tallahassee situation room, canvassing and recount totals were gathered by staffers and volunteers who included Grissom, Erin Isaac, Monica Russell, Martha Edenfield, and the watchful eye of Tim Baker. Isaac was assigned to coordinate messaging with the state Republican Party, Chairman Blaise Ingolia, and other volunteer surrogates; Dan Russell, Will Hall, and Marc Dunbar monitored the materializing legal challenges; and other team members deployed to county canvassing boards throughout Florida. Among them were Ed Pozzuoli, Shari McCartney, Michael Dobson, Brian Stephens, and Daryl Krauza in East Coast counties; they included Chris Sprowls, Melanie Griffin, Adam Ross, Chad Rubin, and Felipe Guerrero on the West Coast and along the I-4 corridor in central Florida; and in rural counties and in north Florida, they included Bo Rivard, Brittany Finkbeiner, Mary Bebout, Cari Roth, and French Brown.[239]

As the recount and the tabulation of overseas and provisional ballots progressed, the governor-elect offered a measured tone toward the process:[240]

"The rule of law is foundational to our society and it must be followed. As governor, I will work diligently with our legislative leaders to make sure all Floridians have continued confidence in our election system and that we address potential deficiencies that have caused this situation in a few counties. A crisis of faith in our election system should not be allowed to fester based on the actions of a few supervisors and I will work to right this situation in future elections. With the election behind us," concluded DeSantis, "it's now time to come together as a state as we prepare to serve all Floridians."

Eleven days elapsed before the machine recount process concluded and Gillum conceded a second time; but once the recount was complete, the initial results from election night were confirmed. Ron DeSantis had been elected governor, and in the process, he became Florida's sixth Republican chief executive of the modern era and the fourth Republican governor in succession.[241]

An Era of New Opportunities

With the Republican emergence onto the statewide scene in Florida came new opportunities for both women and minorities. When the new era began in 1966, there had never been a woman, an African American, or a person of Hispanic heritage selected to hold a statewide elected position in Florida. In addition to the opportunity for partisan successes that came with the Republicans in the two-party system, there was also a new opportunity for diversity that had not been present in the earlier era of the Democratic "Solid South."

Beginning with Paula Hawkins's election to the Florida Public Service Commission and her subsequent election to the U.S. Senate, Florida saw doors of opportunity open for other women to assume prominent statewide posts—Sandra Mortham and Katherine Harris became secretaries of state; Pam Bondi was elected to two terms as the state's attorney general, and she was succeeded in that office by Ashley Moody; Betty Castor won the commissioner of education's post; Alex Sink served a term as the state's chief financial officer; and Toni Jennings, Jennifer Carroll, and Jeanette Nuñez were selected to serve as Florida's lieutenant governor. The modern era also saw five Floridians of Hispanic heritage come to statewide prominence—Florida's second Republican governor, Bob Martinez; U.S. Senator Mel Martinez; Lieutenant Governor Carlos Lopez-Cantera; Lieutenant Governor Jeanette Nuñez; and Florida's two-term U.S. Senator Marco Rubio. Doug Jamison became the first African American to assume a statewide post when he was appointed to serve as the commissioner of education, and Republican Jennifer Carroll became the first African American elected to a statewide office when she won the lieutenant governor's post on the ticket with Rick Scott in his first election.

The opportunities of the modern era have seen twelve statewide elections won by a woman; the era has seen two African Americans assume statewide posts and has witnessed individuals of Hispanic heritage win in six statewide elections. In the aggregate, sixteen of these individuals carried the Republican banner, and three were Democrats.

The diversity that came with the modern era not only manifested itself in the statewide posts; it also found its way into the seats of the state Legislature with increasing frequency as the era matured.

6

REPUBLICAN SENATE

THE FRAGMENTATION OF FLORIDA's executive branch among seven, and more recently four, statewide officials left the state's governor relatively weak in comparison to the chief executives of other states, and the resulting effect was to leave the legislative branch of government in Florida relatively more powerful.[1] Viewed in context, it made Republican voices in the Florida Legislature a Republican Party priority beginning with the election sequence of 1966 and 1967.[2]

While the Republican minority maintained a meaningful policymaking presence in both the Florida Senate—the upper chamber—and the state House of Representatives—the lower chamber—from the time of Claude Kirk, it was to be three more decades before the Republicans claimed the majority status in the Florida Legislature. It came in steps, and it came first in the Florida Senate, but in the early years of the two-party era, the ability of the Republicans to attain the majority status was not always apparent.

The Pork Chop Gang and the End of an Era

Prior to the *Swann v. Adams* court-ordered legislative districts, the Florida Senate was home to the conservative rural lawmakers that the *Tampa Tribune* had labeled the Pork Chop Gang. Prior to the 1966 and 1967 elections, Republican membership in the Senate had been limited to only a few scattered individuals over the first six decades of the twentieth century. In 1928, when Herbert Hoover carried Florida in the presidential election, Albert R. Welsh from St. Petersburg in Pinellas County was elected to the Florida Senate, but Welsh died after his first term in office.[3] When C. W. "Bill" Young was elected to the Florida Senate a generation later in 1961 from Pinellas County, he served as the Republican leader of the Senate for two terms by default because he was the only Republican member of the body, but Young would soon have the company of other Republican colleagues.[4]

The special court-ordered elections of 1967 changed the complexion of the upper legislative chamber in two significant ways—first, a meaningful number of Republicans arrived in the Senate, where they became a relevant minority with new Republican Governor Claude Kirk; and second, a significant change in the majority party caucus materialized with the new Democratic senators from the state's urban areas that had been underrepresented before the *Swann v. Adams* decision. These new senators— "Republicans and Democrats alike—had been changed by their common military experience and shared a vision of Florida not as part of the Old South."[5] These new dynamics were the foundation for the era of two-party politics in the Florida Senate, and the two-party reality in the upper chamber began immediately following the special legislative elections in the spring of 1967.

The new members of the Republican caucus in the Florida Senate— twenty of forty-eight in 1967—began with an impact that was both immediate and enduring. In the decade that followed their initial arrival, many of the Republican senators who came to the Capitol remained for extended lengths of service; they helped to establish an organized alternative to the Pork Chop politics that had preceded them; and with their colleagues in the Florida House, they were significant contributors to the growth of the Republican Party. Like Bill Young, some of the new Republicans remained and rose to be leaders in the Senate, while others followed their service in the Senate by playing significant roles in the growth of the Republican Party. Among the early Republican senators were Tom Slade from Jacksonville; John Ducker and Ken Plante from Orlando; Warren

Henderson from Sarasota; Bill Young, Harold Wilson, Henry Sayler, and John Ware from Pinellas County; Richard Langley from Lake County; Skip Bafalis from Palm Beach County; Clark Maxwell Jr. from Brevard County; and David Lane, Van Poole, and Jim Scott from Broward County.

David Lane, Ken Plante, Warren Henderson, John Ware, Dick Langley, Clark Maxwell, and Jim Scott each rose to become the Republican leader of the Florida Senate, and together, these early-arriving senators combined to lead the Republican caucus for almost two decades.[6] Scott served in the Senate long enough to become not only the body's Republican minority leader but to also become the upper chamber's second Republican president.[7] In addition to their service in the Florida Senate, Tom Slade, Henry Sayler, and Van Poole each went on to become chairmen of the state Republican Party, and each helped to build the growing Republican network at both the state and local level.[8] Both Bill Young and Skip Bafalis followed their service in the state Senate as members of the U.S. Congress.[9]

These early Republican senators were more philosophically conservative than their new Democratic colleagues who arrived from the new urban and suburban districts mandated under the Dauer apportionment plan; however, they did not mirror the same conservative philosophy championed by the members of the Pork Chop Gang.[10] In contrast to the Pork Chop "conservatism" rooted in vestiges of segregation and preserving the status quo of Florida's government institutions, the Republicans brought a philosophy rooted in a limitation on new taxes, enhanced environmental protection, economic development, and support for reforming and modernizing the state's governmental institutions.[11] These philosophical contrasts held significance for the Republicans as they interacted with their Democratic colleagues in the Senate. At times, the Republican philosophy facilitated alliances with the newly arriving members of the majority party because portions of Republican philosophy mirrored the goals of the new urban Democrats.[12] At other times, it provided an opportunity to align with the chamber's remaining conservative Democratic members.[13] The significance of this opportunity to engage in alternating alliances did not materialize immediately as the Legislature adjusted to the new Republican governor, but in time, the contrasting philosophies inside the Democratic caucus created the opportunity for Republican members to remain consistently relevant in the upper chamber's deliberations.[14]

In the new forty-eight-member Senate created by the Dauer apportionment plan in 1967, a few members from the Pork Chop era remained. They included L. K. Edwards from Irvine, L. P. "Pete" Gibson from Perry, J. Emory "Red" Cross from Gainesville, Ben Hill Griffin Jr. from Frostproof, Dempsey Barron from Panama City, and Verle Pope from St. Augustine.[15] Each had begun his legislative career during the 1950s or early 1960s, but by the end of 1968, all but Pope and Barron were gone, and by 1972 only Barron remained.[16]

During their final years, the remaining Pork Choppers enjoyed little of the influence of their early years despite Pope being the body's president during the legislative sessions of 1967 and 1968.[17] Dempsey Barron was the exception, however, and Barron emerged as the de facto leader of the new conservatives in the Democratic caucus. He remained a major influence in the Florida Senate until 1988; he became one of the body's definitive power brokers for nearly two decades; and his presence during the 1970s and 1980s contributed significantly to the influence of the Republican caucus in ways that were initially unexpected.[18]

Funding the Path to Majority

For Republican members in the Senate, as well as those serving in the House, one of the first priorities was to stabilize their new status in the political arena. In addition to engaging themselves in the business of lawmaking, the early Republican leaders also immersed themselves in the partisan political process of bringing more Republican members to the Legislature. Beginning with the priority of reelecting incumbents, Republican leaders also set their sights on supporting the campaigns of new candidates who could increase their numbers. Adequately funding these campaigns was considered one of the keys to success, but garnering support from the traditional sources presented a unique dilemma. These traditional "giving" sources—the interest groups, trade associations, and business lobbyists—were reluctant to consider many of the new Republican contenders, particularly those attempting to win a seat that was held by an incumbent Democrat.[19]

As the modern era began, the Democratic legislative leadership still held the clear majority in both Houses of the Legislature even after the dramatic gains in the 1967 special elections.[20] As Republicans looked to the elections of 1968, the Democrat leadership had made it clear to potential donors that the quick way to suffer the disdain of the majority party was to contribute funds against a Democratic incumbent or contribute to a Republican candidate in a race for an open seat being vacated by a Democratic incumbent.[21] As a result, few from the private sector were willing to part with campaign dollars for individual Republican candidates and risk retribution for their generosity.

To counter this informal "ban" on giving to individual Republican Party candidates, Senate Republican Leader Bill Young and House Republican Leader Don Reed hatched the concept of a Republican Legislative Appreciation Dinner (LAD) under the umbrella of the state Republican Party to raise funds for their candidates; once raised, the funds from the LAD were to be devoted exclusively to legislative races.[22] The Legislative Appreciation Dinner was the Republican response to the majority party's not-so-subtle intimidation of the traditional sources of campaign funds; it was intended as a cooperative effort between the Senate and House Republican legislators; and it was a technique that had not been previously employed by the Democrats in support of their own candidates. With help from their Republican legislative staff members, Young and Reed refined the concept and took it to both Republican caucuses, where the idea was readily received, and in the spring of 1968, a new era of political fund-raising began.[23]

The funds raised at the inaugural LAD were divided equally between the House and Senate caucuses, and the accounts were designated by the state Republican Party as Senate and House Leadership Funds. In the Senate, Young used the funds both to protect his incumbents and to support new candidates attempting to win seats occupied by Democrats. In the House during Reed's tenure as leader, incumbent House Republicans did not receive any of the monies that they helped to raise; the funds were devoted exclusively to bringing new Republicans to Tallahassee in House seats previously held by Democrats.[24]

What Young and Reed began in the spring of 1968 as the first Republican

Early Republican legislative leaders discuss redistricting plans. *Right to left:* first Senate Republican Leader C. W. "Bill" Young with Republican Representatives Douglas Loeffler, James Russell, and John Ducker. Photo courtesy of the State Archives of Florida.

Legislative Appreciation Dinner was later rechristened the Legislative Appreciation Reception (LAR) when the meals and their incidental costs were dropped from the annual event. The LAR continued for more than two decades, and it became one of the important catalysts that allowed Republicans to muster the resources necessary to fund their legislative campaign efforts.[25] A decade later, in 1979, the LAR was supplemented by the fundraising of the Legislative Campaign Committee that Jack Eckerd created at the suggestion of House Republican leader and future State Senator Curt Kiser. The committee was composed of Eckerd, the Republican leaders in both Houses of the Legislature, and the chairman of the state Republican Party; and the committee was initially staffed by Young Republican Jack Latvala.[26] Both funding techniques—the LAR and the Legislative Campaign Committee—were ultimately consolidated and brought directly under the state Republican Party structure during the chairmanship of Tom Slade.[27] But in the early years of the new era, these cooperative fund-raising techniques were a new innovation; they proved successful even from their modest beginnings, and the Republican Leadership Funds became an important part of the campaign efforts that ushered in the era of Republican majorities in both the state Senate and the Florida House.[28]

A "Philosophical Kinship" and Changing District Boundaries

While the cooperative fund-raising efforts by the Senate and the House Republicans took a partisan approach to political campaigns, inside Florida's two legislative chambers the interaction between the Republicans and Democrats manifested itself differently. From the outset of the modern era, the two legislative bodies had characteristically different "personalities" and evolved differently as Republican majorities approached reality. In the Senate, Republicans found influence in both numbers and in their relationship with their Democratic colleagues.[29] When the new era in the Senate began in 1967, Republicans made up more than one-third of the membership, a status they maintained through the next election cycle, but beginning in 1974, it was not a status they would again achieve until 1986.[30] While in raw numbers the Republican progress toward a majority seemed stagnant, the Republican numbers belied their effectiveness. Occasions for partisan party positions were rare, and a philosophical kinship with conservative Democrats in the Florida Senate helped Republicans remain as relevant players.[31] They were not simply numbers on the back row of the Senate chamber.

"I'm not of the loyal opposition. I'm part of the action," explained Warren Henderson, who followed Bill Young as the Republican minority leader in the Senate.[32]

The relationship Henderson described continued under Republican Leaders David Lane and John Ware, who followed him. The relationship included a meaningful voice for Republicans in the Senate's policy debates and committee deliberations; Republicans shared proportionate membership in the Senate's committee structure, and there was permanent staffing for the Senate Republican Minority Office.[33] There was also another benefit from the "philosophical kinship" described by political writer Martin Dyckman.[34] During the years of stagnant aggregate Republican numbers, Democrat presiding officers did not limit their appointments of committee chairmanships to members of their own caucus. Although no Republican senators had been included in leadership positions in the first legislative terms that followed court-ordered reapportionment, that began to change after the legislative redistricting that followed the 1970 census. Under the new apportionment plan, the number of Senate members was reduced from forty-eight to forty, and beginning after the elections in 1974, Republican names began to appear in the Senate organizational structure.[35]

In 1974, the Democratic Senate president, Dempsey Barron, appointed Republican Walter Sims from Orlando to be the Senate Transportation Committee vice chairman and designated Republican Ken Plante from Winter Park to chair Subcommittee C of the powerful Senate Ways and

Republican senators confer on the floor of the Senate chambers. *Left to right:* Jim Scott, Ileana Ros-Lehtinen, Richard Langley, Fred Dudley, and Toni Jennings. Photo courtesy of the Florida Historic Capitol Museum.

Means Committee.[36] Two years later, in 1976, Plante was appointed as the vice chairman of the influential Rules and Calendar Committee, and the appointment was particularly significant because that committee controlled the scheduling of all business coming before the full Senate. By the organizational session for the 1980–82 term, Republican Senators John Ware, Jim Scott, David McClain, Warren Henderson, Van Poole, Clark Maxwell, and Tom Tobiassen had each been appointed as a vice chair for a standing Senate committee, and the appointments continued the precedent started by Barron of including members of the minority Republican caucus in the formal leadership structure of the Senate.[37]

The 1980–82 term was significant for another reason, too. Pursuant to the state's constitution, the Legislature was again tasked to redesign the boundaries of the districts for the seats in the Florida Legislature based upon the population changes identified in the 1980 decennial census.[38] The boundaries for these districts created the blocs of voters that selected the members of the House and Senate, and with changing district boundaries, the opportunities for the voices of new members materialized. Following the court-ordered redistricting in 1967, these new opportunities came to the urban and suburban areas of Florida that had been denied an equal and proportional voice in both legislative bodies by the Pork Chop Gang and its allies.[39] Despite the shift providing voices from the urban centers, however, the same opportunities were not extended to minority voting blocs in the court-ordered plan. The large multimember districts in the court-ordered plan diluted their voices in larger blocs of voters that were predominantly white and predominantly Democratic.[40] In the two election cycles that followed under the plan approved by the federal court in *Swann v. Adams*, no African American legislators were elected to either legislative body; only a single Hispanic senator was elected under the plan, and only two Hispanic members were successful in winning seats in the Florida House.[41]

The redistricting that followed in 1972 was done by the Legislature, and the redesigned districts again met the equal population standard, but the large multimember districts in the urban areas remained. Democrats controlled the placement of the boundary lines for the new districts, and once again, little opportunity was left for minority voices from the densely populated urban and suburban areas that were diluted in larger population groupings of white Democratic voters.[42]

The districts created in the decennial apportionment in 1982 were different, and they eliminated the vestiges of the large multimember districts that had been adopted by the federal court in 1967 and continued by the Legislature in 1972. Although the redistricting plan adopted in 1982 was done in a partisan environment controlled by Democrats, the new single-member districts that the plan created for both the House and Senate opened new opportunities for minority population groupings previously limited by the larger multimember districts.[43] They were opportunities that fully manifested themselves by the end of the decade. There had been no African Americans seated in the Senate following the 1972 elections, but by the end of the decade following the adoption of single-member districting plan in 1982, there were five African American members serving in the Florida Senate. In 1972, Beth Johnson was the only woman serving in the Senate, but after single-member districts had been in effect for a decade, there were six women senators; and by the end of the decade from the districts approved in 1982, there were three Hispanic members serving in Florida Senate where previously there had been none.[44]

Single-member districts made a difference for the Republicans, too. After the elections in 1982, the Republican caucus in the Senate had fallen to its lowest number in the modern era under the Democratic apportionment plan, but under the single-member districting scheme, the Republican numbers in the Senate began to grow once again.[45] By the time of the next decennial redistricting in 1992, Republican senators again totaled more than one-third of the Senate membership.[46] Their increasing numbers, combined with a "philosophical kinship" with conservative members in the Democratic caucus, gave the Republicans a new foundation upon which they could continue to build the numbers in their caucus.[47]

The Coalitions and Increasing Numbers

Within the majority Democratic caucus following the elections in 1982, an internal dynamic also had an impact on the partisan politics in the Senate.

Fractures began to materialize between the conservative and more liberal Democrat senators, and this disruption provided another opportunity for Republicans to exercise their influence and to increase their numbers. The fracture in the Democratic caucus came to a head when some of its members, led by Senator Dempsey Barron, turned their back on the caucus's choice for the next Senate president and joined with Republicans to select the body's next presiding officer.[48] The coalition designated Democratic Senator Curtis Peterson from Polk County as the Senate's president, and in the process, the visibility and role of the Republicans was ratcheted up despite their relatively small numbers.[49] Six of the eight Republican senators were invited to be part of the formal Senate organization, and the kinship with the conservative Democrats helped to stabilize the Republican voice in the Senate. Both Clark Maxwell and Warren Henderson were designated as committee chairmen, and Senators Richard Langley, Mary Grizzle, and Jerry Rehm joined Jim Scott as vice chairs of Senate standing committees.[50]

Curtis Peterson's presidency was to be first of three coalition presidencies during the decade that followed, but the next coalition was preceded by the "hard-core partisan" presidency of Democratic Senator Harry Johnston from Palm Beach County.[51] When Harry Johnston succeeded Peterson in 1984, he garnered sufficient votes from within the Democratic caucus to become the president of the Senate, and there was no need for support from the Republican caucus. After assuming the presidency, Johnston stripped all of the Republicans from the posts they had held as committee chairs and vice chairs, and he returned exclusive control of the Senate hierarchy to the Democrats.

"Harry [Johnston] was so partisan," remembered Senate Republican Toni Jennings, "that he took the television out of the Republican office because he said there's not enough of you to worry about what's going on."[52]

Only two freshman senators were elected in 1984, and both were Republicans—Curt Kiser from Pinellas County and Bob Johnson from Sarasota—and President Johnston extended his partisan ardor to them as well. When the Senate members were asked to continue the tradition of selecting their outstanding colleagues in a series of categories, no freshman was designated as the "Outstanding First-Term Member." When Senate Secretary

Joe Brown was asked why the category had been dropped for the 1984–86 selection process, Brown told Kiser and Johnston that the president had said "it was not worthy of having a vote because there were only Republicans eligible for the honor."[53]

During Harry Johnston's presidency and despite his partisan tenor, the Republican numbers in the Senate began to increase, and by the end of Johnston's term as president, the division in the majority Democratic Party caucus once again appeared. It was a time Senator Toni Jennings described as "a little bit of no-man's-land for Republicans."[54] In 1985, Senator Malcolm Beard from Tampa changed parties and abandoned Johnston and the Democrats to join the Republican caucus, and Ander Crenshaw from Jacksonville joined the Senate Republican caucus following a special election in 1986. Combined with Beard's switch, Crenshaw's election increased the Republican membership in the Senate by two.[55]

As the fall elections of 1986 approached, there was another fortuitous opportunity for the Republicans to join in a coalition with Democratic senators led by Barron, and once again, Republicans were amenable to the invitation.[56] Initially, the Democratic caucus assumed that Senator Ken Jenne, an urban Democrat from Broward County, had secured the votes to become the next president with sufficient votes from within the caucus.[57] The Democratic caucus also assumed that the partisan tenor set by Johnston would continue; but for the second time during the decade, the Democrats' designee for the Senate presidency in the 1986–88 term was rejected in favor of a coalition choice that was supported by the members of the Republican caucus.

Following the 1986 elections that produced a victory for Bob Martinez and gave Republicans their second Florida governor, the Senate Republican caucus led by Senator Toni Jennings was joined by four more new members—Ileana Ros-Lehtinen and Dexter Lehtinen from Miami-Dade County, Fred Dudley from Lee County on the southwest coast, and Marlene Woodson-Howard from Bradenton.[58] With results of the 1986 elections and the conclusion of Johnston's presidency, the numbers in the Republican caucus had increased from ten to fifteen members, and the coalition of conservative Democrats led by Dempsey Barron and the Republican members led by Jennings turned back Jenne's bid for the presidency.[59] Instead of Jenne, the Senate coalition designated conservative Democrat John W. Vogt from Cocoa Beach to lead the Senate.[60]

With Vogt's selection, the Republican caucus was again rewarded for its part in the coalition with a meaningful voice in the business of the Senate, and all of its members were appointed to either chair a Senate committee or to serve as a committee vice chair. The ten Republican committee chairs included Jim Scott (Appropriations); Toni Jennings (Commerce); Mary Grizzle (Executive Business); Tim Deratany (Finance, Tax and Claims); Curt Kiser (Governmental Operations); Doc Myers (Health and Rehabilitative Services); Richard Langley (Judiciary-Civil); Bob Johnson (Judiciary-Criminal); Malcolm Beard (Transportation); and Ander Crenshaw (Select Committee on the Lottery). Vice chairs for the 1986–88 term were awarded to the remaining five Republican senators—Marlene Woodson-Howard (Corrections, Probation and Parole); Fred Dudley (Executive Business); John Grant (Judiciary-Civil); Dexter Lehtinen (Personnel, Retirement and Collective Bargaining); and Ileana Ros-Lehtinen (Health and Rehabilitative Services).[61]

In the next term, the caucus continued to grow. Following the elections in 1988, two more new Republican faces appeared in the Florida Senate when Bill Bankhead arrived from northeast Florida and Javier Souto joined the caucus from Miami-Dade County.[62] The two new Republican members brought the caucus numbers to seventeen in the forty-member Senate, leaving the Senate Republicans led by Senator William "Doc" Myers only four members shy of a majority.[63] As in the prior term and for the third time in the decade, the choice to lead the Senate following the 1988 elections was decided by a coalition of conservative Democrats and Republicans.[64] The coalition's choice as the Senate president was Democrat Bob Crawford from Polk County, and the Republicans were again rewarded for their part in the coalition when Crawford, like his predecessor, appointed each member of the Republican caucus to chair or vice-chair a Senate committee.[65]

Under Crawford's presidency, Republican chairs increased from ten to twelve, and vice chairs increased from six to eleven. Among the Republicans appointed to chair committees were Jim Scott to the influential Rules and

Calendar Committee; freshman Bill Bankhead to the Health Care Committee; Bob Johnson to the Education Committee; Toni Jennings to the Economic, Professional and Utility Regulation Committee; John Grant to the Judiciary-Criminal Committee; Ileana Ros-Lehtinen to the Personnel, Retirement and Collective Bargaining Committee; Fred Dudley to the Ethics and Elections Committee; Mary Grizzle to the Joint Growth Management Implementation Committee; Curt Kiser to the Joint Administrative Procedures Committee; and Dick Langley to the Advisory Council on Intergovernmental Relations. The new vice chairs included freshman Roberto Casas on the Regulated Industries Committee and freshman Javier Souto on the Agriculture Committee.[66]

With increased numbers and an expanded voice in the leadership, Republicans in the Senate were approaching parity as the end of the decade neared. The coalition created with their Democrat colleagues enabled the passage of Governor Martinez's landmark conservation initiative, Preservation 2000, in 1990, and it positioned the Republican caucus in the Senate to be a major factor as the Legislature prepared to reapportion into new districts based upon the 1990 decennial census.

Transition to the Majority and a Shared Senate Podium

Ander Crenshaw, Jim Scott, and Toni Jennings became the sequential Republican leaders who paved the final path for a Republican majority in the Senate.[67] As the 1990s began, Jennings felt it was simply a matter of time before voters became more comfortable with Republican positions on taxes, crime, and even education.[68] With tough economic times and rising crime rates in Florida, the Republican message of lower taxes to stimulate job growth and "tough-on-crime" measures proved to be the right message for voters. It was important, too, that each of the Republican leaders focused on recruiting good candidates and strategically spending campaign dollars from the Republican Leadership Funds.[69] Quite simply, Democrats were not accustomed to recruiting candidates or relying on strategic planning for campaigns, according to Jennings, and she felt that, with the Democrats in the majority for such a long time, they had lost touch with voters and instead spent much of their time fighting each other along liberal and conservative lines.[70] In contrast to the Democrats, remembered Jim Scott, "the Republican caucus was cohesive; they ran better campaigns; and they shared a simple goal—securing the majority."[71]

As Republicans approached majority, there were also signs from the private sector that Democrats were losing touch and that many Democrats were taking their reelections for granted; and in this context, the flow of campaign contributions began to shift more readily toward individual Republican candidates.[72] Staff at the Republican Party also speculated that Democrats were not raising as much money, and the funds that the Democratic Party did raise were not being focused on direct voter contact.[73] At the state Republican Party headquarters, Jim Magill was designated to oversee the upcoming sequence of state Senate campaigns, and Magill's efforts effectively placed the Republican Party's campaign funds to maximize Republicans' chances in tight races. The most obvious of the Republican strategies Magill employed were a strong absentee program, an aggressive direct-mail program, and direct voter contact to turn out Republican supporters on Election Day. As the elections of 1990 approached, Jim Scott remembered that "the Republicans were simply hungrier."[74]

In the 1990 fall elections, though Lawton Chiles defeated Governor Martinez, his popularity did not transfer to other Democratic candidates. While Chiles's "cracker" image served him well as governor, the "cracker" magic was identified with him and did not transfer well to other Democratic candidates. Following the elections, the Republican numbers in the Senate remained unchanged despite Chiles's victory; and there were three new Republican senators seated in the upper chamber—John McKay from Manatee County, Rich Crotty from Orange County, and Lincoln Diaz-Balart from Miami-Dade County—each replacing a retiring member as Senator Ander Crenshaw prepared to succeed Doc Myers as the Republican caucus leader.[75]

With sufficient votes from within the Democrat caucus, Senator Gwynn Margolis was selected to preside over the Senate as its president in the 1990 Organizational Session, but unlike Harry Johnston, Margolis did not take a hard partisan approach to the Senate's organizational structure.[76] Ten of the seventeen Republican senators were appointed to committee leadership posts. Four were designated to chair committees—Mary Grizzle to the Community Affairs Committee; John Grant to the Criminal Justice Committee; Lincoln Diaz-Balart to the Committee on International Trade, Economic Development and Trade; and Javier Souto to the Personnel, Retirement and Collective Bargaining Committee. The other six Republicans were designated as committee vice chairs, and notable among these designations were Ander Crenshaw's appointment as the vice chairman of the Rules and Calendar Committee; Bill Bankhead's appointment as vice chair of the Reapportionment Legislative Subcommittee; and Javier Souto's appointment as the vice chair of the Reapportionment Congressional Subcommittee. Republicans also received proportional representation on both Reapportionment Subcommittees—five of eleven members on the Legislative Subcommittee and six of thirteen on the Congressional Subcommittee.[77]

With both meaningful numbers and key committee assignments, the Republican caucus began the 1990–92 term with a significant voice in the policies to be made, including the reconfiguration of the boundaries for the Senate's forty districts.[78] In a special election in 1991, Locke Burt captured another seat previously held by a Democrat; and the caucus increased its membership to eighteen before the new district boundaries were drawn.[79] When the design of the new districts was complete, the revised boundaries reflected the demographics of the state's shifting population and the growing number of Republican voters.[80]

Ander Crenshaw retained the leadership of the Republican caucus into the 1992 fall elections, and the results from the new districts proved fruitful indeed. Several new Republican faces arrived in the Senate after the 1992 elections, and they included Robert Harden from Fort Walton Beach in the Florida panhandle, Mark Foley from Palm Beach County, Gary Siegel from Orlando, and Don Sullivan from Pinellas County.[81] In addition to these new faces in the redistricted Senate, the total number of Republican senators increased from eighteen to twenty, giving the Republican caucus exactly one-half of the forty-member Senate.[82] With an equal number of senators from each party, there was not to be a fourth coalition Senate president for the two-year term of 1992–94. After three days of jockeying to resolve the deadlock and five formal roll-call votes, the Senate was unable to decide upon a single individual to preside over the body.

"Those were the three longest days," remembered Toni Jennings; "everybody in the Republican caucus just locked down."[83]

Ultimately, the membership of the Senate reached a compromise to share the reins of leadership between the Republican and Democratic caucuses.[84] The terms of the compromise split the presidency of the Senate between Democrat Pat Thomas from Gadsden County and Republican Ander Crenshaw from Jacksonville. Crenshaw was designated to preside as the president of the Senate for the first year of the term, and Thomas was designated to assume the presidency during the second year.[85] When he assumed the role at the 1992 organizational session of the Legislature, Ander Crenshaw became the first Republican Senate president in the state's modern era of two-party politics; and when Democrat Pat Thomas assumed the presidency during the second year of the term, he became the century's last Democrat to hold the title.

The Senate membership approved nineteen standing committees for the 1992–94 term, and thirteen of the committees were chaired by a Republican senator during Crenshaw's tenure. The remaining six committees were chaired by a Democrat.[86] Key chairmanships included the Appropriations Committee, which was headed by Jim Scott; and Republicans Malcolm Beard, Fred Dudley, Doc Myers, and Locke Burt were each selected to chair one of its funding subcommittees. Toni Jennings was designated to chair the Senate Rules and Calendar Committee; Curt Kiser was appointed to chair the Finance, Taxation and Claims Committee; John Grant chaired the Commerce Committee; John McKay was appointed to chair the Health and Rehabilitative Services Committee; Mark Foley chaired the Agriculture Committee; Robert Harden chaired the Governmental Operations Committee; Ginny Brown-Waite chaired the Community Affairs Committee; and Mario Diaz-Balart was picked to chair the Transportation Committee.

Several of these Republican chairs also served as committee vice chairs during Crenshaw's presidency, and the remaining Republican committee vice chairs included John Grant on the Education Committee; Locke Burt on the Personnel, Retirement and Collective Bargaining Committee; and

Senators Ander Crenshaw (*left*) and Pat Thomas (*right*) meeting with Speaker Bolley Johnson (*center*) on the podium of the House Chamber at the beginning of the 1992–94 legislative term. Photo courtesy of the Florida Historic Capitol Museum.

Roberto Casas on the Committee for International Trade, Economic Development and Tourism.[87] During Thomas's tenure the chairmanships and vice chairmanships were flipped from Republican to Democrat, and the sharing of power between the parties in the Senate continued until the results from the fall elections of 1994 were known.[88]

Limiting the Terms of Incumbents

The results from the 1992 elections that brought an equal number of Republicans and Democrats to the Florida Senate had another long-term impact on the partisan composition of Florida's Legislature for another reason, but this impact was not immediately apparent. The long-term consequences only began to manifest themselves as incumbent members of the Legislature were unable to stand for reelection because of a "term limit" amendment to the Florida Constitution that was also approved by the voters in 1992 elections.[89]

Incumbent members of the Legislature, both senators and members of the House, had traditionally been secure in their seats with the ability to serve for extended periods, and defeating an incumbent was a rare occurrence in Florida legislative campaigns. For Republicans, it meant that increasing their numbers by capturing a seat held by an incumbent Democrat was rarely accomplished unless the seat had been reconfigured based on the decennial census or when an incumbent Democrat chose not to seek reelection.[90] The federal courts had previously assured that the decennial redistricting would occur, and Republicans had taken advantage of those opportunities.[91] The 1992 elections assured that there would be more future vacancies in Democratic seats and more opportunities for Republicans with adoption of the constitutional amendment imposing term limits.[92]

The term-limits initiative, labeled "Eight Is Enough," was promoted by Republican and Orlando businessman Phil Handy; and in the 1992 fall elections, Florida voters overwhelming approved the constitutional amendment with more than 77 percent of the total vote.[93] The provisions of "Eight Is Enough" provided that a member of the Legislature was not permitted to seek reelection after being elected to eight consecutive years of service—for House members, after four two-year terms, and for state senators, after two four-year terms.[94] For those members of the Legislature beginning terms after the elections of 1992, the limits on their service did not take effect until the decade was coming to a close, but as the deadline came closer, some legislators began to seek other offices before the limits forced them from office, and by 2002, the full impacts of "Eight Is Enough" affected those who remained.[95] While new restrictions on legislative service applied equally to all legislators, whether Democrat or Republican, once the limits were in full effect, the favorable shift in seats and the shift of political power to the Republican column became obvious.[96]

As the fall elections of 1994 approached, however, the new limits on legislative service were of little consequence. The Senate Republican caucus designated Jim Scott to succeed Ander Crenshaw as its leader during the next term, and both political parties looked to the November elections to break the 20–20 deadlock.[97]

A First Full Term President . . . and the First Two-Term President

In 1994 fall elections, Lawton Chiles eked out a narrow election victory over Jeb Bush for governor, but Democrats lost control of the state Senate.[98] Going into the elections, Democrats had four tough seats to defend, two in central Florida with Patti Grogan and Buddy Dyer, along with one in southwest Florida held by Jim Boczar and one in southeast Florida occupied by Tom Rosin. Dyer and Rosin both won with just under 52 percent of the vote, but the other two other races were in better areas for Republicans.[99] In southwest Florida, Katherine Harris took on the incumbent Democrat, Jim Boczar, and Harris cruised to victory with over 60 percent of the vote. Democrat Patti Grogan had won a squeaker over a Republican candidate in 1992 to capture a seat in the Senate, but in 1994, her reelection efforts to retain the seat fell short. Republican rancher and future Secretary of Agriculture Charlie Bronson captured the Brevard-based seat from Grogan by garnering almost 54 percent of the vote. With Bronson's victory, the Senate was now in Republican hands.[100]

In all, twenty-one Republican senators returned to Tallahassee following the elections, and by a one-member margin, the transition to the first Republican majority in the Florida Senate was complete.[101] The new majority also included Jim Horne from Orange Park, who replaced Ander Crenshaw and future Senate Majority Leader Jack Latvala, who replaced Curt Kiser. With the majority, Jim Scott was designated to lead the body as its president for a full two-year term, and the new Republican era in the Florida Senate began. The other parts of state government—the House of Representatives, the governor's office, and the Florida cabinet—remained in Democratic control; but the change in the Florida Senate was a catalyst for passage of the legislative initiative authorizing charter schools for Florida's students, and it was the harbinger of other changes to come in Florida's capital.

Senate President Jim Scott with his successor, two-term Senate President Toni Jennings. Photo courtesy of the Florida Historic Capitol Museum.

As the new era began under Scott's leadership in the Florida Senate, Republicans carried forward the bipartisan protocol that began during Dempsey Barron's term as president. Senators from both parties were invited into official positions in the Senate's organizational structure, and despite their new minority status, twelve Democrats were appointed to serve as a chair or vice chair of a Senate committee.[102] The tradition of minority party chairmanships that had begun with Barron's presidency was continued by Scott's successor, Toni Jennings, and by each successive Republican Senate president who followed her.

When Jennings assumed the Senate presidency after the 1996 elections, there were even fewer Democratic members in the body. New Republicans included Charlie Clary from Destin, who replaced Robert Harden; and Anna Cowin from Leesburg, who joined the Republican caucus, winning the seat that had been held by Democrat Karen Johnson in the previous term; the other new caucus member was long-serving Senator W. D. Childers from Pensacola, who changed parties to join the Republicans prior to his reelection.[103] The 1996 elections also brought Tom Lee from Brandon to the Republican caucus, replacing retiring Senator Malcolm Beard, and in time, Lee became the Senate's sixth Republican president.[104] What had been a one-member Republican margin for Scott became a three-member margin for Jennings, and Republicans were comfortably in control of the Legislature's upper chamber. Following the 1996 elections, the Republican majority in the Senate was also complemented by a one-member Republican majority in the House of Representatives, giving Republicans the voting majority in both legislative chambers for the first time in the modern two-party era.[105]

It had been long-standing tradition in the Florida Legislature that the presiding officers in the House and the Senate served only a single term, and during their term in office another member from the caucus is selected as the successor to the current leader. The designated successor then carried the title of "designee" into the fall elections and mobilized the campaign efforts for the upcoming term.[106] As the 1998 elections approached, Republican Senators Bill Bankhead from Ponte Vedra, Jim Horne from Clay County, and Mario Diaz-Balart from Miami each stepped forward in an effort to succeed Toni Jennings as the Senate's next president, but none among the three was able to claim the majority support of the Republican caucus for the post.[107] When no consensus among the contenders could be reached, Jennings was approached by her colleagues to remain for a second term as the Senate's president, and ultimately she agreed to do so.[108] In the process, the Senate departed from its prior tradition, and Toni Jennings became the first person in Florida history to serve for two consecutive terms as the upper chamber's presiding officer.[109]

During Jennings's second term as Senate president, the trend of increasing Republican numbers in the body continued with two new additions.

Senate President Toni Jennings presiding from the podium in the Senate chambers. Photo courtesy of the Florida Historic Capitol Museum.

Republican John Laurent from Bartow replaced retiring Democrat Rick Dantzler; and Senator George Kirkpatrick from Gainesville followed the examples of Malcolm Beard and W. D. Childers and switched his affiliation from the Democratic Party to complete the term as a Republican.[110] At the organizational session following the 1998 elections, only fifteen of the forty Senate seats were held by Democrats; but Jennings designated nine members of the minority Democratic caucus to serve as either a chair or a vice chair of a Senate committee as she organized the second term of her presidency.[111]

Growing and Sustaining the Majority

What had been a one-member Republican margin for Jim Scott in 1994 became a five-member margin for Toni Jennings after the elections in 1998, and Republicans held firm control of the Legislature's upper chamber. The

Republican majority in the Senate was complemented by the election of Florida's third Republican governor, Jeb Bush, and a Republican majority in the House of Representatives. Following the 1998 elections, except for three Democrat members of the Florida cabinet, all of the institutions of state government belonged to the Republicans.[112]

When John McKay from Manatee County succeeded Toni Jennings as the Senate's presiding officer after the elections in 2000, Republicans held a stable majority with twenty-five members of the forty-member Senate, and it became a sustainable majority for the Republican presidents who followed. As the new decade began, the impact of term limits also took effect. The migration of House members to the Senate contributed to the new Republican numbers in the upper chamber, and the migration brought six of the next eight Senate presidents from the House of Representatives to the Senate Republican caucus.

In the 2000 and 2002 elections, twenty-nine new senators were elected to open seats, and eighteen of the new senators were Republicans.[113] Among the new Republicans arriving after these elections were former House member and future Senate President Ken Pruitt from Port St. Lucie; former House member and future Senate Majority Leader Alex Villalobos from Miami; former House member and future U.S. Congressman Bill Posey; and future Senate President Pro Tempore Alex Diaz de la Portillas, who was elected to his first full term after winning a special election earlier in 2002.[114]

During John McKay's presidency, Republicans were also handed control of the legislative and congressional redistricting process for the first time in the modern two-party era. Creating the new districts presented the opportunity for Republicans to rebalance the partisan gerrymandering that Democrats had employed to protect their members, and it offered yet another opportunity for Republicans to solidify their base and increase their numbers in the fall elections of 2002.[115]

When Senator Jim King succeeded McKay as Senate president in 2002, there were twenty-six Republican members from the newly apportioned districts, leaving Republicans only one vote shy of a two-thirds supermajority. Of the ten new Republican senators joining King, all had previously served in the Florida House of Representatives. They included Steve Wise from Jacksonville, who had won a special election in 2001; new Senate Majority Leader Dennis Jones from Pinellas County; Evelyn Lynn from Volusia County; Nancy Argenziano from Citrus County; Paula Dockery and future Senate Appropriations Chairman J. D. Alexander from Polk County; future Senate President Pro Tempore Mike Bennett from Manatee County; future Senate President Pro Tempore Mike Fasano from Pasco County; and future Chief Financial Officer and future Senate President Jeff Atwater from Palm Beach County. Future Senate President Mike Haridopolos from Brevard County also joined the Republican caucus the following year when he won a special election in 2003 following the untimely death of Republican Senator Howard Futch.[116]

During King's term as president, there were new policy initiatives imple-

Senate President Jim King (*left*) confers with Senate Majority Leader Dennis Jones (*right*) on the floor of the Senate chambers. Photo courtesy of the Florida Historic Capitol Museum.

mented from the Republican base in the Senate. These included business-friendly reforms to the state's workers' compensation system, tort reform in the medical malpractice arena, funding to increase biomedical research, and incentives to bring new high-tech industries like the Scripps Research Institute into the state. The Legislature also passed enhanced criminal penalties to deter fraudulent auto insurance claims and billing practices, and legislation was enacted to create a smooth transition for portions of funding to Florida's judicial system.[117]

Through the presidencies of Tom Lee, Ken Pruitt, Jeff Atwater, and Mike Haridopolos, the Republican caucus in the Senate never fell below twenty-six members, and changes in state policies continued to be made.[118] Under Lee's presidency following the elections in 2004, the caucus size held at twenty-six, and Senator Carey Baker from Lake County was the only new Republican arrival.[119] During Ken Pruitt's presidency following the elections in 2006, the Republican caucus membership remained at twenty-six, and the new Republican senators included future Senate President Don Gaetz from Niceville, Rhonda Storms from Valrico, and Steve Oelrich from Gainesville.[120] Numbers in the Republican caucus were also unchanged after the 2008 elections, and the new Republican senators arriving during Jeff Atwater's tenure as Senate president were former House members Nancy Detert from Sarasota County, Thad Altman from Brevard County, and future Senate President Andy Gardiner from Orange County.[121]

In the last election cycle under the districting plan approved in 2002, the diversity in the Senate remained stable with a membership that included six African American members, four Hispanic members, and ten women.[122] Republican numbers peaked at twenty-eight members during the 2010–12 term under the presidency of Mike Haridopolos, giving the Republicans more than two-thirds of the total membership and their first supermajority in the Florida Senate. Future Senate President Joe Negron won a special election in August 2009, and among the other new Republican faces arriving after the 2010 elections to serve with Haridopolos were future Majority Leader Lizbeth Benacquisto from Fort Myers; future Senate President Pro Tempore Anitere Flores from Miami; future President Pro Tempore David Simmons from Altamonte Springs; and former House members Rene Garcia from Hialeah, Ellyn Bogdanoff from Fort Lauderdale, and Alan Hays from Umatilla in Lake County. The new senators were joined by Jack Latvala, who had previously served in the Senate and was returning to the body for a second time after an eight-year absence.[123]

Even with a Republican supermajority, the Senate tradition of committee chairs from the Democratic minority was continued under Haridopolos, and for the Senate and its new senators, redistricting was again on the agenda based on the new 2010 decennial census.[124]

New Rules, Similar Results

Unlike prior legislative apportionments, the rules for redistricting based on the 2010 census were different for the Legislature during the 2010–12 term. The new "FairDistricts" amendments to the state constitution were approved by the voters in 2010, and the amendments provided new restrictions and criteria on how the Legislature could configure the legislative and congressional districts.[125] Under the "FairDistricts" standards, priority consideration was to be given to the geographical compactness of the districts; the recognition of city and county boundary lines was also a priority; and the amendments prohibited the creation of district boundaries that were drawn with favoritism toward incumbent members of the Legislature and political parties.[126] The stated objective of the "FairDistricts" constitutional standards was to eliminate the "political gerrymandering" that had been employed by both parties in the three previous decennial apportionments, and the new constitutional amendments abandoned any consideration for communities of common interest or groupings of minority voters.[127]

The 2012 districting plan initially approved for the Florida Senate was challenged in court under the new constitutional standards after its enactment, but while the litigation was pending, the elections in 2012 and 2014 were held under the districting plan approved by the Legislature. Under the presidency of Don Gaetz following the elections in 2012, the Republican majority returned to twenty-six members from the new districts, with nine Republicans taking seats in the Senate for the first time. Two of the new members, Rob Bradley from Clay County and future Senate President-

Left to right: Senators Joe Negron, Lizbeth Benacquisto, Denise Grimsley, and Wilton Simpson converse in front of redistricting maps on the Senate floor. Photo courtesy of the Florida Senate.

designate Wilton Simpson from Pasco, had no prior legislative service; and seven of the new senators—future Senate President Bill Galvano from Manatee County, Aaron Bean from Nassau County, Jeff Brandes from Pinellas County, Denise Grimsley from Highlands County, Dorothy Hukill from Volusia County, John Legg from Pasco County, and Kelli Stargel from Polk County—all arrived with prior service in the Florida House.[128]

Following the 2014 elections, Republican membership in the Senate remained unchanged under President Andy Gardiner, but during Gardiner's term, two years of legal battles over the apportionment of the Senate districts came to an end.[129] The districts for the Senate seats enacted by the Legislature in 2012 were determined not to meet the "FairDistricts" constitutional criteria and were invalidated by the court. New court-ordered districts were created for the Senate at the conclusion of the litigation, and the 2016 elections were held from the judicially mandated districts.[130]

Democratic Party analysts anticipated that "the composition of the chamber could shift dramatically" in 2016 and with good reason.[131] Under the legislative districting plan enacted in 2012, twenty-five of the state Senate districts had more registered Republicans than Democrats, but in the court-ordered plan for the 2016 elections, twenty-one of the Senate seats had a majority of registered Democratic voters.[132] Yet after the elections and despite the Democratic optimism, there was little change in the Senate's partisan composition, and the Republican majority margin that had been achieved in 1998 remained comfortably in place.

Under the challenged legislative plan, the composition of the Senate had included twenty-six Republican members, and under the new court-order plan, twenty-five Republicans returned to the Senate, giving the Democrats a net gain of only a single seat.[133] The Republican majority designated Joe Negron from Martin County as the Senate's new presiding officer at the 2016 organizational session, and the newly arriving Republicans under Negron's presidency included former Bay County Commissioner George Gainer and eight former members of the Florida House—Kathleen Pas-

Left to right: Senators Wilton Simpson, Joe Negron, and Bill Galvano in a sidebar discussion at the Senate podium. Photo courtesy of the Florida Senate.

sidomo from Collier County, Doug Broxson from Escambia County, Dennis Baxley from Marion County, Debbie Mayfield from Brevard County, future U.S. Congressman Greg Steube from Manatee County, Dana Young from Hillsborough County, Keith Perry from Alachua County, and Frank Artiles from Miami-Dade County.[134]

Once the new Senate was seated and organized in 2016, President Negron gathered his new committee chairs and Senate staff to outline the policy objectives for the upcoming session and express the conservative overtones that would govern deliberations in the Senate. Not unlike the message that Claude Kirk and his Republican legislative allies brought to the Capitol fifty years earlier, Negron's points of emphasis were lower taxes, less government intrusion into individuals' lives, consumer protections, and environmental sensitivity toward clean water and the Florida Everglades.[135]

From the court-ordered districts, the 2018 elections saw Republicans lose one seat to Democrats, but Republicans retained a majority in the upper chamber with twenty-three members and designated Senator Bill Galvano as the body's presiding officer. Galvano became the thirteenth successive Republican Senate president; and the new Republicans joining him in the majority caucus included Ed Hooper from Clearwater, Joe Gruters from Sarasota, Gayle Harrell from Stuart, Ben Albritton from Bartow, Manny Diaz Jr. from Hialeah Gardens, and Tommy Wright from Volusia County.[136] All but Tommy Wright had prior legislative service in the Florida House.[137]

Legacy of a Supporting Cast

Like the offices of the statewide elected Republican officials and the personnel from inside the Republican Party organization, the Legislature also provided opportunities for young men and women coming into the world of partisan politics. Some who joined the staff of Republican legislators stayed for long careers in the process, like Jean Berry, who was the longest-serving staff director of the Senate Republican Office; Jim Rathbun, who was staff director in the House Republican Office for three terms before entering the private sector; Bob West, who was a two-term staff director of House Republican Office as the Republicans made the transition into the majority;

Betsy Collins, who began her career in the Florida House and continued her service of more than three decades as the longtime assistant to Senator Dennis Jones; and Marie Robinson, who began on the staff of Republican Leader Don Reed and became one of the longest-serving staff members in the House Republican Office before becoming the inspector general at the Florida Department of Revenue.[138]

Many members of the legislative staff who served while Republicans were a minority voice in the Legislature became part of the transition to a Republican majority in the Legislature. Some chose not to enter the partisan election contests on their own, and they remained on staff to provide policy analysis and support to the elected legislators after the Republicans became the majority party in the Legislature. Others transitioned from the positions on legislative staff to successful careers in the private-sector lobby corps; and still others returned to the Legislature as elected Republican officeholders.

Diane Vanderhoff served in the House Republican Office during four Republican minority leaders; she was part of the leadership staff under four Republican Speakers; and she also served on the staff in the Senate Majority Office.[139] Like Vanderhoff, Doug Bruce, Larry Churchill, Thomas J. "Tom" Randall, Debbie Bergstrom, Sally Bradshaw, Eric Thorn, Gus Corbella, Philip Twogood, Kathy Mears, and Paige Anne LeBoutillier also had tenures in the Republican legislative policy network. Larry Churchill served in the House Republican office for almost two decades, beginning before the Republicans were in the majority and serving until they reached majority status.[140] Like Churchill, Randall also served in the House Republican Office before the party captured a majority of the House for five Republican leaders and then served as the staff director in the office of the Speaker pro tempore for two Republicans after the party came into the majority.[141] Rene Lewis and Paige Anne LeBoutillier both began their careers as legislative aides for Representative R. Z. Safley, and their tenures in the process continued for more than two decades. After leaving her legislative post, Lewis served as senior cabinet aide in both the office of the comptroller and the office of the commissioner of education before becoming director of cabinet affairs at the Department of Environmental Protection. After Safley returned the private sector, LeBoutillier's service in the House continued on the staffs of future Lieutenant Governor Jeff Kottkamp, Representative Gary Aubuchon, and House Majority Leader Dane Eagle.[142]

Doug Bruce began on the staff in the House Republican Office under Leader Don Reed and later continued his service as the staff director in the Senate Republican Office under Republican Leader Ken Plante before entering the private sector.[143] Debbie Bergstrom started as an intern on the staff of Republican Leader Curt Kiser, and she transitioned to an administrative assistant for Representative Peter Dunbar before joining the senior staff of Florida's second Republican governor, Bob Martinez. Sally Bradshaw was recruited to Florida and the state Republican Party by Tom Slade following the presidential campaign of George H. W. Bush in 1992; she served briefly as the staff director of the House Republican Office under Leader Sandra Mortham; she returned to the political arena to manage the gubernatorial campaigns for Jeb Bush; and she served as the governor's chief of staff before leaving the public sector to become a respected political advisor.[144]

Eric Thorn began on the House Republican staff under Representative Dale Patchett and remained in the process to become the House general counsel under the first Republican Speaker, Dan Webster. After transitioning to the private sector, Thorn became a key member of the Republican legal response team that deployed following the Bush-Gore presidential election in 2000.[145] During Philip Twogood's long tenure, he was the staff director of the Republican Office in both the House and Senate; he served in the office of the Senate president; he was a staff director for the Senate Rules and Calendar Committee; and he served for two terms as the secretary of the Florida Senate.[146]

Gus Corbella entered the political arena as a Republican campaign volunteer in 1992; served briefly on the staff of Republican Congressman Cliff Stearns; and returned to Florida in 1995 to begin work as a legislative fellow in the House Republican Minority Office under staff director Bob West. Corbella was one of the staff members who made the transition from the minority to the majority with the Republicans in the Florida House, and at age twenty-four, he succeeded West to become the first staff director of the House Republican Majority Office.[147] When House Majority Leader Jim King was elected to the Senate, Corbella joined King's staff in the Senate

Majority Office, and he became the chief of staff in the office of the Senate president when King assumed the presidency in 2002.[148]

Kathy Mears joined the staff of Republican Speaker Dan Webster in 1996 and remained on his staff when he was elected to the Florida Senate. She followed her service with Webster as the communications director for Senate President Tom Lee and as the deputy chief of staff for Senate President Ken Pruitt before transitioning to the office of Governor Charlie Crist, where she became the deputy chief of staff and director of legislative affairs. After her service in the governor's office, Mears returned to the House of Representatives to be the chief of staff for Republican Speakers Will Weatherford and Steve Crisafulli.[149]

Like Mears, Bob Ward was part of the staff contingent of the first Republican Speaker. In addition to his service for four other Republican House Speakers, Ward also served as an education policy coordinator for Governor Jeb Bush, and he concluded his public service as the clerk of the Florida House of Representatives.[150]

Speaker Marco Rubio and staff in the Speaker's office. *Left to right:* Representative David Rivera (*seated*), Bob Ward, Mat Bahl, George Levesque, and Speaker Rubio with his son Anthony. Photo courtesy of the Florida Historic Capitol Museum.

With majority status, there were more new faces among the Republican legislative staff who continued their services in different ways, among them Robin Safley, Mat Bahl, Kimberly Case, Sarah Bascom, Todd Reid, and Chris Moya. Robin Safley began as contract counsel on the Reapportionment Committee for Senator Ander Crenshaw when Republicans were still in the minority. After serving as the general counsel at the Department of Commerce, she returned to the Florida Senate to become the chief of staff for the Senate's second Republican Senate president, Jim Scott. Following her work in the Senate, Safley served as the chief of staff for Education Commissioner Charlie Crist; she concluded her public service on the senior staff of Republican Agriculture Commissioner Adam Putnam as the division director for Food Nutrition and Wellness.[151]

Mat Bahl entered the political process as the volunteer campaign manager for Republican Representative Trey Traviesa from Hillsborough County and came to the Capitol as his legislative aide following the election.[152] His service continued on the staff of House Majority Whip Ellyn Bogdanoff; he served as deputy chief of staff for House Speaker Larry Cretul; and he concluded his first tenure in the Florida House of Representatives as the chief of staff for Speaker Dean Cannon. After spending four years with Jeb Bush's Foundation for Excellence in Education, Bahl returned to the House of Representatives as the chief of staff for Speaker Richard Corcoran.[153] Todd Reid came from the staff of the Republican National Committee to serve as the communications director under House Speaker Johnnie Byrd; he served on the cabinet affairs staff during Tom Gallagher's tenure as chief financial officer; and he returned to the House under Speakers Cretul and Cannon before becoming the deputy chief of staff for U.S. Senator Marco Rubio.[154]

Kimberly Case was part of the House Majority Office staff during the speakerships of both John Thrasher and Tom Feeney, and she later served as the director of Legislative Affairs for cabinet members Tom Gallagher and Pam Bondi.[155] Her husband, Chip Case, also spent time on the staff in the Florida House, and he served as deputy chief of staff for the fifth Republican Speaker, Allen Bense.[156] Chris Moya entered the political arena as a campaign volunteer in a nonpartisan Miami mayor's race; he joined the staff of Republican Representative Jorge Rodriguez-Chomat following the election of the first Republican Speaker at the encouragement of Gus Corbella; two years later, he joined the staff at the Division of Elections during the administration of Secretary of State Katherine Harris before entering the private sector as a lobbyist and campaign consultant.[157] Sarah Bascom began as the press secretary in the Senate Majority Office; she served as the communications director of the state Republican Party; and she returned to the Senate to serve as the communications director in the office of the Senate president before taking her skills into the private sector.[158]

Other staff members who began their service in the Legislature and continued careers in other parts of state government included Pamela "Pam" Campbell, Harold Reynolds, Cari Roth, Marion Hoffmann, Chris Finkbeiner, Brad Piepenbrink, John Morroni, Joe Gruters, and Jimmy Patronis. Campbell began her career on the House staff of Republican Leader Curt Kiser; her staff work continued in the Florida Senate; and her public service culminated in a nonpartisan capacity as a circuit judge.[159] Reynolds also began as a member of the House Republican staff under Kiser, and like Campbell, he concluded his career of public service as a circuit judge.[160] Cari Roth began as an intern with Republican State Representative Betty Easley. Roth served on the staff of House Republican Leader Dale Patchett; continued her public service as the general counsel of the Department of Community Affairs during the Bush administration; and she was later appointed to serve as a member Florida's Environmental Regulatory Commission by Governors Bush and Crist and as the commission's chair by Governor Rick Scott.[161]

Marion Hoffmann came to Capitol to join the staff in the House Republican Office under Representative Dale Patchett, and she later transitioned to the Office of Treasurer and Insurance Commissioner as a cabinet aide for education and clemency for Tom Gallagher before entering the private sector.[162] Chris Finkbeiner began as a campaign volunteer for Representative Bryan Nelson and became Nelson's legislative aide after the election. Following his service with Nelson, he became the deputy chief of staff for Mike Haridopolos during his term as Senate president; he joined the senior staff of Governor Rick Scott during the governor's first term; and he left the governor's staff near the end of the term to become the deputy campaign manager in Governor Scott's successful reelection.[163] Brad Piepenbrink started as a legislative aide to Senator Garrett Richter; continued his service in the Senate Majority Office under future Senate President Andy Gardiner; and joined the executive branch as a member of the senior staff of Governor Rick Scott.[164]

John Morroni served two terms as legislative aide for Representative Tom Woodruff; in 1992, he was elected to the Legislature and served four terms as a member of the Florida House; and returned to Pinellas County in 2000 to continue his service as a member of the county commission.[165] Jimmy Patronis came to the Capitol in 1995 to serve as an intern in the Florida Senate, and he returned to Tallahassee as an elected member of the Florida House in 2006 to serve four terms before his appointment to the Florida Public Service Commission; in 2017, Governor Scott selected him to be Florida's chief financial officer following the resignation of Jeff Atwater.[166] Joe Gruters served as an intern in the Florida House for Representative Tom Feeney, and he, too, returned to the Legislature, first as an member of the Florida House and then as a state senator.[167]

John Morroni, Jimmy Patronis, and Joe Gruters were not the only young legislative staff members who later returned to the House of Representatives as voting members. Others included R. Z. "Sandy" Safley, John Grant, John McKay, Byron Combee, Sharon Merchant, Lisa Carlton, David Coley, Kurt Kelly, Peter Dunbar, Chris Latvala, John Stargel, Jerry Burroughs, Dave Murzin, Ray Sansom, Jeanette Nuñez, Will Weatherford, Richard Corcoran, Ross Spano, Andy Gardiner, Holly Raschein, Amber Mariano, and Elizabeth Fetterhoff.[168] Grant, McKay, Carlton, and Gardiner followed their service in the House as members of the Florida Senate, and Gardiner rose to be the chamber's thirteenth Republican Senate president.[169]

Jim Scott began as the Broward County delegation attorney and returned to the Florida Senate in 1976 to serve for more than two decades, where he became the second Republican to preside over the body as its president.[170] Ron Richmond accompanied the Pinellas County legislative delegation to Tallahassee as its delegation attorney after the *Swann v. Adams* reapportionment elections; he returned to the House of Representatives as a member in 1972; and he was elected by his colleagues to be the House Republican leader in 1982.[171] John McKay was as a legislative aide in both the Senate and the House, and he later returned as a member of the Senate and rose to become the fifth Republican president to preside over the chamber.[172] Will Weatherford served on the staff of Florida's fifth Republican Speaker, Allan Bense, and he returned to the House as a member and became the ninth Republican House Speaker during his final term in office.[173] Richard Corcoran served on the staff of Florida's sixth Republican Speaker, Marco Rubio, and in 2010, he, too, returned to the House as member. In 2016, Corcoran became the party's eleventh consecutive Republican Speaker.[174]

There were other young men and women who began as aides and legislative staff and took their experience in the process to the private sector as advocates and lobbyists. Among those making a successful transition to lengthy careers in the Capitol hallways as lobbyists were Jon Shebel from the staff of House Republican Leader Don Reed; Rusty Peyton from the staff of Senator Fred Dudley; Michelle McKay from the staff of Senator Curt Kiser; Foyt Ralston from the staff of Senator Bill Bankhead; Missy Timmons and Cameron Yarbrough from the staff of Senator Jack Latvala; Carlos Cruz from the staff of Senator Roberto Casas; Nelson Diaz from the staff of House Speaker Marco Rubio; Nancy Black Stewart from the House Republican Office; Matthew Blair and Mark Anderson from the staff of Senator John Grant; Janet Mabry from the staff of House Republican Leader Ron Richmond; Clark Smith and Emily Duda Buckley from the House Appropriations Committee staff; Allison Carvajal from the Senate Appropriations Committee staff; Ron Pierce from the staff of Senator Tom Lee; Debbie Mortham from the staff of Representative Miguel DeGrandy; David Shepp from the staff of Representative Adam Putnam; and Alison Dudley from the staff of Representative Peter Dunbar.[175]

On a few rare occasions, legislators returned briefly to staff positions to assist other members assuming leadership roles in the process. Senator Carey Baker returned to the staff of the Senate as a coordinator for new member services during the presidency of Mike Haridopolos; Representative Paul Hawkes returned to be the policy chief for Tom Feeney during his speakership; and Representative Dudley Goodlette returned to the House to serve as the chief of staff for Speaker Larry Cretul. After leaving the House as a member, Representative Scott McPherson worked on the staff of the state Republican Party and in the administration of Governor Bush before returning to the permanent post of chief information technology officer for the House of Representatives.[176]

Through the years of emerging Republicanism, the staffing patterns brought a generation of new faces into the political and policy network of the Republican Party, and the support for the Republican agenda continued to expand as the staff members cycled through the structure to other roles in the political process.[177] The influx of new individuals created opportunities for the young staff members; it helped to expand the Republican sphere of influence into the next generation; and it provided an inherent political mentoring process for the others who followed. The collective group of young men and women who were recruited into the system arrived with little public notoriety, but they were important contributors to the Republican Party's continuing success, and many emerged to be part of the next generation of elected Republican leaders.

7

REPUBLICAN HOUSE

THE CONSISTENT PHILOSOPHICAL kinship cultivated between the political parties in the Florida Senate as Republicans progressed toward the majority did not materialize in the Florida House. There were productive times of bipartisan cooperation, but there were times when Republicans had to rely on parliamentary procedures to protect their voices in the process. There were also periodic partisan conflicts from the election cycles that carried over into the relationships between Republicans and Democrats in the House chamber. The contrasting political environments between the Florida Senate and the House of Representatives made the Republican path to the majority in the House different; the path was a bit longer, but following the elections in 1996, it became reality.

Election Night 1996

The now famous photograph commemorating the moment when Republicans claimed the majority membership now hangs prominently in the Majority Office of the House of Representatives. It marks the transition of one of the final vestiges of Florida's governmental institutions to Republican control, and it is a photo that many people thought improbable only a few years earlier. The images in the photograph were taken at 1:29 a.m. on

Representatives John Thrasher (*left*) and Dan Webster (*right*) celebrate the new Republican majority in the House after the final election results are reported. Photo courtesy of the Florida Historic Capitol Museum.

November 6, 1996, and they show Republican Leader Dan Webster and Representative John Thrasher shaking hands triumphantly across a desk in the House Republican Office after learning by phone that Nancy Argenziano had won House District 43 in the state's central West Coast.[1] The victory by the Citrus County Republican secured the sixty-first Republican seat in the 120-member House of Representatives and gave Republicans a majority of the body for the first time since 1876.[2] It seemed to all culminate in the short span of a few hours as the votes from around Florida were tabulated after the polls had closed; but for Webster and his Republican allies it was preceded by more than three years of planning, two election cycles, and the tactical implementation of a well-designed strategy.[3]

Dan Webster came to the House in 1980, and he progressed steadily up the ranks of the caucus leadership. In 1994, his Republican colleagues installed him as the leader of the Republican minority; and two years later, as Republican leader, he became the final architect of the Republican take-over in House of Representatives.[4] Among those contributing to his efforts were Republican Party Chairman Tom Slade, fellow House members John Thrasher and Jim King, and, from the staff at the state party headquarters, Rich Heffley, Gene McGee, Brecht Heuchan, and Jim Magill.[5]

An engineer by profession and a self-proclaimed plodder, Webster me-thodically oversaw the organization, funding, and strategic moves of a plan that was initially deployed in the 1994 election cycle.[6] Dubbed the "ABC Plan" by Webster's campaign team, "the Plan meant the best opportunities to take a seat held by a Democrat received an 'A' while 'B' and 'C' repre-sented smaller odds of success."[7] Under the criteria of the plan, the seats of incumbent Democrats were deemed vulnerable based on changing popula-tion demographics and the voting records of incumbents that were consid-ered inconsistent with the changing moods of voters in the district that they represented.[8]

With limited campaign funds, Webster focused on one race at a time as the ABC Plan prioritized the districts as opposed to diluting the Republican resources among races where there was not a realistic opportunity to win.[9] The strategy included finding and fielding the best possible candidate in the priority districts and then providing each candidate with an effective direct-mail program that contrasted the Republican candidate with his or her Democratic opponent; superior on-the-ground efforts to get out the vote; and enough financial support from the state Republican Party to carry the campaign efforts across the finish line.[10] When the dust settled follow-ing the elections in 1994, Republican numbers in the House increased by twelve, leaving the caucus only four votes short of a majority.[11]

Webster retained the leadership of the Republican caucus into the 1996 election cycle, and the strategies of his ABC Plan were deployed for a sec-ond time. Webster also extended his campaign strategy to protect the newly won seats so that there would be no erosion in the number of Republican gains that had been achieved two years earlier.[12]

As vote totals were tallied throughout the 1996 election evening, results showed that were no losses by Republican incumbents, leaving only four new Republicans needed to capture a majority in the House. In sequence from Polk County, Paula Dockery and Adam Putnam secured two seats previously held by Democrats; in Charlotte County, Lindsey Harrington did the same and captured the third seat; and when Nancy Argenziano was declared the winner in the final seat to be decided on election night, she became the fourth new Republican.[13] With the victories, Webster had secured the majority for his Republican House colleagues and his position as the first Republican Speaker since Reconstruction.

In the ten days that followed Argenziano's victory, there were brief struggles on two fronts in an effort to block Webster's designation as House Speaker at the Legislature's organizational session, but neither was successful. One involved Luis Rojas and Alex Diaz de la Portilla, who led a small group of other Republicans—Jorge Rodriguez-Chomat, Burt Saunders, and Jerry Maygarden—in an attempt to coalesce with the Democrats to deliver the speakership to Rojas.[14] The second attempt by the Democratic caucus employed a different tactic to sidetrack the ascendency of a Republican Speaker. By contesting the election of three Republicans, the Democrats hoped to block the votes of the three challenged Republicans during the designation of the Speaker at the organizational session, but their alternative failed as well.[15]

In a deal brokered between Representative Fred Lippman on behalf the Democrats and Representative John Thrasher on behalf of Webster, former House Republican Leader Curt Kiser was selected to preside over the lengthy roll call at the organizational session, and when the House convened to organize with Kiser presiding, the membership formally designated Webster to lead the body.[16] With Webster's selection, the Republican takeover of the state's legislative branch was complete; but the successes celebrated following the organizational session in 1996 did not come easily.

Republican members in the Florida House of Representatives were a rare breed in the early decades of the twentieth century, and the foundation for a meaningful role in the state House did not begin to appear until mid-century.[17] When it occurred, however, Republicans in the House had the most immediate impact as a functioning minority in the Legislature, even though the House was the last of the two legislative chambers to succumb to

Former Republican Leader Curt Kiser (*right*) presents the gavel to the first Republican Speaker, Dan Webster (*left*), on the rostrum of the House chamber during the organizational session for the 1996–98 legislative term. Kiser family collection.

a Republican majority. The transformation from an afterthought to a meaningful minority voice began in 1967, and the climb toward majority status was built over three decades under a series of House Republican leaders, beginning with three-term Leader Don Reed from Boca Raton.[18]

Reed was succeeded by Jim Tillman from Sarasota County, Bill James from Delray Beach, two-term Leader S. Curt Kiser from Pinellas County, Ronald R. "Ron" Richmond from New Port Richey, three-term Leader R. Dale Patchett from Vero Beach, James Lombard from Sarasota, Sandra Mortham from Largo, and Dan Webster—each building on the efforts of their predecessors. The path of the House Republicans to the majority was similar to that of their Senate colleagues in some ways, but the relationship with their majority Democratic Party colleagues was different. The environment of the House was often more partisan; there was not the "philosophical kinship" in the House that Senator Warren Henderson described in the upper chamber; there were no governing coalitions that contributed to the transition, and House Republicans often made creative use of the body's procedural rules to ensure that their voices could be heard.[19]

Foundation for Change

During the early decades of the twentieth century, an occasional Republican appeared among the assembled members of the House of Representatives, but they were a rare commodity. Lambert M. Ware from St. Andrews in Bay County was seated in 1903 and was the century's first Republican to serve. Other early Republicans included Dr. Henry Clinton Hood from Palm Beach County, who served in 1917; Kenneth W. Kerr from Dunedin, who represented Pinellas County in 1929; A. D. Whitman, who represented Hardee County during the 1931 session; R. Everette Burchard, who served from Hendry County in 1935; and Alex Akerman from Orange County, who was the last of the "single member" Republicans to serve in the House during the legislative session of 1947.[20]

William Cramer was elected from Pinellas County in 1950 to serve during the session of 1951, and he became the first recognized Republican minority leader. His caucus consisted of Donald C. McLaren of St. Petersburg, who served two terms in the House; B. E. Shaffer from Clearwater, who served as a member of the body until 1959; and William C. Coleman Jr., who joined the group from Orange County in 1956.[21] According to long-serving Clerk of the House Allen Morris, it was said, tongue-in-cheek, that "when Bill Cramer called a caucus, the Republicans met in the telephone booth."[22]

There were seven Republican members in the House in 1961; in 1963, there were sixteen Republican members, including Leighton Baker from Lake County, whose son Carey Baker was elected thirty-seven years later to serve as part of the Republican House majority in 2000.[23] In 1965, there were ten Republican members and the Republican leader's committee assignments consisted of Resolutions and Memorials (which handled meaningless legislation), Executive Communications (which received gubernatorial vetoes), and Atomic Energy (which did nothing).[24] These were the

House Republicans before the court-ordered reapportionment election on Capitol steps. *Front row, right to left:* Don Reed, Mary Grizzle, John Ducker, Chuck Rainey; back row, *right to left:* L. S. "Sam" Campbell, James Eddy, L. A. "Skip" Bafalis, John J. "Jack" Savage, Ray Osborne, and Robert Elrod. Photo courtesy of the State Archives of Florida.

limited Republican numbers that preceded the special elections in 1967; and prior to 1967, Republicans had no meaningful roles in the House and no meaningful voice in the chamber's policy deliberations.

Following the two key events of 1966 and early 1967—the election of a Republican governor and the *Swann v. Adams* court-ordered reapportionment of legislative districts—it all changed in dramatic fashion. When the 1967 Legislature was seated for its regularly scheduled session, the House Republicans were instantaneously relevant, meaningful to the decisions being made, and effective in the process as a unified party caucus.[25]

Coalition Speaker

At the time it was little known, and today it is nearly forgotten, that the speakership of Ralph Turlington in 1967 came via a coalition with the Republican minority in the House. It was a unique time in the history of Florida politics—a rare combination of events and individuals that, in a span of six years, permanently changed the face of each branch of Florida's government. Don Reed was one of a small group of policymakers who made an enduring mark on the political landscape of Florida in this unique era.[26] His leadership style, his self-taught knowledge of the rules and protocols in the legislative process, and his vision for building a viable Republican caucus set the standard for the leaders who followed.[27]

Reed's emergence with the House Republicans began obscurely enough at the end of the 1965 legislative session at a time when the Legislature met every two years. At the end of the session, Reed was designated leader of the Republican caucus by the ten Republican members of the Florida House, a House consisting of a total of 113 members.[28] At the time, the leader's post represented little more than a token voice of the loyal opposition in a body where the opposition voice was all but ignored by the majority party; however, the "token" label did not survive until the next gathering of the Legislature in the spring of 1967.

In the general election of 1966, Florida elected Claude Kirk as the state's first Republican governor since the Reconstruction era. After Kirk's election, the election of dozens of Republican legislators followed—in part because of the Republican "tide" and in part because of the special elections in early 1967 mandated by the U.S. Supreme Court in its opinion in *Swann v. Adams*.[29] When the membership of the new House was finally decided following the special elections, there were thirty-nine Republican members, exactly one-third of the body and enough to sustain the veto of the new Republican governor.[30] The veteran Republicans returning to the House with Don Reed were John Ducker from Winter Park, James R. Eddy from Pompano Beach, Mary Grizzle from Indian Rocks Beach, L. S. "Sam" Campbell from DeFuniak Springs, Ray Osborne from St. Petersburg, Charles E. "Chuck" Rainey from Clearwater, and John J. "Jack" Savage from

North Redington Beach.[31] With their freshman colleagues and without other considerations, the Republicans had become a revitalized force in the Legislature for the first time in nearly a century—but that was not the only consideration. One other event raised Leader Reed and his Republicans to an even higher point of prominence, and it became the catalyst for a series of changes that benefited the Republican minority.

In an unfortunate turn of events, the Democrat's designee to assume the speakership for the 1967–68 term, Representative George Stone of Pensacola, was killed in an automobile accident before he could be formally elected Speaker of the House.[32] Two Democrats, Representative Ralph Turlington of Gainesville and Representative Robert T. "Bob" Mann of Tampa, wrestled within the House Democratic caucus to be their party's designee as the next Speaker, but neither could garner enough votes from the members of the Democratic caucus to constitute a majority of the full House of Representatives.[33] Both Turlington and Mann turned to Don Reed for the support of the Republican members of the House.[34]

Reed ultimately threw his support and the support of the Republican caucus to Ralph Turlington, and Turlington claimed the speakership for the 1967–68 term of the Legislature. In exchange for his Republican support, Turlington rewarded seven of the eight returning Republican members with vice chairmanships of a standing committee, and returning Republican Jack Savage with the chairmanship of the House Committee on Standards and Conduct.[35] In further accommodation to the Republicans, Turlington departed from three other House traditions. The new Speaker designated proportional Republican membership on all standing House committees, with the exception of the Appropriations Committee; he permitted the daily calendar of House business to be set in consultation with Reed and the Republicans; and for the first time, the Speaker authorized staffing for the House Republican caucus.[36]

The new members of the Republican caucus in the House all arrived from counties in the urban horseshoe after the 1967 special elections. They included Jack Murphy, A. S. "Jim" Robinson, Don H. Stafford, William H. "Bill" Fleece, and Ed Whitson Jr. from Pinellas County; Richard Bird, Henry J. "Hank" Prominski, Arthur Rude, Joseph Martinez, Charles King,

George Caldwell, and Joel Gustafson from Broward County; Harry Pfeiffer, Clifford McNulty, William E. "Bill" Powell, and Charles E. Davis Jr. from Brevard County; Granville Crabtree, Kent McKinley, and future House Republican Leader Jim Tillman from Sarasota County; Charles "Chuck" Nergard from St. Lucie County; Robert DeYoung, Jack Poorbaugh, Joseph Humphrey, Robert Rust, and future House Republican Leader Bill James from Palm Beach County; and from the Orange-Seminole County districts Robert Shadley, David Lindsey, William D. Gorman, Jan Fortune, Sandy Bassett, and William Gibson.[37]

When the Legislature assembled to begin its business in April 1967, the Republican caucus in the House was primed to play a meaningful role, and the ensuing months produced memorable examples as the newly elected Republican members enjoyed an effective and productive game of "follow-the-leader."

Don Reed—The "Big Kahoona"

Don Reed was unequivocally the "leader," and for the better part of two terms, the Republicans in the House followed him wherever he entered the political thicket on issues before the House.[38] Following the 1967 reapportionment elections, all but eight of Reed's Republican colleagues came to the House with no prior legislative experience.[39] Many came from the ranks of the Young Republican Clubs and fledgling county Republican executive committees recruited by Bill Murfin and party officials in the Republican frenzy following the election of Claude Kirk. Some filed as candidates only to achieve local notoriety for their business ventures, and some were elected to office without running a serious campaign, doing little more than paying their qualifying fee to appear on the ballot.[40]

The new Republican members, in large measure, came with a loyalty to the Republican Party philosophy and without commitments to other outside interests. Campaign funds from traditional sources, of course, had gone to the nominees of the majority party Democrats who had controlled the legislative process for generations. The new Republicans had no mentors. There were no training sessions for new members. There was no legislative staff for individual members to help with orientation to their new roles, and many had never been to the state Capitol before their election. Only one of the new members, former Cocoa Beach Councilman Harry Pfeiffer, had even held prior elected office.[41]

It was a group in need of a cohesive influence, and Don Reed was both willing and able to provide it for the new Republican caucus of thirty-nine. He set up a network of floor whips to help with communication among members; he caucused with them regularly to review policy alternatives on pending legislation; and he made it a practice to record his vote as soon as the voting machine was opened so others could see how he intended to vote on the measures before the House.[42] Most Republicans simply looked to the voting board at the front of the House chambers and followed Reed's button. For the inexperienced Republican members, it offered a reasonably rational path to follow; for Reed, it vested his position as leader with enormous power within the body of the House. And for the new Republican governor, it provided the likely assurance that his vetoes would be sustained.

The most celebrated test for Governor Kirk and the House Republicans came over the state's first billion-dollar budget in 1967. It demonstrated the solidarity of the Republican caucus behind the leader; and it created the first innovative use of the House procedural rules to protect the Republican voice in the debates on the floor of the House.

One of Kirk's key campaign themes had been "No New Taxes"; his Democrat opponent had advocated several, including an increase in the state's sales tax; and Kirk was resolute in his position despite a Democratic House majority that felt new funding sources were essential for maintaining service levels and balancing the budget. Confident that at least one Republican would break ranks by supporting the Democratic majority and overriding a veto by the governor, the 1967 budget was passed not once, but twice, requiring new taxes. But on each occasion the Republican support behind Reed remained solid, and Kirk's vetoes were sustained. After months of work, the Democrats finally conceded defeat, and on the third attempt, the Legislature passed a budget requiring no new taxes as Kirk had demanded. It took three months, two extensions of the regular legislative session, and three special sessions before the issue was finally decided, but in the pro-

Republican Leader Don Reed on the House floor. Photo courtesy of the
Dunbar family collection.

cess, the Florida Legislature arrived at the early stages of a viable two-party
branch of government for the first time.[43]

"Reed established himself as the second most powerful man in the House,
right behind the speaker," reported David Schultz in the *Palm Beach Post-
Times*. "Dubbed the 'Big Kahoona' by a frustrated Democrat in 1967 when
a cherished program went down the drain because of GOP opposition (the
Republicans stuck together like glue to uphold dozens of Kirk vetoes), Reed

proved that tight organization and virtual one-man leadership could make up for lack of numbers. A 'thumbs down' sign from Reed put many bills to death in 1967."[44]

Following the elections in 1968, Republican numbers in the House increased to forty-three of 119, and among the new faces in the Republican caucus were Roger Wilson and John Ware from St. Petersburg; David C. "Dave" Clark and Ray Moudry from West Palm Beach; Lewis Earle from Maitland; Leonard Wood and Cecil Bothwell Jr. from Orlando; Don Heath from Nokomis; Richard Tillman from Cocoa Beach; J. Wertz Nease from Jacksonville; and Lavon Ward from Fort Lauderdale.[45]

The cohesiveness of the caucus under Reed remained solid and effective into the next legislative term, and the tendency to consistently follow the leader's button also held its moments of humor. On one occasion, it was the vote on a bill by Representative Roger Wilson to protect state submerged lands adjacent to Honeymoon Island on Florida's west coast from a massive dredge-and-fill project.[46] Reed had committed to support Wilson and Pinellas County's solid Republican delegation on the protection measure, but, momentarily distracted, he recorded a vote against the bill when the voting machine was unlocked. His staff director recognized the mistake and quietly stepped up behind his chair to remind him of his commitment to the Pinellas members, and he promptly switched his vote. Instantaneously, more than twenty other buttons followed from red to green before the voting machine was locked and the bill passed; but following the vote, more than a dozen Republican members gathered at Reed's desk to plead with him to give more warning on his votes.[47] Passage of the bill avoided the environmental degradation of Honeymoon Island, and five years later, through the bipartisan work of Republican Representative Curt Kiser and Democrat Representative Terrell Sessums, Honeymoon Island was brought into Florida's park system and permanently preserved.[48]

On another occasion, following the "leader" brought a hint of humor to the back-row Republicans as the House handled the business of the day on a consent calendar basis. The consent calendar was an agenda of noncontroversial legislation with little or no opposition, and each bill was handled in a matter of minutes with little debate. For those who have observed the process as it is happening, one will recognize that the consent calendar process is both tedious and monotonous. On this particular day, Reed had his young son Donnie sitting with him at his desk on the House floor. Each time the board opened for members to cast their vote, Donnie turned to his dad and asked how he wanted to vote; with the answer, Donnie then leaned forward and pressed the button as his father instructed.

At one point during the morning, Reed left his chair for a brief conversation in another part of the House chamber. In his absence, Donnie continued to vote his father's button each time the machine was unlocked to record a roll-call vote. When Reed returned to his seat along the back row, Representative Dave Clark from Palm Beach County realized the leader had not been in his seat while Clark and the Republicans had continued to faithfully follow his button on each roll call. Turning to his right, Clark immediately realized that he and the others had been following the lead of a twelve-year-old through a series of votes changing the laws of Florida. Chagrined, Clark turned to Reed and remarked in mock anger that he was willing to follow his leader, but not a twelve-year-old when setting the policy for Florida's future.[49]

Following the Rules

In the Rules of the House of Representatives adopted in 1969, official recognition was given to the minority Republican caucus for the first time, and the old adage concerning rules of parliamentary procedure is that "they are designed to protect the rights of the minority."[50] And so it was with the Rules of the House of Representatives. To know the rules and how to use them, particularly when others did not, gave the knowledgeable individual a distinct advantage in the political arena in the early years of the two-party era.[51]

Beginning with Don Reed, a sequence of Republican leaders, among them Bill James, Curt Kiser, Ron Richmond, Dale Patchett, Sandy Mortham, and Dan Webster, became proficient in the tools that the Rules of the House provided; used them to protect the role of the Republican minority; and accentuated the effectiveness of the Republican members when they did so. As the House Republicans matured as a caucus, each leader encouraged other key members to learn the rules and effectively monitor the flow of business and protect the minority's voice.[52] Over ensuing years, they included Ray Osborne, Richard Langley, Betty Easley, Fred Burrall, Peter Dunbar, Frank Messersmith, John Thrasher, and Paul Hawkes.[53]

Proficiency with the House rules began with Reed, and in the modern era, there was no more proficient student or anyone who made better use of them than Don Reed.[54] His skill and cunning turned the tide on issues when others thought the opportunity lost, and with these magical parliamentary jousts he began the tradition for other Republican House members to follow. His knowledge and skill of the House rules remains one of his

Republican members discussing the application of House Rules with Speaker-designate Tom Gustafson and other Democrats during debate on leadership funds at the desk of House Republican Leader Dale Patchett (*seated*). *Left to right:* Representatives David Thomas, Steve Wise, Art Grindel, Frank Messersmith, Gustafson (D), Mary Figg (D), Dennis Jones, Jim Frishe, Peter Dunbar, Jim Hill, Ron Saunders (D), Tom Woodruff, and Debbie Sanderson. Photo courtesy of the Florida Historic Capitol Museum.

most enduring legacies, and two notable uses of the rules during the 1967 session underscored their effective use.[55]

Daylight Savings Time

The first occasion was an issue before the House to exempt Florida from the annual conversion to daylight savings time. The question before the members was, Would Florida follow the time-conversion format suggested by the U.S. Congress each spring and fall, or would the state opt out to remain on standard time on a year-round basis? The bill was sponsored by Democrat Representative Jim Redman from Plant City, and his legislation proposed the latter. Earlier in the session, the Senate had voted to exempt Florida from the national standard, but in the House the vote was close and the outcome uncertain, with several members undecided on the issue. Retail businesses and the airline industry lined up in favor of daylight savings to keep Florida on the same time schedule as the rest of the eastern seaboard. These interests opposed Redman's bill. Agriculture interests and the movie theater chains lined up in favor of the legislation to keep Florida on standard time throughout the year. The lead advocates for daylight savings time included a bipartisan coalition of urban Democrats and the minority Republican caucus led by Don Reed.[56]

During the debate before the final vote on the bill, both Reed and Redman were passionate and articulate for their cause, but the final outcome remained uncertain as debate came to a close on a Friday afternoon. When the voting machine was locked to record the final tally, the bill passed by a narrow margin, and the Redman-led forces claimed an initial victory. To their surprise, Reed had voted with them and against the position he had advocated during the debate. While the House buzzed in the aftermath of the debate and final vote, Redman sought the recognition of the Speaker, and once recognized, made a humorous presentation to Reed of a container of Morton salt to rub into his "wounds" as the loser of the debate. Reed accepted the salt with a gracious smile and then waved his microphone for recognition by the Speaker from his back-row, aisle seat. The Speaker recognized Reed.

"Mr. Speaker," announced Reed, "I move that the House reconsider the vote by which the bill passed and that the motion to reconsider be left pending."[57]

The members became silent in the face of the procedural motion rarely presented to the House. Initially, for nearly every member, the motion and its significance held little meaning. With time, however, Reed's strategy became clear, and the motion became the catalyst for a delayed victory for the coalition led by the Republican leader.

Under the Rules of the House, the motion to "reconsider and leave pending" placed the final disposition of the vote in the possession of the maker of the motion—in this case, Reed—for three days, at which time the matter was voted on again by the full membership of the House.[58] A key prerequisite of the strategy Reed employed was that the "motion to reconsider" could only be made by a member who voted on the prevailing side of the issue.[59] By voting with Redman against his own position, Reed placed himself in the procedural posture to make the motion and delay the final outcome of the vote.

Over the next three days, supporters of the move to daylight savings used the time to persuade several representatives to change their votes. When the matter was brought back before the House on the third day, the coalition led by Reed was able to defeat the bill by a margin of two votes.[60] Because the House rules provided that a matter could only be reconsidered once during the legislative session, when Reed's parliamentary maneuvering was complete, the bill had been defeated.[61] With the defeat, Florida joined the rest of the eastern seaboard in the annual migration to daylight savings time during the summer months of the year. After the vote, Reed rose again to seek the recognition of the Speaker and used the opportunity to return the container of salt to Representative Redman. The salt remained on Redman's desk for the remainder of the session.[62]

Republicans used a different portion of the House rules six years later to block a second attempt to exempt Florida from the annual change to daylight savings time. In a one-day special legislative session called by Governor Reubin Askew, a procedural approval by two-thirds of the House membership was required to move the legislation to a final vote, but the Republicans led by Representative Curt Kiser kept the House from reaching the required extraordinary majority. Unable to garner the required two-thirds vote, there was no final vote taken on the measure, and the legislation died when the Legislature adjourned at the end of the one-day session.[63]

"Read the Bill"

The House rules played a role in the partisan budget debates, too. During one round of the 1967 budget deliberations, Republicans had prepared an alternative, "no new tax" budget to offer as an amendment to the appropriations bill sponsored by the Democratic leadership. With the state's budget director, Joe Cresse, the House Republican leaders and their staff had worked several long days and into the night to ready their version of the funding plan for Florida's next budget cycle. However, on the day of the budget debate in the House, Speaker Turlington and the Democratic majority had resolved that the Republican alternative was not to be heard on the floor of the House.

During the amendatory process on the bill, instead of recognizing Republican Leader Pro Tempore Ray Osborne to present the massive amendment to the appropriations bill, the Speaker recognized one of his Democratic colleagues for a procedural motion to cut off further amendments to the bill—a motion requiring only a majority of the House for adoption.[64] The motion was promptly adopted in a straight party-line vote, leaving Republicans with no opportunity to present their alternative.

A cumbersome requirement in the House procedures required each bill to be read in full before its final passage.[65] With a waiver of the rules, however, the full reading could be, and was routinely, dispensed with after a motion was adopted providing that "the rules be waived, and the bill be read by its title only." A vote to waive the rules, however, required the approval of two-thirds of the House, and it was a procedural subtlety not lost on Reed, Osborne, and their Republican colleagues.[66] When the motion was made to waive the reading of the appropriations bill in full, the Republican members voted unanimously against the motion, denying the Speaker the two-thirds necessary to move the bill to a final vote.

Frustrated, but with all his other parliamentary options exhausted, Speaker Turlington turned to the reading clerk in the front of the House chamber and simply said, "Read the bill."[67]

The sergeant of arms was ordered to lock the doors, House members were asked to take their seats, and, unless excused by the Speaker to go to the bathroom, members were asked not to leave the chambers while the bill was read in full.[68] As the members grumbled to one another, Representative Bill James turned to his right with a wry smile and muttered with a touch of humor, "Reed, I feel like I'm back in elementary school and need a hall pass. It's a fine mess you've gotten us into this time."[69]

For more than five hours, a team of readers took turns mouthing the words and numbers from the pages of the massive bill to a bored and frustrated House. But by the end of the day, only about a third of the bill had been read as the Rules of the House required. Facing at least one more full day of reading, Turlington acquiesced to the Republicans and permitted their amendment to be offered and debated the following morning.[70] The minority was at least to be heard.

After the amendment was debated, the Democratic majority defeated the Republican proposal and passed the appropriations bill in its original form—after it had been read by title only. It was one of the versions of the bill vetoed by Governor Kirk, and the veto brought the Legislature back into special session to try again. Eventually the Appropriations Act of 1967, consistent with the Republican budget proposal that was initially "not to be heard on the floor of the House," was enacted into law.

This procedure was not forgotten by the leaders who followed Reed. Jim Tillman, Curt Kiser, Ronald R. Richmond, and Dale Patchett all returned to the tactic at various times to keep their membership relevant and to protect their participation as contemplated by the Rules of the House.[71]

Bumps in the Road

Despite the early Republican successes, there were also bumps in the road, and some were significant deterrents to the continued rise of Republican membership in the House of Representatives. The elections in 1970 saw

Claude Kirk lose his reelection bid and only thirty-eight Republicans returned to the House, but there were some new members in the caucus replacing those who retired. From Broward County, Dave Smith, future State Senator George Williamson, and future State Senator and future Party Chairman Van Poole joined the House caucus; new from Sarasota County was future state Senator Bob Johnson; new from Palm Beach County was future State Senator Russell Sykes; Dennis MacDonald joined the caucus from Pinellas County; from Brevard County, the new members included Jane Robinson and Eugene C. "Gene" Tubbs; and from the districts in Orange and Seminole Counties, Harvey Matthews and future State Senator Walter Sims were new.[72]

Reapportionment of the legislative seats based upon the 1970 decennial census greeted the new members, and ultimately a new configuration of districts was passed over the objections of House Republicans on a straight party-line vote. Like the court-ordered reapportionment in 1967, the new districting plan met the "one-person, one-vote" mandate, but the 1972 Democratic plan also preserved the use of large multimember districts and narrowed the opportunity for minority voting blocs in urban centers.[73] Initial concerns by the Republican minority in the Legislature were rejected by the Democratic majority, and subsequent challenges to the plan by both Republicans and the NAACP in the Florida Supreme Court were rejected by the court on a vote of four to three.[74] The resulting districts created a decade of restraint on the potential for Republicans and other minority voting blocs, and from the House districts approved in 1972, there were never more than five African American members serving in the House and never more than a single House member of Hispanic heritage.[75]

Despite the districting disadvantages in the elections, during the tenure of Republican Leaders Don Reed and Jim Tillman, the participation of the Republican caucus continued to grow. There was civil, bipartisan coordination between the Republicans and the Democratic majority under Speakers Ralph Turlington, Fred Schultz, Dick Pettigrew, and Terrell Sessums; and over the initial five-year period, the staff in the House Republican Office grew from the two employees initially authorized by Turlington to eleven staff professionals who coordinated affairs closely with staff in the Speaker's office.[76] The political environment was productive; occasional partisan battles between the parties were civil; and new policy changes continued to pass with bipartisan cooperation between the Republican minority and the progressive urban Democrats in the House.[77]

Beyond the formal lawmaking process inside the House chamber, there was also a political focus by Republicans to build their numbers in the House by effective electioneering. The annual Republican Legislative Appreciation Dinner had been inaugurated to raise campaign funds for new candidates; issue research on the voting records of incumbent Democrats was assembled for use by Republican challengers; and the Republican leaders actively recruited candidates for open seats and to challenge incumbent Democrats. It began with Don Reed, and it was continued by Jim Tillman.

Following the elections in 1972, the Republican caucus under Tillman's leadership increased its numbers to 43 in the 120-member House. New members in the caucus from counties in the horseshoe included Randy Avon and Daniel Bass from Broward County; Jay Reynolds and future U.S. Congressman Tom Lewis from Palm Beach County; Richard Price, future Republican Leader Curt Kiser and future Republican Leader Pro Tempore Betty Easley from Pinellas County; future State Senators Richard Langley and Vince Fechtel from Lake County; and future State Party Chairman Chester Clem from Indian River County.[78] The 1972 elections also pushed the boundaries of Republican influence into Lee County for the first time with the election of Paul Nuckolls from Fort Myers and into Pasco County with the election of future House Republican Leader Ron Richmond from New Port Richey.[79]

Bill James from Delray Beach succeeded Tillman as the Republican House leader in 1974, but the Republican numbers in the House fell to thirty-four members following the fall elections held under the cloud of the unfolding Nixon Watergate scandal. There were a few bright spots, and new members in the House caucus replacing retiring Republicans following the elections included Laurent "Larry" Belanger and George Hieber from Pinellas County and future State Senator Clark Maxwell from Brevard County. The elections also brought Fred Burrall from Charlotte County and Mary Ellen Hawkins from Collier County to the caucus, and their elections stretched the Republican influence farther south along Florida's west coast.[80] As the 1976 election approached, Republican leaders looked to rebuild their numbers, but the cloud of the Watergate break-in remained. Only twenty-eight Republicans returned to the House when the election cycle concluded, and the caucus fell to its lowest membership in the modern era. Nine of the twenty-eight Republicans were new, and they included Thomas E. "Tom" Danson and Ted Ewing from Sarasota; Dorothy Sample and T. M. "Tom" Woodruff from St. Petersburg; Marilyn Evans-Jones from Brevard County; future House Republican Leader R. Dale Patchett from Indian River County; and Larry Kirkwood, future Senate President Toni Jennings, and future U.S. Congressman John Mica from Orange County.[81]

Another consequence from the 1976 elections also had an impact on the effectiveness of the Republican caucus and its new members when they were seated in the House. In the summer of 1976, new Republican House Leader Bill James had recruited Tallahassee attorney Taylor Moore in the hope of upsetting incumbent Democratic Speaker Don Tucker in the fall elections.[82] The Speaker was successfully reelected in a bitter and relatively close race featuring an expensive new desk that Tucker had ordered for his office in the Capitol, but the bitterness toward James and the Republicans remained.[83] When the House met in organizational session on November 16, 1976, the civility that had existed between Republican Leaders Reed and Tillman and Speakers Turlington, Schultz, Pettigrew, and Sessums evaporated.[84] In one of his first decisions, Tucker all but eliminated James's staff in the House Republican Office; and Tucker's remarks on the occasion were chronicled by House Clerk Allen Morris: "What I'm getting at is, we have positions authorized for the House Majority office and the Speaker's office that total 11 positions; there are 11 positions authorized for the Minority office. We don't need that and we're not going to have it. The Minority office will have a secretary and an aide; the Majority office will have a secretary and an aide."[85]

Not only did Tucker slash the staffing for Republicans, others serving at the time remembered that he also refused to work or communicate directly with James as the Republican leader. Limited communications with the Republican caucus by Tucker were conducted through future Republican Leader Ron Richmond, and bipartisan cooperation during Tucker's speakership faded from the House chamber.[86] When James relinquished his leadership post at the end of the term in 1978, it fell to the successor Republican leaders to begin to rebuild the caucus numbers and restore the civility between the two parties.

Civility and Single-Member Districts

Curt Kiser was the first Republican leader to begin the rebuilding process, and under his leadership, the 1978 fall elections returned thirty-one Republicans to the House. Among the new first-term members were Jim Watt from Palm Beach County; future Senate Republican Leader William "Doc" Myers from Martin County; Bill Bankhead and Fred Tygart from Duval County; Tim Deratany from Brevard County; future Lieutenant Governor Bobby Brantley from Seminole County; Tom Bush from Broward County; and Dennis Jones, Bob Melby, Peter Dunbar, and James Harrison "Jim" Smith from Pinellas County.[87] The civil dialogue between the Republican and Democratic leadership also returned with the selection of Democrat Hyatt Brown from Volusia County as the House Speaker; and with restoration of bipartisan working relationships, renewed reforms and the implementation of new policies followed.[88]

In the 1980 elections, Republicans under Kiser continued to rebuild their numbers in the Florida House, which jumped from thirty-one to thirty-nine members. The net gains included Reid Moore Jr., Bernard "Bernie" Kimmel, and future Republican Leader Pro Tempore Frank Messersmith from Palm Beach County; Robert M. Woodburn from Broward County; Jason Steele from Brevard County; James K. "Jim" Brodie, Scott McPherson, and John "Gus" Plummer from Miami-Dade County; Thomas B. "Tom" Drage Jr., Bruce McEwan, and future House Speaker Dan Webster from Orange County; and the era's first Republican House member from Hillsborough County, John Grant.[89] For Republicans, however, the new numbers did not restore the minority caucus to a third of the chamber. It took three more election cycles before Republican numbers exceeded one-third of the body and restored the protection afforded by the Rules of the House that could not be waived without Republican support.

Kiser served two terms as the Republican leader, and the bipartisan cooperation between Republicans and Democrats restored under Brown continued under his successor, Ralph Haben.[90] Republican House members were appointed to chair subcommittees; the Republican leadership had a voice in setting the Special Order Calendar of business that came before the full House; and the occasional partisan battles were civil and respectful.[91] Politically during Kiser's final term as leader, Republican attention also turned to the required decennial reapportionment of legislative districts and the elimination of the large multimember districts that had diluted voices of minority population groupings and Republican voters in the state's urban areas—a districting scheme that had kept Republican membership in the House between thirty-one and thirty-nine with little opportunity for increasing their numbers in the preceding decade.[92]

Prior to the formal legislative consideration of a new apportionment plan in 1982, Kiser had elicited a public commitment from the House Apportionment Committee chairman, Lee Moffitt, that single-member districts would be a consideration if there was public support for the districting scheme. Moffitt also promised to hold public hearings throughout the state to take public input. In the public hearing sequence that followed, Republicans and leaders from the African American community organized testimony in support of single-member districts, whereas Democrats did little to organize initial testimony for an alternative districting scheme. In the final Miami public hearing, however, Democrats made efforts to offer testimony in support of a continued multimember districting plan in the state's urban areas, but proponents of single-member districts recruited former Democratic Governor Reubin Askew as their final witness in support of single-member districts, effectively ending the debate.[93]

When the Legislature completed the 1982 decennial apportionment plan, Ron Richmond assumed the post of Republican leader. All of the new districts in both the House and the Senate were single-member districts, and while some political gerrymandering remained, the districts offered new opportunities for minorities, women, and Republicans to add to their numbers. As it had in the Florida Senate, the new plan brought a decade of changes to the membership in the House of Representatives.[94]

Within two election cycles under the new House districting scheme, the number of women serving in the House had increased from thirteen to twenty-two; the members of Hispanic heritage increased from a single member to eight, including new Miami-Dade Republicans Roberto Casas, Ileana Ros-Lehtinen, Rudy Garcia, Al Gutman, Javier Souto, Arnhilda Gonzalez-Quevedo, and future Speaker Pro Tempore Luis Morse; and the African American House membership grew from four members to ten.[95] Also new to the Republican caucus after the elections in 1982 were Byron Combee from Clearwater, Fred Dudley from Fort Myers, Carol Hanson from Boca Raton, Art Grindle from Altamonte Springs, Carl Self from Casselberry, Bob Shelly from Pompano Beach, and future State Senator Debbie Sanderson from Fort Lauderdale. In the spring of 1984, Republicans added another new member to the caucus when Dixie Sansom from Satellite Beach won a special election from a district in Brevard County.[96]

Republican Leader R. Dale Patchett from Vero Beach followed Richmond at the conclusion of the 1984 legislative session, and Republicans continued to add to their numbers in the fall elections. When the House was seated after the 1984 elections, the Republican caucus led by Patchett had increased to include forty-three members, and among the new faces in the caucus were Jim Frishe from Pinellas Park; Frances L. "Chance" Irvine from Orange Park in Clay County; Harry Jennings, David L. "Dave" Thomas, and future House Republican Leader James M. "Jim" Lombard from Sarasota County.[97] With new and growing numbers, the bipartisan coexistence between the party caucuses in the House began to change; and for Patchett and the Republican caucus, new challenges began to materialize on the horizon.

Rekindling the Partisan Fires

During the initial legislative sessions following the decennial reapportionment in 1982, the bipartisan cooperation did continue under Republican Leaders Richmond and Patchett and Democratic Speakers Lee Moffitt and James Harold Thompson; Republicans continued to chair House subcommittees; and the formal order of business was decided cooperatively.[98] Bipartisan cooperation under Patchett's leadership produced the state's landmark growth management initiative; a new policy to regulate stormwater runoff protecting the state's surface waters was enacted; and a bipartisan House initiative created Florida's first coordinated environmental protections for the coastal estuaries below the mean high waterline with the creation of the Florida Marine Fisheries Commission cosponsored by Democrat James Harold Thompson and Republican Peter Dunbar.[99]

The collegial cooperation and civil partisan disagreements that had been present during the tenures of Curt Kiser and Ron Richmond and Dale Patchett's first term as Republican leader came to an abrupt end following the elections of 1986, however. With the election of Bob Martinez and the seating of Florida's second Republican governor in the modern era, Patchett found a return to many of the partisan challenges that confronted Don Reed after the 1967 special elections as he began his second term as Republican leader. House Speaker Jon Mills stripped all Republicans of their subcommittee chairmanships; cooperation setting the Special Order Calendar for the House business changed; and on multiple occasions, Patchett and his leadership team had to lead Republicans in votes to block the waiver of the House rules to ensure that their voices could continue to be heard.[100]

Republican numbers in the House increased by two in the 1986 elections, and among the new Republicans replacing retiring members and joining Patchett's team in the new heightened partisan environment were J. J. "Toby" Holland from Manatee County, Stan Bainter from Eustis, Frank Stone from Casselberry, Tom Banjanin from Pensacola, David Troxler from Jacksonville, Robert J. "Bob" Starks from Maitland, future House Majority Leader and future Senate President Jim King from Jacksonville, and future House Republican Leader and future Secretary of State Sandra Mortham from Largo.[101]

During the ensuing legislative session following the 1986 elections, the tax battles returned. The infamous services tax was passed initially with support from members of both party caucuses, but when the bipartisan support for the tax disintegrated, it was quickly repealed in a special session called by the new Republican governor. The partisan disagreements continued over

Republican Leader Dale Patchett (*right*) and Representative Frank Messersmith (*left*) take part in the 1990 gas tax debate in the House chamber. Photo courtesy of the Florida Historic Capitol Museum.

a proposed increase in the state's gas tax in the legislative sessions that followed, and it was a tax increase supported by the House Democrats and opposed by Governor Martinez and the House Republicans.

The discord between the party leaders in the House spilled over into the elections, too. As Patchett led the House Republicans into the 1988 election, the party challenged the reelection of the Democrats' designee for Speaker, Sam Bell.[102] Unlike Bill James's attempt to unseat Don Tucker in 1976; however, the Republican effort in 1988 was successful, and Richard S. "Dick" Graham from Volusia County defeated Bell, ending his fourteen-year legislative career.[103] Two years later, Democrats returned the favor by successfully challenging the reelection of Republican leader-designate John Renke from Pasco County, ending his career in the House of Representatives after only three terms.[104]

The partisan rancor over the House Democrats' proposed gas tax increase culminated in 1990. After its passage by the Democratic majority, it was vetoed by Governor Martinez, and the House Republicans sustained his veto. Led by House Appropriations Committee Chair T. K. Wetherell, partisan disagreement among Democrats also extended to the permanent funding initiative for Governor Martinez's Preservation 2000/Florida Forever environmental program.[105] Although the landmark program passed the Legislature in 1990, permanent funding for the environmental protection program did not. Funding for the program became an annual debate until Florida voters placed the program into the state constitution in 2014, and the implementing legislation for the initiative was passed two years later, sponsored by future Senate President Joe Negron and Representative Gayle Harrell.[106]

Despite the growing partisan discord, numbers in the Republican caucus continued to grow during Patchett's final term as the Republican leader. Following the 1988 elections, the new Republicans joining Dick Graham in the House included Joe Arnall from Jacksonville Beach; George Albright from Ocala; Bruce Hoffmann from Coral Gables; R. Z. "Sandy" Safley and Jeffery C. "Jeff" Huenink from Clearwater; Luis Rojas from Hialeah; Carlos Valdez from Miami Springs; Mario Diaz-Balart from Miami; and, in a special election in 1989, Miguel De Grandy from Miami.

By the time Jim Lombard succeeded Patchett following the 1990 elections, there were forty-six Republican members in the House, and they included new Republicans Chris Corr from Apollo Beach; Charles W. "Charlie" Sembler from Sebastian; future District Court of Appeals Judge Paul Hawkes from Citrus County; future Circuit Judge John Laurent from Polk County; future Circuit Judge Patricia "Trish" Muscarella from Clearwater; future House Speaker Tom Feeney from Orlando; future Senate President Ken Pruitt from Port St. Lucie;[107] and, in a 1991 special election, Buddy Johnson from Plant City.[108]

During Lombard's tenure as Republican leader, the Legislature approved its decennial redistricting plan to be effective for the 1992 elections, and the format of single-member House districts was continued. By the time Lombard passed the leadership reins to Sandra Mortham following the 1992 elections, Republican members in the House totaled forty-nine. Among the new members replacing retiring Republicans were future House Speaker John Thrasher from Clay County; future Republican Party Chairman Dave

Bitner from Charlotte County; Bruno Barreiro Jr. from Miami; future State Senators Howard Futch from Brevard County and Alex Villalobos from Miami-Dade County; and future U.S. Congressman Bill Posey from Brevard County. In addition, there were three more new representatives from counties beyond the horseshoe—Bob Casey was elected from Alachua County; James P. "Jim" Kerrigan was elected from Santa Rosa County; and Jeff Stabbins came to the House from Hernando County.[109]

Gains for women and minorities also continued to be made following the 1992 decennial redistricting. By the time Sandra Mortham, who was the first woman designated to lead either party in the House of Representatives, passed the Republican leader's post to Dan Webster following the elections in 1994, there were twenty-three women serving in the House; the House membership included fourteen African American members; and there were eleven serving House members of Hispanic heritage.[110]

Former Republican leaders on the House Speaker's podium. *Left to right:* Ronald Richmond, Bill Cramer, Curt Kiser, Dan Webster, Jim Lombard, Dale Patchett, and Jim Tillman. Photo courtesy of the Florida Historic Capitol Museum.

In total, fifty-seven Republican members came to the House following the 1994 elections, including Alex Diaz de la Portilla from Miami-Dade County; Rob Wallace from Hillsborough County; Jerry Burroughs from Escambia County; and future House Republican Majority Leaders Mike Fasano from Pasco County and Jerry Maygarden from Pensacola.[111] In the next election cycle, the Republican caucus needed only four more seats to capture a majority of the lower chamber's membership.

Arrival of the Republican Majority

It happened in the fall elections of 1996, and the photograph of Dan Webster and John Thrasher captured the moment. Four more Republicans had joined the party caucus, and among the new members were Nancy Argenziano; future House Speaker Johnnie Byrd from Plant City; future Speaker Pro Tempore Lindsay Harrington from Punta Gorda; and future State Senator Paula Dockery from Polk County. Tom Feeney had left the House in 1994 to run unsuccessfully for lieutenant governor with Jeb Bush, but he returned to the House in 1996 at Dan Webster's urging to become part of the new majority and a future Republican Speaker.[112] As the party had in the Senate two years earlier, Republicans claimed a one-vote majority of the seats in the House of Representatives for the first time in the modern era, and it came nearly three decades after the climb toward the majority began under the leadership of Don Reed.[113]

When the House Republicans joined their Senate colleagues in the majority, there were also reforms that were immediately apparent in the process. The practice of ramrodding huge, complex bills through the House and Senate in the late-night hours of the final days came to an end; the regular sessions began to conclude at the end of a normal working day and not as the clock approached midnight on the final day; and over time, legislative deliberations in the Capitol became increasingly transparent.[114]

Initially, the Republican majority in the House was only a single seat, but as it had in the state Senate, the margin continued to grow in each successive election with new faces and new names. When John Thrasher succeeded Webster as the House Speaker in 1998, there were eleven more Republican members seated in the House chamber, and among the new members were future House Speaker Allan Bense from Panama City; future House Rules Chairman Dudley Goodlette from Naples; Fred Brummer from Apopka; Chris Hart IV from Tampa; Randy Johnson from Celebration; Bev Kilmer from Quincy; Gaston Cantens, Gustavo Barreiro, and Manuel "Manny" Prieguez from Miami; Leslie Waters from Seminole; future U.S. Congressmen Jeff Miller from Escambia County; and Gus Bilirakis from Palm Harbor.[115] During Thrasher's speakership, the Legislature passed the A+ Plan, bringing new accountability to the state's public schools; the Florida Forever land conservation program was renewed; and significant tort reform and tax cuts were enacted.[116]

As the new decade approached, the impact of term limits that had passed in 1992 took effect as well, and the ensuing elections in 2000 brought sixty-five new members to the 120-member House.[117] When Republican Tom Feeney assumed the Speakership following the 2000 elections, Republicans had won thirty-five of the sixty-five open seats, and the Republican Party caucus in the House claimed seventy-seven seats and a seventeen-member majority. The incoming freshman members also continued the trend that developed future Republican leaders, and among the new Republicans were future Speaker Pro Tempore Marsha "Marty" Bowen from Haines City; future Speaker Pro Tempore and future State Senator Dennis Baxley from Ocala; future Senate Presidents Mike Haridopolos from Melbourne and Joe Negron from Stuart; future Circuit Judge Mark Mahon from Jacksonville; future U.S. Congressmen Dennis Ross from Lakeland and Connie Mack IV from Fort Lauderdale; future Lieutenant Governor Jeff Kottkamp from Cape Coral; future Senate President and future Chief Financial Officer Jeff Atwater from North Palm Beach; and future House Speaker and future U.S. Senator Marco Rubio from Miami.

Joe Pickens from Palatka, Jerry Paul from Port Charlotte, and future State Senator Aaron Bean from Fernandina Beach also joined the House in 2000. Pickens's election extended the Republican influence in northeast Florida into Putnam County; Paul continued the Republican tradition from the state's southwest coast; and Bean's election brought a Republican to the Legislature from Nassau County for the first time since Reconstruction.[118]

During Tom Feeney's speakership, Republicans were in the majority for the decennial redistricting Legislature for the first time, and like their counterparts in the Florida Senate, the House Republican members took full advantage of the opportunity. In the 2002 elections that followed in the newly reconfigured districts, Republicans captured eighty-one of the 120 House seats, and when Johnnie Byrd became the fourth Republican Speaker, the party claimed a two-thirds supermajority in the chamber.[119]

New members joining the Republican caucus in the House in 2002 who contributed to the new supermajority included future House Majority Leader Adam Hasner from Delray Beach; future Speaker Larry Cretul from Ocala; future Speaker Pro Tempore Ron Reagan from Bradenton; future Circuit Judge John Stargel from Lakeland; future U.S. Congressman David Riviera from Miami; and future U.S. Congresswoman Sandra Adams from Orlando. Also new to the caucus from Miami-Dade County were Marcelo Llorente, J. C. Planas, Julio Robaina, and Juan Zapata; and from other regions of the state came Tom Anderson from Dunedin; Kevin Ambler from Lutz; Ed Homan from Tampa; future State Senator Charlie Dean from Inverness; Mike Davis from Naples; future Senate President Bill Galvano from Bradenton; Carl Domino from Jupiter; Ray Sansom from Destin; Dave Murzin from Pensacola; Ralph Poppell from Vero Beach; John "Q" Quinones from Kissimmee; Baxter Troutman from Winter Haven; and future State Senator Thad Altman from Melbourne, who joined the Republican House caucus after a special election in 2003.[120]

The first redistricting plan done by the Republican majority also continued the single-member districting scheme, and in addition to increased Republican numbers, the plan also brought a record number of women and minorities to the Florida House following the 2002 elections. Among the membership under Byrd's speakership, the composition of the House of Representatives included twenty-eight women, seventeen African American members, and thirteen members of Hispanic heritage.[121]

In the elections of 2004, Republicans captured eighty-four of the 120 House seats, and the supermajority continued under the leadership of Speaker Allan Bense from Panama City. Among the new Republican members and those replacing retiring Republicans under the Bense Speakership

House Speaker Allan Bense (*center*) confers with Representative Jeff Kottkamp (*left*), Speaker-designate Marco Rubio, and Representative Joe Pickens (*far right*). Photo by Mark Foley; courtesy of the State Archives of Florida.

were Rich Glorioso from Plant City; David Coley from Marianna; Paige Kreegel from Punta Gorda; Trey Traviesa from Tampa; William L. "Bill" Proctor from St. Augustine; Susan Goldstein from Weston; future Speaker Dean Cannon from Orlando; future Speaker Pro Tempore John Legg from Port Richey; future House Majority Leader and future Lieutenant Governor Carlos Lopez-Cantera from Miami; future Senate President Pro Tempore Anitere Flores from Miami; and future State Senators Dorothy Hukill from Port Orange and Alan Hays from Umatilla. New, too, was future State Senator Denise Grimsley from Lake Placid, whose election extended the Republican influence into Highlands, Glades, and Hendry Counties. Following the untimely death of David Coley during his first year in office, he was succeeded by his wife and future Speaker Pro Tempore Marti Coley in a special election in 2005.[122]

House Republicans maintained their margins at or near a two-thirds majority through the balance of the decade and into the next reapportionment cycle. After the 2006 elections, Speaker Marco Rubio led a House with seventy-nine Republican members—fourteen of them new—that included Gary Aubuchon from Cape Coral; Doug Holder from Sarasota; future State Senator Ed Hooper from Clearwater; Bryan Nelson from Apopka; Rob Schenck from Spring Hill; William Snyder from Stuart; future State Senator and Senate President Pro Tempore Garrett Richter from Naples; future Circuit Judge Nicholas "Nick" Thompson from Fort Myers; future Chief Financial Officer Jimmy Patronis from Panama City; and future House Speaker Will Weatherford from Wesley Chapel.[123] Between the regular elections of 2006 and 2008, six new Republicans were elected to the House in special elections, and they included Clay Ford from Gulf Breeze; Kurt Kelly from Ocala; Ron Schultz from Crystal River; Charles McBurney from Jacksonville; Chris Dorworth from Lake Mary; and future Speaker Pro Tempore Matt Hudson from Naples.

Speaker Larry Cretul had eighty-one Republicans in the House after the elections in 2008; twenty-one of the Republicans were new; and among these new members of the caucus from north Florida were Janet Adkins from Fernandina Beach; Michael "Mike" Weinstein and Lake Ray from Jacksonville; Brad Drake from Eucheeanna in Jackson County; Charles Van Zant from Keystone Heights; and Ronald "Doc" Renuart from Ponte Vedra Beach. New from central Florida were future District Court of Appeals Judge Eric Eisnaugle from Orlando; Marlene O'Toole from Lady Lake; Mike Horner from Kissimmee; John Wood from Winter Haven; Scott Plakon from Longwood; future House Speaker Steve Crisafulli from Merritt Island; future House Rules Chairman Rich Workman from Melbourne; and future State Senators Debbie Mayfield from Vero Beach and Kelli Stargel from Lakeland. Kenneth Roberson from Port Charlotte was new from the West Coast, and new from Miami-Dade County was Esteban Bovo.[124]

Speaker Dean Cannon's House also had eighty-one Republicans during the 2010–12 term, when the legislative districts for the House and Senate were redrawn once again for the elections beginning in 2012. Among the first-term members joining the Republican caucus following the 2010 elections were future State Senator Ben Albritton from Wauchula in Hardee County; Larry Ahern from St. Petersburg; James Grant from Tampa; Jimmie Smith from Inverness in Citrus County; Matt Caldwell from Lehigh Acres in Lee County; George Moraitis from Fort Lauderdale; Michael Bileca, Carlos Trujillo, and Jose Felix Diaz from Miami-Dade County; future Circuit Judge Larry Metz from Yalaha in Lake County; Clay Ingram from Pensacola; future Speaker Richard Corcoran from Pasco County; future Lieutenant Governor Jeanette Nuñez from Miami-Dade County; future House Majority Leader and future State Senator Dana Young from Tampa; and future U.S. Congressman Matt Gaetz from Fort Walton Beach.[125] The incoming Republican House members also included future State Senators Jeff Brandes from St. Petersburg; Kathleen Passidomo from Naples; Keith Perry from Gainesville; Greg Steube from Parrish; Doug Broxson from Gulf Breeze; and Frank Artiles from Miami; and, in a special election in 2011, future Speaker Jose Oliva also joined the House Republican caucus.[126]

The House districts in the legislative apportionment plan for the new decade beginning with the 2012 elections—the second redistricting completed by a Republican majority—was a plan that continued the single-member format. Unlike the 2012 districting plan approved for the Florida Senate, however, the House plan met the new "FairDistricts" standards of the state constitution, and the district configurations were not challenged further in the courts. Following the elections in 2012, there was no regression in the number of diverse voices in the House of Representatives from the numbers that emerged from the districts created in 2002, and the House that was seated after the 2012 elections included twenty-seven women, twenty-two African American members, and fourteen Hispanic members.

Will Weatherford assumed the speakership after the 2012 elections, and Republican numbers in the House dipped to seventy-six of 120, and the eighty-vote supermajority was temporarily lost.[127] The effects of term limits continued to bring new members to the House to replace those who had served their allotted time, however, and new Republicans joining the caucus in 2012 included Halsey Beshears from Monticello in Jefferson County; Neil Combee from Polk City in Polk County; Travis Cummings from

Orange Park in Clay County; Charles David "Dave" Hood and David Santiago from Volusia County; Mike La Rosa from St. Cloud in Osceola County; Jake Raburn and future U.S. Congressman Ross Spano from Hillsborough County, Heather Fitzenhagen and future House Majority Leader Dane Eagle from Lee County; Cary Pigman from Avon Park in Highlands County; future Majority Leader Ray Rodriguez from Estero in Lee County; future Speaker Pro Tempore MaryLynn Magar from Tequesta in Martin County; future State Senators Manny Diaz from Hialeah and Travis Hutson from Elkton in St. Johns County; and Holly Raschein from Key Largo and the state's southernmost House district.[128] Following a special election in June 2013, Mike Hill from Pensacola was seated in the House, increasing to seventy-seven the Republican numbers in the caucus.[129]

Left to right: Speaker Steve Crisafulli conversing with Representative and future U.S. Congresswoman Sandra Adams, Representative and past Speaker Pro-Tempore Marty Coley, Representative and future State Senator Dorothy Hukill, and Representative Steve Precourt. Photo by Meredith Hill Geddings; courtesy of the State Archives of Florida.

After the 2014 elections, the Republican supermajority in the House was restored when eighty-one Republicans returned to serve during Steve Crisafulli's speakership. Among the newly arriving Republicans were Jennifer Sullivan from Mount Dora in Lake County; Danny Burgess from Pasco County; Colleen Burton from Polk County; Chris Latvala from Clearwater; Mike Miller from Winter Park; Robert "Bob" Cortes from Maitland; Rene "Coach P" Plasencia from Orlando; Julio Gonzalez from Venice; Bryan Avila from Hialeah; Jay Fant from Jacksonville; Chairman of the State Republican Party Blaise Ingoglia from Spring Hill; and Chris Sprowls from Palm Harbor, who was designated as a future House Speaker shortly after the 2014 elections. In special elections in April 2015, Paul Renner from Palm Coast and Cyndi Stevenson from Ponte Vedra Beach also joined the House Republican caucus.[130]

When Richard Corcoran was designated Speaker of the House following the 2016 elections, the Republican dominance in the House remained basically unchanged. Republicans in the chamber numbered seventy-nine, and twenty-one of the members were new to the caucus. From northwest Florida, Frank White from Pensacola, Jayer Williamson from Pace in Santa Rosa County, and Mel Ponder Fort Walton Beach were new; from northeast Florida, Cord Byrd from Jacksonville Beach, Clay Yarborough and Jason Fischer from Jacksonville, and Bobby Payne from Palatka in Putnam County were new; and the new Republicans from central Florida included Stan McClain from Ocala, Dan Hahnfeldt from the Villages in Marion County, and Sam Killebrew from Polk County.

The new Republicans for House districts along the west coast were Ralph Massullo from Citrus County; Amber Mariano from Pasco County; Jackie Toledo from Tampa; Alex Miller and future State Senator Joe Gruters from Sarasota; and Byron Donalds and Bob Rommel from Collier County. From districts along the east coast, the new members were Tom Leek from Volusia County; Randy Fine from Brevard County; Erin Grall from Vero Beach; and Rick Roth from Palm Beach Gardens.[131] During the term there were changing faces in the caucus from special elections to fill vacancies, and four Republicans—Robert "Bobby O" Olszewski from Winter Garden, Daniel Perez from Miami, Josie Tomkow from Polk City,

Speaker-designate Chris Sprowls delivering the nominating speech for Speaker Richard Corcoran with (*left to right*) U.S. Senator Marco Rubio, Lieutenant Governor Carlos Lopez-Cantera, and Senator Dana Young in the foreground. Sprowls family collection.

and Lawrence McClure from Dover—replaced other Republicans vacating those seats.[132]

The elections of 2016 marked fifty years since the federal court mandates of *Swann v. Adams* reapportioned Florida's Legislature that facilitated the emergence of the Republican minority.[133] By 1996, the Republican minority in the House of Representatives had become a one-vote majority, and in less than two decades, what had begun as a one-vote majority hovered near or above a two-thirds supermajority, and the results from the 2018 elections continued that trend.

As the House of Representatives convened the 2019 regular session under Speaker Jose Oliva, it began the third decade of Republican control of the House chamber, and the Republican House caucus gaveled in with seventy-three members. Among the twenty-four new Republicans replacing retiring members or replacing incumbent Democrats were Alex Andrade and Chuck Brannon from Pensacola in Escambia County; Wyman Duggan from Jacksonville in Duval County; Elizabeth Fetterhoff from Deland in Volusia County; David Smith from Winter Springs in Seminole County; Anthony Sabatini from Howey-in-the-Hills in Lake County; Brett Hage from Oxford in Sumpter County; Ardian Zika from Land O'Lakes in Pasco County; Tyler Sirois from Merritt Island in Brevard County; Melony Bell from Bartow in Polk County; Mike Beltran from Lithia in Hillsborough County; Nick DiCeglie from Belleair Bluffs in Pinellas County; Will Robinson from Bradenton in Manatee County; Tommy Gregory from Sarasota and James Buchanan from Venice in Sarasota County; Spencer Roach from North Fort Myers in Lee County; Toby Overdorf from Palm City in Martin County; Mike Caruso from Delray Beach in Palm Beach County; Chip LaMarca from Lighthouse Point in Broward County; Ana Maria Rodriguez from Doral and Vance Aloupis, Anthony Rodriguez, and Juan Fernandez-Barquin from Miami in Miami-Dade County; and Mike Hill from Pensacola, who was returning to the House as a member from Escambia County after a two-year absence.[134] With their successful elections, each took their place as part of the continuing Republican legacy.

8

WASHINGTON AND
THE FLORIDA REPUBLICANS

AT THE BEGINNING of the modern era, Republican voices from Florida were sparse in the nation's capital, and the impact of the Republican members of the U.S. House of Representatives and the U.S. senators was limited by the short durations of their service in Washington, where long tenures of service and seniority have historically been important. Initially and in contrast, it was the support of Florida voters for the Republican nominees in presidential elections that proved significant as the modern, two-party era began to emerge in the state.

Early successes in the presidential campaigns motivated party loyalists and energized the growth of local grassroots by the Republican Party faithful, particularly in the horseshoe counties of the state. The Republican successes also created opportunities for some Floridians to take posts and positions in the new presidential administrations. As the modern era matured, Florida voters became much sought after and increasingly important to both political parties in races for the presidency.[1] With the state's increasingly large number of electoral votes as the population continued to grow, Floridians often had the ability to be one of the deciding factors in the races for the nation's highest office.

Beginnings in the Presidential Elections

Florida's electoral votes in the disputed presidential election between Republican Rutherford B. Hayes and Democrat Samuel Tilden in 1876 contributed to the end of the Reconstruction era and ushered in nearly a century of Democratic dominance in the state; and the return of the Republican voice to Florida politics began in the same way it vanished, in races for the presidency.[2] In the counties of the urban horseshoe, voters carried a majority of the popular vote for Republican Thomas Dewey in 1948, and although the horseshoe majorities were insufficient to put the state's electoral votes on the Republican side of the ledger, it was a meaningful beginning for Republicans. In the presidential elections of 1952 and 1956, all of the state's electoral votes went to Dwight Eisenhower by comfortable percentages of the popular vote—by more than 10 percent in 1952 and by almost 15 percent in 1956—and with the Eisenhower victories, the Republican optimism that began in 1948 fully manifested itself.[3]

The Republican trend among Florida voters continued in the race between Richard Nixon and John Kennedy when Nixon carried the state in 1960, and Nixon easily won all of Florida's electoral votes in both 1968 against Hubert Humphrey with a margin of almost 10 percent in the popular vote and in 1972 against George McGovern with a margin of more than 43 percent of the popular vote.[4] Ronald Reagan also won the state's electoral votes by wide margins in both of his successful presidential runs—by 17 percent over Jimmy Carter in 1980 and by more than 30 percent over Walter Mondale in 1984.[5] George H. W. Bush continued the trend in 1988 and kept Florida comfortably in the Republican column, beating Michael Dukakis by a margin of more than 20 percent of the popular vote in his race for the presidency.[6]

Beginning with Eisenhower, the Republican dominance in the presidential elections over the four-decade period that began in 1952 was interrupted on only two occasions. The first was in 1964, when Democrat Lyndon Johnson narrowly carried the state in his race against Barry Goldwater by a margin of 2.3 percent of the popular vote; and the second occurred in 1976, when Democrat Jimmy Carter narrowly bested Gerald Ford by a margin of slightly more than 5 percent under the shadow of the Watergate break-in.[7] Between 1952 and 2004, Florida's electoral votes went to the Republican candidate eleven times and to the Democratic candidate on only four occasions; and on all but two occasions, in 1960 and 1992, Florida's electoral votes appeared in the column of the winning presidential candidate.[8]

The predominant Republican preference in presidential elections in the last half of the twentieth century produced two responses by Florida Democrats. The first came in 1964, and it was an orchestrated move of the statewide races for the governor and the Florida cabinet to an election cycle that did not coincide with the presidential race; and the other response came in 1992 when a Democratic initiative attempted to apportion the state's electoral votes based upon the popular vote by congressional district instead of the "winner-take-all" result based upon the statewide popular vote total.[9] Ultimately, the proposition to apportion the state's electoral votes did not garner enough support to pass the state Legislature, and Florida continued to award all of its electoral votes to the victor regardless of how close the final total in the popular vote.

Ironically, as a clear Republican dominance began to emerge in statewide races and races for the state Legislature, by 1996 the trend of strong Republican margins for the national ticket began to wane. Democrat Bill Clinton narrowly lost Florida's electoral votes to George H. W. Bush when Clinton won his bid for the White House in 1992, and Clinton was able to reverse the loss when he captured Florida's electoral votes in the 1996 presidential race, carrying the popular vote by a 6 percent margin over Republican Bob Dole.[10] As the twenty-first century began, Florida was no longer considered a solid Republican "Red" state in national elections, and Florida transitioned into the nation's largest swing state. The presidential race in 2000 underscored its new swing-state image on the national political stage.

Like the race in 1876 between Hayes and Tilden, in the presidential election of 2000, it was once again Florida's electoral votes that ultimately decided the nation's presidency. In the race between Democrat Al Gore and Republican George W. Bush, more than 5.9 million Floridians cast votes, and following a mandatory recount of the machine totals, Bush claimed a scant and disputed 537-vote margin of victory.[11]

To preserve the victory, the Florida Republican Party organized and deployed in new ways with its young volunteers and lawyers to steadfastly defend the narrow margin in the face of multiple challenges from their Democratic counterparts. The challenges to the results came with recount efforts in individual counties and in legal proceedings in both the state and federal courts.

From the state Republican Party headquarters, executive director Randy Enwright deployed young volunteers in minivans to monitor county canvassing boards and support the Republican efforts where ballots were in question, among them David Johnson, Travis Blanton, Frank Terraferma, Cameron Yarbrough, Steve Madden, future Party Executive Director Andy Palmer, and future Party executive director Mike Grissom.[12] At the Division of Elections under the direction of Clay Roberts and at Republican Party headquarters, lawyers were deployed to defend the narrow Republican victory margin, and they included Carrie Carpenter, Paul Kraft, Jon Sjostrom, Debbie Kearney, Hayden Dempsey, Eric Thorn, Ken Wright, Ed Pozzuoli, Richard Coates, and Bucky Mitchell.[13] Mac Stipanovich and Marc Reichelderfer helped coordinate communications on the unfolding events; and at the Leon County Public Library, Marc Dunbar joined other young Republican volunteers who sat around tables next to Republican governors and U.S. senators from other parts of the country as punch-card ballots and hanging chads from Palm Beach, Broward, and Miami-Dade Counties were being examined.[14]

"During the recount, we were in rooms at the Leon County Public Library. We had to be there at 6:00 a.m. and couldn't leave," remembered Marc Dunbar. "Judge Harold Reynolds was supervising the examination of the punch cards while we observed, and I was using my Palm Pilot VII to communicate with the outside. I would raise the small antenna on the Palm and periodically send my updates until Judge Reynolds noticed it and said, 'if I see that antenna one more time, you're out of here.'"[15]

Ultimately, their counting efforts were for naught. Bush's narrow victory was ultimately confirmed by the U.S. Supreme Court before the recount at the library could be completed, and it was the work of the Republican legal teams that carried the day. After weeks of uncertainty, the final 537-vote margin delivered all of Florida's electoral votes and the presidency to George W. Bush.[16]

In the presidential elections that followed, the popular vote margins in the presidential races remained close, and all of Florida's electoral votes continued to go to the winning candidate. In 2004, Florida remained in the Republican column when President Bush carried the popular vote in the state by a 5 percent margin over Democrat John Kerry in his successful reelection campaign.[17] In 2008, the state swung Democratic for Barack Obama when the new president managed a 3 percent margin in the popular vote over Republican John McCain and captured Florida's electoral votes; and by a margin of slightly less than 1 percent, President Obama kept Florida in the Democratic column when he defeated Republican Mitt Romney in his successful reelection bid in 2012.[18]

In 2016, Florida was again the nation's largest battleground state in the race for the presidency.[19] The candidates from the two major political parties made more visits and spent more campaign dollars in Florida than in any other state, and, as in the previous elections of the new century, it was a narrow victory in the popular vote for the winning candidate.[20] Republican Donald Trump's margin was less than 2 percent over Democrat Hillary Clinton, but the margin was enough to capture all twenty-nine of Florida's electoral votes and, with them, the nation's presidency.[21]

Political analyst and Democratic campaign consultant Steve Schale underscored the competitive "Purple" swing-state status of Florida over more than two decades of presidential campaigns in his postscript to the 2016 presidential election this way: "And just to drive home the point of Florida's competitiveness—when you go back to 1992, the year where Florida became a true battleground state, there have been more than 50 million votes cast for President, and Republicans and Democrats are separated by 12,000 votes. No, that isn't a typo—12,000 votes, or right at 0.02%."[22]

Appointees and Ambassadors

Following Donald Trump's victory in 2016, opportunities for Florida Republicans that began with earlier Republican presidents presented themselves once again. As in previous contests, when the national election had been decided and a new president and his new administration were being assembled, there were offices to be filled and appointments to be made. With the Republican victories, there were party loyalists, financial donors, and campaign workers to be remembered, and during the modern era, Republican presidents remembered and rewarded Floridians with posts in their administrations.

Following Richard Nixon's victory in 1968, the president selected Florida as one of the states where his federal-state revenue-sharing initiative was to be unveiled, and he sent Vice President Spiro Agnew to Florida's Capitol to address a joint session of the Legislature on the initiative. It was the first time that either a president or vice president had done so. He also extended an invitation for two prominent Floridians to join the new administration. Republican Party State Chairman Bill Murfin was appointed serve as the director of the Small Business Administration, and joining Murfin was the environmental advisor from Claude Kirk's administration, Nathaniel P. Reed.[23] Reed accepted a post as the assistant secretary for Fish, Wildlife and Parks at the U.S. Department of the Interior, and he served at the Department of Interior under the presidencies of both Richard Nixon and Gerald Ford.[24]

During the Ford administration, Reed was joined by Pinellas County drugstore chain founder Jack Eckerd and Palm Beach County banker Jerry Thomas. Eckerd had his roots in Pinellas County with the ICY Machine; he helped to organize the Republican Legislative Campaign Committee to support local legislative candidates; he unsuccessfully challenged Claude Kirk's reelection in the 1970 Republican primary; and he had been the Republican Party nominee for the U.S. Senate in 1974 but lost to Democrat Richard Stone in the general election.[25] The following year, President Ford brought Jack Eckerd to Washington to head the General Services Administration and also named Eckerd to the Board of Governors of the USO.

Jerry Thomas had served in the Florida Legislature as a Democrat but became a political convert and was the Republican Party's nominee for governor in 1974 in a losing campaign against incumbent Reubin Askew.[26] In 1976, President Ford rewarded Thomas by appointing him to be the nation's undersecretary of the treasury.[27]

Vice President Spiro Agnew (*center left*) being escorted into the Florida House chambers by Republican Leaders Senator Warren Henderson (*front*), Governor Reubin Askew (*center*), and Representative Don Reed (*right*), with Governor Askew followed by Republican Senators Beth Johnson and David Lane (*left*). House Republican Staff Director Peter Dunbar and Representatives Tommy Stevens, Jack Poorbaugh, and Tom Danahy observe from the right rear. Dunbar family collection.

Eckerd returned to Florida after serving in the Ford administration and made his third attempt at statewide office in 1978 but lost to Democrat Bob Graham in the race for governor. Despite the defeat, Eckerd remained active in Florida Republican politics, and during Ronald Reagan's presidency, he was asked by the president to return to Washington as a member the Grace

Commission's private-sector panel on government cost control.[28] During the Reagan administration, other Floridians were invited to take roles in Washington as well. Among them was Jose Sorzano, who was appointed as an ambassador and U.S. deputy to the United Nations, and he later served as a special assistant to President Reagan for national security.[29]

Al Cardenas was part of the Reagan transition team at the U.S. Department of Commerce. During the course of the administration, Cardenas was appointed by the president as a special ambassador to the Caribbean nation of St. Kitts and Nevis; he was appointed to serve as a member of the Advisory Council on Minority and Small Business Affairs; and he was later tapped by Reagan to serve on the Board of Directors of the Federal National Mortgage Association. Lanny Wiles was also a Reagan appointee to the President's Advisory Council on Minority and Small Business Affairs; former State Senator Van Poole was appointed to the National Advisory Council on Educational Research; State Representative Peter Dunbar was a two-term appointee to the National Sea Grant Panel in the Department of Commerce; future House Republican Leader Jim Lombard served as assistant secretary of the Department of Education; and House Republican Leader Dale Patchett was appointed to the South Atlantic Fishery Management Council of NOAA and continued his service on the Council under George H. W. Bush.[30]

When George H. W. Bush succeeded President Reagan following the 1988 campaign, the new president brought other Floridians to the administration following his inauguration. Kevin Michael "Mike" Moore was among the new appointees, and he was invited to Washington from his post as the U.S. attorney for the Northern District of Florida to become the director of the U.S. Marshal Service in 1989. Moore brought attorney Andrea Hillyer from the legal staff of Governor Bob Martinez to serve as general counsel for the Marshal Service during his tenure.[31] Following Bob Martinez's unsuccessful reelection bid, President Bush invited Governor Martinez to join his administration at a cabinet level post as the director of the National Drug Control Office—the country's "drug czar"—replacing William Bennett.[32] Jim Magill from Martinez's Florida staff accompanied him to Washington to serve in the National Drug Control Office and then returned to Florida

Right to left: Tom Slade and Van Poole greet President George H. W. Bush and Congressman Cliff Stearns in front of Air Force One. Green family collection.

after his Washington service to continue his contributions to the emerging Republican presence—first on the staff of House Republican Leader Jim Lombard and later as part of the Republican Party campaign staff as Republicans captured the majority membership in the Florida Senate.[33] There were also opportunities for other young staffers with roots in Florida. David Hart served in roles at both the U.S. Department of Transportation and the Peace Corps during the administration; Trey Evers also served at the Department of Transportation as a congressional relations officer at the Department of Transportation; and Marty Fiorentino joined the staff of the Federal Railroad Commission.

During the 1988 presidential campaign, St. Petersburg shopping center developer Melvin Floyd "Mel" Sembler and Pinellas County developer and businessman Joseph Zappala had served as the Florida cochairmen of the National Finance Committee for George H. W. Bush, and both were major donors to the Bush campaign. In 1989, President Bush rewarded both cochairmen with appointments to serve as United States ambassadors. Sembler's appointment by the Republican president was to be the country's representative in Australia and Nauru.[34] Zappala's appointment was to represent the United States as its ambassador to Spain.[35]

Mel Sembler was rewarded again a decade later by President George W. Bush for his commitment and generosity to Bush's narrow victory over Al Gore in 2000. His second appointment was also an ambassadorial post, and in 2001, it was to represent the United States as the ambassador to Italy.[36] President George W. Bush also picked three other major donors from Florida to be ambassadors during his presidency. In 2004, the president appointed Jacksonville developer John D. Rood to be the United States ambassador to the Commonwealth of the Bahamas; and in 2005, two other Floridians accepted posts to represent the country abroad. The first was Alfred "Al" Hoffman Jr., the founder of WCI Communities, Inc., whom the president selected to be the United States ambassador to Portugal.[37] The other was Francis Rooney from Naples, the majority owner of Manhattan Construction Company, who was appointed as the United States ambassador to the Holy See at the Vatican.[38]

President Bush also brought another Floridian to the administration as a member of his cabinet. In 2001, Mel Martinez from Orlando became the second Florida Republican to serve at the cabinet level in the administration of a U.S. president. Martinez had previously served as the elected mayor of Orange County, and during the 2000 presidential campaign, he was the Florida cochairman of the Bush-Cheney Republican ticket. Following the inauguration in 2001, the new president selected Martinez to be an initial part of his new administration as the secretary of Housing and Urban Development.[39] Among the other Floridians who served during the presidency of George W. Bush were former U.S. Senator Connie Mack, who was selected to chair the President's Advisory Panel for Tax Reform; former State Representative Jerry Paul, who joined the administration as deputy administrator of the National Nuclear Security Administration at the U.S. Department of Energy; and former executive director of the state Republican Party Randy Enwright, who served as Florida's political consultant for the White House from 2001 to 2007.[40]

The next Republican elected to the U.S. presidency was Donald Trump, and following Donald Trump's victory in 2016, Floridians were again invited to positions of prominence with the new president. Tallahassee attorney-lobbyist Brian Ballard, Mel Sembler, and Palm Beach resident Laura Perlmutter were invited to help plan the inaugural; Attorney General Pam Bondi and Susie Wiles from Jacksonville Beach, who had managed the president's Florida campaign, were named to the Trump transition team; and two Floridians were initial appointees to the President's cabinet as Trump organized his new administration. Veteran private-equity investor Wilbur Ross from Palm Beach was named the secretary of the Department of Commerce, and West Palm Beach resident Ben Carson was designated as the secretary of Housing and Urban Development.[41] State Representative Carlos Trujillo from Miami was one of the president's initial ambassadorial appointments, and he was named first as one of the U.S. representatives to the United Nations General Assembly and later as the United States ambassador to the Organization of American States.[42]

Others accepting invitations from Trump included Jesse Panuccio, who had previously served in several capacities during the administration of Governor Rick Scott; Panuccio accepted the post of principal deputy attorney general in the Justice Department.[43] Former deputy attorney general Carlos Muniz was selected to be the new general counsel at the U.S. Department of Education; and former Florida Commissioner of Education and Lieutenant Governor Frank Brogan also accepted a post at the Department of Education as the assistant secretary for elementary and secondary education.[44]

Former senior advisor to Governor Scott Mary Anne Carter became a senior White House advisor to the National Endowment for the Arts; former Hillsborough County Republican Chairwoman Deborah Cox Roush assumed a post in the public affairs office at the U.S. Department of Education; Miamian Helen Aguirre Ferre joined the White House staff as a special assistant to the president and director of media affairs; and Tallahasseans Matthew Leopold, Jahan Wilcox, and John Konkus accepted positions at the Environmental Protection Agency.[45] State Representative Neil Combee joined the Trump administration as director of the U.S. Department of Agriculture's Farm Service Agency; Justin Sayfie from Fort Lauderdale accepted an appointment to the President's Commission on White House Fellows; and Pam Bondi followed her work on the transition team by accepting an appointment to the President's Opioid and Drug Abuse Commission.[46]

The presidential appointments were rewards and recognitions for the contributions to campaigns and support for the Republican Party's presidential nominee, and they were part of the growing Republican Party foundation. Those receiving recognition through the appointment process were the indirect beneficiaries of the voters who gave their support to the Republican nominee, but there were other Floridians who earned their way to Washington in direct appeals to Florida voters.

Florida Republicans in the Senate

Through much of the early twentieth century, Florida's two U.S. Senate seats were held by Democrats. The initial Democratic senators were Duncan Fletcher, who was elected by the Legislature in 1908, and Park Trammell, who was elected by the voters in 1916, and both Democrats served until their deaths in 1936 just one month apart.[47] In 1936, Democrat Claude Pepper ran unopposed to fill Fletcher's vacancy, and Democrat Charles Andrews won 81 percent of the vote against Republican H. C. Babcock in the race to replace Trammell. Pepper served until 1950, when he was defeated in the Democratic primary by George Smathers, and Smathers served until 1969, when he retired from public service. Andrews served until 1946, when he was succeeded by former Democratic Governor Spessard Holland, and Holland served as a member of the U.S. Senate until 1971, when he was succeed by Democrat Lawton Chiles.[48]

The infighting among Republican Party leaders thwarted several Republican opportunities to capture seats in the U.S. Senate, and even the victories turned out to be disappointments when successful Republican Senate candidates failed to hold onto their offices after their initial elections. Claude Kirk's election in 1966 and a renewed battle between the conservative and liberal factions inside the Democratic Party offered enough momentum for the Republicans to break the cycle of Democratic dominance in the U.S. Senate seats for the first time in 1968. The victory in the fall of 1968 went to Republican and World War II veteran Ed Gurney, who became the first Republican in history to be elected to the U.S. Senate from Florida.[49]

Like the gubernatorial primary battle between Democrats Haydon Burns and Robert King High that opened the door for Claude Kirk, the Democratic primary for the U.S. Senate nomination between former Governor LeRoy Collins and State Attorney General Earl Faircloth did the same for Ed Gurney. Gurney became the beneficiary of a bitter Democratic primary battle that was ultimately won by Collins, but the campaign left Collins vulnerable and gave Ed Gurney and the Republicans plenty of political ammunition to defeat the Democratic nominee in the general election. Gurney did not complete his six-year term, however, and resigned amid a political scandal in 1974, four years after his landmark election.[50] Following Gurney's resignation, the seat returned to Democratic hands when their nominee, Dick Stone, won in a three-way contest with 43.4 percent of the vote in a race against Republican Jack Eckerd and third-party candidate Dr. John Grady.[51]

Republicans had another opportunity to take Florida's other Senate seat in 1970, but the momentum from Claude Kirk's election in 1966 and Gurney's victory in 1968 was lost, in large part by the rivalry between Claude Kirk and U.S. Congressman Bill Cramer. Cramer's 1970 bid to succeed Spessard Holland following Holland's retirement was caught in the intraparty fight with Kirk, and without a unified Republican Party, Lawton Chiles turned back Cramer's effort to win the Senate post by capturing 53.9 percent of the vote in the general election.[52]

The second Florida Republican to capture a seat in the U.S. Senate came in 1980, twelve years after Ed Gurney had become the first. Paula Hawkins accomplished the feat when she beat Democrat Bill Gunter in 1980 following the retirement of Democrat Dick Stone. Unlike Gurney, Paula Hawkins completed a full six-year term, but her bid for reelection and a second term was turned back in 1986 by former Governor Bob Graham, and she served only one term in the Republican caucus of the U.S. Senate.[53]

Following Hawkins's defeat, Florida elected its third Republican U.S. senator in 1988 after the retirement of Democratic incumbent Lawton Chiles. Republican Congressman Connie Mack III beat Robert Merkle in the primary to earn the Republican Party's nomination, and in a narrow

Paula Hawkins campaigning for U.S. Senate. Photo courtesy of the Florida Historic Capitol Museum.

Senator Connie Mack visits with Representatives Faye Culp (*center*) as (*left to right*) Representatives Ken Pruitt, George Albright, John Thrasher, and Jim King observe on the floor of the Florida House chamber. Photo courtesy of the Florida Historic Capitol Museum.

contest that separated the candidates by less than 1 percent in the final vote total, Mack bested Democratic Congressman Buddy MacKay to win the Senate seat.[54] Six years later, Mack was reelected to the U.S. Senate by an overwhelming margin, capturing 71 percent of the vote and winning every Florida county against Democrat Hugh Rodham to become the first Florida Republican to win a second term.[55] With the seniority earned during his second term, Mack began to have a meaningful impact; he rose to become the chairman of the Senate Republican Conference; and among his accomplishments, he cosponsored and was able to help engineer the passage of the Everglades Restoration Act.[56]

Connie Mack retired from the Senate at the end of his second term, and Democrat Bill Nelson defeated Republican Bill McCollum in 2000 to fill the vacancy. This returned the seat to the Democratic column, and both senators were once again Florida Democrats.[57] Four years later, in 2004, Bob Graham followed Connie Mack into retirement after serving three terms, and his retirement presented another opportunity for Florida Republicans to return a voice to the U.S. Senate. Republican Mel Martinez filled the vacancy left by Graham, winning a narrow victory over Democrat Betty Castor in the 2004 general election; and with the victory, Martinez became Florida's fourth Republican to serve in the U.S. Senate.[58] Martinez also became the first person of Cuban American heritage to serve in the U.S. Senate; but like his Republican predecessor, Ed Gurney, Martinez's time in the U.S. Senate did not include a full six-year term.[59]

For reasons personal to Martinez, he resigned his seat in the Senate before the end of his first term in 2009, and Governor Charlie Crist appointed Republican George Lemieux to fill the remaining months of his term. Lemieux had been a previous chair of the Broward County Republican Executive Committee; he had run unsuccessfully as a Republican for the Florida House; and he was the former chief of staff and a close political ally of Crist. But Lemieux's tenure in the Senate also was brief, and there was no meaningful legacy identified with his service. After only months of service, he opted not to seek a full term in office and deferred instead to Charlie Crist, who attempted to capture the U.S. Senate seat vacated by Martinez.[60]

Ironically, Lemieux's decision to defer to Crist contributed to the Republican's success in filling the seat he vacated when Crist opted to leave the Republican Party and run as an Independent. In a three-way contest in 2010 that included Democrat Kendrick Meek, Crist running as an Independent, and former State House Speaker Marco Rubio carrying the Republican banner, Meek garnered 20.2 percent of the vote; Crist managed only 29.7 percent of the vote; and Rubio captured 48.9 percent of the vote to win the race and keep the seat in the Republican column.[61]

After making an unsuccessful effort to capture the Republican presidential nomination in 2016, Rubio returned to Florida to seek a second term in the U.S. Senate, and in the November general election, Rubio comfortably bested Democratic Congressman Patrick Murphy by more than 720,000 votes to win reelection.[62] Rubio's victory marked the second time during the modern era that a Florida Republican had been reelected to the body, and it was a new opportunity for a Florida Republican to begin to garner important seniority as a member of the U.S. Senate. As his second term began, Rubio emerged quickly as a frequent spokesman from within the Senate Republican caucus on national issues, and he gained key recognition when he preserved the child tax credit for families in the 2017 tax bill.[63]

Rubio was joined by another Republican in the Senate following the elections in 2018, but it would not be a victory easily won. Unlike the other statewide contests appearing on the 2018 ballot that featured contests for open seats, the U.S. Senate race was not a battle for a vacant post but was, rather, a challenge to defeat a long-serving Democratic incumbent. The race pitted Governor Rick Scott against incumbent Bill Nelson, and it came with national attention and campaign funding from around the country. Before it ended, it became "the most expensive Senate contest in American history," and it remained a close contest from the outset, with polling never showing the lead by one candidate or the other to be outside the margin of error.[64] When vote tabulations were complete on election night, Rick Scott claimed a narrow victory in the race, but because of the margin, the race was not finally decided until both a machine recount and a hand recount mandated by Florida law had been completed.[65]

What Nelson and the Democrats could not accomplish at the ballot box,

Governor Rick Scott (*right*) and Chief Financial Officer Jimmy Patronis enjoy a relaxing moment during the 2018 general election campaign. Photo courtesy of Stone family collection.

they tried to achieve in the courtroom while the recounts were pending; and it immediately revived memories of the presidential election between George Bush and Al Gore. During the 2000 recount in the election between Bush and Gore, forty-seven lawsuits were filed in state and federal court before the U.S. Supreme Court finally confirmed the vote totals. During the recounts in 2018, a similar pattern emerged. Nelson and the Democratic Senatorial Campaign Committee and the Democratic National Committee on his behalf filed multiple lawsuits in state and federal courts, and these were accompanied by challenges at county canvassing boards in the hope that the results reported on election night might be reversed.[66] At one point during the recount at the Lake County canvassing board, a Nelson attorney went so far as to claim that a write-in vote for country singer Willie Nelson should be counted as a vote for Bill Nelson—a claim that was rejected by the canvassing board.[67] In the end, the "flurry of increasingly and unsuccessful post-election lawsuits couldn't change the outcome," and the contests at the canvassing boards produced no change to the final results.[68]

Rick Scott's narrow margin of slightly more than 10,000 votes was confirmed when the recounts were completed, and after twelve days of skirmishing, Nelson finally conceded defeat.[69] In a year when pundits, pollsters, and Democrats predicted a Democratic "Blue Wave," the results proved a devastating blow for Democrats. For Republicans, it was another history-making milestone in the modern era. When Rick Scott joined Marco Rubio in the U.S. Senate, both Florida seats in the U.S. Senate were occupied by Republicans for the first time since Reconstruction.[70]

Florida Republicans in the U.S. Congress

In the other congressional body, the U.S. House of Representatives, there were more than two seats from Florida to be contested between the two major political parties when the modern two-party era began to emerge, and the opportunities for Republicans were more readily available. The seats in the U.S. Congress are allocated, or reallocated, among the fifty states every ten years based upon changing population demographics identified in the nation's decennial census; and in the process, some states lose seats in Congress while others gain membership and expanded representation. During the modern era, Florida has been consistently one of the gainers. Based on the 1950 decennial census, Florida was apportioned eight seats in the U.S. House of Representatives, but in the same 1952 election when Florida voters delivered all of the state's electoral votes to Republican Dwight Eisenhower in race for the presidency, voters sent Democrats to Washington to fill all eight seats in the state's congressional delegation. It was to be the last solid Democratic congressional delegation from Florida as the new two-party era emerged.

Republican presence in Florida's delegation to the U.S. House of Representatives followed a growth pattern not unlike that of the bodies in the state's Legislature. It began with a toehold and a single member in 1954, when Bill Cramer became the first Republican in the modern era to capture a congressional seat.[71] While all the remaining congressmen were Democrats, as the state's population grew and the Republicans began to build their party infrastructure, the number of congressional seats increased and the number of Republicans occupying those seats grew as well. The 2010 census marked Florida as the country's third-largest state, and based upon its population growth from the time of Bill Cramer's election in 1954, its representation in the Congress more than tripled from eight to twenty-seven members, in the process providing new opportunities for Republicans as the population grew.[72]

Like the seats in state's legislative bodies, the decennial census required periodic redistricting for the congressional seats to ensure groupings of equal population.[73] Politically in the early years of the era as the district boundary lines for Florida's congressional seats were redesigned, the new boundaries were approved by a state Legislature controlled by the Democrats. The boundaries dictated the partisan advantages from the choices made by the Legislature, and the advantages defined the likely outcome of elections held within many of the districts. The Democratic Party's choice of the boundary lines often constrained the efforts of minority voting blocs to elect candidates to Congress, and that included constraints on the Republicans.[74] Despite the partisan disadvantages in the selection of the district boundaries, however, as the number of seats in the Florida congressional delegation increased, Republicans began to take advantage of the new opportunities that accompanied the state's changing population.

Following the federal census in 1960, four new seats in Congress were allocated to Florida, bringing the total to twelve based on the state's increased population.[75] Through the preceding decade, Bill Cramer had continued to hold the single Republican seat in the state's congressional delegation, but from the new districting scheme that followed in 1962, Republican Ed Gurney from Winter Park was able to win one of the new seats and joined Cramer in the Florida delegation to Congress.[76] Two years later, in 1966, Republican J. Herbert Burke from Broward County won another seat, and with Cramer and Gurney, Burke's victory gave Republicans one-fourth of the membership in the state's delegation to Washington.[77] Republican Lou Frey from Orlando was elected to fill the seat vacated by Ed Gurney when Gurney ran for the U.S. Senate in 1968, and Bill Young replaced Bill Cramer when Cramer vacated his seat to run for the U.S. Senate in 1970.[78] As the 1960s came to a close, Republicans continued to hold three seats in the state's congressional delegation as the state Legislature prepared to again redistrict based on the 1970 decennial census.

The new census figures brought three more seats in the U.S. Congress to the state, and Florida began the new decade with fifteen members of Congress. Once the boundaries for the new congressional districts were approved by the Democratic majority in the Legislature, the 1972 elections that followed saw Young, Frey, and Burke retain their seats; Skip Bafalis from Palm Beach County was able to win one of the three new seats; and Republicans began the new decade with four members of the state's delegation returning to Congress. Two years later, in 1974, Republican Richard Kelly from Pasco County won a seat vacated by a Democrat in central Florida, and the Republican membership increased to five during the middle of the decade; but in 1978 their numbers were again reduced to three with the departure of Lou Frey, whose vacant seat was won by a Democrat, and the defeat of Herb Burke.[79]

By 1980, Republican Bill McCollum had defeated Republican incumbent Richard Kelly, who had been caught in the ABSCAM scandal, and McCollum kept the central Florida congressional seat in the Republican column as the new census was being completed. Clay Shaw's victory in southeast Florida in 1980 returned the district that had been previously occupied by Herb Burke to the Republican column as well, and the Republican members again numbered four of the fifteen-member delegation as the 1970s came to a close.[80]

The population increase reflected in the 1980 census allocated four more new congressional seats to Florida, and the state's delegation to Washington increased to nineteen members beginning in 1982. In the 1982 elections, six Florida Republicans captured seats in the U.S. House of Representatives, and Republicans in the delegation included returning veterans Bill Young, Bill McCollum, and Clay Shaw. The new Republican members joining these veterans were former State Representative Tom Lewis from Palm Beach County, who replaced retiring Congressman Skip Bafalis; Connie Mack III from Lee County, who won one of the newly reconfigured seats on the state's southwest coast; and Mike Bilirakis from Tarpon Springs in north Pinellas County, who won the newly reconfigured seat in the Tampa Bay area.[81] Despite the new faces, however, Republicans remained in the minority of the delegation, and their numbers accounted for slightly less than one-third of the state's representation in the nation's capital.

In 1984, incumbent Congressman Andy Ireland from Polk County left the Democratic Party and was reelected as a Republican, bringing the delegation's Republican numbers to seven.[82] As the end of the decade neared, Republican Porter Goss from Lee County replaced Connie Mack; Republican Craig James from Deland in Volusia County defeated Democrat incumbent William Chappell; Republican Cliff Stearns from Marion County captured the seat being vacated by Democrat Buddy MacKay; and for the first time, Republican numbers began to approach majority status in the delegation as their numbers rose to nine of nineteen members.[83] In the final year of the decade, that goal was finally realized.

In a special election following the death of Democratic Congressman Claude Pepper in 1989, Republican State Senator Ileana Ros-Lehtinen captured the vacant seat. In addition to being the first woman and the first Cuban American to be elected to the U.S. Congress from Florida, Ros-Lehtinen also brought the number of Republicans in the delegation to ten; and as the decade closed and the new decennial census approached, Republicans held a majority of the Florida seats in the U.S. Congress for the first time.[84]

As the Republican Party organization grew and matured, many of the emerging candidates for national office came from those individuals who had begun successful careers in the state Legislature and in the offices of local government. Once successful at the state and local level, these officeholders became viable candidates for the new seats in Congress being assigned to Florida or for those existing seats being vacated by Democratic incumbents. From the beginning of the modern era through the population growth and redistricting based on the 2010 decennial census, forty-nine individual Re-

Future U.S. Congresswoman Ileana Ros-Lehtinen confers with Senator Roberto Casas on the floor of the state Senate chambers. Photo courtesy of the Florida Historic Capitol Museum.

publicans from Florida took seats in the U.S. Congress, and from among that group, twenty-four had previously served as a member of the Florida Legislature, and eight more had held offices at the county or city level.[85] As the next round of redistricting approached based upon the 1990 census, several of these local officials prepared to seek seats in Congress.

The 1990 decennial census confirmed Florida's continued population growth, and with the growth, the state's delegation to the U.S. Congress increased from nineteen to twenty-three members. Democrats still maintained control of both Houses in the state Legislature, but, confronted with a coalition of African American and Republican lawmakers challenging the majority's districting plan, the Democrat-controlled Legislature was unable to complete the decennial redistricting task.[86] Led by attorney and Republican State Representative Miguel De Grandy, the coalition demanded more opportunities for minority voting blocs and took their cause to the federal courts.[87] In the face of the mounting judicial challenges that followed, the Legislature ultimately adjourned without completing a congressional redistricting plan and left the task to the federal courts to create the boundaries for Florida's new districts.[88]

From the twenty-three new court-ordered districts following the elections in 1992, Republican candidates won thirteen seats and preserved their new majority status in the state's congressional delegation.[89] Members returning to Congress included veterans Bill Young, Bill McCollum, Mike Bilirakis, Cliff Stearns, Porter Goss, Tom Lewis, Clay Shaw, and Ileana Ros-Lehtinen. The new Republicans joining the state's congressional delegation included former Jacksonville council member Tillie Fowler; former State Representative John Mica from Orlando; former State Representative Charles Canady from Polk Count; former State Senator Lincoln Diaz-Balart from Miami-Dade County; and Dan Miller from the new district anchored by Sarasota County on Florida's west coast. From the new court-ordered districts, there were also minority voices in the delegation that included three African American members and two members of Hispanic heritage.[90]

In 1994, Republicans extended their delegation majority by two when Joe Scarborough from Pensacola won a seat previously held by Democrat Earl Hutto, and Dave Weldon from Brevard County won the seat held previously by Democrat Jim Bacchus.[91] While elections through the balance of the decade produced some new Republican faces in the delegation—Ander Crenshaw replaced Tillie Fowler; Mark Foley succeeded Tom Lewis from Palm Beach County; and Ric Keller replaced Bill McCollum—the total number of Republicans in the twenty-three-member delegation remained stable at fifteen.[92]

The decennial census at the turn of the century documented once again the continuing increase in Florida's population, and when the Legislature gathered in 2002 to create the boundaries for the state's congressional districts, there were two more new seats, bringing the state's total to twenty-five. For the first time in the modern era, the boundaries for the new congressional districts were drawn by a Legislature with a majority of Republicans in both the House and Senate; and from the newly drawn districts, eighteen Republicans emerged with victories in the fall elections, with the remaining seven seats going to Democrats.[93] By the end of the decade, the new districts drawn by the Republican-controlled Legislature also saw a Florida delegation to Congress that included three Hispanic members and four African American members.[94]

The Republican incumbents seeking reelection in 2002 from the new districts were all returned to office, and new Republican members in the state's delegation included former State Representative and future Agriculture Commissioner Adam Putnam from Polk County, who replaced Charles Canady; former State Senator Katherine Harris from Sarasota County, who replaced Dan Miller; and former State Representative Jeff Miller from Pensacola, who replaced Joe Scarborough. Also new to the delegation were the members who won the new seats, and these included former House Speaker Tom Feeney from Seminole County; former State Senator Ginny Brown-Waite from Hernando County; and former State Senator Mario Diaz-Balart, who joined his brother Lincoln in the congressional delegation from Miami-Dade County.

Through the balance of the decade there were other new Republican faces in the state's congressional delegation, but the total number of Republicans stabilized between seventeen and eighteen members. In the middle of the decade, former State Representative Connie Mack IV replaced Porter Goss from the district on Florida's southwest coast to occupy the seat previously held by his father, Connie Mack III; like Mack, former State Representative Gus Bilirakis replaced his father, Mike, in the seat anchored in Pinellas County on the state's central west coast; and Vern Buchanan from Sarasota replaced Katherine Harris. In the final two elections from the districts created in 2002, Tom Rooney, Richard Nugent, Allen West, and former state legislators Dan Webster, Dennis Ross, Bill Posey, Sandy Adams, and David Riviera all won seats in the Congress replacing retiring Republicans.[95]

Demographic shifts in the state's population near the end of the decade saw Republicans lose one of the seats on the lower east coast to a Democrat but also saw Republican Steve Southerland from Panama City win the Sec-

Future U.S. Congressmen Dan Webster (*right*) and Bill Posey (*left*) in a sidebar discussion on the floor of the Florida Senate. Photo courtesy of the Florida Senate.

ond Congressional District in the Florida Panhandle that had been previously held by Democrat Allen Boyd.[96] As Florida awaited the next decennial census, the Republican majority in the state's congressional delegation remained unchanged.

New Rules, Similar Results

When it was completed, the 2010 decennial census produced two more seats for the Florida congressional delegation, and for the second time in the modern era, the boundaries of the twenty-seven new districts were drawn by a state Legislature controlled by Republicans. Like the new districts drawn for the state Senate in 2010, however, the boundaries created for the new congressional districts were immediately challenged in state court for their failure to comply fully with the new criteria of the "FairDistricts" amendments to the Florida constitution. While the court challenge was pending, the 2012 and 2014 election cycles were held under the Legislature's districting plan, but at the conclusion of the state court proceedings, new court-ordered districts were mandated for the congressional elections in 2016.[97]

In the first two election cycles under the Legislative plan, there were no aggregate numerical gains for the Democrats, and the Republican numbers in the delegation remained stable at seventeen members, with Democrats claiming the remaining ten seats. Though the elections produced no net gains for the Republicans in 2012 and 2014, there were new Republican faces in the state's delegation to Congress. They included Ted Yoho from Alachua County, who replaced Republican Cliff Stearns, and Republican and future Governor Ron DeSantis from Flagler County, who was elected from one of the two new congressional seats assigned to Florida by the 2010 census.[98]

Following the elections in 2016 from the court-ordered congressional districts, the Democrats gained only a single seat in the state's delegation to Washington, bringing their total to eleven. The other sixteen seats continued to be occupied by Republicans. The retirement of incumbents and the reconfigured districts did bring five new Republican faces to the delegation in 2016, and they included former State Representative Matt Gaetz from Okaloosa County, Neal Dunn from Bay County, John Rutherford from Duval County, Brian Mast from Martin County, and former U.S. Ambassador to the Vatican Francis Rooney from Collier County.[99]

The 2018 midterm elections saw congressional contests in suburban swing districts extend to states across the country, and Florida was no exception. When the final results from the midterms were known, two seats in suburban Miami previously held by the Republicans went to Democrats, but Republicans defended their remaining seats and retained majority status in the delegation by capturing fourteen of the twenty-seven districts. Among the fourteen Republicans were three new faces in the delegation—Ross Spano replaced retiring Dennis Ross; Greg Steube won the seat being vacated by retiring Tom Rooney; and Michael Waltz was the victor in the open seat previously occupied by Florida's new governor, Ron DeSantis.[100] Each became a part of Florida's representation in Washington, D.C., which included two Republican U.S. senators for the first time in the modern era.

Continuing Legacy

The offices of the Republican U.S. senators and the Republican members of the U.S. Congress from Florida, like the offices of Republican governors, cabinet members, and state legislators, provided an introduction to the political process and to the Republican Party for young interns and staff members. Many of these staff members and interns, too, became part of the growing Republican base and part of the expanding network of future leaders. Some served long careers on the congressional staffs; and for others, it was a foundation for different roles in the Republican Party structure or a path to elected office. Among those spending time in the offices of congressional leaders and who later moved on to political careers of their own were John Mica, George Cretekos, Oscar Juarez, David Troxler, Jamie Wilson, Tom Rooney, Dana Young, Greg Steube, Chris Sprowls, and Mike Miller.

John Mica served as a young intern for Congressman Bill Young, and his service in Washington began a political career that took Mica first to the Florida House of Representatives and then back to the U.S. Congress as member.[101] George Cretekos spent more than three decades on the staff of Congressman Young before he returned to Pinellas County after his retirement to become a two-term mayor of Clearwater.[102] Jamie Wilson and Tom Rooney served as members of the staff of U.S. Senator Connie Mack. After an unsuccessful attempt to win a seat in the Florida Senate, Wilson was tapped to be the executive director of the state Republican Party by Chairman Al Cardenas, and Tom Rooney returned to Washington following the elections in 2002 as a member of the U.S. Congress representing a portion of Florida's Southeast Coast.[103] Oscar Juarez began on the staff of Congressman Lou Frey, and his career continued as a longtime Republican consultant and lobbyist.[104]

David Troxler from Jacksonville, Dana Young from Tampa, and Greg Steube from Manatee County all served as congressional interns before their service in the Florida Legislature; Mike Miller from Winter Park worked for both Senator Mack and Congressman Bill McCollum before his election to the Florida House of Representatives; and Chris Sprowls was sponsored by

Congressman Mike Bilirakis as part of the congressional page program that began his interest in the political process. It led Sprowls to work in local Republican campaigns and to a seat in the Florida House of Representatives, where his colleagues designated him to be the thirteenth consecutive Republican Speaker.[105]

Like the other individuals in the growing and emerging Republican network, each, in their own way, contributed to the successes and accomplishments that came with the modern, two-party era.

9

POLITICS, POLICY, AND CONTRIBUTIONS

A VIABLE TWO-PARTY SYSTEM has been a reality in Florida since the election sequence of 1966–67, and with it came the new ideas, policy alternatives, and initiatives that changed and modernized Florida's governmental institutions.[1] When the federal court ordered the reapportionment of the state Legislature, the decision and the subsequent special elections "effectively ended the political domination by the North Florida/Panhandle legislative delegation, called the Pork Chop Gang."[2] It opened the door for a new political era that included meaningful Republican voices, and the special elections brought a new group of leaders to the Capitol who became a catalyst for changes in state government and to important parts of Florida's public policy.[3] They were changes that had not been attainable under the one-party rule of the Democrats prior to the Republican emergence, and Republicans were essential contributors to the changes that followed—first as a contributing minority and later as the uncontested majority.[4]

With the early successes at the ballot box, new Republican leaders brought ideas and philosophies with them to the Capitol fully intending to contribute to the changes.[5] In the early years, they contributed to the restructuring of the institutions of state government and to innovations that modernized state policies that had stagnated before the two-party era arrived.[6] As the modern era matured, there were transformations in the state's policies on the environment, public education, and taxes; and the new two-party environment brought reforms that revitalized the state's criminal justice system.[7]

These ideas and innovations modernized governmental structures; created more governmental accountability to executive branch agencies; and brought choices to the state's education system and new protections for Florida's environment. Each of these can be traced to the Republican campaign messages that began with Claude Kirk, and the messages contrasted in significant ways to the prior rural and conservative policies of the Pork Chop–era Democrats. Many of the new ideas found commonality with the urban Democrats who arrived with a properly apportioned Legislature in 1967, but not all of the changes met with universal approval during the decades that followed.[8] If the growing Republican successes at the ballot box were any indication, however, the policy changes and innovations they offered were embraced by many Florida voters who aligned with the new Republican dogma and supported the Republican Party candidates.[9] With growing Republican successes at the ballot box, the policy pendulum in Florida's Capitol also began to swing toward the ideas that the new officeholders brought with them.

A Modern State Governmental Structure

The first meaningful changes of the new political era began after the election of Claude Kirk and the Republican legislators who followed him into office in 1967. During Kirk's term in office, Republican partisans brought support from their ranks for the state's new constitution and modernization of the state's executive branch government.[10] In his initial address to the joint session of the Legislature on April 4, 1967, Kirk addressed the Republican Party policy for both initiatives.

As your first order of business I urge you to present to the people of this state their long-awaited new constitution. The constitution under which we now function is a patchwork document of rare inadequacy. It not only fails to meet today's needs—it is totally incapable of providing for tomorrow. In this session, I recommend you look searchingly into the structure and operation of various state boards and commissions such as the Florida Installment Land Sales Board, the Florida Milk Commission, and others. It may be possible through consolidation and revision—and, in some cases, elimination—to provide greater service and effectiveness, while, at the same time, effecting substantial savings.[11]

By the middle of Kirk's term, the Legislature had responded by proposing a new constitution with bipartisan support in both the House of Representatives (by a vote of 94–16) and the Florida Senate (by a vote of 37–9) that totaled more than the three-fifths required to present the issue to Florida voters for its ratification.[12] In the fall of 1968, the new constitution was approved at the ballot box, and following ratification by the voters, the institutional changes in Florida's governmental structure began. Under the mandates of the new constitution, the Legislature transformed and completely reorganized the state's executive branch of government, consolidating more than three hundred boards, commissions, and agencies into the modern structure that permits no more than twenty-five executive agency departments.[13]

Once enacted, the governmental reorganization initiative gave rational structure to the executive branch; it provided direct responsibility for each of the agencies to the governor and cabinet; and it created statutory guidance and limitations on the powers and activities of the agencies. Without Don Reed and the House Republicans, however, the final version of the reorganizational initiative would not have passed in the Florida House, and the efforts to modernize Florida's government structures would have been frustrated once again.[14]

Many give credit for much of these executive branch reforms to the new, moderate and liberal Democrats who arrived in the reapportioned Legislature—especially to Democrat Richard Pettigrew in the House of Representatives and Democrat Welborn Daniel in the Florida Senate.[15] Yet in the words of former Democrat Governor Buddy MacKay, the Republicans were an essential ingredient to Pettigrew's final successes in the House, which were achieved by maintaining a coalition of new urban Democrats and the members of the minority Republican Party in support of the reforms.

"Pettigrew understood how all the pieces fit together and had the leadership to keep the forces of reform united and motivated," remembered MacKay. "He did this by developing an effective urban coalition with moderate House Republican leaders like the minority leader, Don Reed, from Palm Beach, and Joel Gustafson, from Broward County."[16]

To provide accountability for the state's newly reorganized executive agencies, adoption of the Administrative Procedures Act (APA) followed. The APA institutionalized the formal protections and procedural due process for citizens and businesses dealing with the agencies of state government, and like the reorganization of the executive agencies, it was enacted with the bipartisan support of both Democrats and Republicans. The legislation was sponsored in the House of Representatives by Republican Curt Kiser and in the Senate by Democrat Dempsey Barron. Final passage took two years of work by the sponsors of the legislation, and under their leadership, the APA was finally enacted into law in 1974 with unanimous bipartisan votes in both Houses of the Legislature.[17] Following its passage, Florida's Administrative Procedures Act was looked to as a model by other states and by the federal government. Following its enactment, Representative Kiser was invited to testify on three occasions before the U.S. Congress and in a variety of other states as those other jurisdictions looked to Florida's APA as a model for their own legislation.[18]

The fundamental changes that followed the adoption of the 1968 constitution did not end with the APA and executive agency reorganization, and the Republicans continued to be part of other innovations. Following the adoption of the new constitution, Republican House Leader Don Reed sponsored the "resign-to-run" law and changed the dynamics of Florida's elections so a sitting officeholder could not retain his or her position while seeking another office.[19] Consistent with the mantra of a more accountable state government and with an objective of protecting Florida ratepayers, Representative Kiser also sponsored legislation to create the Office of Public Counsel at the Florida Public Service Commission to provide representation for consumers in rate-increase cases brought by the state's regulated utilities.[20]

Changes were not just limited to the early years of the new era, either. Governor Martinez led efforts to reform the Florida Department of Corrections, and the new policies relieved overcrowding and limited the early release of prisoners that resulted from the inattention to the problems in the state's correction system by those who preceded him. His administration implemented the Florida Lottery that was authorized by the voters in 1986 with a structure that permitted it to mature into one of the nation's most efficient and productive state-sponsored lotteries.[21] Martinez also used his line-item veto to temper the growth of state government and block indiscriminate spending of state tax dollars, vetoing more than $210 million of items in the appropriations bills during his first two years in office.[22] He also successfully challenged the efforts of the Democratic majority in the Legislature to hide special appropriations and insulate them from the governor's line-item veto authority by placing directives in legislative computer "working papers" and withholding them from the official appropriations bill.[23]

House Republican Leader Sandra Mortham led her caucus in a bipartisan initiative to create the Department of Juvenile Justice during the Democratic administration of Governor Chiles, and with the arrival of Republican Governor Jeb Bush, other reforms manifested themselves during his two terms as governor.[24] During Bush's tenure, he brought new attention and better services to Floridians with special challenges, and he was the principal advocate for the creation of the Agency for Persons with Disabilities as a permanent part of Florida's executive branch governmental structure.[25] Bush began initiatives to privatize some of the government's functions to make them more cost-efficient, including the delivery of personnel services, the administration of foster care, and the management of state parks.[26] The Bush era also saw the beginnings of a reduction in Florida's state workforce in relation to its population.[27] By the time the Republican administration of Governor Rick Scott was nearing its end, Florida's employee ratio to its population had dropped to the lowest of any state in the country; and Florida government was "proportionately, smaller and less expensive than any other state administration in the country."[28]

A Modern Legislature

The state's executive branch of government was not the only institution that underwent transformation. There were significant changes in the legislative branch as well. At the beginning of the modern era, Florida's Legislature met every other year; members were paid one hundred dollars per month; there was no professional staff to support the institution; and there was no staff to assist individual members of the House and Senate with their official duties. In a rating by the National Conference of State Legislatures, Florida ranked forty-seventh among the fifty states as the two-party era began, but changes to the legislative institution began almost immediately after the 1967 regular session convened.[29] Some of the changes were sponsored by the new Republicans, and other reforms came with the bipartisan support offered by both party caucuses.

Professional staffing was provided to the newly created House Republican Office as the 1967 session began, and expense allocations were made available to individual members for their district offices in the same year. After voters approved the new constitution in 1968, the Legislature moved to annual sessions; interim committee work was instituted between regular legislative sessions; and professional staffing was extended to individual members of the Legislature and to the standing committees in both the House and the Senate beginning in 1969.[30]

The rules of parliamentary procedure for the Legislature were reformed. The use of proxy votes by legislators was eliminated; provisions advanced by Don Reed and the House Republicans were incorporated into the rules to provide for official recognition of the minority party; and due process protections were adopted for investigative hearings conducted by the Legislature.[31] The new constitution provided for an organizational session following the general election and provided opportunities for the selection of legislative leaders and adoption of formal rules to govern legislative proceedings in advance of the regular sessions.[32] An independent legislative auditor general was established to provide accountability checks on state spending, and the pay for members was increased from one hundred dollars a month to one thousand dollars per month. The legislative pay raise was sponsored by House Republican Leader Don Reed, and it recognized the demands on legislators' time and their commitment to the duties of their office.[33]

During the interim time between Republican Governors Kirk and Martinez, Republicans in the Legislature provided bipartisan support for the creation of Florida's Ethics Commission.[34] The legislation also prohibited conflicts of interest between the public duties and private interests of government officers and employees to protect the public trust.[35] The legislation creating the Ethics Commission was named the "John J. Savage Memorial Act of 1974" in honor of the Representative Jack Savage.[36] Savage chaired the House Committee on Standards and Conduct from 1967 through 1970, and he was the first House Republican committee chairman of the modern era.[37]

With annual sessions, professional staffing, proper apportionment, and the bipartisan cooperation from the modern two-party era, Florida began the 1970s with its Legislature acknowledged to be among the nation's most respected.[38]

Environmental Policy Changes

Beyond the institutional changes, Republicans were also a catalyst for other policy reforms that had been stymied during the era of Democratic Pork Chop politics.[39] Notable in the early years of the modern era was the new attention to Florida's environmental policies. Beginning with Claude Kirk's campaign for governor, the environment became a focal point for Republicans.

Kirk's campaign platform focused on the impacts of development and the lack of environmental policy that had begun to leave noticeable effects on the state's coastlines, inland water bodies, and natural uplands. Kirk's efforts to pursue a conservationist agenda began immediately after he assumed office, and his efforts were rooted in three factors, according to biographer Edmund Kallina. They included his personal appreciation for the state's natural features, the fact that those responsible for the detriments to the environment were Democrats, and the fact that a number of environmentalists, notable among them Nathaniel ("Nat") Reed, had helped in Kirk's campaign and persuaded him of the importance of the environmental policy platform planks Kirk brought to his campaign.[40]

Among the subsets of environmental policy outlined in Kirk's sixty-four-page campaign white paper were concerns about the polluting effects of stormwater runoff, habitat destruction from dredge-and-fill projects in the coastal wetlands, problems with declining gamefish populations, pollution in the spawning grounds of oysters and shellfish, and the lack of environmental protections below the mean high-water line in the state's coastal zones.[41] The concerns of the new Republican governor also included the saltwater intrusion and low water levels in Lake Okeechobee, which affected the health of the Florida Everglades.

During Kirk's term in office, the governor put Nathaniel Reed in charge of his initial environmental reforms, and two of the administrations initiatives centered on the Randall Act and a bill to create the Florida Air and Water Commission. Under the Randall Act, the effort was to make it more difficult to secure approval for the destructive dredge-and-fill operations in the state's coastal waters, and with its passage, the sale of sovereign submerged lands for dredging was brought to a virtual halt.[42] Under Kirk's initiative to create the Air and Water Commission, new restrictions were enacted to regulate waste disposal, to enforce air- and water-quality standards, and to provide other enhanced environmental protections.[43] Governor Kirk also stepped out prominently to stop state support for the continued construction of the Cross-Florida Barge Canal, and Kirk subsequently persuaded President Richard Nixon to support his position by terminating federal funding for the canal project.[44]

After Kirk's departure, Republicans in the Legislature continued to be visible partners in bipartisan environmental initiatives. The 1974 Legislature passed legislation to protect wetlands and other environmentally sensitive lands with support from the Republican minority, and the Legislature named the measure the "Warren S. Henderson Wetlands Protection Act of 1974" in honor of State Senator and noted Republican environmentalist Warren Henderson.[45]

Republican Representative A. S. "Jim" Robinson sponsored a severance tax initiative that provided mandates to fund the reclamation of lands that

State Senator and future Republican Party Chairman Henry Sayler (*left*) and Senator Warren Henderson (*right*), sponsor of the Wetlands Protection Act, converse on the floor of the Florida Senate. Photo by Don Dughi; courtesy of the State Archives of Florida.

had been mined for phosphate.[46] The Wilson-Grizzle Act, sponsored by Republican Senator Harold Wilson and Republican Representative Mary Grizzle, stopped the runoff of polluted stormwater into the estuary waters of Tampa Bay, leading to its restoration.[47] Legislation sponsored by Republican Representatives Peter Dunbar and R. Z. Safley expanded the state's environmental policies into the saltwater coastal estuaries for protection of the fisheries habitat found below the mean high-water line along Florida's coast; and initiatives sponsored by Republican Senator Jack Latvala and Representative Safley ushered in a new era of regional water supply for the Tampa Bay region.[48] Their water-supply initiative eliminated the region's stresses from the excessive pumping of groundwater and facilitated the construction of new and diversified supply sources that included surface waters and one of the largest desalination facilities in the Western Hemisphere.[49]

During Governor Martinez's term, many of the policy themes were similar to those from the Kirk years, but the Martinez successes were more significant and greater in number.[50] It can be argued that his environmental initiatives were unsurpassed by any prior Florida chief executive in a single term of office. His efforts began with the Surface Water Management and Improvement Act (SWIM). With bipartisan support from the Legislature, the SWIM act was enacted into law in the spring of 1987, creating uniform policies and coordinated procedures to manage and protect Florida's surface waters for the first time.[51] The governor resisted efforts to turn away from Florida's Growth Management Act, and at his direction, Secretary Tom Pelham at the Department of Community Affairs oversaw the final implementation of the act.[52] Martinez also advocated new funding resources for marine research, coastal resource protection, and coastal habitat restoration.[53] He worked for the conservation of threatened and endangered marine life and for the protection of the state's natural coral reefs.[54] He searched for ways to eliminate the sources of ocean dumping and coastal pollution, and he fought vigorously to stop the exploration for oil off the Florida coasts.[55]

In the second year of Governor Martinez's administration, the bureaucratic paralysis among state leaders over the restoration of the Kissimmee River Basin finally started to wane.[56] In that fiscal year, 1989–90, the state budget allocated $8 million for the initial purchase of properties in the Kissimmee floodplain by the South Florida Water Management District. The funding was considered the first step necessary to begin major restoration of the Kissimmee Basin, and it was followed the next year with an additional $5 million to continue the land acquisition phase for the restoration of the wetlands in the river's basin.[57]

Passage of the Preservation 2000 initiative on the final day of the 1990 session of the Florida Legislature marked the crowning achievement in a four-year environmental record for Bob Martinez.[58] When the governor announced the new initiative, support from the environmental community and from the state's daily newspapers was virtually unanimous.

"It's a grandiose scheme to rescue Florida's remaining wild places from the indomitable growth machine that gobbles up earth and spits out condos," observed Booth Gunter of the *Tampa Tribune* following the formal announcement of the initiative.[59]

"Credit Governor Bob Martinez for the political vision to see the need to secure now the state's environmental legacy," opined the *Miami Herald* editorial page.[60]

"If he can convince the Legislature to go along with it, the Governor's so-called Preservation 2000 will stand as a landmark achievement in the struggle to preserve natural Florida from the consequences of the State's rapid growth," echoed the *Gainesville Sun*. "We hope the Legislature will join him in ensuring that large tracts of Florida remain forever in the public trust for future generations to enjoy."

Martinez did convince the Legislature of the program's merits, and the landmark initiative was the last measure passed in 1990 before the Legislature concluded its business and adjourned. The "grandiose scheme" embraced in Preservation 2000 was renewed and expanded during the administration of Governor Jeb Bush, and the initiative was renamed "Florida Forever."[61] In 2014, two and half decades after Governor Martinez introduced the program, the essence of the program was permanently added to the constitution of Florida with overwhelming support from the state's electorate, lifting the environmental legacy to constitutional status.[62] In 2016, legislation sponsored by Republican Senator Charlie Dean provided statutory structure for the new constitutional initiative, and the legislation also included the Florida Springs and Aquifer Protection Act to provide comprehensive protections for Florida's natural springs and other inland water bodies.[63] In the same year, Republican Representative Gayle Harrell and Republican Senator Joe Negron sponsored legislation that established permanent statutory allocations for the funds set aside under the constitutional initiative.[64] By the end of 2017, the combined initiatives of Preservation 2000 and Florida Forever had contributed to the protections of more than 2.4 million acres in Florida.[65]

Focus on the plight of the Florida Everglades began with Claude Kirk and his environmental advisor Nat Reed; it was championed by Democrats Bob Graham and Lawton Chiles during their tenures as governor; and the bipartisan efforts to restore the Everglades continued through the administrations of each successive chief executive.[66] Significant to the restoration efforts during the twenty years that spanned the Republican administra-

Senator Charlie Dean (*left*), sponsor of the Florida Springs and Aquifer Protection Act, and Senator Jack Latvala (*right*), sponsor of regional water supply legislation, confer in the Senate chambers. Photo courtesy of the Florida Senate.

tions of Governors Bush, Crist, and Scott were the reductions in pollutant discharges of phosphorus into the Everglades ecosystem, and during their tenures these discharges were reduced by more than 50 percent.[67] Other innovations ranging from "water farming" to land acquisition for stormwater treatment areas also came to fruition during their Republican administrations, and all the innovations continued the initial steps that had begun with Nat Reed during the administration of Claude Kirk.[68]

Like his Republican predecessors, after his election in 2018, Governor Ron DeSantis also stepped forward to promote a variety of initiatives for the protection of Florida's environment. The day after formally assuming office, he announced his support for the continued funding of the restoration and protection of the Everglades; he created a task force focused on the toxic algae blooms in the state's coastal waters; he called for the creation of a state office to direct integrated scientific research and analysis on the state's environmental priorities; and he appointed a chief science officer to direct the research on current and emerging environment concerns most pressing to Floridians.[69]

Tax Policy and Economic Incentives

In his famous 1964 nationally televised "Time for Choosing" speech in support of Republican presidential nominee Barry Goldwater, Ronald Reagan promoted a message of lowering taxes, fostering a business-friendly environment, and reducing government spending that became the backbone of national Republican Party tax policy.[70] In keeping with this Republican dogma of reduced taxes, economic development incentives, and a business-friendly environment, the modern two-party era in Florida has seen a variety of innovations to complement these themes. Starting with Claude Kirk, Florida Republicans have consistently embraced the messages, and once in power, the record of Republican policymakers has been an aggressive program of tax incentives and tax cuts that has extended from the time of Claude Kirk to the business-friendly administration of Rick Scott.[71]

Republicans believed that less government spending and lower taxes promoted economic growth and placed more dollars back into the hands of private-sector taxpayers. The Republican tax policies were in stark contrast to the actions taken by Democrats throughout the 1970s, 1980s, and early 1990s. During this era of Democratic dominance in the Legislature, Floridians saw an increase of 50 percent in the state's sales tax.[72] There were also increases in the documentary stamp tax on new home purchases; gas tax increases; hotel tax increases; increases in utility taxes; increases in the corporate income tax; new hospital taxes; and an increase in "sin taxes" on both alcohol and cigarettes.[73]

The difference between the parties on taxes was a policy trend that created one of the vital wedge issues that frequently separated Republicans from Democrats on the campaign trail. While Republicans remained in the minority in the Legislature, they represented the loyal opposition in many of the policy debates to increase taxes, and when the Republicans attained a majority in both Houses of the Legislature, the changes to Florida's previous tax policies began to promptly move in the opposite direction.[74]

After securing the majority in both legislative chambers following the 1996 elections, Republicans enacted the first back-to-school "sales-tax holiday" that provided a temporary exemption for school supplies; and for Republicans, it met the basic ideals of promoting economic activity and saving people money.[75] It was an initiative renewed almost every year for more than two decades, and it was followed by similar exemptions and tax-free holidays on other items including online computer services in 1997, agricultural equipment in 1998, hurricane preparedness supplies in 2005, energy-efficiency products in 2007, personal computers and computer accessories in 2013, and college meal plans and children's car seats in 2014.[76] After two decades of sales-tax holidays, Florida Tax Watch, the non-profit, nonpartisan government watchdog, found that these holidays had met their intended objectives and proved to be beneficial not only for Florida consumers but for retail businesses as well by increasing their foot traffic and generating a significant positive economic impact.[77]

With the election of Jeb Bush in 1998, the Republican mantra for tax relief took on an enhanced dimension. The first promise Governor Bush made was to simply never raise taxes, "period."[78] Republican legislators became even more aggressive on tax cuts when the first class of term-limited state lawmakers arrived in the Capitol following the 2000 elections and organized the "Freedom Caucus" to oppose both tax and fee increases.[79] This new dimension of the Republican tax-cut dogma made it easy for Bush and his legislative allies to keep the promise to not raise taxes; to pursue the continuation of the incentives and exemptions that started in 1996; and to reduce and eliminate some taxes altogether.[80]

During his tenure as governor, Jeb Bush placed particular emphasis on eliminating what he called the "insidious," "evil" intangibles tax that had been enacted during the Great Depression on stocks, bonds, and mutual funds.[81] At the time, the tax was seen as a "soak-the-rich tax," but as more and more Floridians relied on stocks and bonds for saving and investing, it was viewed as an increasingly punitive tax on average Floridians. One piece at a time, Bush and his legislative allies engineered the complete repeal of the intangibles tax by 2006, and the ensuing tax savings for Floridians approached $600 million per year.[82] In total during the eight-year tenure of Governor Bush, the combined tax reductions spearheaded by the Governor and Republican legislative majorities reached a total of $19 billion.[83] It was a stark contrast to the prior policies of the Democrats.

The era also saw amendments to the state constitution to provide property tax relief. Notably in 1994, voters approved a constitutional initiative spearheaded by Lee County Republican Property Appraiser Ken Wilkinson, branded "Save Our Homes," that limited the annual increases to the assessed value for homesteaded real estate to 3 percent or to the change in the Consumer Price Index, whichever was lower.[84] The benefits of "Save Our Homes" were expanded significantly just over a decade later during the Senate presidency of Republican Ken Pruitt in a measure sponsored by Senator Mike Haridopolos to amend the state's constitution.[85] The new amendment, approved by the voters in 2008, increased Florida's Homestead exemption from $25,000 to $50,000; it permitted the portability of the accumulated assessment savings from "Save Our Homes" to new home purchases; and it extended the benefits of the amendment to nonhomestead properties by placing a 10 percent cap on tax increases to those properties as well.[86] The Legislature followed these constitutional amendments by offering two more proposed tax exemptions to the voters in 2010 and 2012. These constitutional amendments, too, were approved, and the new provisions provided property tax relief for deployed military personnel and for disabled military veterans.[87]

Tax incentives for new sporting venues were another Republican fiscal innovation. When the two-party era began, Florida was the home of one major professional sports franchise—the Miami Dolphins. By the turn of the twenty-first century, with bipartisan support for the Republican-sponsored tax incentive to facilitate the construction of new stadiums and sports arenas, Florida was home to three NFL football teams, two Major League Baseball teams, two National Hockey League teams, and two National Basketball Association franchises. In the three decades that followed passage of the tax incentive, the newly constructed venues hosted nine Super Bowls, three

World Series, the Major League Baseball All Star game, three NHL Stanley Cup finals, and seven NBA finals.[88] During the same period, Florida teams occupying the venues captured the Stanley Cup, the Super Bowl's Lombardi Trophy, Major League Baseball's World Series Championship trophy, and three NBA Championship trophies. There were other incentives that expanded beyond the world of sports, too.

Changes to the state's corporate income tax offered tax relief to Florida employers; they provided incentives for economic development; and they offered new educational choices through opportunity scholarships for Florida students. Exemptions and credits to the 5.5 percent corporate tax rate were offered to create jobs in rural and intercity areas; to encourage research and development activities; to provide community revitalization incentives; and to create and retain jobs in the private business sector.[89] There were also tax incentives for farm machinery used in agricultural production; incentives for the space and semi-conductor industries; incentives for manufacturing equipment; incentives for new and expanded renewable energy facilities; and initiatives to incentivize the cleanup of contaminated "brownfield" sites.[90] Beginning in 2001, the first Republican-sponsored tax incentives were enacted to promote the educational choice policies championed by Governor Bush, and the incentives provided credits for corporations making donations to non-profit scholarship-funding organizations.[91] The new incentives became the foundation for student choices under the Florida Tax Credit Scholarships and Opportunity Scholarships programs; and by 2010, these incentives had been expanded to provide $140 million in tax-credit scholarship programs for Florida students.[92]

The Republican commitment to avoid tax increases and provide tax relief that began during the era of Jeb Bush continued under his successors, particularly during the administration of Governor Rick Scott. During Scott's two terms in office, the sales tax holidays were continued and expanded; new tax credits and corporate income tax exemptions were directed at economic development; Florida motor vehicle owners received a reduction in their annual tag fees; and the Florida Tax Credit Scholarship Program begun under Governor Bush was expanded.[93]

By 2017, as Scott's second term neared its conclusion, Florida's bonded indebtedness had been reduced by $10 billion, and Florida residents could claim that they paid "the third-lowest total taxes at $2.385 per capita" in the country.[94] The state's overall tax policy was summarized by Florida Tax Watch president and chief executive officer Dominic Calabro in the spring of 2017 this way: "Florida's tax climate makes it an attractive option for families and businesses alike. A lower tax burden allows businesses to create more jobs and expand, while allowing taxpayers to have more money in their pockets that can then be spent and funneled back into the economy."[95]

For Republican leaders, Calabro's summary was a validation of their tax policy objectives.[96]

Education Innovations

With the bipartisan support from the Republican minority to improve Florida's public schools and its institutions of higher learning, the Pork Chop era of stagnation and segregation was left behind. So, too, was the disparate funding for the state's sixty-seven school districts. In 1974, bipartisan support helped to ensure adequate funding for all of the state's school districts when the Legislature enacted the Florida Education Finance Program (FEFP) that became the permanent foundation for the state's public education funding.[97] It was an achievement that had not been possible during the Pork Chop era, and through the ensuing decades, other education innovations followed the FEFP.[98] Some enhanced funding, others provided new opportunities for Florida students, and all had Republican support or began as Republican initiatives.

In 1987, following the election of Florida's second Republican governor, the Martinez administration was charged with organizing the new Florida Lottery. The Lottery had been created when voters approved its authorizing constitutional amendment in the fall 1986, and the state-sponsored gambling initiative was billed as an initiative to enhance the funding of the state's public education system. It fell to the administration of Bob Martinez to implement the constitutional amendment, and the governor designated Lieutenant Governor Brantley to oversee the administration's efforts.

"We opposed the Lottery during the campaign," remembered Brantley, "but we promised to implement it like a business if it passed to maximize the funding for public education. It was like starting a Fortune 100 company from the ground up. We had to find a building; hire the staff; and resist more government control by the Legislature so it would operate like a successful business."[99]

As implementation began, Brantley took charge of the project and served as the first Lottery secretary, and in his new role, he awarded the check to the first million-dollar winner on a day when he forgot his wallet and had no money in his pocket.[100] From its inception, the Florida Lottery met the objectives of Governor Martinez and his administration, and through the first three decades of the Lottery's operation, it grew to become an industry leader and has contributed more than $30 billion to Florida's public education system.[101] Even with the new monies produced by the Lottery, however, "decades of Democratic dominance in Florida politics had not brought serious change to Florida's education system."[102] That changed when Republicans became the majority in the Florida Senate during the 1994–96 term, and the first charter school authorization was enacted under the sponsorship of Senate Education Committee Chairman Don Sullivan.[103] Under the initiative, elementary and secondary schools operating under state-approved performance contracts offered students new options not previously available in Florida. The options included theme-based, technology-rich curriculums accompanied by rigorous instructional methods. The curriculums provided specialized and innovative academic programs free from many of the traditional regulations, while preserving the basic accountability standards for the academic results of their student populations. From their beginning, charter schools found a relevant place in the state's educational offerings; and since their initial authorization, they are among the state's fastest-growing school choice options. By the 2015–16 school year, Florida had more than 270,000 students enrolled in more than 652 charter schools that had been created under the Republican education initiative sponsored by Senator Sullivan.[104]

Innovations to the state's education system extended beyond charter schools under the new Republican majority. In 1997 and a decade into the Lottery's successful implementation, Republican State Representative Ken Pruitt originated an innovation with legislation that capitalized on the Lot-

Bright Futures sponsor Representative Ken Pruitt (*right*) visiting with House Speaker and future U.S. Senator Marco Rubio (*left*) on the House podium. Photo courtesy of the Florida Historic Capitol Museum.

tery's success. His initiative created the Florida's Bright Futures Scholarship Program, funded solely from Lottery proceeds. Under the Bright Futures Program, college scholarships were made available to academically qualifying Florida high school students to continue their higher education in the state's community colleges and universities.[105]

When Jeb Bush arrived in the governor's office two years later, "he saw the issue of education as a way of testing new conservative ideas," and more education initiatives emerged following his election in 1998. At the core of his new reforms was the A+ Plan. Its basic premise was accountability based on student assessment tests, and it became the number-one priority during the governor's first year in office.[106] The specific criteria in the A+ Plan called for letter grades to be assigned to schools based upon assessment tests, and schools were ranked from A to F with incentive funding available for those achieving the top rankings.

The A+ Plan also permitted students attending F-rated schools to transfer to another public school with a rating of C or better; it made vouchers available from public funds for students in F-rated schools to attend private schools; and it included a merit pay raise program for teachers based upon the performance of their students. Although the initial voucher plan that relied on public funding was ultimately found to be unconstitutional, it was later replaced by the Florida Tax Credit Scholarship Program, which relied on private funds; and the new Tax Credit Scholarship Program did not restrict the vouchers only to students from F-rated schools.[107] Following the implementation of these reforms advocated by Bush, Florida's public school system provided more options for students than at any time in the state's history, and other programs for students with special educational needs followed.

In 1999, Republican Senator John McKay pioneered a new school voucher program for students with a wide range of disabilities. Once enacted, the McKay Scholarship Program provided meaningful new choices and opportunities for students with intellectual disabilities, speech and language impairments, behavioral disabilities and limitations, and autism spectrum disorders. These choices afforded the students options to attend eligible public and private schools and to pursue meaningful educational opportunities that otherwise had not been available.[108] It was the first program of its kind in the country, and by the 2015–16 school year, more than thirty thousand students were taking advantage of the opportunities in the McKay Scholarship Program.[109]

The educational offerings for students with disabilities were expanded even further during the tenure of Republican Senate President Andy Gardiner in 2016. Under program elements of the Gardiner Scholarship Program, new funding was made available to customize educational programs for students and to provide specialized services such as speech and occupational therapy, instructional materials, and tuition at eligible private schools for qualifying students.[110] The Gardiner Scholarship Program also included postsecondary educational opportunities for students. Funding was set aside to start programs at Florida's colleges and universities for students with special needs and "unique abilities," and among the initial institutions establishing programs were the University of Central Florida and the University of North Florida.[111]

The Career and Professional Employment Act (CAPE Act) was the brainchild of Republican Senator Don Gaetz, and it became another innovation from the Republican majority for the state's public education system.[112] Beginning in 2007, the CAPE Act set out to change the image of the vocational technical model offered in Florida high schools from a "second-class option with second-rate teachers and second-rate students" to one that attracted college-bound students as well as those on a vocational track.[113] The CAPE Act pioneered programs where students earned industry-recognized certifications; it refined educational offerings to competencies

Sponsor of the CAPE Act, Senator Don Gaetz (*left*), confers with Senator John McKay (*right*), sponsor of the scholarship initiative for students with special needs, on the floor of the Senate chambers as Senator Charlie Dean (*center rear*) looks on. Photo courtesy of the Florida Senate.

needed by area employers; and it created internships and apprenticing opportunities in businesses that matched educational offerings with the skills needed in the workplace.[114] From its modest first year that saw only 954 certificates earned, participation increased steadily, and by the 2015–16 school year, more than 367,000 students were participating in the program.[115]

Florida's colleges and universities system saw changes, too. Florida Polytechnic University was authorized as the twelfth institution in the State University System; and new medical schools were authorized at Florida State University, the University of Central Florida, and Florida International University.[116] The college of law, eliminated in the closing years of the Pork Chop era, was restored at Florida A&M University after a thirty-five-year hiatus.[117] A new college of law was authorized at Florida International University dedicated to provide opportunities "for minorities to attain representation within the legal profession"; and new colleges of engineering and business were approved at Florida Gulf Coast University.[118] In 2001, the curriculum was also expanded in the state's community college system by authorizing four-year degree programs and making degree options more accessible for Florida students.[119]

Crime and Criminal Justice

In the criminal justice arena, Republicans championed reforms and offered new policy alternatives in the name of public safety, and it began during Claude Kirk's gubernatorial campaign with his "War on Crime" platform plank. Kirk's campaign message was for safer communities for Florida residents. After his election, it was highlighted in his first speech to the joint session of the Florida Legislature in April 1967, and the messaging continued in Kirk's words and pronouncements in many of his public appearances as governor.[120] There was a focus on confronting organized crime activities in the state; Kirk advocated compensation for crime victims; and his administration saw the creation of the Florida Bureau of Law Enforcement as the state's first statewide law enforcement agency.[121]

Faced with a Legislature controlled by the opposition party, the balance of Kirk's "War on Crime" initiatives met with only limited success, but the "tough-on-crime" and public safety mantra had found a permanent home in the Republican Party platform.[122] It was a theme that resurfaced consistently in the Republican administrations that followed, and it was in contrast to the Democratic administrations that preceded them.

Following Claude Kirk in the intervening years of Democratic Governors Askew and Graham, little attention was afforded to the state's criminal justice system or the state's rising crime rate, and this lack of attention helped to strengthen the Republican Party's relationship with Florida voters.[123] By the time Bob Martinez was seated as Florida's second Republican governor in 1987, Florida's prison system was in disarray. The system was badly overcrowded; the food service was deemed to be constitutionally deficient; medical care for inmates was found to be substandard; and the entire corrections system had been under continuous scrutiny from the federal courts for more than a decade.[124] From 1971 through 1986, only 5,574 new prison beds were actually funded by the Legislature to house the influx of more than 30,000 new prisoners, and as the end of 1986 approached under the administration of Governor Graham, prisoners were serving only about 30 percent of their actual sentences.[125] It fell to the new Republican governor to confront these challenges that had manifested during the terms of his predecessors.

Within a matter of months after Martinez assumed office, a special session of the Legislature was called and new policies were enacted to stop the indiscriminate release of hardened inmates; the initial steps to stabilize the Department of Corrections were begun under the new department secretary, Richard Dugger; and by 1990, the construction of 27,000 new prison beds had been authorized.[126] As Martinez's term came to an end, the reforms for the system were being implemented; new prisons were under construction; and within three years, control of Florida's corrections system had been relinquished back to the state from the federal courts.[127]

Other criminal justice initiatives of note occurred during the Martinez administration. The Crime Prevention and Law Enforcement Study Commission, chaired by former FBI agent Phil McNiff, was created to evaluate new crime-prevention initiatives. There were new and innovative programs to support the victims of criminal acts; Martinez placed a strong emphasis on combating the use and sale of illegal drugs; and there was a renewed com-

Governor Bob Martinez with his legislative affairs staff with the bills from the 1990 session, including the Preservation 2000 legislation and initiatives from the Crime Prevention and Law Enforcement Study Commission. *Left to right:* Mike Gomez, General Counsel Peter Dunbar, Tom Katina, Mark Purvis, and Legislative Affairs Director Amy Baker. Photo courtesy of the Gomez family collection.

mitment to carrying out the death penalty, which included the execution of serial killer Ted Bundy.[128]

To deal with the long delays in death-penalty appeals, Martinez made diligent efforts to process death warrants and designated Deputy General Counsel Andrea Hillyer to push the sequence of appeals that impeded the process. During his four years, the governor signed 139 warrants to bring Florida's death-row inmates closer to their final punishment.[129]

In 1988, Florida voters passed the Victims' Rights Amendment to the state constitution, and following its passage, Governor Martinez initiated a blueprint for implementing its provisions as well.[130] First, by executive order, Martinez created the Governor's Coordinating Council on Victims'

Rights and Services and designated Deborah Huey from his staff as its executive director.[131] The Council's purpose was to assist with the orderly implementation of the new rights and services for victims embraced by the amendment and to help with efforts to reorganize and consolidate existing programs on victims' rights.

The implementing legislation that Martinez signed into law after the passage of the constitutional amendment guaranteed the opportunity for victims to be present and to be heard at all stages of the criminal justice process; it extended to victims the right to submit an impact statement concerning the effects of the crime on the victim; it gave victims the right to testify at parole hearings and be notified when a criminal was being released; and it afforded the victim of a crime the opportunity to seek restitution for the damages caused by the criminal act.[132] During the tenure of Governor Martinez, Florida also increased its funding for the Crime Compensation Trust Fund to compensate victims for their losses; and within less than two years under his stewardship, Florida had effectively implemented a new and unified foundation for victims' rights embraced by the constitutional amendment.[133]

Focus on Florida's illicit drug problems had been predominantly one-dimensional, with an emphasis on tougher penalties and longer prison sentences, before Martinez arrived in the governor's office, but without capacity in the state's prisons, the concept of tougher penalties was little more than a hollow reply to an escalating problem. During Martinez's years, the emphasis changed, and in addition to the construction of new prison facilities, the state's antidrug strategy took on a new multidimensional approach. Its foundation was the governor's fifteen-member Drug Policy Task Force.[134] From the Task Force's deliberations came support for initiatives that included drug-free school zones.[135] A year later, it included the expansion of the drug-free zones to public housing projects, university campuses, public parks, and public recreation areas.[136] The Legislature enacted a drug-free workplace initiative advocated by the governor; and the governor's multidimensional approach was evident in such social-awareness programs as "Project Graduation," "Safe Homes," and the "Red Ribbon Campaign" from the Florida Informational Parents Network.[137]

The governor's antidrug strategy included initiatives on the supply side of the drug equation and put renewed emphasis on the interdiction efforts of law enforcement. The governor directed the use of prison inmate labor to help with the destruction of "crack houses," and he introduced new cooperative interdiction efforts involving the Florida National Guard and the federal military. For the most notorious of the drug traffickers—those moving the largest volumes of illicit drugs (150 kilograms of cocaine or 30 kilograms of heroin or other narcotics)—Governor Martinez advocated the death penalty, and in 1990, the Legislature enacted his recommendation into law.[138]

Between 1990 and 2009 and building on the reforms from the Martinez era, the length of time served by inmates in Florida prisons increased dramatically by 166 percent, and with an appropriately functioning corrections system, more new laws assured that the state's prison facilities were put to use.[139] With the arrival of Governor Jeb Bush and Republican majorities in both legislative bodies, the "tough-on-crime" message took on new dimensions both for criminals and for citizens seeking the right to protect themselves from criminal conduct.

Governor Bush began his administration by implementing his "10-20-Life" campaign pledge.[140] Under the governor's initiative, a person convicted of a crime while carrying a gun received a mandatory ten-year prison sentence, a twenty-year sentence if the gun was fired, and a sentence of twenty-five years to life if a person was injured or killed by gunfire during the commission of a crime.[141] As the Bush era continued, there were also initiatives to increase mandatory minimum prison sentences for career criminals; new penalties for gang-related criminal activity; and new criminal penalties for cyber-stalking.[142]

Beyond harsher penalties for the criminal elements in the population, there were also significant and controversial new protections for gun owners, and gun rights became a central tenet as "Governor Bush and the Republican legislature methodically and completely changed gun regulation in Florida during his terms."[143] It began with a measure that expanded the right of Florida citizens to carry concealed weapons;[144] it was followed by Republican Senator Charlie Bronson's initiative that extended the right to carry a concealed firearm to non-Floridians;[145] and "the most comprehen-

"Castle Doctrine" sponsor Senator Dennis Baxley (*right*) conferring on the Senate floor with Senator David Simmons (*left*). Photo courtesy of the Florida Senate.

sive and controversial gun legislation during Bush's tenure, the law known as "Stand-Your-Ground," was enacted in 2005, when the Legislature, with the support of the governor, vastly expanded the so-called "Castle Doctrine."[146] Sponsored in the House by Republican Representative Dennis Baxley, the expanded Castle Doctrine allowed citizens to stand their ground in the face of an imminent peril of death or great bodily harm, and it permitted Floridians to use deadly force to defend themselves from the imminent peril.[147]

Despite the controversies, the emphasis on public safety, the "tough-on-crime" initiatives, and the protections for gun owners remained a constant part of the Republican criminal justice dogma. Over time the Republican criminal justice initiatives produced palpable results, and there was visible satisfaction among Republican officials as they reflected on the changes in the crime rate.[148] From the time that the Florida Department of Law Enforcement began tracking the state's crime statistics in 1971, the drop in Florida's crime rate into the early decades of the twenty-first century was discernible. In the department's 2014 annual report, the crime rate had stabilized at its lowest point in the modern two-party political era.[149] By 2018, during Governor Scott's last year in office, Florida's crime rate had continued to drop, and it reached a forty-seven-year low as the governor was concluding his tenure as the state's chief executive.[150]

Acknowledging Injustice

As the two-party era matured, a different side of the criminal justice system became evident. This dimension, too, contrasted with the segregationist policies of the earlier era of the Pork Chop Gang. Three examples of the different side of the system were found in the release of James Richardson from Florida's death row; the public exoneration of the men known as the Groveland Four; and the acknowledgment and subsequent apology for the brutality and abuses that had occurred in the juvenile detention centers at the Dozier School in Marianna and the Florida School for Boys in Okeechobee.

In 1988, when the racial overtones and the prosecutorial misconduct in the case of itinerant farm laborer James Richardson were brought to the attention of Governor Bob Martinez, he appointed State Attorney Janet Reno as a special prosecutor to reopen the case. Reno's investigation confirmed the miscarriage of justice in the case, and her report to the governor and presentation to the court led to Richardson's release after nearly two decades in prison.[151] In the process of reopening the case, Martinez was able to help find some measure of justice for a man whom the criminal justice system had all but forgotten.[152]

Two other miscarriages of justice from the dark times of an earlier era were addressed with the unanimous bipartisan support from both political parties during the 2017 legislative session.[153] The first involved the 1949 case of Charles Greenlee, Walter Irvin, Samuel Shepherd, and Ernest Thomas— four African Americans known as the "Groveland Four"—all of whom were accused of the rape of a young white woman that they did not commit. In what Republican Representative Chris Sprowls described as one of Florida's "greatest moral failings," two of the men were murdered under the watch of racially motivated Lake County Sheriff Willis McCall, and the other two were ultimately convicted of the crime.[154]

When the full depth of the miscarriage of justice was revealed in Gilbert King's Pulitzer Prize–winning book *Devil in the Grove*, the current era of public officials stepped forward to address the injustices.[155] In a resolution brought to the House of Representatives by Democratic Representative Bobby DuBose and Republican Representative Jason Fischer, and cosponsored by 117 of their legislative colleagues, the House of Representatives unanimously issued formal apologies to all four members of the Groveland Four and their families.[156] In addition to the apologies, the resolution also called for the expedited clemency of the Groveland Four to provide complete exoneration for the miscarriage of justice that the four men had endured in the earlier era of the Pork Chop Gang.[157] At the first meeting of the Florida cabinet following his inauguration, Governor Ron DeSantis was joined by Chief Financial Officer Jimmy Patronis, Attorney General Ashley Moody, and Agriculture Commissioner Nikki Fried in unanimously granting the clemency.[158]

The other "shameful part of Florida history" addressed during the 2017 legislative session was the systematic abuse that had occurred at the Dozier School for Boys in Marianna, which opened in 1900, and the Florida School for Boys at Okeechobee, which opened in 1955.[159] The abuses included frequent brutal beatings, widespread mental and sexual abuse, and more than fifty suspicious deaths that took place between the 1940s and the 1960s. In a similar bipartisan effort, the myriad of injustices at Dozier and Okeechobee were addressed in twin legislative initiatives, one sponsored by Democratic Representative Tracie Davis, joined by 116 of her colleagues in the Florida House, and the other sponsored by Republican Representative Shawn Harrison and Democratic Representative Cynthia Stafford. When passed unanimously, the Davis concurrent resolution issued a formal public apology for the multitude of institutional abuses that had occurred in the earlier era.[160] The Harrison-Stafford legislation supplemented the formal apology with state funding for the internment of the inmates' remains discovered at the Dozier School and funds for the placement of permanent monuments in both Marianna and Tallahassee to assure that the brutal transgressions from an earlier era would not be forgotten.[161]

Extending Consumer Protections

Over the decades of the modern era, there were also protections for Floridians that reached beyond the realm of criminal conduct, and these were significant, too. Some of the protections created marketplace balance for Florida home buyers, and others created safety nets for vulnerable and aging Floridians.

The initial consumer protections in Florida's Condominium and Cooperative Acts that passed in 1976 were the bipartisan work product of Democratic Representative Alan Becker and Republican Representative Curt Kiser.[162] The initial statutory protections for the state's mobile-home owners that passed the same year were sponsored by Representative Kiser; and the comprehensive protections of the Florida Mobile Home Act enacted in 1984 and the initial regulation of community association managers that passed in 1987 were also Republican-sponsored initiatives.[163]

Once in the majority in both chambers, Republicans introduced new laws to expand protections for senior citizens, persons with disabilities, and military service members and their families from deceptive and unfair trade practices.[164] Republican Senator Joe Negron passed a measure to protect citizens from unauthorized surveillance by drones.[165] New penalties were put into place to prevent price-gouging during periods of declared emergency; and consumer reforms to the state's foreclosure laws were enacted to protect Florida homeowners.[166] A series of protections were also added to the "bill of rights" for persons with developmental disabilities, residents of assisted-living facilities, residents of nursing homes, and residents of adult family care homes after Republican majorities came to the Legislature.[167]

Initiatives by Republican State Representative Kathleen Passidomo and Republican State Senator Nancy Detert reformed and modernized Florida's guardianship laws to protect Floridians who were unable to act

Representative and future State Senator Kathleen Passidomo presents the guardianship reform initiative to her colleagues in the House chamber. Passidomo family collection.

on their own behalf.[168] New safeguards were enacted to protect minors from abuse; enhanced services were put in place for those children who had been abused; and measures were enacted to protect other vulnerable Floridians from exploitation by guardians and other agents who were authorized to act on their behalf. These were also sponsored by Representative Passidomo.[169]

This collection of consumer protection measures, combined with the traditional "tough-on-crime" initiatives that began with Claude Kirk and were continued through other Republican administrations, are part of the legacy of policy changes that matured as Republicans strengthened their majority status in Tallahassee. Each represented a tangible policy change consistent with the Republican core messages to protect Floridians and provide a safer living environment.

The Legacy from the Strategic War of Ideas

When Republicans arrived on the political scene in Florida, their ideas for change and reform arrived with them—party campaign platform planks called for changes to stagnant policies on the environment, changes to a struggling public education system, reforms for a deteriorating criminal justice system, and changes to other political doctrine that had dominated since the end of Reconstruction. Before the Republicans arrived in the state Capitol in meaningful numbers, the Legislature had been badly malapportioned, and Florida's executive branch government was little more than a hodgepodge of random boards, commissions, departments, and executive offices. There were no choices for students in the state's one-dimensional education system; and the state's correctional system was deteriorating. At the beginning of the new era, Florida was without meaningful laws to protect much of its environment—phosphate miners had no mandates or incentives to reclaim the land being mined; Florida's sensitive submerged lands were being sold off to private developers for dredge-and-fill projects; there were no policies to protect or restore the Everglades; no policies had been enacted to protect the state's wetlands; and there was no cleanup responsibility imposed on those who spilled pollutants into Florida's coastal seaports. With the emergence of Republicanism, it all began to change.

The Republicans contributed initially to the bipartisan effort to present a new constitution to Florida voters, and after the ratification of the new constitution by the electorate in 1968, Republican policymakers contributed to the modernization of all three branches of state government during the ensuing legislative sessions. Changing the status quo of other policies also followed. Beginning with Claude Kirk and early-era Republicans like Bill Young, Don Reed, Mary Grizzle, Harold Wilson, Jim Robinson, and Warren Henderson, the void in environmental policies began to be filled.

Republicans who followed like Bob Martinez, Jeb Bush, Jack Latvala, R. Z. Safley, Charlie Dean, David Simmons, Gail Harrell, and Joe Negron continued to sustain the party's environmental priorities as Republicans transitioned into the majority.

During the Pork Chop era, the policy stagnations were not just in the environmental arena, and these other stagnations, too, began to be addressed. Republicans contributed to bipartisan efforts with urban Democrats to facilitate some changes, but on other reforms, there was little or no Democratic support, and Republicans ultimately prevailed with changes that were uniquely their own. In the criminal justice arena during the tenure of Bob Martinez, bipartisan responses to the state's deteriorating corrections system saw new policies implemented to stabilize the system, new rights were enacted for the victims of crime, and Florida began to adopt a new view toward crime and criminals. Under the spectrum of Republican ideas when the century turned, bipartisan alliances with Democrats played no meaningful role in the expansion of the rights for Florida gun owners, and there was no bipartisan support for the expansion of the Castle Doctrine that permitted Floridians to "stand their ground" in the face of threats to their property and personal safety.

In the early decades of the political era, Republicans were bipartisan contributors to initiatives that stabilized the funding for the state's public education system, but as Jeb Bush's second term came to an end, the roots of the other alternative ideas became exclusively Republican. School-choice initiatives were introduced and grew significantly as the new century unfolded in the Capitol. Under the Republican-sponsored education proposals, Florida students were afforded more options for their education than at any time in history; there were new opportunities for those students with disabilities and special abilities that had not existed during earlier eras; and the Republican education mantra for accountability in the public education system contrasted significantly with the policies that preceded it under a Democratic majority.

The Republican commitment to reduce taxes, limit the size of government, and modernize the institutions of governance took on new meaning during the Bush administration. New technologies were implemented to manage the business of state agencies; and when the government reforms by the Bush administration were fully implemented, taxes were lowered, the size of state government was reduced, and the new policy trend to limit the size of government continued consistently through the administration of Governor Rick Scott.

In retrospect, Florida is radically different as the result of transition into an era of two-party politics. In the strategic battle of ideas, Florida has been transformed by the Republicans and the ideas they brought with them. Some of the changes have been universally accepted; some were made possible with bipartisan support; others have been considered controversial; and still others have been trend-setting, not only in Florida but around the country. Reflecting on the modern history of the two-party system in Florida, the impact of the Republican contributions has been palpable, and the policies of the modern era bear little resemblance to those that existed prior to their arrival.

10

CHALLENGES IN AN
EVER-CHANGING POLITICAL
ENVIRONMENT

THE FIRST ITERATION of Republicanism that appeared in Florida in 1865 was radically different from the second Republican emergence that came nearly a century later. The national issues of the day that followed the Civil War dictated the Republican presence in the South during Reconstruction, and when the Reconstruction era came to an end with the election of Rutherford B. Hayes, the southern Republican voice disappeared.[1] Basically, Republicans appeared in majority status in a virtual political instant at the end of the Civil War, and their presence vanished as quickly as it had appeared. The Republicans neither began as a minority voice in the state's political arena in the 1860s, nor did they claim any role following the end of Reconstruction. The initial Republican voice in Florida simply disappeared from the political landscape.

In contrast, the modern version of the Republican Party emerged differently, and it has maintained a sustained presence for more than a half century. The modern version of Florida Republicanism was built as an organization; it planted political roots in a growing network of party loyalists; it offered a meaningful alternative to an unorganized Democratic majority; and, with the Republican Party's emergence, the pendulum of political power began to swing in a new direction.

An Eye on the Pendulum's Arc

Once the shift began in earnest, it took only three decades for the pendulum to move from the Democratic dominance of the Pork Chop Gang to an era of alternative Republican governance. The collective factors that brought the Republican Party to prominence were dynamic and multifaceted, and each facet contributed to the party's emergence. The population growth and the changing partisan demographics that accompanied it contributed to the Republican cause.[2] The commitment to an effective party organization permitted Republicans to take advantage of the organizational void left by Florida Democrats.[3] Republican regulars refined and implemented campaign fund-raising and communication techniques; and the Republican Party and its candidates maintained consistent philosophical messaging on core issues as the momentum of the political pendulum moved away from the Democrats.[4]

In each of these facets, there were setbacks along the way for Republicans, and the arc of the pendulum did not always swing in a Republican direction. The changing population demographics were not always beneficial to the Republican base, and there were intraparty struggles like those between Claude Kirk and Congressman Bill Cramer. The shadow of the national Watergate scandal had impacts and brought reductions to the number of Republicans serving in the state capital; there were Democratic legislative leaders like Don Tucker and Harry Johnston who made concerted efforts to isolate Republican voices; and the embarrassment of Jim Greer's tenure as the state Republican Party chairman tempered the party's ability to fundraise for its candidates. But unlike their first appearance on Florida's political landscape, Republicans in the modern era were better prepared; persevered in the face of challenges; and overcame the setbacks along their path to the majority.[5]

Beginning with the elections in 1996 and 1998, two decades of Republican control in both the executive and legislative branches of state gov-

294 THE MODERN REPUBLICAN PARTY IN FLORIDA

ernment followed. Republican majorities in the House and Senate that began with one-vote margins quickly grew to margins that left them unchallenged as the dominant voice of both legislative chambers into the new century.[6] Entering the 2018 election cycle, Florida had not elected a Democrat governor since 1994, and the Democrats had lost fourteen of the last fifteen statewide cabinet races, leaving a clear Republican legacy in Florida's executive branch agencies.[7]

As the second decade of Republican dominance in Florida's capital neared its close in 2018, however, there were signs that the swing of the political pendulum might trend back toward the Democrats and a more competitive political environment. These signs included concerns that some of the new Republican policies had become too extreme; that the political leanings of Florida's newly arriving populations might not align with Republican policies; and that changes in the Republican Party's organizational structure had left a void in fund-raising and campaign expertise. There were signs, too, of a return to intraparty struggles between members of the majority Republican Party like those that had appeared in the ranks of the Democrats at the beginning of the two-party era.[8]

Projecting what the future may hold for the Republican majority became speculative at best as the new century's third decade loomed; and continued Republican dominance became dependent on the ability of its network to adapt to evolving changes in the political arena as it had in earlier decades. It also became dependent on the ability of the Republican network to persevere and overcome the setbacks that materialize in the ever-changing world of partisan politics.

Modernizing the Messages

Consistent messaging that connected with Florida voters was important to the Republicans' rise to majority status.[9] At the beginning of the modern era, getting loyalist voters to the polls and encouraging swing voters to support Republican candidates on Election Day involved effective messaging. Republicans relied on the themes found in the planks of the party platform, and consistent messaging on these main themes served the party's candidates well as Republicans rose in prominence.[10] The conversion of the campaign messages into new state policies followed and manifested themselves initially in coalitions with the urban Democrats while Republicans remained in the minority. In time, however, the bipartisan coalitions became less frequent. Once Republicans attained the majority, changes in state policies became more pronounced, and the philosophical distinctions between the Republican and Democratic Party platforms grew wider in contrast.[11]

During the years of Republican control, Florida's education options continued to evolve; the rights for individuals to protect their property and personal safety were expanded; taxes and the size of state government were continually reduced; and there were new incentives created for Florida's business community that encouraged job growth in the private sector.[12] Water conservation, water quality, and restoration of the Everglades remained dominant environmental priorities during the Republicans' tenure in the majority; and following the 2018 announcement from the Trump administration of its intent to permit oil drilling off the Florida coastline, Republicans, led by Governor Rick Scott, renewed their opposition to the federal plan as Governor Bob Martinez had done three decades earlier.[13]

On environmental issues, there has been little contrast between the two political parties on the major initiatives during the years of Republican dominance, and new environmental policies continued to find bipartisan support in the modern era. Initiatives included the Florida Springs and Aquifer Protection Act, permanent funding for the state's land and water conservation programs, and continued restoration of the Everglades.[14] Each was enacted without partisan wrangling. In response to the Republican opposition to offshore oil exploration espoused by Governor Scott in 2018, the bipartisan cooperation extended to that issue as well, and the Democratic answer was little more than "me too." Yet in other areas of policy, the contrast and countermessaging by Democrats continued to grow and become more apparent and more acute.[15]

Democrats maintained that the evolving Republican education policies diverted needed funding from the state's public education system and that school-choice policies threatened to erode Florida's commitment to public education.[16] The Democratic response to the reduction in the tax base and the size of state government was that these Republican policies meant the loss of meaningful government services; and the Democratic counter-messages to the Republican criminal justice policies and the expansion of rights for Floridians to carry personal firearms was that the policies threatened public safety and that more gun control was the appropriate policy alternative.[17]

Through the 2016 election cycle, Democrats struggled to find effective messages to unify voters behind their candidates, and the countermessages they offered produced little meaningful impact on the election outcomes.[18] As qualifying for the 2018 elections approached, however, current events on the national scene and the tragic shooting at the Marjory Stoneman Douglas High School in Broward County became potential harbingers of change in Florida's political arena.[19] Following the shooting, an emotional outpouring from the tragedy renewed the focus on a generation of Republican policies and the "right to bear arms" mantra from the National Rifle Association. The Democratic alternative message of gun control seemed to take on new life, and Democrats made an all-out effort "to put Republicans on record as opposing a ban on the sale of assault weapons, believing it [could] change the outcome of elections in a year that already appeared very uncertain for Republicans."[20] Once the votes had been tabulated, however, the contrasting debate on the right to bear arms versus more stringent gun control produced little change in the partisan makeup of Florida's legislative chambers, where Republicans continued to maintain comfortable margins.[21]

Another element of uncertainty for Florida Republicans had, on occasion, been tied to messages emanating from Washington. Concerns about impacts from national political debates have been present from the outset of the modern era when the Democrats moved Florida's statewide elections to the off-presidential election years beginning in 1966. While both political parties have been sensitive to the personalities and issues on the national scene, the "coattail" effect from national trends has historically been minimal on in-state elections, but there have been exceptions. For Republicans, there were noticeable benefits during the tenure of President Ronald Reagan and noticeable negative impacts following the events of Watergate and the resignation of Richard Nixon; otherwise national politics had little influence on Republicans in the Florida political arena. Following the 2016 election of Donald Trump, attention once again focused on the national scene and the administration of President Trump. With the renewed focus came widespread speculation among pundits that a "Blue Wave" for Democrats would push the Florida statewide elections in a Democratic direction in 2018.[22]

The unorthodox and polarizing style of the Trump administration created new rallying points for the opposition on issues ranging from immigration to gun control, and from international affairs to domestic racial relations. As the 2018 midterm elections approached, Democrats believed President Trump had become a decisive issue in the erosion of the Republican base and the foundation for new opportunities for Florida Democrats.[23] The belief that Trump's style could impact the midterm elections further was enhanced when Ron DeSantis, Trump's hand-picked candidate to succeed Governor Rick Scott, captured the Republican gubernatorial nomination.[24]

Not lost on Republicans and perhaps overlooked by pundits and pollsters, however, were the new Floridians like those retiring to communities like The Villages in central Florida—identified as the fastest-growing metropolitan area in the United States in 2016—where voters delivered support for Trump by a margin of 39 percent over his opponent in 2016.[25] The unanswered questions as the elections of 2018 approached were (1) the extent to which the debate on the national scene might impact the ballot box in Florida election contests; (2) the extent to which the DeSantis nomination might bring the Trump factor into the governor's race; and (3) the extent to which the national debate might undercut the efforts of Republicans and Governor Rick Scott to unseat incumbent Democratic U.S. Senator Bill Nelson.

How voters aligned or realigned behind the contrasting messages and personalities offered by the political parties during the 2018 campaign cycle remained an open question until the votes were tabulated.[26] In the end, there was no "Blue Wave" creating a tidal surge to wash away Republican majorities in the Legislature; victory in the governor's race by Trump's hand-picked candidate dispelled the belief that national politics would reverse the trend in the Florida political arena; Rick Scott's narrow victory in the U.S. Senate race gave Republicans both U.S. Senate seats for the first time; and the arc of the pendulum edged in the Republican direction once again.[27]

Adapting to Changes in the Arena

Historically, another key factor in the Republicans' rise to power had been their ability to seize upon the void in the party structure left by the Democrats, and much of the Republicans' success during the modern political era can be attributed to the Republican Party's formal organization.[28] The organized Republican network was the vehicle that developed campaign professionals; it was the catalyst to raise the funds for its candidates; and it was the organization that turned out voters on Election Day. Republicans systematically assembled a network of local organizations; they activated clubs for party loyalists and volunteers; and the party recruited and trained a staff of political consultants, fund-raisers, and field operatives to support Republican candidates and their campaigns.[29] The organized network served Republicans well as they transitioned into the majority, but maintaining party structure as an effective campaign tool faced new challenges as the new century brought innovations to the political arena.

Among the new challenges was the relocation of campaign technicians and consultants to offices outside the formal party structure.[30] In the early decades of the new century, the maturing cadre of campaign advisors and consultants was increasingly found in a series of independent consulting operations; notable among those taking advantage of the opportunities outside the formal Republican Party structure were Randy Enwright, Jim Rimes, Rich Heffley, Pat Bainter, Tim Baker, Meredith O'Rourke, Randy Nielson, Marc Reichelderfer, David Johnson, Melissa Stone, and Debbie Aleksander.[31] While these independent consultant campaign shops remained aligned with the Republican cause, their services were provided independent of the formal party structure.[32]

It was also significant that the state Republican Executive Committee turned away from the choice of Governor Rick Scott to head the Republican Party in 2015. Spurning Scott's choice, the committee selected State

Representative Blaise Ingoglia to chair the state party and, in the process, diluted the organization's fund-raising options without the support of their Republican governor.[33] The dilemma faced by the party and Chairman Ingoglia as Scott concluded his second term as governor was the ability to maintain relevance and effectiveness on behalf of the next generation of candidates flying the Republican banner, particularly in light of the changing dynamics of campaign fund-raising.[34]

Coordinated party fund-raising for Republican candidates began with the Republican Legislative Appreciation Dinners and the Legislative Campaign Committee, and these individual events were consolidated inside the formal Republican Party structure by Tom Slade after he became the party chair in 1993. During Slade's tenure, the Republican Party became the source of financial strength for the margins of victory on Election Day, but traditional fund-raising under the Republican umbrella began to change following the passage of the McCain-Feingold Act of 2002 by Congress and the subsequent decision from the U.S. Supreme Court in the case of *Citizens United v. Federal Election Commission* in 2010.[35]

The initial impact of McCain-Feingold placed limits on the amounts that political parties were permitted to provide in direct support for their candidates, and with the limits in place, the financial resources available directly through both political parties began to wane. Over time, the impact of McCain-Feingold began to erode the power and significance that the parties exercised in the partisan political arena.[36] The U.S. Supreme Court's decision in *Citizens United v. Federal Election Commission* accentuated the changes that began with McCain-Feingold by opening the door to new campaign-funding alternatives.

The Supreme Court's decision expanded the ability of "independent committees" not formally aligned with either political party to raise unlimited campaign dollars; it created new sources of "soft-money" campaign dollars from wealthy donors; and it further undercut the dominant role that the political parties had previously held earlier in the era. Under the giving options permitted by *Citizens United*, donors were able to bypass the contribution limits to individual campaigns found in McCain-Feingold and the Florida Election Code, and it opened the door for wealthy donors to open their wallets and escalate their political soft-money contributions to political committees organized under Section 527 of the Internal Revenue Code.[37]

"Another consequence," wrote Jane Mayer in her 2016 book *Dark Money*, "was that the *Citizens United* decision shifted the balance of power from parties built on broad consensuses to individuals who were wealthy and zealous enough to spend millions of dollars from their own funds."[38]

Instead of, and in addition to, contributions from the accounts of the state Republican Party as the third decade of dominance began, campaign funds were increasingly found in the soft-money accounts of Section 527 political committees.[39] As the 2018 statewide elections approached, committees supporting Republican candidates included "Let's Get to Work," affiliated with Rick Scott; "Florida Grown," affiliated with Adam Putnam; "Fund for Florida's Future," affiliated with Ron DeSantis; "Saving Florida's Heartland," affiliated with Denise Grimsley; "Friends of Matt Caldwell"; "Friends of Ashley Moody"; "United Conservatives," affiliated with Frank White; "Liberty and Justice for All," affiliated with Ross Spano; and "Treasure Florida," affiliated with Jimmy Patronis.[40]

On the Democratic side, there were similar political committees, and funding for these committees came from wealthy individual donors with alternative, "left-leaning" political philosophies like George Soros, Tom Steyer, Michael Bloomberg, Norman Lear, Tyler Perry, and others affiliated with the Democracy Alliance committed to "liberal causes."[41] Heading into the final weeks of the 2018 gubernatorial election, Democratic nominee Andrew Gillum "attracted a flock of billionaires" and more than $9.1 million to support his "unapologetically progressive" messaging as the campaign entered its final month.[42]

As a matter of custom, each of these soft-money accounts—whether left-leaning like Gillum's or conservative like DeSantis's Fund for Florida's Future—was maintained outside the formal party structure. The funds from these accounts were meted out with more individual discretion, and the effect was to diminish the role of political parties and empower individuals outside the traditional party network.[43]

At the beginning of the two-party era, the Republican Party had become a key clearinghouse for campaign fund-raising, and its efforts did not disburse funds to candidates in the primary contests. Party dollars instead were used after the primary elections to support Republican nominees in general election contests in the tradition begun by legislative leaders Bill Young and Don Reed. The same traditions were not extended to the new, individual soft-money accounts; and the new accounts opened up the opportunity for soft-money campaign funds to be used in Republican primary contests.[44] As a result, the new giving options heightened the risk of factions inside the network; they encouraged hard-fought primary contests between Republican candidates; and they opened the door to intraparty struggles for the soul of the Republican Party like those that occurred among Democrats at the beginning of the era typified by the contests between Haydon Burns and Robert King High.[45]

The innovations permitting campaign expenditures from alternative individual soft-money accounts and the network of campaign professionals found outside the party structure became two more factors with the potential to move the pendulum's arc in Florida's political arena, but there were others. Perhaps the most closely watched factor with the ability to shift the direction of power continued to be the composition of Florida's newly arriving voters.[46]

A Watchful Eye on New Arrivals

As the foundation for two-party politics in Florida was being laid into place, the rebalancing of partisanship in the electorate has largely mirrored the growth in the state's population.[47] The growth that spurred the new political foundation also brought Florida increasing representation in the U.S. Congress; it brought the state to the forefront of presidential politics; and it made Florida the nation's third-most-populous state. As the population continued to grow into the new century, Florida continued to be the destination where new residents with regional and cultural differences merged. With the influx of these new cultural differences, the rebalancing of the partisan base in the political arena continued to evolve.[48]

The Republican foundation began in the urban horseshoe, but as the growth and demographics changed, there were shifts in the voter base of both political parties. The horseshoe counties remained important for Republicans, but over the decades, the population demographics showed that the core Democratic vote had a tendency to aggregate in the urban centers, including those located in the horseshoe counties.[49] In counterbalance, Republican influence expanded into suburban regions in central Florida; into the growing population of Brevard County and Florida's Space Coast; into the new arriving populations in the counties along the southwest coast that included Collier, Lee, Manatee, and Charlotte; into the new populations settling in the Florida Panhandle; and into the populations found in Florida's rural counties.[50]

As the core Democratic base expanded in the urban centers of Broward, Palm Beach, and Miami-Dade Counties, Republicans successfully countered with support from new voters in The Villages and the other retirement communities found in Lake, Marion, Flagler, and Putnam Counties.[51] By the time Jeb Bush successfully captured his second term as governor, support for Republican candidates had expanded into the state's more rural counties and into the agricultural communities that had traditionally been aligned with Florida Democrats.[52] With the emergence of voters identifying with Tea Party faction, a *New York Times* poll showed that more than three-quarters of its supporters identified as Republicans, and Republican candidates were the overwhelming choice of those voters, too.[53]

On the eve of the 2018 elections, political reporter Jim Saunders described the evolving voter demographics this way:

> While registered Democrats outnumber Republicans in the state's urban counties, the GOP has the advantage in large swaths of the state, including dominating in mid-sized counties. The GOP has a registration edge in 42 of the 67 counties heading into the general election. Voters in much of Florida have always been conservative, but the days of the traditional Southern Democrats are largely gone. Democrats still have more registered voters in many rural parts of the state, but 25 counties have flipped from Democrat to Republican in the registration advantages since 1998.[54]

Results at the ballot box in 2016 demonstrated the continued adaptability of the Republican network to the changing voter demographics, and the continued successes were underscored by Republican House Speaker Richard Corcoran following the 2016 legislative elections. "We successfully defended every single House GOP incumbent," observed Corcoran after the elections, "and [we also] flipped a Democrat seat to the GOP."[55]

Yet the challenge of a growing population has never been a stagnant issue in the maturing two-party era. Seeking out and recruiting the flood of new voters remained a relevant and constant priority for both political parties because new arrivals have historically been a significant factor in determining the partisan composition of the electorate.[56] Some of the migration patterns of earlier decades that trended toward the Republican base have remained and include retiring military veterans and new residents arriving from the Midwest and Northeast, but there were also other changes in the patterns.[57] The influx of residents from Cuba waned, and the new migration from Puerto Rico, Venezuela, and other Caribbean and Latin American countries brought new voters who tended to be "a Democratic-leaning counterweight to Miami's Republican-leaning Cuban population."[58]

Republicans demonstrated an unwillingness to concede the influx of these new voters to the Democrats as the 2018 elections neared, however.[59] To counter Democratic efforts, the conservative-leaning Libre Institute launched outreach programs to assist citizens arriving from Puerto Rico and relocating to Florida, and the Institute supplemented their assistance with political messages of smaller government, school choice, and a business-friendly environment that were found at the heart of the traditional Republican Party platform.[60] In addition, and perhaps little noticed, were the personal efforts made by Governor Rick Scott to reach out to this segment of the electorate. Beginning in 2011, Governor Scott began learning Spanish; he made eight personal visits to Puerto Rico to assist with those displaced by Hurricane Maria in 2017; and he was unwilling to concede the new arrivals to the Democratic voting bloc.[61]

Another factor that has added to the uncertainty about the political leanings among the Florida electorate since the turn of the twenty-first century has been the voters choosing not to affiliate with either party.[62] The demographic trend among Floridians opting to align with neither party—voters known in campaign parlance as the NPAs—presented a different kind of challenge for the partisan loyalists in both parties, and the evolving partisan composition of the electorate was summarized by political reporter Steve Bousquet in the fall of 2017:[63] "Statewide, Florida had 12.8 million voters on Sept. 30, [2017], with Democrats holding a narrow statewide lead in total registration over Republicans, 37.5 percent to 35.4 percent. But the fastest-growing segment of the voting population is NPAs who made up 26.7 percent of all voters."[64]

As the number of voters aligning under the NPA banner increased, they altered the focus of campaigns. By increasing numbers, the NPAs became the segment of the electorate where races in the modern era were decided.[65] In large measure, the ranks of the NPA segment tended toward the middle of the political spectrum; and voters registering with no party affiliation were not afforded the opportunity to participate in either the Republican or Democratic primary elections.[66] In the party primaries, candidates showed a tendency not to seek those in the middle of the political spectrum and battled instead for the support of loyalists who embraced the more extreme side of their party's political spectrum—those more conservative in the Republican primaries and those more liberal in the Democratic primaries.[67] The ensuing challenge for the successful nominees emerging from the Democratic and Republican primaries became finding a way to capture the moderate NPA voters in a general election. More than any segment on the changing political landscape, it was the new voters and the voters aligning with neither party—the NPAs—who held the power to move the arc of the pendulum between the political parties.

Election Recount, 2018

By the time the 2018 Election Day came to a close, the results for twenty-three congressional seats, nineteen seats in the state Senate, eighty-five seats in the Florida House of Representatives, and the statewide races for Florida's chief financial officer and attorney general had been decided by undisputed margins; but in six races, the results remained close and in doubt.[68] Two of the undecided races were for seats in the Florida House; one was for a seat in the Florida Senate; and the remaining three were statewide races. It was on these statewide contests that the attention of both parties immediately focused. In the governor's race, Ron DeSantis led Democrat Andrew Gillum by more than 33,000 votes; Rick Scott held a smaller lead over incumbent Bill Nelson in the U.S. Senate race; and Republican Matt Caldwell trailed his Democratic opponent by a small margin in the race for commissioner of agriculture. Reporter James Call's observations seemed to typify the contemporary view of Florida's political environment.

"Florida has become the epicenter of the midterm and a preview of the 2020 election," wrote Call. "Democratic heavy hitters including former President Barack Obama and former Vice President Joe Biden along with Vermont Sen. Bernie Sanders have stumped for Gillum. President Trump campaigned this past week in Fort Myers and Pensacola for DeSantis. Trump told supporters they had a choice 'between greatness and gridlock.'"[69]

"Once again," echoed Jeffrey Schweers in his reporting for the *Tallahassee Democrat*, "the Sunshine State is heading into election overtime—but this time with an unprecedented three statewide races in the balance critical to Republicans maintaining a 20-year-old grip on the state capital and to flipping a U.S. Senate seat red."[70]

With the recounts came close scrutiny of the vote totals; examination of questionable and provisional ballots; and questions about the proficiency of the county election supervisors, particularly in Broward and Palm Beach Counties. From the polling precincts on Election Day, the three statewide contests moved into forums for "legal battles and skirmishes in the theater of public opinion" where assembled teams of attorneys and volunteers stepped up to protect the vote totals for DeSantis and Scott to preserve their margins of victory.[71]

As they did in 2000 for the presidential recount, the Republican network deployed its party officials, volunteers, and attorneys to monitor county canvassing boards; they observed the recount process and the examination of provisional ballots; and they advocated in the courtrooms where Democrats were challenging the election tabulations. Some of the faces had been present in 2000, including Ed Pozzuoli, Marc Dunbar, Mike Grissom, Jason Unger, Richard Coates, and Bucky Mitchell. New faces in the network included Jennifer Ungru, Melanie Griffin, Dan Russell, Will Hall, Kirk Pepper, Erin Isaac, Tim Cerio, George Levesque, Greg Black, Ben Gibson, and Chris Carmody, and their efforts offered tangible confirmation that the Republican network was still firmly in place as the final election results from 2018 were certified.[72]

The narrow margins in each of the major races brought speculation about the comparative contemporary strength of the competing political parties, and when viewed in isolation, the close races and the recount process demonstrated that in parts of Florida, the state was balanced and nearly equal in its party loyalties.[73] It was also a demonstration that some of the political strength had shifted to that portion of the electorate that claimed "No Party Affiliation."

From a broader perspective, however, the Republican network continued to deliver margins that brought victory for its candidates. Following the elections in 2018, Republican majorities remained in both of the state's legislative chambers; Florida began its third decade under the administration of a Republican governor and a Republican majority on the Florida cabinet; Republicans continued to be a majority in the state's delegation to the U.S. Congress; and for the first time in the modern era, both of Florida's U.S. senators were Republicans.[74]

Changes in the Arc

For those who have immersed themselves in the world of partisan politics, Florida's two-party system has planted deep political roots where both parties have remained viable, but some have looked to the future and see a change in the pendulum's swing back toward the Democrats.[75] Others see the arc of the power pendulum remaining with the Republicans.[76] No matter which projection proves true, none have predicted that the swing will be so extreme that Republicans will vanish from the political arena as they did following the end of the Reconstruction era.

The future and the foundation for Republicans in Florida depends, as it does for Democrats, on their adaptation to the complexities of the new era—their organizational acumen; their adjustment to the new fund-raising parameters for campaigns; capitalizing on the new media options for message delivery; finding the messages that motivate the electorate to support their candidates, particularly among voters opting for NPA status; and, in the legislative and congressional arenas, surviving the decennial realignment of district boundary lines.[77]

With the arrival of the twenty-first century, the two-party era had become an entrenched part of Florida's political landscape where both Republicans and Democrats vied for the support of the state's voters. In each election cycle, the object of both political parties was to win and to move the arc of the pendulum in their direction; and for more than two decades, the election cycles have produced results that have left Republicans as the dominant voice in Florida's political arena. The close voting margins and the skirmishes in the theater of public opinion in the aftermath of the 2018 elections raise the unanswered question, "Can the Republican momentum be sustained?"

In the contemporary political parlance, states dominated by Republicans were considered "Red" states; those dominated by Democrats were considered "Blue" states; and states where neither party consistently dominated were considered "Purple" swing states. Beginning in 1998 and for more than two decades, Florida voted as a "Red" state in state elections. In the same window of time, however, Florida had become the penultimate "Purple" swing state in national elections, giving its electoral votes to the Republican presidential nominees on three occasions and to the Democratic presidential nominees on two other occasions.

While historic trends can be a guide to the future path of the pendulum's arc, current events and changing demographics in the political arena can disrupt those trends. In this context, as the third decade of the century loomed, there were predictions that Republicans in Florida would maintain their dominance, but there was alternative speculation that the dominance of the Republicans would wane. Perhaps the more likely scenario as the decades unfold will be that elections for statewide office and the contests for control of Florida's legislative bodies will take on a more "Purple" hue in a political arena where the electorate remains evenly divided; where the role of the political parties is uncertain; where the messages from competing sides provide contrasting extremes; and where the influence of soft money continues to grow.[78]

ACKNOWLEDGMENTS

The authors wish to express their appreciation for the more than 140 individuals who gave us their time and shared their memories about the events they witnessed as the modern two-party era emerged in the Florida political arena.

The interviews helped us to identify many of the people who contributed to the growing Republican network as its foundation was laid and matured. They provided firsthand accounts that chronicled the Republican Party's growth; they helped to identify those who contributed to the transformation of the Republican network into a viable political force; and they helped to provide the narrative of how Republicans transitioned into the majority in Florida's political arena.

These individuals were part of the transformation, and they represent the contributions of others in a much wider network of Republican partisans. There have been many, many more who were also important contributors to the emerging network that we were not able to identify during our interviews and research or name during the completion of the book, and we regret the omissions.

The authors wish to thank, too, those who helped with the editing, fact-checking, and research of our narrative, particularly Frank Messersmith, Ken Pruitt, R. Z. Safley, Michael Dobson, Theresa Zerkle, Jennifer Ungru, John Wharton, Chris Finkbeiner, and Martha Edenfield. Our appreciation also extends to Tiffany Baker at the Florida Historic Capitol

Museum, Katie Betta at the Florida Senate, and Shane Baldetti for their assistance in assembling the graphic images that accompany the text. Finally, our appreciation as well to Meredith Babb, who conceived the project and supported it through the peer reviews, editing, and publication.

NOTES

Chapter 1. Foundation of Florida's Political History

1. Wells, *Inside "Bush v. Gore,"* x.

2. Randy Enwright, interview by Peter Dunbar, March 22, 2018.

3. Colburn, *From Yellow Dog Democrats to Red State Republicans*, 14.

4. Corrigan, *Conservative Hurricane*, 10.

5. Morris, *The Florida Handbook 1987–1988*, 362.

6. Lemieux and Mize, *Florida Made*, 16–17.

7. Hare, *Tallahassee: A Capital City History*, 49.

8. David Stewart, www.historynewsnetwork.org.

9. Carol Ebel, "George Mathews (1739–1812)," *New Georgia Encyclopedia,* www.georgia encyclopedia.org.

10. Corrigan, *Conservative Hurricane*, 9; Morris, *The Florida Handbook 1987–1988*, 182.

11. Hare, *Tallahassee: A Capital City History*, 20.

12. Morris, *The Florida Handbook 1987–1988*, 369.

13. Hare, *Tallahassee: A Capital City History*, 23, 24.

14. Lemieux and Mize, *Florida Made*, 177.

15. Morris, *The Florida Handbook 1987–1988*, 290.

16. Corrigan, *Conservative Hurricane*, 11.

17. Morris, *The Florida Handbook 1987–1988*, 87–88.

18. Karl, *The 57 Club*, 191.

19. Fla. Const. art. III, § 1.

20. Fla. Const. of 1885, art, VII, § 26.

21. Swann v. Adams, 263 F.Supp. 225 (1967).

22. Hare, *Tallahassee: A Capital City History*, 27.

23. Senate Handbook 1976–1978, 48.

24. Morris, *The Florida Handbook 1987–1988*, 219–21.

25. Hare, *Tallahassee: A Capital City History*, 49.

26. Morris, *The Florida Handbook 1987–1988*, 236.

27. "Historical Background of Mosquito Lagoon," www.dep.state.fl.us.

28. The Hernandez-Capron Trail, The Historical Marker Database, www.hmdb.org.

29. Hare, *Tallahassee: A Capital City History*, 54.

30. "Missouri Compromise," Library of Congress, www.loc.gov.

31. Hare, *Tallahassee: A Capital City History*, 53.

32. "Florida's Role in the Civil War: 'Supplier to the Confederacy,'" www.fcit.usf.edu.

33. "Florida's Role in the Civil War: 'Supplier to the Confederacy,'" www.fcit.usf.edu.

34. Hare, *Tallahassee: A Capital City History*, 63.

35. "Historical Events of the Republican and Democratic Parties: United States Senate Vote," www.govtrack.us.

36. Allen Morris, "It's a New Kind of Ball Game in Tallahassee," *Florida Times-Union*, March 29, 1970.

37. Tunnell, "Creating the Propaganda of History," 789–822.

38. Colburn, *From Yellow Dog Democrats to Red State Republicans*, 12.

39. Morris, *The Florida Handbook 1987–1988*, 362.

40. Corrigan, *Conservative Hurricane*, 16.

41. "Rutherford B. Hayes," http://whitehouse.gov.

42. Corrigan, *Conservative Hurricane*, 14.

43. Corrigan, *Conservative Hurricane*, 14.

44. Morris, *The Florida Handbook 1987–1988*, 308.

45. Morris, *The Florida Handbook 1987–1988*, 308.

46. Florida Jim Crow—Finding Sources, https://www.jimcrowhistory.org.

47. Colburn, *From Yellow Dog Democrats to Red State Republicans*, 35. See also Fla. Const. of 1885, art. IV, § 20.

48. Corrigan, *Conservative Hurricane*, 29.

49. Adkins, *Making Modern Florida*, 7.

50. "Growth of Florida's Railroads," www.fcit.usf.edu.

51. Lemieux and Mize, *Florida Made*, 19.

52. Colburn, *From Yellow Dog Democrats to Red State Republicans*, 16.

53. Corrigan, *Conservative Hurricane*, 22.

54. Lemieux and Mize, *Florida Made*, 47.

55. Glover, "Henry B. Plant—Genius of the West Coast," http://etc.usf.edu.

56. Morris, *The Florida Handbook 1987–1988*, 181.

57. Lemieux and Mize, *Florida Made*, 111–12. See also Davis, *The Gulf: The Making of an American Sea*, 357.

58. "The Hoosier Barnum: Carl G. Fisher," http://www.indianahistory.org.

59. "Former Secretaries," www.fdot.gov.

60. "The Great Florida Land Boom," http://www.floridahistory.org.

61. See Fla. Const. art. VII, §7; and art. 10, §4.

62. Corrigan, *Conservative Hurricane*, 24.

63. Bullock, *The New Politics of the Old South*, 2nd ed., 267.

64. Morris, *The Florida Handbook 1987–1988*, 309.

65. Morris, *Reconsiderations—The Emergence of a Party*, 1.

66. Adkins, *Making Modern Florida*, 9.

67. "Florida during World War II," https://www.floridamemory.com.

68. Glines, *The Doolittle Raid*, 28–30; Dunbar, *Before They Were the Black Sheep*, 42, 101; www.campblanding-museum.org/history.htlm. See also "Amphibious Training Base—Ft. Pierce"; and "Amphibious Landing Training at Carrabelle Beach," https://www.florida memory.com.

69. Morris, *The Florida Handbook 1987–1988*, 282; Colburn, *From Yellow Dog Democrats to Red State Republicans*, 17.

70. Morris, *The Florida Handbook 1987–1988*, 352.

71. Green, "A Brief History of Air Conditioning."

72. Colburn, *From Yellow Dog Democrats to Red State Republicans*, 19.

73. DDT and Its Derivatives, 3.2 Productive and Use, http://www.INChem.org. See also Davis, *The Gulf: The Making of an American Sea*, 416.

74. Mormino, "1958: The Dawn of Modern Florida."

75. Colburn, *From Yellow Dog Democrats to Red State Republicans*, 25.

76. Morris, *The Florida Handbook 1967–1968*, 463.

77. Morris, *The Florida Handbook 1987–1988*, 571, 572.

78. Wells, *Inside "Bush v. Gore,"* x.

Chapter 2. Foundations of Emerging Republicanism

1. Randy Enwright, interview by Peter Dunbar, March 22, 2018.

2. Official Results, November 2, 1948 General Election, Florida Department of State, Division of Elections.

3. 270 to Win, "Presidents," "Historical Presidential Elections," www.270towin.com. See also Congressman John L. Mica, *Congressional Record*, October 20, 2003.

4. Official Results, November 8, 1966 General Election, Florida Department of State, Division of Elections; Official Results, November 5, 1968 General Election, Florida Department of State, Division of Elections; *The Clerk's Manual, 1968–1970*.

5. Official Results, November 4, 1980 General Election, Florida Department of State, Division of Elections.

6. Official Results, November 8, 1988 General Election, Florida Department of State, Division of Elections.

7. Colburn, *From Yellow Dog Democrats to Red State Republicans*, 1.

8. Baker v. Carr, 369 U.S. 186, 210 (1962).

9. Bullock, *The New Politics of the Old South*, 2nd ed., 267.

10. Population total of 968,470.

11. Morris, *The Florida Handbook 1987–1988*, 572.

12. Morris, *The Florida Handbook 1987–1988*, 571.

13. Key, *Southern Politics in State and Nation*, 22.

14. Key, *Southern Politics in State and Nation*, 22.

15. Colburn, *From Yellow Dog Democrats to Red State Republicans*, 3.

16. Colburn, *From Yellow Dog Democrats to Red State Republicans*, 25.

17. Dyckman, *Reubin O'D. Askew and the Golden Age of Florida Politics*, 87.

18. Bill Cotterell, "Democrats Have a Long Comeback Ahead of Them," *Tallahassee Democrat*, November 17, 2016.

19. Ray Hill, "Claude Pepper of Florida," *Knoxville Focus*, November 29, 2015.

20. Official Results, November 7, 1950 General Election, Florida Department of State, Division of Elections.

21. Morris, *The Florida Handbook 1987–1988*, 316.

22. Phelps, *The People in Lawmaking in Florida 1822–2001*.

23. Corrigan, *Conservative Hurricane*, 28; Enwright, interview.

24. Phelps, *The People in Lawmaking in Florida 1822–2001*.

25. "Governor Thomas LeRoy Collins," http://cms.leoncountyfl.gov. See also Morris, *The Florida Handbook 1987–1988*, 316.

26. Colburn, *From Yellow Dog Democrats to Red State Republicans*, 33.

27. Lemieux and Mize, *Florida Made*, 159–60.

28. Official Results, November 6, 1956 General Election, Florida Department of State, Division of Elections.

29. Official Results, November 8, 1960 General Election, Florida Department of State, Division of Elections.

30. Karl, *The 57 Club*, 232.

31. Morris, *Reconsiderations—The Emergence of a Party*, 1.

32. Official Results, November 2, 1948 General Election, Florida Department of State, Division of Elections.

33. Official Results, November 4, 1952 General Election, Florida Department of State, Division of Elections.

34. Dwight D. Eisenhower: Campaigns and Elections, Miller Center, http://millercenter.org.

35. Dwight D. Eisenhower: Campaigns and Elections, Miller Center, http://millercenter.org.

36. Official Results, November 4, 1952 General Election, Florida Department of State, Division of Elections.

37. Official Results, November 6, 1956 General Election, Florida Department of State, Division of Elections.

38. Official Results, November 8, 1960 General Election, Florida Department of State, Division of Elections.

39. Official Results, November 8, 1960 General Election, Florida Department of State, Division of Elections.

40. Karl, *The 57 Club*, 191.

41. "What Is the Coattail Effect?," http://uspolitics.

42. Colburn, *From Yellow Dog Democrats to Red State Republicans*, 57.

43. "Haydon Burns Is Dead; Ex-Governor of Florida," *New York Times*, November 24, 1987.

44. Official Results, November 8, 1960 General Election, Florida Department of State, Division of Elections.

45. Karl, *The 57 Club*, 232.

46. Cotterell, "Democrats Have a Long Comeback Ahead of Them."

47. Kenneth Plante, interview by Mike Haridopolos, January 15, 2009.

48. Halberstam, "Claude Kirk and the Politics of Promotion," *Harper's Magazine*, April 30, 1968.

49. Karl, *The 57 Club*, 195.

50. Lloyd C. Hagaman, interview by Ben Houston, July 1, 2000.

51. Morris, *The Florida Handbook 1987–1988*, 32.

52. Baker v. Carr, 369 U.S. 186, 210 (1962).

53. Baker v. Carr, 206 F.Supp. 341, 344 (1962).

54. Morris, *The Florida Handbook 1967–1968*, 113.

55. Colburn, *From Yellow Dog Democrats to Red State Republicans*, 35.

56. Corrigan, *Conservative Hurricane*, 34.

57. Adkins, *Making Modern Florida*, 34.

58. Swann v. Adams, 378 U.S. 553 (1964).

59. Swann v. Adams, 258 F.Supp. 819, 822 (1966).

60. Adkins, *Making Modern Florida*, 66.

61. Adkins, *Making Modern Florida*, 66.

62. Swann v. Adams, 385 U.S. 440 (1967).

63. *Journal of the Senate*, April 4, 1967.

64. *The Clerk's Manual, 1966–1968*.

65. Swann v. Adams, 385 U.S. 440 (1967).

66. Adkins, *Making Modern Florida*, 161.

67. Swann v. Adams, 263 F.Supp. 225, 226 (1967).

68. Swann v. Adams, 263 F.Supp. 225, 226 (1967).

69. *The Clerk's Manual, 1966–1968*.

70. *The Clerk's Manual, 1966–1968*.

71. Adkins, *Making Modern Florida*, 160.

72. Phelps, *The People in Lawmaking in Florida 1822–2001*.

73. "The Final Nail in the 'Pork Chop Gang' Coffin," *Tampa Tribune*, September 1, 2013.

74. Adkins, *Making Modern Florida*, 163.

75. *The Clerk's Manual, 1966–1968*.

76. *The Clerk's Manual, 1966–1968*.

77. Martin Dyckman, "The Loyal Opposition," *St. Petersburg Times*, April 8, 1971.

78. Tom Slade, interview by Mike Haridopolos, June 4, 2009.

79. Allen Morris, "It's a New Kind of Ball Game in Tallahassee," *Florida Times-Union*, March 29, 1970.

80. Bobby Brantley, interview by Peter Dunbar, July 13, 2016.

81. "State to Become GOP Stronghold, Leaders Predict," *Sarasota Herald-Tribune*, December 21, 1983.

82. Plante, interview.

83. Brantley, interview.

Chapter 3. Planting Local Republican Roots

1. Scher, *Politics in the New South*, 2nd ed., 144.

2. Dyckman, *Reubin O'D. Askew and the Golden Age of Florida Politics*, 3.

3. Ronald Richmond, interview by Peter Dunbar, October 4, 2016. See also Colburn, *From Yellow Dog Democrats to Red State Republicans*, 98.

4. James Brodie, interview by Peter Dunbar, October 4, 2016.

5. Colburn, *From Yellow Dog Democrats to Red State Republicans*, 178.

6. Official Results, November 2, 1948 General Election, Florida Department of State, Division of Elections.

7. S. Curtis Kiser, interview by Peter Dunbar, October 4, 2016.

8. Wolfgang Saxon, "William C. Cramer, 81, A Leader of G.O.P. Resurgence in South," *New York Times*, October 27, 2003.

9. Hathorn, "Cramer v. Kirk: The Florida Republican Schism of 1970," 404.

10. Congressman John L. Mica, *Congressional Record*, October 20, 2003.

11. Biographical Directory of the United States Congress, s.v. "William Cato Cramer," 888.

12. Richmond, interview, April 5, 2016; and May 3, 2016.

13. Dara Kam and David Royse, "C. W. 'Bill' Young, in Congress since '71, Dies at Age 82," *News Service of Florida*, October 18, 2013.

14. Kam and Royse, "C. W. 'Bill' Young, in Congress since '71, Dies at Age 82."

15. Biographical Directory of the United States Congress, s.v. "C. W. "Bill Young," http://bioguide.congress.gov.

16. Dyckman, *Reubin O'D. Askew and the Golden Age of Florida Politics*, 3.

17. Richmond, interview, May 3, 2016.

18. Richmond, interview, May 3, 2016; Kiser, interview by Dunbar, October 4, 2016.

19. Kiser, interview by Dunbar, May 3, 2016.

20. Don McBride, "Ford Blasts Carter for Not Keeping Campaign Promises," *Evening Independent*, September 18, 1980.

21. Sandra Mortham, interview by Peter Dunbar, April 17, 2018.

22. "Charles E. 'Chuck' Rainey, Consummate Pinellas Politician Dies at 77," *Tampa Bay Times*, June 23, 2010; Scott Taylor Hartzell, "Herman Goldner Dubbed a 'Pre-eminent Mayor,'" *St. Petersburg Times*, August 21, 2002; Craig Basse and Curtis Krueger, "Former State Attorney Dies," *Tampa Bay Times*, January 3, 2006; Curtis Krueger, "Local GOP Leader Aims Higher," *St. Petersburg Times*, December 31, 2002.

23. Phelps, *The People in Lawmaking in Florida 1822–2001*.

24. Donald H. Reed Jr., meeting with Peter Dunbar, July 1967.

25. Kenneth Plante, interview by Mike Haridopolos, January 15, 2009.

26. Plante, interview.

27. Phelps, *The People in Lawmaking in Florida 1822–2001*.

28. *The Clerk's Manual, 1966–1968*.

29. *The Clerk's Manual, 1966–1968*.

30. Phelps, *The People in Lawmaking in Florida 1822–2001*.

31. *The Clerk's Manual, 1966–1968*.

32. Kiser, interview by Dunbar, October 4, 2016.

33. Mortham, interview, October 4, 2016.

34. Tom Gallagher, interview by Peter Dunbar, October 4, 2016; "Charles Bronson," Florida Agricultural Hall of Fame, http://floridaaghalloffame.org; "Former FAU President Brogan Leaving Florida," *Sun Sentinel*, August 7, 2013; *The Clerk's Manual, 1996–1998*.

35. "Charlie Crist," Florida Department of State, museumoffloridahistory.com; Biographical Directory of the United States Congress, http://bioguide.congress.gov; "About Pam Bondi," www.pambondi.com; *The Clerk's Manual, 2006–2008*.

36. Biographical Directory of the United States Congress, http://bioguide.congress.gov.

37. Morris, *Reconsiderations—The Emergence of a Party*.

38. *The Clerk's Manual, 1966–1968 through 1992–1994*.

39. Kam and Royse, "C. W. 'Bill' Young, in Congress since '71, Dies at Age 82."

40. *The Clerk's Manual, 1966–1968* through *1992–1994*.

41. *The Clerk's Manual, 1966–1968* through *1992–1994*.

42. *The Clerk's Manual, 1992–1994* through *2018–2020*.

43. *The Clerk's Manual, 1992–1994* through *2018–2020*.

44. *The Clerks Manual, 1966–1968*.

45. Phelps, *The People in Lawmaking in Florida 1822–2001*.

46. Phelps, *The People in Lawmaking in Florida 1822–2001*.

47. *The Clerks Manual, 1992–1994*.

48. Phelps, *The People in Lawmaking in Florida 1822–2001*.

49. *The Clerk's Manual, 2002–2004*.

50. *The Clerk's Manual, 1984–1986*.

51. Phelps, *The People in Lawmaking in Florida 1822–2001*.

52. *The Clerk's Manual, 1996–1998*.

53. *The Clerk's Manual, 2004–2006*.

54. Biographical Directory of the United States Congress, http://bioguide.congress.gov.

55. Biographical Directory of the United States Congress, http://bioguide.congress.gov.

56. Biographical Directory of the United States Congress, http://bioguide.congress.gov.

57. *The Clerk's Manual, 1996–1998*.

58. Phelps, *The People in Lawmaking in Florida 1822–2001*.

59. *The Clerk's Manual, 1986–1988*.

60. Stephen Shiver, interview by Peter Dunbar, July 1, 2016.

61. Official Results, November 8, 1994 General Election, Florida Department of State, Division of Elections.

62. *The Clerk's Manual, 2004–2006; The Clerk's Manual, 2012–2014.*

63. Swann v. Adams, 263 F.Supp. 225 (1967).

64. Morris, *The Florida Handbook 1973–1974,* 189.

65. Kiser, interview by Dunbar, May 3, 2016.

66. *The Clerk's Manual, 1972–1974.*

67. Phelps, *The People in Lawmaking in Florida 1822–2001;* Kiser, interview by Dunbar, May 3, 2016.

68. *The Clerk's Manual, 1982–1984.*

69. Kiser, interview by Dunbar, May 3, 2016.

70. Brodie, interview, October 4, 2016.

71. *The Clerk's Manual, 1982–1984.*

72. Biographical Directory of the United States Congress, http://bioguide.congress.gov.

73. *The Clerk's Manual, 1996–1998.*

74. *The Clerk's Manual, 1984–1986.*

75. *The Clerk's Manual, 1986–1988; The Clerk's Manual, 1988–1990.*

76. Phelps, *The People in Lawmaking in Florida 1822–2001.*

77. Biographical Directory of the United States Congress, 1774–Present, http://bioguide.congress.gov.

78. Phelps, *The People in Lawmaking in Florida 1822–2001.*

79. Phelps, *The People in Lawmaking in Florida 1822–2001.*

80. *The Clerk's Manual, 1982–1984.*

81. *The Clerk's Manual, 2002–2004; The Clerk's Manual, 2008–2010; The Clerk's Manual, 2014–*2016; *The Clerk's Manual, 2016–2018; The Clerk's Manual, 2018–2020.*

82. Rich Heffley, interview by Mike Haridopolos, December 10, 2008; Martin Dyckman, "The Loyal Opposition," *St. Petersburg Times,* April 8, 1971.

83. *The Clerk's Manual, 1966–1968; The Clerk's Manual, 1998–2000; The Clerk's Manual, 2002–2004; The Clerk's Manual, 2006–*2008; *The Clerk's Manual, 2014–2016; The Clerk's Manual, 2016–2018.*

84. Cari Roth, interview by Peter Dunbar, April 30, 2016.

85. Bobby Brantley, interview by Peter Dunbar, July 13, 2016; Brodie, interview, March 14, 2017; Kiser, interview by Dunbar, April 5, 2016; Mary Ellen Klaus and Amy Sherman, "Former Congressman E. Clay Shaw, Jr. Dies after Battle with Cancer," *Miami Herald,* September 11, 2013; *The Clerk's Manual, 1972–1974; The Clerk's Manual, 1980–1982; The Clerk's Manual, 1986–1988; The Clerk's Manual, 1996–1998; The Clerk's Manual, 2000–2002; The Clerk's Manual, 2006–2008; The Clerk's Manual, 2014–2016.*

86. Richmond, interview, May 3, 2016; *The Clerk's Manual, 1972–1974; The Clerk's Manual, 1986–1988; The Clerk's Manual, 1992–1994; The Clerk's Manual, 1996–1998; The Clerk's Manual, 2000–2002; The Clerk's Manual, 2002–2004; The Clerk's Manual, 2006–2008; The Clerk's Manual, 2010–201;* and *The Clerk's Manual, 2014–2016.*

87. *The Clerk's Manual, 1984–1986; The Clerk's Manual, 1998–2000; The Clerk's Manual, 2002–2004; The Clerk's Manual, 2008–2010; The Clerk's Manual, 2010–2012.*

88. Don Gaetz, "Work with Thrasher," *Tallahassee Democrat,* September 29, 2014; Frank

Messersmith, interview by Peter Dunbar, October 4, 2016; Allison DeFoor, interview by Mike Haridopolos, April 19, 2009; Frank Messersmith to Peter Dunbar, memorandum, November 16, 2016; *The Clerk's Manual, 1992–1994*; *The Clerk's Manual, 1998–2000*; *The Clerk's Manual, 2008–2010*; *The Clerk's Manual, 2010–2012*.

89. Lieutenant Governor of Florida, www.flgov.com; Phelps, *The People in Lawmaking in Florida 1822–2001*.

90. Steve Bousquet, "Governor Scott Picks Rep. Mike Fasano to Be Pasco's New Tax Collector," *Tampa Bay Times*, August 7, 2013; Manatee County Supervisor of Elections, www.votemanatee.com; Eloisa Ruano Gonzalez, "Lake Property Appraiser Carey Baker Settling into New Job," *Orlando Sentinel*, December 9, 2012.

91. "About Rich Crotty," *Orlando Sentinel*, October 15, 2015.

92. Richmond, interview, May 3, 2016.

93. Brantley, interview.

94. Van Poole, interview by Peter Dunbar, April 5, 2016; Kiser, interview by Dunbar, October 4, 2016; Jim Turner, "Florida GOP Says It Can Fend off 'Blue Wave,'" *Tallahassee Democrat*, April 8, 2018; Marc Dunbar, interview by Peter Dunbar, November 13, 2018; William Sklar, interview by Peter Dunbar, October 23, 2018; Frank Messersmith to Peter Dunbar, memorandum, November 16, 2016.

95. Brodie, interview, March 14, 2017; Scott McPherson, interview by Peter Dunbar, March 14, 2017; Colburn, *From Yellow Dog Democrats to Red State Republicans*, 158; Alberto Cardenas, interview by Peter Dunbar, January 12, 2017.

96. Ken Pruitt, interview by Mike Haridopolos, January 17, 2017; David Hart interview, interview by Peter Dunbar, October 30, 2018.

97. Kiser, interview by Dunbar, October 4, 2016.

98. Cardenas, interview; Bebout interview, November 7, 2018; Marc Dunbar, interview, October 10, 2016.

Chapter 4. Organizing to Spread the Influence

1. Bobby Brantley, interview by Peter Dunbar, July 13, 2016.

2. Rich Heffley, interview by Mike Haridopolos, December 10, 2008.

3. Colburn, *From Yellow Dog Democrats to Red State Republicans*, 13.

4. Lloyd Dunkelberger, "Democratic Race Raises Questions," *Tallahassee Democrat*, January 8, 2017.

5. Brendan Farrington, "Florida Politics Remain Lopsided," *Tallahassee Democrat*, June 27, 2017.

6. Dyckman, *Reubin O'D. Askew and the Golden Age of Florida Politics*, 3.

7. Dyckman, *Reubin O'D. Askew and the Golden Age of Florida Politics*, 286.

8. Colburn, *From Yellow Dog Democrats to Red State Republicans*, 21.

9. Dyckman, *Reubin O'D. Askew and the Golden Age of Florida Politics*, 4.

10. Jack Latvala, interview by Peter Dunbar, September 22, 2016, St. Petersburg.

11. Alberto Cardenas, interview by Peter Dunbar, January 12, 2017.

12. Martin Dyckman, "The Loyal Opposition," *St. Petersburg Times*, April 8, 1971; Halberstam, "Claude Kirk and the Politics of Promotion," 36.

13. §103.091, F.S.

14. Colburn, *From Yellow Dog Democrats to Red State Republicans*, 99.

15. Heffley, interview by Haridopolos.

16. Stephen Shiver, interview by Peter Dunbar, July 1, 2016.

17. Genean Hawkins McKinnon, interview by Peter Dunbar, May 18, 2018; Colburn, *From Yellow Dog Democrats to Red State Republicans*, 159.

18. *The Clerk's Manual, 1966–1968*.

19. *The Clerk's Manual, 1982–1984*.

20. *The Clerk's Manual, 1998–2000*.

21. *The Clerk's Manual, 1998–2000*.

22. *The Clerk's Manual, 1988–1990*.

23. Kurt Kelly, interview by Peter Dunbar, February 9, 2017.

24. *The Clerk's Manual, 1966–1968*; *The Clerk's Manual, 1978–1980*; *The Clerk's Manual, 1984–1986*; *The Clerk's Manual, 1992–1994*; *The Clerk's Manual, 1996–1998*; *The Clerk's Manual, 2000–2002*; *The Clerk's Manual, 2010–2012*.

25. *The Clerk's Manual, 1978–1980*; *The Clerk's Manual, 1984–1986*; *The Clerk's Manual, 1992–1994*; *The Clerk's Manual, 2000–2002*; *The Clerk's Manual, 2006–2008*; *The Clerk's Manual, 2012–2014*; Mike Fasano, interview by Mike Haridopolos, January 13, 2009.

26. *The Clerk's Manual, 1966–1968*; *The Clerk's Manual, 1984–1986*; *The Clerk's Manual, 1992–1994*; *The Clerk's Manual, 1998–2000*; *The Clerk's Manual, 2000–2002*; *The Clerk's Manual, 2002–2004*; *The Clerk's Manual, 2012–2014*.

27. Shiver, interview.

28. "William F. Murfin (1925–2008)," *Northwest Florida Daily News*, October 16, 2008.

29. Official Results, November 5, 1968 General Election, Florida Department of State, Division of Elections.

30. "William F. Murfin (1925–2008)."

31. Mike Miller, interview by Peter Dunbar, August 18, 2016.

32. Cardenas, interview.

33. Latvala, interview by Dunbar.

34. Official Results, November 7, 1972 General Election, Florida Department of State, Division of Elections.

35. "Paula Hawkins," *Orlando Sentinel*, December 5, 2009.

36. Robert M. Press, "Reagan's Southern Supporters Confident but Not Complacent," *Christian Science Monitor*, July 25, 1984.

37. Official Results, November 2, 1976 General Election, Florida Department of State, Division of Elections.

38. Marian Johnson, interview by Peter Dunbar, September 13, 2018.

39. Official Results, November 2, 1982 General Election, Florida Department of State, Division of Elections and *The Clerk's Manual, 1982–1984*.

40. Michael Griffin, "GOP's Jeanie Austin Dies at 66," *Orlando Sentinel*, April 24, 2000.

41. Official Results, November 8, 1988 General Election, Florida Department of State, Division of Elections.

42. Official Results, November 6, 1990 General Election, Florida Department of State, Division of Elections.

43. Official Results, November 3, 1992 General Election, Florida Department of State, Division of Elections.

44. Heffley, interview by Haridopolos.

45. Colburn, *From Yellow Dog Democrats to Red State Republicans*, 143.

46. Frank Terraferma, interview by Peter Dunbar, August 17, 2016.

47. Official Results, November 3, 1998 General Election, Florida Department of State, Division of Elections.

48. Official Results, November 3, 1998 General Election, Florida Department of State, Division of Elections.

49. Colburn, *From Yellow Dog Democrats to Red State Republicans*, 172.

50. *The Clerk's Manual, 2000–2002.*

51. Official Results, November 7, 2000 General Election, Florida Department of State, Division of Elections.

52. Shiver, interview.

53. Official Results, November 2, 2004 General Election, Florida Department of State, Division of Elections.

54. *The Clerk's Manual, 2004–2006.*

55. Official Results, November 7, 2006 General Election, Florida Department of State, Division of Elections.

56. Aaron Deslatte and Rene Stutzman, "Florida GOP ex-Chairman Jim Greer Leaves Jail after Being Indicted," *Orlando Sentinel*, June 2, 2010.

57. Randy Enwright, interview by Peter Dunbar, March 22, 2018.

58. Matt DeLong, "Ex-Florida GOP Chairman Jim Greer Indicted on Six Felony Counts," *Washington Post*, June 2, 2010.

59. Jeremy Wallace, "Republican Chairman Dave Bitner Dies after ALS Battle," *Sarasota Herald-Tribune*, September 8, 2011.

60. Official Results, November 2, 2010 General Election, Florida Department of State, Division of Elections and *The Clerk's Manual, 2010–2012.*

61. Latvala, interview by Dunbar.

62. Brantley, interview.

63. Florida Federation of Republican Women, http://www.ffrw.net/?page_id=2.

64. Florida Federation of Republican Women, http://www.ffrw.net/?page_id=2.

65. *The Clerk's Manual, 2008–2010.*

66. Dyckman, *Reubin O'D. Askew and the Golden Age of Florida Politics*, 147; *The Clerk's Manual, 1978–1980.*

67. *The Clerk's Manual, 1982–1984;* Phelps, *The People in Lawmaking in Florida 1822–2001.*

68. *The Clerk's Manual, 1994–1996.*

69. *The Clerk's Manual, 1982–1984;* Phelps, *The People in Lawmaking in Florida 1822–2001.*

70. *The Clerk's Manual, 2008–2010.*

71. *The Clerk's Manual, 1996–1998.*

72. *The Clerk's Manual, 1982–1984.*

73. *The Clerk's Manual, 1966–1968.*

74. *The Clerk's Manual, 1982–1984;* Phelps, *The People in Lawmaking in Florida 1822–2001.*

75. *The Clerk's Manual, 1988–1990.*

76. https://www.irctax.com/

77. 2016–2018 Senate Handbook.

78. *The Clerk's Manual, 1984–1986.*

79. *The Clerk's Manual, 2008–2010.*

80. *The Clerk's Manual, 1982–1984.*

81. *The Clerk's Manual, 2006–2008.*

82. *The Clerk's Manual, 1998–2000.*

83. *The Clerk's Manual, 2004–2006.*

84. *The Clerk's Manual, 1994–1996.*

85. Sandra Mortham, interview by Peter Dunbar, October 4, 2016; Brantley, interview.

86. Lou Frey, interview by Mike Haridopolos, July 14, 2009.

87. Colburn, *From Yellow Dog Democrats to Red State Republicans,* 103.

88. S. Curtis Kiser, interview by Peter Dunbar, April 5, 2016; and May 3, 2016.

89. Brantley, interview.

90. *The Clerk's Manual, 1966–1968.*

91. Frey, interview.

92. *The Clerk's Manual, 1966–1968;* Biographical Directory of the United States Congress, http://bioguide.congress.gov.

93. *The Clerk's Manual, 1972–1974; The Clerk's Manual, 1978–1980.*

94. Phelps, *The People in Lawmaking in Florida 1822–2001.*

95. *The Clerk's Manual, 1972–1974; The Clerk's Manual, 1994–1996.*

96. Frey, interview.

97. *The Clerk's Manual, 1972–1974; The Clerk's Manual, 1978–1980; The Clerk's Manual, 2000–2002.*

98. Garcia, "Heavy Hitter"; *The Clerk's Manual, 1978–1980;* Chris Sprowls, interview by Peter Dunbar, September 27, 2016.

99. Phelps, *The People in Lawmaking in Florida 1822–2001;* Kiser, interview by Dunbar, May 3, 2016.

100. *The Clerk's Manual, 1968–1970; The Clerk's Manual, 1972–1974; The Clerk's Manual, 1986–1988.*

101. *The Clerk's Manual, 2006–2008.*

102. Brantley, interview.

103. *The Clerk's Manual, 1968–1970; The Clerk's Manual, 1980–1982; The Clerk's Manual, 1982–1984; The Clerk's Manual, 2014–2016.*

104. *The Clerk's Manual, 1968–1970; The Clerk's Manual, 1984–1986; The Clerk's Manual, 1998–2000; The Clerk's Manual, 2000–2002.*

105. *The Clerk's Manual, 1972–1974*; *The Clerk's Manual, 1982–1984*; *The Clerk's Manual, 1992–1994*; *The Clerk's Manual, 1996–1998*; *The Clerk's Manual, 1998–2000*; *The Clerk's Manual, 2004–2006*.

106. *The Clerk's Manual, 1972–1974*; *The Clerk's Manual, 1982–1984*.

107. *The Clerk's Manual, 1972–1974*; *The Clerk's Manual, 1982–1984*.

108. *The Clerk's Manual, 1988–1990*.

109. *The Clerk's Manual, 1982–1984*; *The Clerk's Manual, 1988–1990*; *The Clerk's Manual, 1998–2000*; *The Clerk's Manual, 2012–2014*.

110. Phelps, *The People in Lawmaking in Florida 1822–2001*.

111. Official Results, November 4, 1986 General Election, Florida Department of State, Division of Elections.

112. Official Results, November 7, 2006 General Election, Florida Department of State, Division of Elections.

113. Phelps, *The People in Lawmaking in Florida 1822–2001*; Linda Florea, "EDC to Recognize Orange County Ex-Mayor Crotty," *Orlando Sentinel*, February 7, 2011.

114. Latvala, interview by Dunbar.

115. Brendan Farrington, "Florida Politics Remain Lopsided," *Tallahassee Democrat*, June 27, 2017.

116. Heffley, interview by Haridopolos.

117. Colburn, *From Yellow Dog Democrats to Red State Republicans*, 143.

118. Bill Cotterell, "Democrats Have a Long Comeback Ahead of Them," *Tallahassee Democrat*, November 17, 2016.

119. Latvala, interview by Dunbar.

120. Donald H. Reed Jr., personal Kirk Campaign file.

121. Enwright, interview; Mike Harrell, interview by Peter Dunbar, October 4, 2018; Jennifer Ungru, interview by Peter Dunbar, November 8, 2018; David Johnson, interview by Peter Dunbar, November 28, 2018; Kirk Pepper, interview by Peter Dunbar, November 8, 2018.

122. Kiser, interview by Dunbar, May 3, 2016; Brantley, interview.

123. R. Z. Safley, interview by Peter Dunbar, May 3, 2016; Kiser, interview by Dunbar, May 3, 2016.

124. Ronald Richmond, interview by Peter Dunbar, April 5, 2016.

125. Colburn, *From Yellow Dog Democrats to Red State Republicans*, 143.

126. Chris Finkbeiner, interview by Peter Dunbar, July 14, 2016.

127. Shiver, interview.

128. Latvala, interview by Dunbar, September 22, 2016.

129. Enwright, interview, March 22, 2018.

130. Shiver, interview; Latvala, interview; Terraferma, interview.

131. Amy Baker, interview by Peter Dunbar, April 10, 2017.

132. Latvala, interview by Dunbar; Lanny Wiles, interview by Peter Dunbar, January 9, 2017.

133. Frank Terraferma, interview by Peter Dunbar, August 17, 2016.

134. Marian Johnson, interview by Peter Dunbar, September 13, 2018.

135. *The Clerk's Manual, 2000–2002*; *The Clerk's Manual, 2016–2018*.

136. Wiles, interview.

137. Jon Johnson, interview by Peter Dunbar, February 13, 2017.

138. Colburn, *From Yellow Dog Democrats to Red State Republicans*, 143.

139. Cardenas, interview; Dane Eagle, interview by Peter Dunbar, October 22, 2018.

140. Jennifer Ungru, interview, November 26, 2018; Enwright, interview.

141. Rich Heffley, interview by Peter Dunbar, March 21, 2018.

142. Fasano, interview; Gene McGee, interview by Mike Haridopolos, January 7, 2009; Schorsch, "Brightest Minds in Florida Politics: David Johnson," *SaintPetersBlog,* 2017, http://staintpetersblog.com.

143. Shelley Green, interview by Peter Dunbar, November 28, 2018.

144. John Thrasher, interview by Mike Haridopolos, January 6, 2009.

145. Gene McGee, interview by Peter Dunbar and Mike Haridopolos, October 25, 2016.

146. Shiver, interview.

147. Eagle, interview.

148. *The Clerk's Manual, 1996–1998*; Brecht Heuchan, interview by Mike Haridopolos, March 16, 2009; Terraferma, interview, August 17, 2016.

149. Cardenas, interview.

150. *The Clerk's Manual, 2000–2002*.

151. Shiver, interview.

152. Andy Palmer, interview by Peter Dunbar, December 4, 2017.

153. Marc Caputo, "Andy Palmer to Lead Republican Party of FL as Executive Director," *Miami Herald*, January 11, 2011.

154. Pepper, interview.

155. Mat Bahl, interview by Peter Dunbar, November 11, 2016; Derek Whitis, interview by Mike Haridopolos, October 23, 2018; Brian Jogerst, interview by Peter Dunbar, March 10, 2017; Charlie Dudley, interview by Peter Dunbar, October 24, 2018; Finkbeiner, interview, July 14, 2016.

156. Terraferma, interview, August 17, 2016; Shiver, interview.

157. Colburn, *From Yellow Dog Democrats to Red State Republicans*, 99.

158. Morris, *The Florida Handbook 2013–2014*, 18.

159. Dyckman, *Reubin O'D. Askew and the Golden Age of Florida Politics*, 15.

160. Colburn, *From Yellow Dog Democrats to Red State Republicans*, 68; Toni Jennings, interview by Mike Haridopolos, July 15, 2009.

161. Cardenas, interview.

162. Jennings, interview.

163. Dyckman, *Reubin O'D. Askew and the Golden Age of Florida Politics*, 87.

164. Kirk Address to the Joint Session of the Legislature, April 4, 1967.

165. Dyckman, *Reubin O'D. Askew and the Golden Age of Florida Politics*, 31, 87.

166. Bullock, *The New Politics of the Old South,* 2nd ed. See also Scher and Colburn, *Florida's Gubernatorial Politics in the Twentieth Century*, 73.

167. Colburn, *From Yellow Dog Democrats to Red State Republicans*, 24.

168. Dyckman, "The Loyal Opposition," *St. Petersburg Times*, April 8, 1971.

169. Dunbar, personal staff notes.

170. Morris, *The Florida Handbook 2013–2014*, 19.

171. Bousquet, "$1 Billion Tax Cuts Top Florida Governor's 2016 Priorities."

172. Claude Kirk, White Papers, 1966.

173. Kiser, interview by Dunbar, October 4, 2016; Richmond, interview, October 4; Mario Diaz-Balart, interview by Mike Haridopolos, July 15, 2009; Mortham, interview, October 4, 2016.

174. Dyckman, *Reubin O' D. Askew and the Golden Age of Florida Politics*, 87.

175. Kirk, White Paper on Conservation and Recreation, 1966; Kirk, White Paper on Finance and Taxation, 1966.

176. Dyckman, *Reubin O' D. Askew and the Golden Age of Florida Politics*, 35.

177. Chapter 74–310, *Laws of Florida*; Dyckman, *Reubin O' D. Askew and the Golden Age of Florida Politics*, 85; Chapter 89–175, *Laws of Florida*.

178. Costello v. Wainwright, 430 U.S. 325, (1977).

179. Special Session A, 1987.

180. Special Session A, 1987. See also Chapter 87–298, *Laws of Florida*.

181. Lloyd Dunkelberger, "Martinez Riding Environmental Wave," *Gainesville Sun*, February 19, 1990.

182. Corrigan, *Conservative Hurricane*, 171; Latvala, interview by Dunbar.

183. Harrell, interview.

184. Diaz-Balart, interview; Jeb Bush, interview by Mike Haridopolos, December 21, 2009; see also Colburn, *From Yellow Dog Democrats to Red State Republicans*, 50, 103.

185. James Brodie, interview by Peter Dunbar, October 4, 2016.

186. Cardenas, interview.

187. David Bitner, interview by Mike Haridopolos, June 22, 2009.

188. Kiser, interview by Dunbar, October 4, 2016; Frank Messersmith, interview by Peter Dunbar, October 4, 2016; Brodie, interview, August 2, 2016.

189. Tom Feeney, interview by Mike Haridopolos, December 16, 2008.

190. Corrigan, *Conservative Hurricane*, 63.

191. Colburn, *From Yellow Dog Democrats to Red State Republicans*, 58; Morris, *The Florida Handbook 2013–2014*, 23.

192. Morris, *The Florida Handbook 2013–2014*, 23.

193. Tom Slade, interview by Mike Haridopolos, June 4, 2009; see also Phelps, *The People in Lawmaking in Florida 1822–2001*.

194. Mac Stipanovich, interview by Mike Haridopolos, August 5, 2009.

195. Biographical Directory of the United States Congress, 1774–Present, http://bioguide.congress.gov.

196. Phelps, *The People in Lawmaking in Florida 1822–2001*; Biographical Directory of the United States Congress, 1774–Present, http://bioguide.congress.gov.

197. Colburn, *From Yellow Dog Democrats to Red State Republicans*, 96; *Jerry Thomas*

Confirmation Hearing, 94th Cong., transcript, U.S. Senate Committee on Finance, April 1, 1976, 7 and 8.

198. Phelps, *The People in Lawmaking in Florida 1822–2001*.

199. "Chronology of the Chief Justices of Florida."

200. Phelps, *The People in Lawmaking in Florida 1822–2001*.

201. Phelps, *The People in Lawmaking in Florida 1822–2001*.

202. "Melbourne's Harry Goode Dies at 75," *Space Coast Daily*, December 29, 2013.

203. Phelps, *The People in Lawmaking in Florida 1822–2001*.

204. Jim Ross, "Former Sheriff Joins Campaign for State House," *St. Petersburg Times*, April 20, 2002; *The Clerk's Manual, 2014–2016*.

205. *The Clerk's Manual, 1994–1996*.

206. *The Clerk's Manual, 2006–2008*.

207. Jennings, interview.

208. *The Clerk's Manual, 2008–2010*.

209. *The Clerk's Manual, 1966–1968*; *The Clerk's Manual, 2014–2016*.

210. *The Clerk's Manual, 2014–2016*.

211. *The Clerk's Manual, 2014–2016*.

212. Phelps, *The People in Lawmaking in Florida 1822–2001*.

213. *The Clerk's Manual, 2014–2016*; Phelps, *The People in Lawmaking in Florida 1822–2001*.

214. *The Clerk's Manual, 2014–2016*.

215. Phelps, *The People in Lawmaking in Florida 1822–2001*.

216. *The Clerk's Manual, 2016–2018*.

217. Dana Young, interview by Peter Dunbar, March 20, 2017.

218. Phelps, *The People in Lawmaking in Florida 1822–2001*.

219. Hillsborough County, http://www.hillsboroughcounty.org.

220. "A Moderate on a Mission," *News Press*, December 25, 2016.

221. "A Moderate on a Mission." See also *The Clerk's Manual, 2014–2016*.

222. *The Clerk's Manual, 2006–2008*.

223. *The Clerk's Manual, 1986–1988*.

224. *The Clerk's Manual, 2010–2012*.

225. *The Clerk's Manual, 2008–2010*.

226. *The Clerk's Manual, 2010–2012*; *The Clerk's Manual, 2008–2010*; Phelps, *The People in Lawmaking in Florida 1822–2001*.

227. Phelps, *The People in Lawmaking in Florida 1822–2001*.

228. Phelps, *The People in Lawmaking in Florida 1822–2001*.

229. Richard Perez-Pena, "Charlie Crist, Ex-Governor of Florida, Announces Run for Congress," *New York Times*, October 20, 2015; Official Results, November 4, 2014 General Election, Florida Department of State, Division of Elections.

230. Official Results, November 8, 2016 General Election, Florida Department of State, Division of Elections.

231. Marian Johnson, presentation to the Florida Outdoor Advertising Association Convention, St. Petersburg, September 22, 2016.

232. Feeney, interview; Bitner, interview, June 22, 2009.

233. R. Z. Safley, interview, November 26, 2018; Jennings, interview, July 15, 2009; Dan Webster, interview by Mike Haridopolos, June 12, 2009; Charlotte Audie, interview by Peter Dunbar, October 24, 2018.

Chapter 5. A Statewide Two-Party Reality

1. Fla. Const. art. IV, § 20.

2. *Congressional Quarterly,* https://library.cqpress.com/cqalmanac/document.php?id =cqal66-129950.

3. Kallina, *Claude Kirk and the Politics of Confrontation*; Morris, *The Florida Handbook 2013–2014,* 73.

4. Official Results, November 3, 1964 General Election, Florida Department of State, Division of Elections.

5. Kenneth Plante, interview by Mike Haridopolos, January 15, 2009.

6. Karl, *The 57 Club,* 195; Lloyd C. Hagaman, interview by Ben Houston, July 1, 2000.

7. S. Curtis Kiser, interview by Mike Haridopolos, January 15, 2009.

8. Lou Frey, interview by Mike Haridopolos, July 14, 2009.

9. Plante, interview.

10. Plante, interview.

11. Donald H. Reed Jr. to Robert E. Lee, June 17, 20, and 24, 1966, Peter Dunbar's personal files.

12. Donald H. Reed Jr. personal Kirk campaign file, 1966.

13. R. Z. Safley, interview by Peter Dunbar, May 3, 2016.

14. Hagaman, interview.

15. Frey, interview.

16. Claude R. Kirk Jr. to Verle Pope and Ralph Turlington, May 3, 1967.

17. Claude Kirk, White Papers, 1966.

18. Kirk, Address to the Joint Session of the Legislature, April 4, 1967.

19. Plante, interview.

20. Colburn, *From Yellow Dog Democrats to Red State Republicans,* 60.

21. Robin Safley, interview by Peter Dunbar, October 12, 2016.

22. Donald H. Reed Jr., meeting with Peter Dunbar, June 1968.

23. Donald H. Reed Jr., meeting with Peter Dunbar, May 1969.

24. Kiser, interview by Haridopolos.

25. Dyckman, *Reubin O'D. Askew and the Golden Age of Florida Politics,* 32.

26. Martin Waldron, "Ex-Aides of Nixon Help Kirk Rival," *New York Times,* March 5, 1970; Colburn, *From Yellow Dog Democrats to Red State Republicans,* 76.

27. Hathorn, "Cramer v. Kirk: The Florida Republican Schism of 1970," 403.

28. Hathorn, "Cramer v. Kirk: The Florida Republican Schism of 1970," 403.

29. Dyckman, *Reubin O'D. Askew and the Golden Age of Florida Politics,* 84, 87; MacKay, *How Florida Happened,* 16.

30. Phelps, *The People in Lawmaking in Florida 1822–2001*.

31. R. Z. Safley, interview by Peter Dunbar, November 26, 2018.

32. Dara Kam and David Royse, "C. W. 'Bill' Young, in Congress since '71, Dies at Age 82," *News Service of Florida*, October 18, 2013.

33. Phelps, *The People in Lawmaking in Florida 1822–2001*.

34. Mac Stipanovich, interview by Peter Dunbar, January 5, 2018.

35. Stipanovich, interview by Dunbar.

36. S. Curtis Kiser interview by Peter Dunbar, February 7, 2017.

37. Nora Herron, interview by Peter Dunbar, March 17, 2017.

38. *The Clerk's Manual, 1970–1972*.

39. *The Clerk's Manual, 1990–1992*.

40. Phelps, *The People in Lawmaking in Florida 1822–2001*.

41. Bill Montgomery, "200 from Campuses Aim to Help in Poverty Areas," *Tallahassee Democrat*, February 18, 1969.

42. Tom Gallagher, interview by Peter Dunbar, October 4, 2016

43. Dyckman, *Reubin O'D. Askew and the Golden Age of Florida Politics*, 69.

44. Kiser, interview by Dunbar, October 4, 2016.

45. Kiser, interview by Dunbar, October 4, 2016.

46. Fla. Const. art. IV, § 1 (f).

47. Morris, *The Florida Handbook 1987–1988*.

48. David Stout, "Paula Hawkins, 82, Florida Ex-Senator Dies," *New York Times*, December 4, 2009.

49. Dyckman, *Reubin O'D. Askew and the Golden Age of Florida Politics*, 146.

50. Dyckman, *Reubin O'D. Askew and the Golden Age of Florida Politics*, 147.

51. Genean Hawkins McKinnon, interview by Peter Dunbar, May 18, 2018.

52. "Paula Hawkins," *Orlando Sentinel*, December 5, 2009.

53. McKinnon, interview.

54. Women in Congress: Paula Fickes Hawkins, http:// womenincongress.house.gov/ member-profiles/profile.html?intID=103.

55. "In Our Opinion: Senator Paula Hawkins," *Deseret News*, December 5, 2009.

56. Colburn, *From Yellow Dog Democrats to Red State Republicans*, 124.

57. David Dahl, "Governor Urged to Take His Time Finding New Chief of Staff," *St. Petersburg Times*, October 24, 1987.

58. Mac Stipanovich to Bob Martinez, memorandum, 1983; Stipanovich, interview by Dunbar.

59. Noonan, *What I Saw at the Revolution*, xiii.

60. Lloyd Dunkelberger, "Martinez First Prominent GOP to Announce Governor Bid," *Ocala Star-Banner*, March 2, 1985.

61. Official Results, September 30, 1986 General Election, Florida Department of State, Division of Elections.

62. Official Results, September 30, 1986 General Election, Florida Department of State, Division of Elections.

63. Colburn, *From Yellow Dog Democrats to Red State Republicans*, 124; Official Results, September 30, 1986 Primary Election, Florida Department of State, Division of Elections.

64. Stipanovich, interview by Dunbar.

65. Stipanovich, interview by Dunbar.

66. Official Results, November 4, 1986 General Election, Florida Department of State, Division of Elections.

67. Tom Gallagher, interview by Peter Dunbar, August 2, 2016.

68. Stipanovich, interview by Dunbar.

69. Morris, *Reconsiderations—The Emergence of a Party*, 1988; Morris, *The Florida Handbook, 1983–1984*.

70. Morris, *The Florida Handbook, 1987–1988*.

71. *The Clerk's Manual, 1990–1992*; Morris, *The Florida Handbook, 1989–1990*.

72. Colburn, *From Yellow Dog Democrats to Red State Republicans*, 131; Stipanovich, interview by Dunbar.

73. Stipanovich, interview by Dunbar.

74. Debbie Bergstrom, meeting with Peter Dunbar, April 1990.

75. *New York Times* Public Opinion Poll, April 25, 1989.

76. Official Results, September 4, 1990 Primary Election, Florida Department of State, Division of Elections.

77. Official Results, September 4, 1990 Primary Election, Florida Department of State, Division of Elections.

78. *New York Times* Public Opinion Poll, October 13, 1990, personal notes of Peter Dunbar, November 7, 1990.

79. Official Results, November 6, 1990 General Election, Florida Department of State, Division of Elections.

80. Colburn, *From Yellow Dog Democrats to Red State Republicans*, 139; Official Results, November 6, 1990 General Election, Florida Department of State, Division of Elections.

81. Bill Cornwell and Morris Kennedy, "Chiles Buries Martinez to Win Governor's Race," *Tampa Tribune*, November 7, 1990.

82. David Hill, presentation to Martinez staff, March 1990, personal notes of Peter Dunbar, March 16, 1990.

83. Colburn, *From Yellow Dog Democrats to Red State Republicans*, 134–35.

84. *The Clerk's Manual, 1988–1990*.

85. *Senate Handbook 1992–1994*.

86. *The Clerk's Manual, 1994–1996*.

87. *Legislative Legacy*, Florida Legislative Research Center, FLRCM.gov.

88. Diane Hirth, "Official Wins Seat on PSC—Legislator Joins Utility Regulator," *Sun Sentinel*, June 13, 1990.

89. Amy Baker, interview by Peter Dunbar, April 10, 2017.

90. Chris Finkbeiner, interview by Peter Dunbar, December 1, 2016.

91. Allison DeFoor, interview by Mike Haridopolos, April 19, 2009.

92. Cari Roth, interview by Peter Dunbar, April 30, 2016.

93. Jon Johnson, interview by Peter Dunbar, February 13, 2017.

94. Bill Cotterell, "Roy Moore and the Albatross Aura of Trump," *Tallahassee Democrat*, December 14, 2017.

95. Wilson, "Florida Lobbyist Turning Trump Ties into Mega-millions," Center for Public Integrity, http://www.publicintegrity.org.

96. Jim Magill, interview by Peter Dunbar, February 6, 2017.

97. Van Poole interview by Peter Dunbar, April 5, 2016.

98. Nada Hassanein, "A Nest Egg," *Tallahassee Democrat*, May 29, 2017; Lucy Morgan, "Inside Southern Strategy, Connections Help," *St. Petersburg Times*, March 7, 2004.

99. Brian Jogerst, interview by Peter Dunbar, March 10, 2017.

100. Cathy Quick, interview by Peter Dunbar, August 3, 2018; Mike Gomez, interview by Peter Dunbar, November 23, 2018.

101. "Hayden Dempsey Rejoins Greenberg Traurig to Lead Florida Governmental Affairs Practice," *Business Wire*, http://www.businesswire.com, September 13, 2011.

102. Morris, *The Florida Handbook 1987–1988*.

103. Steve Bousquet, "GOP Rule Started with a Democrat," *St. Petersburg Times*, January 23, 2012.

104. Morris, *The Florida Handbook 1987–1988*, 6.

105. Corrigan, *Conservative Hurricane*, 4.

106. Morris, *The Florida Handbook 1987–1988*, 1.

107. Colburn, *From Yellow Dog Democrats to Red State Republicans*, 171.

108. Fla. Const. art. IV, § 4.

109. Fla. Const. art. IV, § 4.

110. Morris, *The Florida Handbook 2013–2014*, 101.

111. Official Results, November 8, 1988 General Election, Florida Department of State, Division of Elections.

112. Official Results, November 8, 1994 General Election, Florida Department of State, Division of Elections and Official Results, November 3, 1998 General Election, Florida Department of State, Division of Elections.

113. Official Results, November 8, 1994, General Election, Florida Department of State, Division of Elections and Official Results, November 7, 2000 General Election, Florida Department of State, Division of Elections.

114. Gallagher, interview, August 2, 2016.

115. "Florida Forever," Florida Department of Environmental Protection, http://dep.state.fl.us.

116. Morgan, "Inside Southern Strategy, Connections Help."

117. Paul Mitchell, interview by Peter Dunbar, January 24, 2018.

118. Clay Roberts, interview by Peter Dunbar, March 20, 2017.

119. *The Clerk's Manual, 1994–1996*; *The Clerk's Manual, 1996–1998*; *The Clerk's Manual, 2000–2002*.

120. *The Clerk's Manual, 1996–1998*; *The Clerk's Manual, 1998–2000*.

121. Doug Darling, interview by Peter Dunbar, January 27, 2017.

122. Rick Mahler, interview by Peter Dunbar, March 15, 2017.

123. Official Results, November 6, 2018 General Election, Florida Department of State, Division of Elections.

124. Emmett Mitchell, interview by Peter Dunbar, March 27, 2017.

125. Marc Dunbar, interview by Peter Dunbar, May 2, 2016.

126. Tom Slade, interview by Mike Haridopolos, June 4, 2009.

127. "Betty Castor," Bureau of Educational and Cultural Affairs, United States Department of State, https://eca.state.gov.

128. Official Results, November 8, 1994 General Election, Florida Department of State, Division of Elections; and Slade, interview, June 4, 2009.

129. Official Results, November 8, 1994 General Election, Florida Department of State, Division of Elections.

130. Official Results, November 3, 1998 General Election, Florida Department of State, Division of Elections.

131. Official Results, November 7, 2000 General Election, Florida Department of State, Division of Elections.

132. Colburn, *From Yellow Dog Democrats to Red State Republicans*, 159.

133. Official Results, November 8, 1994 General Election, Florida Department of State, Division of Elections.

134. Corrigan, *Conservative Hurricane,* 64.

135. Corrigan, *Conservative Hurricane,* 64; Official Results, September 1, 1998, Primary Election, Florida Department of State, Division of Elections.

136. Colburn, *From Yellow Dog Democrats to Red State Republicans*, 163–64.

137. Colburn, *From Yellow Dog Democrats to Red State Republicans*, 163–64.

138. Corrigan, *Conservative Hurricane,* 65.

139. Official Results, November 3, 1998 General Election, Florida Department of State, Division of Elections.

140. Official Results, November 3, 1998 General Election, Florida Department of State, Division of Elections.

141. *The Clerk's Manual, 1998–2000*; Colburn, *From Yellow Dog Democrats to Red State Republicans*, 163, 171.

142. Colburn, *From Yellow Dog Democrats to Red State Republicans*, 157.

143. Corrigan, *Conservative Hurricane,* 156–57; Colburn, *From Yellow Dog Democrats to Red State Republicans*, 164–65.

144. Official Results, September 10, 2004 Primary Election, Florida Department of State, Division of Elections.

145. Howard, "Jeb's Legacy."

146. Official Results, November 5, 2002 General Election, Florida Department of State, Division of Elections.

147. *The Clerk's Manual, 1996–1998*; *The Clerk's Manual, 2004–2006*.

148. Howard, "Jeb's Legacy."

149. Corrigan, *Conservative Hurricane,* 66; Howard, "Jeb's Legacy."

150. Corrigan, *Conservative Hurricane*, 174–75.

151. Pudlow, "Sen. Flores Was Raised to 'Love the Constitution' and the Rule of Law."

152. "President Donald J. Trump Announces Intent to Nominate Carlos G. Muniz to the Department of Education," The White House, Office of the Press Secretary, http://white house.gov.

153. Schorsch, "Jose Oliva Names Carol Gormley as Chief of Staff," *Florida Politics*, November 14, 2018, https://floridapolitics.com/archives/281269-personnel-note-carol-gormley; Jennifer Ungru, interview by Peter Dunbar, November 26, 2018.

154. Marc Caputo, "Return of the GOP King: Jeb Bush's Political Team Staffs up in Tallahassee," *Miami Herald*, January 29, 2015; Ungru, interview, November 26, 2018.

155. Buddy Nevins, "New Chairwoman Brings Hope to Democrats," *South Florida Sun-Sentinel*, June 11, 2005; Ed O'Keefe, "Meet the People Who Will Try to Get Jeb Bush Elected President," *Washington Post*, June 15, 2015.

156. "Mark Kaplan Named UF Vice President for Government and Community Affairs," UF News, www.news.ufl.edu.

157. Mark Silva, "Jeb Bush's Southern Puppet Master," *USA Today*, June 12, 2015.

158. Brian Yablonski, http://perc.org.

159. Slater Bayliss, interview by Peter Dunbar, December 5, 2017.

160. Mike Harrell, interview by Peter Dunbar, October 4, 2018.

161. David Hart, interview by Peter Dunbar, October 30, 2018; Harrell, interview; Bradford L. Thomas, http://www.1dca.org.

162. Jeb Bush, interview by Mike Haridopolos, December 21, 2009.

163. Foundation for Florida's Future, http://afloridapromise.org.

164. Patricia Levesque, http://milkeninstitute.org.

165. Mat Bahl, interview by Peter Dunbar, November 11, 2016.

166. Ward Harkavy, "The Bush-Cheney Gazillions Tour," *Village Voice*, October 23, 2003; Foundation for Florida's Future, http://afloridapromise.org.

167. Julie Hauserman, "Democrats May Lose Agriculture Post," *St. Petersburg Times*, December 20, 2000.

168. *The Clerk's Manual, 1994–1996*.

169. Charles Bronson—Agricultural Hall of Fame, http://floridaaghalloffame.org/ 2012.

170. Official Results, November 5, 2002 General Election, Florida Department of State, Division of Elections and Official Results, November 7, 2006 General Election, Florida Department of State, Division of Elections.

171. *The Clerk's Manual, 1996–1998*.

172. Biographical Directory of the United States Congress, 1774–Present, http://bioguide.congress.gov.

173. Official Results, November 4, 2014 General Election, Florida Department of State, Division of Elections.

174. Official Results, November 6, 2018 General Election, Florida Department of State, Division of Elections.

175. Official Results, November 5, 2002 General Election, Florida Department of State, Division of Elections.

176. Official Results, November 5, 2002 General Election, Florida Department of State, Division of Elections.

177. Official Results, November 5, 2002, General Election, Florida Department of State, Division of Elections.

178. Colburn, *From Yellow Dog Democrats to Red State Republicans*, 10.

179. Official Results, November 7, 2006 General Election, Florida Department of State, Division of Elections.

180. Official Results, August 24, 2010 Primary Election, Florida Department of State, Division of Elections.

181. Official Results, November 2, 2010 General Election, Florida Department of State, Division of Elections.

182. Official Results, November 4, 2014 General Election, Florida Department of State, Division of Elections.

183. Official Results, November 6, 2018 General Election, Florida Department of State, Division of Elections.

184. Official Results, November 5, 2002 General Election, Florida Department of State, Division of Elections.

185. Official Results, November 7, 2006 General Election, Florida Department of State, Division of Elections.

186. Official Results, November 2, 2010 General Election, Florida Department of State, Division of Elections.

187. Official Results, November 4, 2014 General Election, Florida Department of State, Division of Elections.

188. Official Results, November 6, 2018 General Election, Florida Department of State, Division of Elections.

189. Brendan Farrington, "Tale of 2 Parties: Florida GOP High, Democrats Low Ahead of 2018 Races," *Tallahassee Democrat*, January 15, 2017.

190. Official Results, September 5, 2006 Runoff Primary Election, Florida Department of State, Division of Elections.

191. Official Results, November 7, 2006 General Election, Florida Department of State, Division of Elections.

192. Kiser, interview by Dunbar, November 1, 2016; Corrigan, *Conservative Hurricane,* 184.

193. Matt DeLong, "Ex-Florida GOP Chairman Jim Greer Indicted on Six Felony Counts," *Washington Post*, June 2, 2010; Henry Fountain, "Florida—Election Results 2010," *New York Times*, www.nytimes.com/2010/results/florida.

194. Official Results, November 2, 2010 General Election, Florida Department of State, Division of Elections and Official Results, November 4, 2014 General Election, Florida Department of State, Division of Elections.

195. Official Results, November 8, 2016 General Election, Florida Department of State, Division of Elections.

196. Ungru, interview, November 26, 2018.

197. Dan Balz, "Fla. Governor Picks Confidant for Senate," *Washington Post*, August 29, 2009.

198. "About Eric Eikenberg," *Sun Sentinel*, July 5, 2013.

199. Ungru, interview, November 26, 2018.

200. Kathy Mears, interview by Peter Dunbar, October 4, 2016, Tallahassee.

201. Peter Schorsh, "Ron DeSantis Taps Shane Strum for Chief of Staff," *Florida Politics*, http://floridapolitics.com.

202. Gary Fineout, "Scott a Model, Warning for Trump," *Tallahassee Democrat*, November 26, 2016.

203. Official Results, August 24, 2010 Primary Election, Florida Department of State, Division of Elections.

204. Official Results, August 24, 2010 Primary Election, Florida Department of State, Division of Elections and "Florida Governor-Scott vs. Sink (RPC Poll Average)," http://www.realclearpolitics.com.

205. "Florida Elections 2010: Kendrick Meek, Rick Scott Score Big Wins," August 24, 2010, http://www.huffingtonpost.com.

206. Angie Drobnic Holan, Amy Sherman, and Joshua Gillin, "Rating Gov. Rick Scott on his 2010 Campaign Promises," *Miami Herald*, September 6, 2014.

207. Fineout, "Scott a Model, Warning for Trump."

208. Padgett, "Rick Scott's Tea-Friendly Budget Cuts: Too Deep?" *Time*, February 11, 2011.

209. Fountain, "Florida—Election Results 2010," *New York Times*, www.nytimes.com/2010/results/florida.

210. Official Results, November 2, 2010 General Election, Florida Department of State, Division of Elections.

211. Holan, Sherman, and Gillin, "Rating Gov. Rick Scott on his 2010 Campaign Promises."

212. Fineout, "Scott a Model, Warning for Trump."

213. Fineout, "Scott a Model, Warning for Trump."

214. Official Results, August 26, 2014 Primary Election, Florida Department of State, Division of Elections.

215. Official Results, August 26, 2014 Primary Election, Florida Department of State, Division of Elections.

216. Adam C. Smith and Marc Caputo, "How Rick Scott Won Re-election as Florida Governor," *Tampa Bay Times*, November 4, 2014.

217. Official Results, November 4, 2014 General Election, Florida Department of State, Division of Elections.

218. James Brodie, interview by Peter Dunbar, August 2, 2016; and December 6, 2016.

219. James Call, "A Lame Duck, A Laser Focus on New Jobs," *Tallahassee Democrat*, December 4, 2016; Official Results, November 4, 2014 General Election, Florida Department of State, Division of Elections; *The Clerk's Manual, 2010–2012*; *The Clerk's Manual,*

2012–2014; The Clerk's Manual, 2014–2016; and Official Results, November 8, 2016 General Election, Florida Department of State, Division of Elections.

220. Finkbeiner, interview, December 1, 2016.

221. "Did Rick Scott's Chief-of-Staff News Just Ring the Opening Bell for the Senate Race?," *Sunshine State News*, March 26, 2018.

222. Steve Bousquet, "Gov. Rick Scott Names Jackie Schutz Zeckman Chief of Staff," *Miami Herald*, May 16, 2017.

223. Jeff Woodburn, interview by Peter Dunbar, March 31, 2017.

224. Marc Dunbar, interview by Peter Dunbar, May 2, 2016.

225. Peter Schorsch, "Jesse Panuccio Taking Job with Donald Trump Administration," *Florida Politics,* http://floridapolitics.com/archives.

226. "Dueling Profiles," *Tallahassee Democrat*, November 6, 2018.

227. Ana Ceballos, "DeSantis Hopes 'Top Conservative' Cred Will Win Out," *Tallahassee Democrat*, November 6, 2018.

228. Eve Samples, "Looking at DeSantis, the Environment," *Tallahassee Democrat*, November 6, 2018; DeSantis, Tallahassee Breakfast Reception, October 22, 2018.

229. Lloyd Dunkelberger, "Ron DeSantis Has a President's Hand on His Shoulder," *News Service of Florida*, August 16, 2018.

230. Ungru, interview, November 26, 2018.

231. "Dueling Profiles," *Tallahassee Democrat*, November 6, 2018.

232. Caitlin Ostroff, Emily L. Mahoney, and Ben Wieder, "National Megadonors, with Eyes on 2020, Flood Florida Governor's Race with Cash," *Miami Herald*, October 23, 2018.

233. Scott Maxwell, "Blue Wave? Not in Florida as Ron DeSantis, GOP Keep State Red," *Orlando Sentinel*, November 6, 2018.

234. Maxwell, "Blue Wave? Not in Florida as Ron DeSantis, GOP Keep State Red."

235. Official Results, November 6, 2018 General Election, Florida Department of State, Division of Elections.

236. Langston Taylor and Adam Smith, "High Voter Turnout Isn't Helping Democrats: Here's Why," *Tampa Bay Times*, November 7, 2018.

237. Peter Schorsch, "'Calm in the Chaos': How Jones Walker Navigated Recount for Ron DeSantis," *Florida Politics*, December 10, 2018, https://floridapolitics.com/archives/282867-jones-walker-recount-desantis.

238. Ungru, interview, November 26, 2018

239. Erin Isaac, interview by Dunbar, November 14, 2018; Ungru, interview, November 8, 2018.

240. Marc Caputo, "Scott Goes Trump as DeSantis Goes 'Statesman' in Florida Recount," *Politico*, November 13, 2018.

241. Ashley White, "Gillum Concedes Race for Governor," *Tallahassee Democrat*, November 18, 2018; Official Results, November 6, 2018 General Election, Florida Department of State, Division of Elections.

Chapter 6. Republican Senate

1. Dyckman, *Reubin O'D. Askew and the Golden Age of Florida Politics*, 9.

2. Donald H. Reed Jr., meeting with Peter Dunbar, July 1967.

3. Morris, *Reconsiderations—The Emergence of a Party*, 5.

4. *The Clerk's Manual, 1966–1968*.

5. MacKay, *How Florida Happened*, 16.

6. Phelps, *The People in Lawmaking in Florida 1822–2001*.

7. *The Clerk's Manual, 1994–1996*.

8. Rich Heffley, interview by Mike Haridopolos, December 10, 2008.

9. Biographical Directory of the United States Congress, 1774–Present, http://bioguide. congress.gov.

10. Martin Dyckman, "The Loyal Opposition," *St. Petersburg Times*, April 8, 1971.

11. Colburn, *From Yellow Dog Democrats to Red State Republicans*, 24, 31.

12. MacKay, *How Florida Happened*, 16.

13. Dyckman, "The Loyal Opposition."

14. Toni Jennings, interview by Mike Haridopolos, July 15, 2009.

15. *The Clerk's Manual, 1966–1968*.

16. Phelps, *The People in Lawmaking in Florida 1822–2001*.

17. *The Clerk's Manual, 1966–1968*.

18. Garcia, "Heavy Hitter"; Jim Scott, interview by Mike Haridopolos, January 7, 2009.

19. Donald H. Reed Jr., staff conference with Peter Dunbar, January 1968.

20. *The Clerk's Manual, 1966–1968*.

21. Reed, staff conference with Dunbar, January 1968.

22. Heffley, interview by Haridopolos.

23. Kenneth Plante, interview by Mike Haridopolos, January 15, 2009.

24. Reed, staff conference with Dunbar, January 1968.

25. Heffley, interview by Haridopolos.

26. S. Curtis Kiser, interview by Mike Haridopolos, January 15, 2009.

27. Heffley, interview by Haridopolos.

28. Plante, interview.

29. S. Curtis Kiser, interview by Peter Dunbar, August 2, 2016.

30. *The Clerk's Manual, 1972–1974*; *The Clerk's Manual, 1986–1988*.

31. Dyckman, "The Loyal Opposition."

32. Dyckman, "The Loyal Opposition."

33. *The Clerk's Manual, 1970–1972*.

34. Dyckman, "The Loyal Opposition."

35. *The Clerk's Manual, 1974–1976*.

36. *The Clerk's Manual, 1974–1976*.

37. *The Clerk's Manual 1978–1980*; *The Clerk's Manual, 1980–1982*.

38. Fla. Const. art. III, § 16.

39. Swann v. Adams, 263 F.Supp. 225 (1967).

40. Tom Feeney, interview by Mike Haridopolos, December 16, 2008.

41. *The Clerk's Manual, 1970–1972.*

42. Kiser, interview by Dunbar, October 4, 2016.

43. Jim Scott, interview.

44. *The Clerk's Manual, 1972–1974; The Clerk's Manual, 1990–1992; The Clerk's Manual, 1992–1994.*

45. *The Clerk's Manual, 1982–1984.*

46. *The Clerk's Manual, 1990–1992.*

47. Jim Scott, interview.

48. Jennings, interview.

49. *The Clerk's Manual, 1982–1984.*

50. *The Clerk's Manual, 1982–1984.*

51. Kiser, interview by Dunbar, August 2, 2016.

52. Jennings, interview.

53. Kiser, interview by Dunbar, April 5, 2016.

54. Jennings, interview.

55. Phelps, *The People in Lawmaking in Florida 1822–2001.*

56. Jim Scott, interview.

57. Jimmy Patronis, interview by Peter Dunbar, August 23, 2018.

58. Official Results, November 4, 1986 General Election, Florida Department of State, Division of Elections.

59. Kiser, interview by Dunbar, August 2, 2016.

60. *The Clerk's Manual, 1984–1986.*

61. *The Clerk's Manual, 1986–1988.*

62. Official Results, November 8, 1988 General Election, Florida Department of State, Division of Elections.

63. *The Clerk's Manual, 1988–1990.*

64. Jim Scott, interview.

65. *Journal of the Senate*, November 22, 1988.

66. *The Clerk's Manual, 1988–1990.*

67. *The Clerk's Manual, 1990–1992; The Clerk's Manual, 1992–1994; The Clerk's Manual, 1994–1996.*

68. Jennings, interview.

69. Jennings, interview.

70. Jennings, interview.

71. Jim Scott, interview.

72. Tom Slade, interview by Mike Haridopolos.

73. Gene McGee, interview by Mike Haridopolos, January 7, 2009.

74. Jim Scott, interview.

75. Phelps, *The People in Lawmaking in Florida 1822–2001.*

76. Kiser, interview by Dunbar, October 4, 2016.

77. *The Clerk's Manual, 1990–1992.*

78. Jim Scott, interview.

79. *The Clerk's Manual, 1992–1994.*

80. *Senate Handbook 1992–1994.*

81. Phelps, *The People in Lawmaking in Florida 1822–2001.*

82. *The Clerk's Manual, 1992–1994.*

83. Jennings, interview.

84. Morris, *The Florida Handbook 2013–2014*, 226.

85. Jim Scott, interview.

86. *The Clerk's Manual, 1992–1994.*

87. *The Clerk's Manual, 1992–1994.*

88. Kiser, interview by Dunbar, November 1, 2016.

89. Fla. Const. art. VI, § 4.

90. Kiser, interview by Dunbar, May 3, 2016.

91. Swann v. Adams, 385 U.S. 440 (1967); Swann v. Adams, 263 F.Supp. 225 (1967).

92. "Legislative Term Limits: An Overview," National Conference of State Legislatures, March 13, 2015, www.ncsl.org.

93. Waczewski, "An Analysis of the Impact of Term Limits on the Legislature," 6, 18.

94. Fla. Const. art. VI, § 4.

95. Feeney, interview.

96. Waczewski, "An Analysis of the Impact of Term Limits on the Legislature," 26.

97. *The Clerk's Manual, 1994–1996.*

98. *The Clerk's Manual, 1994–1996.*

99. Official Results, November 8, 1994 General Election, Florida Department of State, Division of Elections.

100. Jennings, interview; *The Clerk's Manual, 1994–1996.*

101. Jennings, interview.

102. Jennings, interview.

103. *The Clerk's Manual, 1996–1998*; Phelps, *The People in Lawmaking in Florida 1822–2001.*

104. Official Results, November 5, 1996 General Election, Florida Department of State, Division of Elections.

105. The Clerk's Manual, 1996–1998.

106. Mario Diaz-Balart, interview by Mike Haridopolos, July 15, 2009.

107. Jack Latvala, interview by Peter Dunbar, September 22, 2016.

108. Jennings, interview.

109. *The Clerk's Manual, 1998–2000.*

110. Phelps, *The People in Lawmaking in Florida 1822–2001.*

111. *The Clerk's Manual, 1998–2000.*

112. Morris, *The Florida Handbook 1998–2000.*

113. *The Clerk's Manual, 2000–2002*; *The Clerk's Manual, 2002–2004.*

114. *The Clerk's Manual, 2000–2002.*

115. Diaz-Balart, interview.

116. *Senate Handbook 2002–2004.*

117. Agustin Corbella, interview by Peter Dunbar, December 15, 2016; Sandra Mortham, interview by Peter Dunbar, May 7, 2018.

118. *The Clerk's Manual, 2004–2006; The Clerk's Manual, 2006–2008; The Clerk's Manual, 2008–2010.*

119. *The Clerk's Manual, 2004–2006.*

120. *Senate Handbook 2006–2008.*

121. *The Clerk's Manual, 2008–2010.*

122. *Senate Handbook 2010–2012.*

123. *The Clerk's Manual, 2010–2012.*

124. *The Clerk's Manual, 2010–2012.*

125. Official Results, November 2, 2010 General Election, Florida Department of State, Division of Elections.

126. Fla. Const. art. III, § 20 and 21.

127. "The People Have Spoken: We Want FairDistricts Now!" http://fairdistrictsnow.org/mission/.

128. *The Clerk's Manual, 2012–2014.*

129. *The Clerk's Manual, 2014–2016.*

130. League of Women Voters v. Detzner, Case no. 2012-CA-2842 (2nd Circuit, Leon County).

131. Jeremy Wallace and Mary Ellen Klaus, "Florida Legislature Won't Appeal Redistricting Ruling," *Tampa Bay Times*, January 20, 2016.

132. Lauren Flannery and Michael Van Sickler, "Democrats Could Have Won Back Florida's Senate on Tuesday," *Tampa Bay Times*, November 4, 2016.

133. Patricia Mazzei, "Gobsmacked by Election, Florida Democrats try to Refocus," *Miami Herald,* November 12, 2016.

134. Official Results, November 8, 2016 General Election, Florida Department of State, Division of Elections.

135. James Call, "Negron: Senate Isn't Moderate," *Tallahassee Democrat*, December 13, 2016.

136. Official Results, November 6, 2018 General Election, Florida Department of State, Division of Elections.

137. *The Clerk's Manual, 2018–2020.*

138. *The Clerk's Manual, 1984–1986; The Clerk's Manual, 1986–1988; The Clerk's Manual, 1988–1990; The Clerk's Manual, 1994–1996; The Clerk's Manual, 1996–1998;* Kiser, interview by Dunbar, August 2, 2016.

139. *The Clerk's Manual, 1990–1992; The Clerk's Manual, 1992–1994; The Clerk's Manual, 1994–1996; The Clerk's Manual, 1996–1998; The Clerk's Manual, 2004–2006; The Clerk's Manual, 2006–2008; The Clerk's Manual, 2012–2014; The Clerk's Manual, 2014–2016.*

140. *The Clerk's Manual, 1982–1984* through *The Clerk's Manual, 1994–1996.*

141. *The Clerk's Manual, 1990–1992; The Clerk's Manual, 1992–1994; The Clerk's Manual; The Clerk's Manual, 1996–1998; The Clerk's Manual, 2004–2006.*

142. R. Z. Safley, interview by Peter Dunbar, November 26, 2018.

143. Doug Bruce, interview by Peter Dunbar, September 30, 2016.

144. Mortham, interview, May 7, 2018.

145. Eric Thorn, interview by Peter Dunbar, March 19, 2018.

146. *The Clerk's Manual, 1992–1994; The Clerk's Manual, 1994–1996; The Clerk's Manual, 2002–2004; The Clerk's Manual, 2008–2010; The Clerk's Manual, 2010–2012.*

147. Corbella, interview.

148. *The Clerk's Manual, 2002–2004.*

149. Kathy Mears, interview by Peter Dunbar, October 4, 2016.

150. Steven Birnholz, "Florida Council of 100 Names Bob Ward President and Chief Executive Officer," August 26, 2016, Florida Council of 100, www.fc100.org.

151. Robin Safley, interview by Peter Dunbar, October 12, 2016.

152. *The Clerk's Manual, 2004–2006.*

153. Mat Bahl, interview by Peter Dunbar, November 11, 2016; *The Clerk's Manual, 2006–2008; The Clerk's Manual, 2010–2012; The Clerk's Manual, 2016–2018.*

154. Todd Reid, interview by Peter Dunbar, January 9, 2017.

155. *The Clerk's Manual, 1998–2000; The Clerk's Manual, 2000–2002.*

156. *The Clerk's Manual, 2004–2006.*

157. Chris Moya, interview by Peter Dunbar, January 5, 2017.

158. Peter Schorsch, "Brightest Minds in Florida Politics: Sarah Bascom, *SaintPetersblog*, http://saintpetersblog.com.

159. Pamela Campbell, interview by Peter Dunbar, August 8, 2016.

160. Kiser, interview by Dunbar, November 8, 2016.

161. Cari Roth, interview by Peter Dunbar, April 30, 2016.

162. Marion Hoffmann, interview by Peter Dunbar, December 14, 2017.

163. Chris Finkbeiner, interview by Peter Dunbar, July 14, 2016.

164. *The Clerk's Manual, 2010–2012.*

165. John Morroni, interview by Peter Dunbar, May 24, 2016.

166. Patronis, interview; *The Clerk's Manual, 2012–2014.*

167. Joe Gruters, interview by Peter Dunbar, September 3, 2018.

168. Kurt Kelly, interview by Peter Dunbar, February 9, 2017; Phelps, *The People in Lawmaking in Florida 1822–2001; The Clerk's Manual, 2014–2016;* John Stargel, interview by Peter Dunbar, March 9, 2017; *The Clerk's Manual, 2002–2004; The Clerk's Manual, 2006–2008; The Clerk's Manual, 1996–1998;* Marc Dunbar, interview by Peter Dunbar, October 10, 2016; *The Clerk's Manual, 2016–2018.*

169. *The Clerk's Manual, 2014–2016.*

170. Jim Scott, interview, January 7, 2009.

171. Ronald R. Richmond, interview by Peter Dunbar, April 5, 2016.

172. *The Clerk's Manual, 1990–1992.*

173. Mears, interview by Dunbar, October 4, 2016; *The Clerk's Manual, 2012–2014.*

174. *The Clerk's Manual, 2016–2018.*

175. Marc Dunbar, interview, April 1, 2018; Matthew Blair, interview by Peter Dunbar, April 6, 2018; Mortham, interview, May 7, 2018; Moya interview, October 22, 2018.

176. Finkbeiner, interview, December 1, 2016; *The Clerk's Manual, 2000–2002;* Scott MacPherson, interview by Peter Dunbar, March 14, 2017.

177. Stephen Shiver, interview by Peter Dunbar, July 1, 2016.

Chapter 7. A Republican House

1. Dan Webster, interview by Mike Haridopolos, June 12, 2009.

2. Official Results, November 5, 1996 General Election, Florida Department of State, Division of Elections.

3. Webster, interview.

4. Phelps, *The People in Lawmaking in Florida 1822–2001.*

5. John Thrasher, interview by Mike Haridopolos, January 6, 2009; Webster, interview; Rich Heffley, interview by Mike Haridopolos, December 10, 2008.

6. Marc Caputo, "The Curious Case of Dan Webster, a 'Plodder,' Not a Prophet,'" *Miami Herald,* January 7, 2015.

7. Brecht Heuchan, interview by Mike Haridopolos, March 16, 2009.

8. Thrasher, interview.

9. Heuchan, interview.

10. Heffley, interview.

11. *The Clerk's Manual, 1994–1996.*

12. Webster, interview.

13. Official Results, November 5, 1996 General Election, Florida Department of State, Division of Elections.

14. Luis Rojas, interview by Mike Haridopolos, January 15, 2009.

15. Thrasher, interview.

16. Thrasher, interview; and S. Curtis Kiser, interview by Peter Dunbar, April 5, 2016, and May 3, 2016.

17. Morris, *Reconsiderations—The Emergence of a Party,* 3.

18. Kiser, interview by Dunbar, April 5, 2016.

19. Frank Messersmith, interview by Peter Dunbar, November 1, 2016.

20. Morris, *Reconsiderations—The Emergence of a Party,* 3; see also Phelps, *The People in Lawmaking in Florida 1822–2001.*

21. Genean Hawkins McKinnon, interview by Peter Dunbar, May 18, 2018.

22. Morris, *Reconsiderations—The Emergence of a Party,* 10 and 11.

23. *The Clerk's Manual, 2000–2002.*

24. Morris, *Reconsiderations—The Emergence of a Party,* 11; David Schultz, "Rep. Don Reed King: Among GOP Legislators," *Palm Beach Post-Times,* April 25, 1971.

25. Adkins, *Making Modern Florida,* 118.

26. Allen Morris, "It's a New Kind of Ball Game in Tallahassee," *Florida Times-Union,* March 29, 1970.

27. Kiser, interview by Dunbar, April 5, 2016.

28. Morris, *Reconsiderations—The Emergence of a Party,* 18.

29. Swann v. Adams, 385 U.S. 440 (1967).

30. *The Clerk's Manual, 1966–1968.*

31. Phelps, *The People in Lawmaking in Florida 1822–2001.*

32. Bruce Stone, interview by Peter Dunbar, July 30, 2010.

33. Phelps, *The People in Lawmaking in Florida 1822–2001*; Donald H. Reed, meeting with Peter Dunbar, July 1967.

34. Adkins, *Making Modern Florida*, 107.

35. *The Clerk's Manual, 1966–1968*, 11–22.

36. Reed, meeting with Dunbar, July 1967.

37. *The Clerk's Manual, 1966–1968.*

38. Schultz, "Rep. Don Reed King: Among GOP Legislators."

39. *The Clerk's Manual, 1966–1968.*

40. Reed, meeting with Dunbar, July 1967.

41. *The Clerk's Manual, 1966–1968.*

42. Donald H. Reed Jr., staff conference with Peter Dunbar, April 1967.

43. Peter Dunbar, personal staff notes, July 1972.

44. Schultz, "Rep. Don Reed King: Among GOP Legislators."

45. *The Clerk's Manual, 1968–1970.*

46. Kiser, interview by Dunbar, February 7, 2017.

47. Peter Dunbar, personal staff notes, 1969.

48. Kiser, interview by Dunbar, February 7, 2017.

49. Peter Dunbar, personal staff notes, 1969.

50. Morris, *The Florida Handbook 2013–2014,* 227; Ronald R. Richmond, interview by Peter Dunbar, October 4, 2016.

51. Kiser, interview by Dunbar, October 4, 2016; Messersmith, interview, October 4, 2016.

52. Richmond, interview, April 5, 2016, and May 3, 2016.

53. Kiser, interview by Dunbar, April 5, 2016, and May 3, 2016.

54. Kiser, interview by Dunbar, October 4, 2016.

55. Richmond, interview, October 4, 2016.

56. Reed, staff conference with Dunbar, May 1967.

57. Peter Dunbar, personal staff notes, May 1968.

58. Rule 10.8, *The Rules*, Florida House of Representatives, 1980/1982.

59. Rule 10.8, *The Rules*, Florida House of Representatives, 1980/1982.

60. Elvis Lane, "Don Reed in a Hurry to Get to Washington," *Palm Beach Post-Times,* August 24, 1969.

61. Rule 10.10, *The Rules*, Florida House of Representatives, 1980/1982.

62. Peter Dunbar, personal staff notes, May 1968.

63. Kiser, interview by Dunbar, October 4, 2016.

64. Rule 10.14 (c), *The Rules*, Florida House of Representatives, 1980/1982.

65. Rule 8.10, *The Rules*, Florida House of Representatives, 1980/1982.

66. Rule 15.2, *The Rules*, Florida House of Representatives, 1980/1982.

67. Peter Dunbar, personal staff notes, June 1967.

68. Allen Morris, "Of Shipwrecks, Duels and Filibusters," *Floridian*, April 5, 1970.

69. Peter Dunbar, personal staff notes, June 1967.

70. Peter Dunbar, personal staff notes, June 1967.

71. Richmond, interview, May 3, 2016; Messersmith, interview, November 1, 2016.

72. *The Clerk's Manual, 1970–1972*.

73. Jim Scott, interview by Mike Haridopolos, January 7, 2009.

74. "Staff Report #1," House Republican Office, July 15, 1971, 38–39; "Staff Report #2," House Republican Office, October 11, 1971; Milton, et al., v. Smathers, 351 SO.2d 24 (Fla. 1977); Alberto Cardenas, interview by Peter Dunbar, January 12, 2017.

75. *The Clerk's Manual, 1972–1974*; *The Clerk's Manual, 1974–1976*; *The Clerk's Manual, 1978–1980*; *The Clerk's Manual, 1980–1982*.

76. Dyckman, *Reubin O'D. Askew and the Golden Age of Florida Politics*, 88.

77. Dyckman, *Reubin O'D. Askew and the Golden Age of Florida Politics*, 29.

78. Ed Taylor, "51 Years a Vero Beach Lawyer," *Indian River Guardian*, February 11, 2014.

79. *The Clerk's Manual, 1972–1974*.

80. *The Clerk's Manual, 1974–1976*.

81. *The Clerk's Manual, 1978–1980*.

82. Official Results, November 2, 1976 General Election, Florida Department of State, Division of Elections.

83. Morris, *Reconsiderations—The Speakers: Donald LeGrand Tucker*, 6.

84. Kiser, interview by Dunbar, August 2, 2016.

85. Morris, *Reconsiderations—The Speakers: Donald LeGrand Tucker*, 1.

86. Kiser, interview by Dunbar, May 3, 2016; Richmond, interview by Dunbar, May 3, 2016.

87. *The Clerk's Manual, 1978–1980*.

88. Kiser, interview by Dunbar, October 4, 2016.

89. *The Clerk's Manual, 1980–1982*.

90. Morris, *Reconsiderations—The Speakers: Ralph Harris Haben, Jr.*, 6.

91. Kiser, interview by Dunbar, October 4, 2016.

92. James Brodie, interview by Dunbar, November 1, 2016.

93. Kiser, interview by Dunbar, May 3, 2016; Richmond, interview by Dunbar, May 3, 2016.

94. *The Clerk's Manual, 1982–1984*; Cardenas, interview.

95. *The Clerk's Manual, 1984–1986*.

96. *The Clerk's Manual, 1984–1986*.

97. *The Clerk's Manual, 1984–1986*.

98. Richmond, interview by Dunbar, May 3, 2016; Dale Patchett, interview by Peter Dunbar, March 14, 2017.

99. Jeff Klinkenberg, "Marine Fisheries Commission," *St. Petersburg Times*, June 12, 1983.

100. Sandra Mortham, interview by Peter Dunbar, October 4, 2016; Messersmith, interview, November 1, 2016.

101. *The Clerk's Manual, 1986–1988.*

102. *The Clerk's Manual, 1988–1990.*

103. Phelps, *The People in Lawmaking in Florida 1822–2001.*

104. Phelps, *The People in Lawmaking in Florida 1822–2001.*

105. Messersmith, interview, November 1, 2016.

106. Chapter 2016–201, *Laws of Florida.*

107. *The Clerk's Manual, 1990–1992.*

108. *The Clerk's Manual, 1992–1994.*

109. *The Clerk's Manual, 1992–1994.*

110. *The Clerk's Manual, 1994–1996.*

111. *The Clerk's Manual, 1994–1996.*

112. Tom Feeney, interview by Mike Haridopolos, December 16, 2008.

113. *The Clerk's Manual, 1996–1998.*

114. Bill Cotterell, "Education Bill Is Logrolling on Steroids," *Tallahassee Democrat*, November 23, 2017.

115. *The Clerk's Manual, 1998–2000.*

116. Thrasher, interview.

117. *The Clerk's Manual, 2000–2002*, 196–97.

118. *The Clerk's Manual, 2000–2002;* Aaron Bean, interview by Peter Dunbar and Mike Haridopolos, October 25, 2016, Ocala.

119. *The Clerk's Manual, 2002–2004.*

120. *The Clerk's Manual, 2002–2004.*

121. *The Clerk's Manual, 2002–2004.*

122. *The Clerk's Manual, 2004–2006.*

123. *The Clerk's Manual, 2006–2008.*

124. *The Clerk's Manual, 2008–2010.*

125. *The Clerk's Manual, 2010–2012.*

126. *The Clerk's Manual, 2012–2014.*

127. *The Clerk's Manual, 2012–2014.*

128. *The Clerk's Manual, 2012–2014.*

129. *The Clerk's Manual, 2014–2016.*

130. *The Clerk's Manual, 2014–2016.*

131. *The Clerk's Manual, 2016–2018.*

132. *The Clerks' Manual, 2018–2020.*

133. Swann v. Adams, 385 U.S. 440 (1967).

134. Official Results, November 6, 2018 General Election, Florida Department of State, Division of Elections.

Chapter 8. Washington and the Florida Republicans

1. Steve Schale, "Florida 2016 in the Rearview Mirror," http://steveschale.com/blog.

2. Morris, *The Florida Handbook 1987–1988*, 624.

3. 270 to Win "Historical Presidential Elections," www.270towin.com.

4. 270 to Win, "Historical Presidential Elections," www.270towin.com.

5. Official Results, November 4, 1980 General Election, Florida Department of State, Division of Elections and Official Results, November 6, 1984 General Election, Florida Department of State, Division of Elections.

6. Official Results, November 8, 1988 General Election, Florida Department of State, Division of Elections.

7. Presidential Elections, http://uselectionatlas.org.

8. Historical Presidential Elections, www.270towin.com.

9. S. Curtis Kiser, interview by Peter Dunbar, October 4, 2016.

10. Official Results, November 3, 1992 General Election, Florida Department of State, Division of Elections and Official Results; November 5, 1996 General Election, Florida Department of State, Division of Elections.

11. Official Results, November 7, 2000 General Election, Florida Department of State, Division of Elections.

12. Randy Enwright, interview by Peter Dunbar, March 22, 2018; Cameron Yarbrough, interview by Peter Dunbar, November 14, 2018; Andy Palmer, interview by Peter Dunbar, November 19, 2018; David Johnson, interview by Peter Dunbar, November 28, 2018; Mike Grissom, interview by Peter Dunbar, November 8, 2018.

13. Clay Roberts, interview by Peter Dunbar, March 20, 2017; Eric Thorn, interview by Peter Dunbar, March 19, 2018; Enwright, interview; Richard Coates, interview by Peter Dunbar, October 22, 2018; Emmett Mitchell, interview by Peter Dunbar, March 27, 2017.

14. Marc Reichelderfer, interview by Peter Dunbar, October 23, 2018; Marc Dunbar, interview by Peter Dunbar, October 10, 2016; Wells, *Inside "Bush v. Gore,"* 66.

15. Marc Dunbar, interview by Peter Dunbar, April 1, 2018.

16. Bush v. Gore, 531 U.S. 98 (2000).

17. Official Results, November 2, 2004 General Election, Florida Department of State, Division of Elections.

18. Official Results, November 4, 2008 General Election, Florida Department of State, Division of Elections and Official Results, November 6, 2012 General Election, Florida Department of State, Division of Elections.

19. Adam Smith and Alex Leary, "Donald Trump Is Elected 45th President of the U.S. with Florida's Help," *Tampa Bay Times*, November 9, 2016.

20. Steven Lemongello, "Trump Takes Florida over Clinton," *Orlando Sentinel*, November 9, 2016.

21. Official Results, November 8, 2016 General Election, Florida Department of State, Division of Elections.

22. Schale, "Florida 2016 in the Rearview Mirror," http://steveschale.com/blog.

23. "William F. Murfin (1925–2008)," *Northwest Florida Daily News*, October 16, 2008.

24. Kiser, interview by Dunbar, October 4, 2016; Nathaniel P. Reed, http://nathaniel-preed.blogspot.com.

25. Official Results, November 5, 1974 General Election, Florida Department of State, Division of Elections.

26. Phelps, *The People in Lawmaking in Florida 1822–2001*; Official Results, November 5, 1974 General Election, Florida Department of State, Division of Elections.

27. *Jerry Thomas Confirmation Hearing,* 94th Cong., April 1, 1976, 7 and 8.

28. "Jack Eckerd, Drug Store Pioneer, Philanthropist and Founder of Eckerd Youth Program Dies," PR Newswire, May 19, 2004.

29. Alberto Cardenas, interview by Peter Dunbar, January 12, 2017.

30. Van Poole, interview by Peter Dunbar, March 14, 2017; Dale Patchett, interview by Peter Dunbar, March 14, 2017; Cardenas, interview.

31. Kevin Michael Moore, U.S. District Courts for the Districts of Florida, History of the Federal Judiciary, Federal Judicial Center, www.fjc.gov.

32. Robert "Bob" Martinez, Florida Department of State, dos.myflorida.com.

33. Jim Magill, interview by Peter Dunbar, February 6, 2017.

34. "Mel Sembler: Executive Profile & Biography—Businessweek," September 5, 2016, www.bloomberg.com.

35. Karl Vick, "Zappala Confirmed as Ambassador to Spain," *St. Petersburg Times,* October 4, 1989.

36. "Mel Sembler: Executive Profile & Biography—Businessweek," September 5, 2016, www.bloomberg.com.

37. "John D. Rood, Ambassador to the Bahamas," U.S. Department of State Archive, January 20, 2009; "Alfred Hoffman, Jr., Ambassador to Portugal," U.S. Department of State Archive, January 20, 2009.

38. "Francis Rooney, Ambassador to the Holy See," U.S. Department of State Archive, January 20, 2009.

39. Lemongello, "Mel Martinez," *Time,* August 22, 2005.

40. Enwright, interview.

41. Vogel, "Florida's Richest 25"; Paul Davidson, "Ross Is New Face of American Business," *USA Today,* December 1, 2016; Trip Gabriel, "Trump Chooses Ben Carson to Lead HUD," *New York Times,* December 5, 2016.

42. Mary Ellen Klaus and Patricia Mazzei, "Carlos Trujillo Named as U.S. Ambassador to OAS," *Tampa Bay Times,* October 26, 2017.

43. Peter Schorsch, "Jesse Panuccio Taking Job with Donald Trump Administration," http://floridapolitics.com/archieves.

44. "President Donald J. Trump Announces Intent to Nominate Carlos G. Muniz to the Department of Education," The White House, Office of the Press Secretary, http://whitehouse.gov; Mary Ellen Klaus, "Trump Picks Bush Ally Frank Brogan to Be Assistant Secretary of Education," *Tampa Bay Times,* March 29, 2018.

45. Adam C. Smith, "Here's the Latest Florida Five from the Daily Buzz," enews@email1.tampabay.com; James Call, "Capital City Represented in Trump's EPA," *Tallahassee Democrat,* September 8, 2017; Patricia Mazzei, "Miami's Helen Aguirre Ferre Gets Trump White House Job," *Miami Herald,* January 19, 2017; Michael Biesecker, "EPA Appointee Approved to Consult for Clients," *Tallahassee Democrat,* March 6, 2018.

46. Amy Hollyfield, "Rep. Neil Combee Resigning to Take Federal Farm Service Job," *Tampa Bay Times*, November 9, 2017; "Ballard Partners, Ft. Lauderdale," *Florida Trend*, May 7, 2018; Smith, "Here's the Latest Florida Five from the Daily Buzz," enews@email1.tampabay.com.

47. Allen, *The Florida Handbook 1995–1996*, 648–49.

48. Allen, *The Florida Handbook 1995–1996*, 648–49.

49. Official Results, November 5, 1968 General Election, Florida Department of State, Division of Elections.

50. Colburn, *From Yellow Dog Democrats to Red State Republicans*, 65–66.

51. Official Results, November 5, 1974 General Election, Florida Department of State, Division of Elections.

52. Official Results, November 3, 1970 General Election, Florida Department of State, Division of Elections.

53. Official Results, November 4, 1986 General Election, Florida Department of State, Division of Elections.

54. Official Results, November 8, 1988 General Election, Florida Department of State, Division of Elections.

55. Official Results, November 8, 1994 General Election, Florida Department of State, Division of Elections.

56. Senator Connie Mack III, Congress.Gov, Library of Congress, https://www.congress.gov.

57. Official Results, November 7, 2000 General Election, Florida Department of State, Division of Elections.

58. Official Results, November 2, 2004 General Election, Florida Department of State, Division of Elections.

59. Morris, *The Florida Handbook 2013–2014*, 300.

60. Dan Balz, "Fla. Governor Picks Confidant for Senate," *Washington Post*, August 29, 2009.

61. Official Results, November 2, 2010 General Election, Florida Department of State, Division of Elections.

62. Official Results, November 8, 2016 General Election, Florida Department of State, Division of Elections.

63. Herb Jackson, "Final Version of GOP Tax Bill a Winner for Rubio and Corker," *USA Today*, December 16, 2017.

64. Reid Wilson, "Midterms in 2018 Become Most Expensive in History," *The Hill*, October 16, 2018.

65. Manuel Roig-Franzia and Amy Gardner, "Nelson's Chance at Win in Florida Senate Race Dwindles as Key Counties Complete Hand Recount," *Washington Post*, November 17, 2018.

66. Jeffrey Schweers, "Seven Lawsuits and Counting: Tallahassee Is Ground Zero," *Tallahassee Democrat*, November 14, 2018.

67. Robert Bridges, "As for Nelsons, 'Willie' Doesn't Mean 'Bill' on Write-in Ballots," *Lake City Reporter*, November 15, 2018.

68. Steve Bousquet and Steve Contorno, "Bill Nelson's Ending: Sluggish Campaign Couldn't Overcome Rick Scott's Millions," *Tampa Bay Times*, November 17, 2018.

69. John McCarthy, "Recount: Scott Defeats Nelson," *Florida Today*, November 19, 2018.

70. Official Results, November 6, 2016 General Election, Florida Department of State, Division of Elections.

71. Congressman John L. Mica, *Congressional Record*, October 20, 2003.

72. Morris, *The Florida Handbook 2013–2014*, 304.

73. Reynolds v. Sims, 377 U.S. 533 (1964).

74. Morris, *The Florida Handbook 2013–2014*, 261.

75. Morris, *The Florida Handbook 1967–1968*, 187.

76. Biographical Directory of the United States Congress, 1774–Present, http://bio guide.congress.gov.

77. Biographical Directory of the United States Congress, 1774–Present, http://bio guide.congress.gov.

78. Official Results, November 5, 1968 General Election, Florida Department of State, Division of Elections and Official Results, November 3, 1970 General Election, Florida Department of State, Division of Elections.

79. Official Results, November 7, 1978 General Election, Florida Department of State, Division of Elections.

80. Official Results, November 4, 1980 General Election, Florida Department of State, Division of Elections.

81. Official Results, November 2, 1982 General Election, Florida Department of State, Division of Elections.

82. Biographical Directory of the United States Congress, 1774–Present, http://bio guide.congress.gov.

83. Official Results, November 2, 1982 General Election, Florida Department of State, Division of Elections; Morris, *The Florida Handbook 1995–1996*, 660.

84. Morris, *The Florida Handbook 2013–2014*, 261, 518.

85. Phelps, *The People in Lawmaking in Florida 1822–2001*; *The Clerk's Manual, 2008–2010*; *The Clerk's Manual, 2010–2012* and Biographical Directory of the United States Congress, 1774–Present, http://bioguide.congress.gov.

86. Morris, *The Florida Handbook 2013–2014*, 261.

87. Mary Ellen Klaus and Steve Bousquet, "Florida Hands Redistricting to Courts for Only the Second Time in History," *Tribune New Service*, August 24, 2015.

88. Johnson v. DeGrandy, 515 U.S. 997 (1994).

89. Official Results, November 3, 1992 General Election, Florida Department of State, Division of Elections; Morris, *The Florida Handbook 1995–1996*, 662.

90. Morris, *The Florida Handbook 1995–1996*, 662.

91. Official Results, November 8, 1994 General Election, Florida Department of State, Division of Elections and Biographical Directory of the United States Congress, 1774–Present, http://bioguide.congress.gov.

92. Morris, *The Clerk's Manual, 2002–2004*.

93. Official Results, November 5, 2002 General Election, Florida Department of State, Division of Elections.

94. Morris, *The Florida Handbook 2013–2014*, 349–50.

95. Official Results, November 5, 2002 General Election, Florida Department of State, Division of Elections; *The Clerk's Manual, 2000–2002*; Official Results, November 5, 2002 General Election, Florida Department of State, Division of Elections.

96. Biographical Directory of the United States Congress, 1774–Present, http://bio guide.congress.gov.

97. League of Women Voters of Florida v. Detzner, 172 SO.3d 363 (Fla. 2015).

98. Morris, *The Florida Handbook 2013–2014*, 302.

99. Official Results, November 8, 2016 General Election, Florida Department of State, Division of Elections.

100. Official Results, November 6, 2018 General Election, Florida Department of State, Division of Elections.

101. *Congressional Record*, October 20, 2003.

102. MyClearwater.com, www.clearwater-fl.com/gov.

103. Stephen Shiver, interview by Peter Dunbar, July 1, 2016; Biographical Directory of the United States Congress, 1774–Present, http://bioguide.congress.gov.

104. Harry Straight and Donna Blanton, "Taped Talk," *Orlando Sentinel*, March 16, 1986.

105. *The Clerk's Manual, 1986–1988*; *The Clerk's Manual, 2010–2012*; Mike Miller, interview by Peter Dunbar, August 18, 2016, Orlando; Chris Sprowls, interview by Peter Dunbar, February 27, 2017.

Chapter 9. Politics, Policy, and Contributions

1. Tom Slade, interview by Mike Haridopolos, June 4, 2009.

2. Barlow, *Our Florida Legacy*, 122.

3. Allen Morris, "It's a New Kind of Ball Game in Tallahassee," *Florida Times-Union*, March 29, 1970.

4. Dyckman, *Reubin O'D. Askew and the Golden Age of Florida Politics*, 29.

5. Donald H. Reed Jr., meeting with Peter Dunbar, June 1968.

6. MacKay, *How Florida Happened*, 29.

7. Colburn, *From Yellow Dog Democrats to Red State Republicans*, 129–30, 153; Jack Latvala, interview by Peter Dunbar, September 22, 2016, St. Petersburg.

8. Dyckman, *Reubin O'D. Askew and the Golden Age of Florida Politics*, 87.

9. Toni Jennings, interview by Mike Haridopolos, July 15, 2009.

10. Adkins, *Making Modern Florida*, 164, 165; Dyckman, *Reubin O'D. Askew and the Golden Age of Florida Politics*, 29.

11. Claude Kirk Jr., address to the Joint Session of the Legislature, April 4, 1967.

12. Dyckman, *Reubin O'D. Askew and the Golden Age of Florida Politics*, 20.

13. Fla. Const. article IV, § 6.

14. Dyckman, *Reubin O' D. Askew and the Golden Age of Florida Politics*, 29.

15. MacKay, *How Florida Happened*, 29; Karl, *The 57 Club*, 160.

16. MacKay, *How Florida Happened*, 29.

17. §120.51, Fla. Stat.

18. S. Curtis Kiser, interview by Peter Dunbar, May 3, 2016.

19. Peter Dunbar, personal staff notes, April 1968.

20. Kiser, interview by Dunbar, April 5, 2016; Dyckman, *Reubin O' D. Askew and the Golden Age of Florida Politics*, 179.

21. Bobby Brantley, interview by Peter Dunbar, July 13, 2016.

22. Patty Woodworth, meeting with Peter Dunbar, January 10, 1989.

23. Martinez v. Florida Legislature, 542 SO.2d 358 (Fla. 1989).

24. Sandra Mortham, interview by Peter Dunbar, May 15, 2018.

25. Chapter 2005–21, *Laws of Florida*.

26. Corrigan, *Conservative Hurricane*, 68.

27. Amy Baker, interview by Peter Dunbar, April 10, 2017.

28. "State Personnel System Annual Workforce Report," Florida Department of Management Services, January 22, 2014; Cotterell, "Think State Government Is Big and Bloated? Guess Again," *Tallahassee Democrat*, March 8, 2018.

29. Donald H. Reed Jr., meeting with Dunbar, July 1967

30. Morris, *The Florida Handbook 2013–2014*, 19, 172.

31. Rules 6.55 and 6.56, Rules of the House of Representatives.

32. Fla. Const. art. III.

33. Dyckman, *Reubin O' D. Askew and the Golden Age of Florida Politics*, 26, 27.

34. Dyckman, *Reubin O' D. Askew and the Golden Age of Florida Politics*, 181.

35. Commission on Ethics, *Guide to the Sunshine Amendment*, 1.

36. §112.3191, Fla. Stat.

37. *The Clerk's Manual, 1968–1970*; *The Clerk's Manual, 1966–1968*.

38. Morris, *The Florida Handbook 2013–2014*, 248.

39. Adkins, *Making Modern Florida*, 15, 17, 92.

40. Kiser, interview by Dunbar, May 3, 2016.

41. Claude Kirk, White Paper on Conservation and Recreation, 3, 4, 7.

42. Davis, *The Gulf: The Making of an American Sea*, 404.

43. Kirk, State of the State Address, January 28, 1969.

44. Coburn, *From Yellow Dog Democrats to Red State Republicans*, 71.

45. Chapter 84–310, *Laws of Florida*; see also Barlow, *Our Florida Legacy*, 19.

46. Dyckman, *Reubin O' D. Askew and the Golden Age of Florida Politics*, 85.

47. Latvala, interview by Dunbar. See also § 403.086 (1) (c), Fla. Stat.; chapter 71–259, *Laws of Florida*.

48. Chapter 89–175, *Laws of Florida*.

49. "Water Supply Sources," Tampa Bay Water, http://tampabaywater.org.

50. Colburn, *From Yellow Dog Democrats to Red State Republicans*, 129–30.

51. Chapter 87–97, *Laws of Florida*; § 373.453, Fla. Stat.

52. Bob Martinez, conference with Thomas Pelham and Peter Dunbar, January 6, 1989.

53. Chapter 89–270, *Laws of Florida*; §379.2201 (1) (a), Fla. Stat.

54. Chapter 89–270, *Laws of Florida*; §379.2201 (1) (a), Fla. Stat.

55. Spill Response Task Force meeting, October 16 and 17, 1989; Bob Martinez, meeting with President George H. W. Bush, January 6, 1989.

56. Estus Whitfield and David Gluckman, meeting with Peter Dunbar, March 27, 1989; Estus Whitfield, Charles Lee, and David Gluckman, meeting with Peter Dunbar, April 6, 1989.

57. Patty Woodworth, Estus Whitfield, and John Scherer, meeting with Peter Dunbar, May 1, 1989.

58. Chapter 90–217, *Laws of Florida*. See §259.105, Fla. Stat.

59. Booth Gunter, "It's a Grandiose Scheme to Rescue Florida's Remaining Wild Places," *Tampa Tribune*, February 4, 1990.

60. "Credit Gov. Bob Martinez for Political Vision," editorial, *Miami Herald*, January 28, 1990.

61. Corrigan, *Conservative Hurricane*, 166. See also *Florida Forever Act*, Chapter 99–246, *Laws of Florida* and § 259.105, Fla. Stat.

62. Fla. Const. art. X, § 28.

63. Chapter 2016–1, *Laws of Florida*.

64. Chapter 2016–201, *Laws of Florida*.

65. "What Florida's Good At," *Florida Trend*, May 2018, 81.

66. Kiser, interview by Dunbar, October 4, 2016.

67. Andy Reid, "South Florida Growers Meet Yearly Everglades Cleanup Requests," *Sun Sentinel*, August 8, 2016.

68. "Stormwater Treatment Areas," South Florida Water Management District, https://my.sfwmd.gov.

69. Executive Order 19-12, January 10, 2019.

70. Reagan, "Time for Choosing" speech, October 27, 1964.

71. Kirk Budget Address, April 26, 1967; Brandon Larrabee, "Scott Budget Could Face Legislative Squeeze," *News Service of Florida*, January 31, 2017.

72. *2016 Florida Tax Handbook*, 155.

73. *2016 Florida Tax Handbook*, 74, 127, 98, 91, 58, 93, 46, 50.

74. David Schultz, "Rep. Don Reed King: Among GOP Legislators," *Palm Beach Post-Times*, April 25, 1971.

75. Adam J. Cole, "Sales Tax Holidays: Timing Behavior and Tax Incidence," https://deepblue.lib.umich.edu, 12.

76. *2016 Florida Tax Handbook*, 157, 158.

77. Florida Tax Watch, "Supporting Sunshine State Shoppers," February 2017.

78. Corrigan, *Conservative Hurricane*, 153.

79. Connie Mack, "Responsibility, Not Higher Taxes, Needed," *Sun Sentinel*, February 11, 2002.

80. *2016 Florida Tax Handbook*, 58, 59.

81. Sullivan, "As Governor, Jeb Bush Catered Tax Cuts to the Wealthy."

82. Chapter 2006–312, *Laws of Florida*. See also *2016 Florida Tax Handbook*, 119.

83. Joshua Gillin, "Jeb Bush Says He Cut Florida Taxes by $19 Billion, but Did He Really?," http://politifact.com.

84. "Save Our Homes," http://pcpao.org.

85. Ken Pruitt to Peter Dunbar, January 4, 2019.

86. "Florida Save Our Homes, Amendment 1 (January 2008)," https://ballotpedia.org.

87. Official Results, November 2, 2010 General Election, Florida Department of State, Division of Elections and Official Results, November 6, 2012 General Election, Florida Department of State, Division of Elections.

88. "NFL History-Super Bowl Winners," www.espn.com/nfl/superbowl; "World Series History" and "All-Star Game History," www.baseball-almanac.com; "Stanley Cup Champions and Finalists," www.nhl.com; "NBA Finals: All-Time Champions," www.nba.com/history/finals.

89. Chapter 97–50, *Laws of Florida*; *2016 Florida Tax Handbook*, 59.

90. Chapter 2012–117, *Laws of Florida*; *2016 Florida Tax Handbook*, 65, 157, 158.

91. *2016 Florida Tax Handbook*, Florida Revenue Estimating Conference, 59.

92. Chapter 2003–391, *Laws of Florida*; Chapter 2009–108, *Laws of Florida*; Chapter 2010–24, *Laws of Florida*.

93. *2016 Florida Tax Handbook*, 61, 62; Chapter 2014–06, *Laws of Florida*; Chapter 2011–123, *Laws of Florida*.

94. Jimmy Patronis, speech to FOAA, January 24, 2018; Carrie Salls, "Florida Residents Pay 6th Lowest State Taxes; Some Say Burden Can Be Still Be Lowered," FloridaWatchdog.org, http://watchdog.org.

95. Salls, "Florida Residents Pay 6th Lowest State Taxes."

96. Patronis, speech to FOAA.

97. Colburn, *From Yellow Dog Democrats to Red State Republicans*, 80.

98. Corrigan, *Conservative Hurricane*, 118.

99. Brantley, interview.

100. Brantley, interview.

101. Florida Lottery—History, www.flalottery.com.

102. Corrigan, *Conservative Hurricane*, 122.

103. Robin Safley, interview by Peter Dunbar, October 12, 2016. See also Chapter 96–186, *Laws of Florida*.

104. "Charter Schools," Florida Department of Education, http://www.fldoe.org.

105. CS/CS/SB 858—1997 and Section 1009.537, *Florida Statutes*.

106. Corrigan, *Conservative Hurricane*, 121, 126.

107. § 220.186, Fla. Stat. See also Corrigan, *Conservative Hurricane*, 122–23.

108. § 1002.39, Fla. Stat.

109. The John M. McKay Scholarships for Students with Disabilities, https://www.edchoice.org. See also s. 1002.39, Fla. Stat.

110. Chapter 2016–2, *Laws of Florida.*

111. Beth Kassab, "Gardiner Scholarships a Win for Florida's Special Needs Students," *Orlando Sentinel,* January 29, 2016.

112. Chapter 2007–216, *Laws of Florida.*

113. "CAPE Crusade."

114. § 1003.492 (2), Fla. Stat.

115. "CAPE Crusade."

116. Chapter 2012–129, *Laws of Florida;* Chapter 2000–303, *Laws of Florida;* Chapter 2006–58, *Laws of Florida.*

117. Julie Kay, "Saving the School."

118. Chapter 2002–387, *Laws of Florida;* § 1004.39 (6), Fla. Stat. See also Florida Gulf Coast University, http://www.fgcu.edu.

119. Lloyd Dunkelberger, "State Colleges Defend 4-Year Degrees," *Tallahassee Democrat,* February 11, 2017.

120. Claude Kirk Jr., Address to the Joint Session of the Legislature, April 4, 1967; Kirk, *A Man and His Words,* 18–36; Kirk, Message on Crime to the Florida Legislature, May 3, 1967.

121. Kirk, State of the State Address, January 28, 1969.

122. Kiser, interview by Dunbar, February 7, 2017.

123. Colburn, *From Yellow Dog Democrats to Red State Republicans* 98.

124. See Costello v. Wainwright, 397 F.Supp. 20 (1975); and Costello v. Wainwright, 430 U.S. 325 (1977).

125. Richard Dugger and Patti Woodworth, staff conference with Peter Dunbar, January 4, 1989. See also "Prison Construction," Florida House of Representatives, October 22, 1993.

126. *Journal of the House of Representative,* Special Session A, 1987. See also "Prison Construction," Florida House of Representatives, October 22, 1993.

127. "Florida Conditions Lawsuit Settled after 21 Years," *Prison Legal News,* 14.

128. Peter Dunbar, personal staff notes from the Bundy execution, January 4, 1989.

129. Andrea Hillyer, interview by Peter Dunbar, November 19, 1990.

130. Fla. Const. art I, §.

131. Executive Order 89–34.

132. § 960.001 and § 960.0015, Fla. Stat.

133. § 960.21, Fla. Stat.; Deborah Huey, interview by Peter Dunbar, October 31, 1990.

134. Executive Order 88–134.

135. Chapter 89–281 and Chapter 89–524, *Laws of Florida.*

136. § 893.13 (1), Fla. Stat.

137. § 112.0455, Fla. Stat. enacted as part of Chapter 89–173, *Laws of Florida;* Huey, interview.

138. Bob Martinez, Address to Joint Session of the Legislature, April 3, 1990; see also Chapter 90–112, *Laws of Florida.*

139. "Time Served," PEW Center on the States, 2012, 13.

140. Corrigan, *Conservative Hurricane,* 83.

141. § 775.087, Fla. Stat.

142. Chapter 97–78, *Laws of Florida*; Chapter 98–284, *Laws of Florida*; Chapter 97–194, *Laws of Florida*.

143. Corrigan, *Conservative Hurricane,* 83, 84.

144. Chapter 97–72, *Laws of Florida;* Chapter 97–102, *Laws of Florida.*

145. Chapter 99–132, *Laws of Florida.*

146. Chapter 97–72, *Laws of Florida*; Chapter 97–102, *Laws of Florida* Corrigan; Chapter 99–132, *Laws of Florida; Conservative Hurricane,* 85.

147. Chapter 2005–27, *Laws of Florida.*

148. "Florida Crime Rate Drops Almost 5 Percent," *Pensacola News Journal,* May 20, 2015; Latvala, interview.

149. "2014 Annual Uniform Crime Report," Florida Department of Law Enforcement, http://www.fdle.state.fl.us/Content/FSAC/UCR-Home.aspx.

150. Tyler White, "Gov. Scott Announced 6-Percent Drop in Crime 2017 for the Sunshine State," First State News, May 22, 2018; see also Sanchez, "Investigating Claims about Crime," *Tallahassee Democrat,* October 8, 2018.

151. Janet Reno, Circuit Court Hearing before Judge Clifton Kelly, April, 25, 1989.

152. Constance Johnson, "Richardson Released after 21 Years in Prison: Judge Rules Murder Trial Wasn't Fair," *Orlando Sentinel,* April 26, 1989.

153. Senator Gary Farmer and Representative Bobby DuBose, Groveland Four Press Conference, April 18, 2018; Larry Lee, speech to the House of Representatives, March 8, 2018.

154. Representative Chris Sprowls, Groveland Four Press Conference, April 18, 2018.

155. King, *Devil in the Grove.*

156. *Journal of the House of Representative,* April 18, 2017.

157. CS/HCR 631 (SCR 920): Groveland Four, 2017.

158. Jo, Turner, "'A True Vindication' for Groveland Four," *Tallahassee Democrat,* January 12, 2019.

159. Senator Darryl Rouson, Testimony before Senate Rules Committee, April 25, 2017.

160. CS/HCR 1335 (SCR 920): Arthur G. Dozier School for Boys and Florida School for Boys at Okeechobee, 2017.

161. Chapter 2017–69, *Laws of Florida.*

162. Chapter 76–222, *Laws of Florida*; Kiser, interview by Dunbar, August 2, 2016.

163. Kiser, interview by Dunbar, August 2, 2016; Chapter 1984–80, *Laws of Florida*; Chapter 1987–343, *Laws of Florida.*

164. Chapter 2003–179, *Laws of Florida* and Chapter 2013–210, *Laws of Florida.*

165. Chapter 2013–33, *Laws of Florida.*

166. Chapter 2005–238, *Laws of Florida*; Chapter 2013–137, *Laws of Florida.*

167. Chapter 2000–263, *Laws of Florida*; Chapter 2000–349, *Laws of Florida*; Chapter 2000–367, *Laws of Florida.*

168. Chapter 2014–124, *Laws of Florida*; Chapter 2015–83, *Laws of Florida*; Chapter 2016–40, *Laws of Florida.*

169. Chapter 99–168, *Laws of Florida*; Chapter 2014–124, *Laws of Florida;* Chapter 2014–200, *Laws of Florida*.

Chapter 10. Challenges in an Ever-Changing Political Environment

1. Colburn, *From Yellow Dog Democrats to Red State Republicans*, 12.

2. Bullock et al., *The New Politics of the Old South,* 2nd ed., 267.

3. Colburn, *From Yellow Dog Democrats to Red State Republicans*, 21.

4. Rich Heffley, interview by Mike Haridopolos, December 10, 2008.

5. Jon Mills, interview by Mike Haridopolos, June 10, 2009.

6. James Call, "Florida Democratic Party's Problems with Numbers," *Tallahassee Democrat*, January 6, 2018.

7. Brendan Farrington, "Tale of 2 Parties: Florida GOP High, Democrats Low Ahead of 2018 Races," *Tallahassee Democrat*, January 15, 2017.

8. Alberto Cardenas, interview by Peter Dunbar, January 12, 2017; Ken Pruitt to Peter Dunbar, March 23, 2017.

9. Jeb Bush, interview by Mike Haridopolos, December 21, 2009.

10. Stephen Shiver, interview by Peter Dunbar, July 1, 2016.

11. Bush, interview.

12. Steve Bousquet, "With One Year to Go, Numbers Sum up Rick Scott's Governing Legacy," *Miami Herald*, January 4, 2018.

13. Ledyard King, "Massive Off-shore Drilling Proposed," *Tallahassee Democrat*, January 5, 2018.

14. Chapter 2016–1, *Laws of Florida;* Chapter 2016–201, *Laws of Florida*.

15. Ledyard King, "White House Excludes Florida from Drilling," *Tallahassee Democrat*, January 10, 2018.

16. Emily Mahoney, "Battle Royale: Florida House Gears up for What Could Be Its Biggest Debate of the Session," *Tampa Bay Times*, February 7, 2016.

17. James Call, "Critics Say It Shortchanges Schools and State Workers," *Tallahassee Democrat*, March 12, 2018; Rich Templin, testimony before House Appropriations Committee, February 23, 2018; Alex Leary, "Florida Democrats Say School Massacre a Call for Gun Control," *Tampa Bay Times*, February 15, 2018.

18. Howard, "Arrows and Wheels."

19. Mac Stipanovich, interview by Peter Dunbar, January 5, 2018.

20. Steve Bousquet, "Democrats Demand Assault Weapons Ban; Republicans Call It 'Politically Motivated,'" *Tampa Bay Times*, February 22, 2018.

21. Kirby Wilson, "Here's What the Florida Legislature Looks Like after the 2018 Elections," *Tampa Bay Times*, November 9, 2018.

22. Stipanovich, interview by Dunbar.

23. Stipanovich, interview by Dunbar. See also Dara Kam, "Democrats Hope Tuesday Is a Sign of a 'Blue Wave,'" *Tallahassee Democrat*, February 15, 2018.

24. Greenblatt, "Can Andrew Gillum Break Republicans' Winning Streak in Florida?"

25. Nate Cohn, "A 'Blue' Florida? There Are No Quick Demographic Fixes for Democrats," *New York Times*, February 1, 2018.

26. Jim Turner, "Florida GOP Says It Can Fend off 'Blue Wave,'" *Tallahassee Democrat*, April 8, 2018.

27. Official Results, November 6, 2018 General Election, Florida Department of State, Division of Elections.

28. Colburn, *From Yellow Dog Democrats to Red State Republicans*, 21.

29. Heffley, interview by Haridopolos.

30. Chris Sprowls, interview by Peter Dunbar, December 20, 2017.

31. Heffley, interview by Dunbar, March 21, 2018; Dan Webster, interview by Haridopolos, June 12, 2009; Randy Enwright, interview by Peter Dunbar, March 22, 2018.

32. Enwright, interview.

33. Adam Smith and Eli Zhang, "The Florida House Speaker Who Bashes Special Interests Spends Their Money Lavishly," *Tampa Bay Times*, December 14, 2017.

34. Heffley, interview by Dunbar.

35. Bipartisan Campaign Reform Act of 2002, Pub.L. 107–155; Citizens United v. Federal Election Commission, 55 U.S. 310 (2010).

36. Heffley, interview by Dunbar.

37. Frederka Schouten and Christopher Schnaars, "Wealthy Donors Set Spending Records," *USA Today*, July 23, 2018; Mayer, *Dark Money*, 4499 of 9271; Citizens United v. Federal Election Commission, 55 U.S. 310 (2010).

38. Mayer, *Dark Money*, 4727–28 of 9271.

39. Heffley, interview by Dunbar.

40. Michael Dobson to Peter Dunbar, March 12, 2018.

41. Maggie Severns and Marc Caputo, "Progressive Billionaires Fall for Florida Gillum," *Politico*, October 1, 2018; Caitlin Ostroff, Emily L. Mahoney, and Ben Wieder, "National Megadonors, with Eyes on 2020, Flood Florida Governor's Race with Cash," *Miami Herald*, October 23, 2018; Melanie Payne, "DeSantis Leads with Big Donors in Governor Race," *Fort Myers News-Press*, October 30, 2018.

42. Severns and Caputo, "Progressive Billionaires Fall for Florida Gillum."

43. Enwright, interview.

44. James Call, "The Fight for the GOP's Soul," *Tallahassee Democrat*, January 6, 2018.

45. Toni Jennings, interview by Haridopolos, July 15, 2009; Heffley, interview by Dunbar.

46. Bullock et al., *The New Politics of the Old South,* 2nd ed., 267.

47. Steve Bousquet, "With One Year to Go, Numbers Sum up Rick Scott's Governing Legacy," *Miami Herald*, January 4, 2018; Bullock et al., *The New Politics of the Old South,* 2nd ed., 267.

48. Jose De Cordoba and Arian Campo-Flores, "Like the Cubans before Them, Venezuela Exiles Are Transforming Florida Politics," *Wall Street Journal*, December 14, 2017.

49. Chris Finkbeiner, interview by Peter Dunbar, April 10, 2018; Stipanovich, interview by Dunbar.

50. Cohn, "A 'Blue' Florida? There Are No Quick Demographic Fixes for Democrats."

51. Shiver, interview.

52. Official Results, November 5, 2002 General Election, Florida Department of State, Division of Elections.

53. Mayer, *Dark Money*, 3348 of 9271; James Call, "Gov. Scott Mum on 2018 Run," *Tallahassee Democrat*, December 27, 2017.

54. Jim Saunders, "Numbers Count the Ways Voters Have Changed," *Tallahassee Democrat*, October 28, 2018.

55. Smith and Zhang, "The Florida House Speaker Who Bashes Special Interests Spends Their Money Lavishly."

56. De Cordoba and Campo-Flores, "Like the Cubans before Them, Venezuela Exiles are Transforming Florida Politics."

57. Cohn, "A 'Blue' Florida? There Are No Quick Demographic Fixes for Democrats."

58. Carmen Sesin, "Puerto Ricans Could Transform Florida Politics, and Parties Are Taking Notice," NBC News, November 27, 2017, https://www.nbcnews.com; De Cordoba and Campo-Flores, "Like the Cubans Before Them, Venezuela Exiles are Transforming Florida Politics"; Garcia, "Influx."

59. Michael Van Sickler, "Florida Politicians Are Courting Displaced Puerto Ricans," *Tampa Bay Times*, January 11, 2018.

60. "As Influx of Puerto Ricans Continues, Koch-Backed Group Starts Seeking Them out in Florida," *Washington Post*, January 8, 2018.

61. Rick Scott, interview by Mike Haridopolos, November 30, 2018.

62. Steve Bousquet, "Online Voter Registration Favors Democrats over GOP in Early Run," *Tampa Bay Times*, November 20, 2017.

63. Howard, "Arrows and Wheels."

64. Howard, "Arrows and Wheels."

65. Stipanovich, interview by Dunbar.

66. Stipanovich, interview by Dunbar. See also §101.021, Fla. Stat.

67. Steve Bousquet, "People Want to Vote out Politicians Who Oppose Gun Control: History Isn't on Their Side," *Tampa Bay Times*, March 5, 2018; Evan Bayh, CNBC interview on *Power Lunch,* January 22, 2018.

68. Official Results, November 6, 2018 General Election, Florida Department of State, Division of Elections.

69. James Call, "Gillum and DeSantis Make Closing Case in Governor's Race," *Tallahassee Democrat*, November 6, 2018.

70. Jeffrey Schweers, "Rescinding Concession, Gillum Calls for Count," *Tallahassee Democrat*, November 11, 2018.

71. John McCarthy, "Vote Counting Spills into the Court System," *Florida Today,* November 13, 2018.

72. Jennifer Ungru, interview by Peter Dunbar, November 8, 2018; Marc Dunbar, interview by Peter Dunbar, November 21, 2018; Greg Black, interview by Peter Dunbar, November 16, 2018.

73. John McCarthy, "Recount Better Than '00, but Fixes Needed," *Florida Today,* November 18, 2018.

74. Official Results, November 6, 2018 General Election, Florida Department of State, Division of Elections.

75. Stipanovich, interview by Dunbar.

76. Sprowls, interview, December 20, 2017.

77. Heffley, interview, March 21, 2018; Marc Dunbar, interview by Peter Dunbar, March 17, 2018.

78. McCarthy, "Recount Better Than '00, but Fixes Needed."

BIBLIOGRAPHY

Primary Sources

Interviews (by Peter Dunbar unless otherwise noted)

Audie, Charlotte. October 24, 2018.
Bahl, Mat. November 11, 2016.
Baker, Amy. April 10, 2017.
Bayh, Evan. CNBC interview on *Power Lunch*. January 22, 2018.
Bayliss, Slater. December 5, 2017.
Bean, Aaron. By Peter Dunbar and Mike Haridopolos. October 25, 2016. Ocala.
Bebout, Mary. November 7, 2018.
Bitner, David. By Mike Haridopolos. June 22, 2009.
Black, Greg. November 16, 2018.
Blair, Matthew. April 6, 2018.
Brantley, Bobby. July 13, 2016.
Brodie, James. August 2, 2016; October 4, 2016; November 1, 2016; December 6, 2016; and March 14, 2017.
Bruce, Doug. September 30, 2016.
Bush, Jeb. By Mike Haridopolos. December 21, 2009.
Campbell, Pamela. December 8, 2016. Ponte Vedra.
Cardenas, Alberto. January 12, 2017.
Coates, Richard. October 22, 2019.
Corbella, Agustin. December 15, 2016.
Darling, Doug. January 27, 2017.
DeFoor, Allison. By Mike Haridopolos. April 19, 2009.
Diaz-Balart, Mario. By Mike Haridopolos. July 15, 2009.
Dudley, Charlie. October 24, 2018.
Dunbar, Marc. May 2, 2016; October 10, 2016; April 1, 2018; and November 13 and 21, 2018.

Eagle, Dane. October 22, 2018.

Enwright, Randy. March 22, 2018.

Fasano, Mike. By Mike Haridopolos. January 13, 2009.

Feeney, Tom. By Mike Haridopolos. December 16, 2008.

Finkbeiner, Chris. July 14, 2016; December 1, 2016; and April 10, 2018.

Frey, Lou. By Mike Haridopolos. July 14, 2009.

Gallagher, Tom. August 2, 2016; and October 4, 2016.

Gomez, Mike. November 23, 2018.

Green, Shelley. November 28, 2018.

Grissom, Mike. November 8, 2018.

Gruters, Joe. September 3, 2018.

Hagaman, Lloyd C. By Ben Houston. July 1, 2000. University of Florida Samuel Proctor Oral History Program.

Harrell, Mike. October 4, 2018.

Hart, David. October 30, 2018.

Heffley, Rich. By Mike Haridopolos. December 10, 2008.

———. March 21, 2018.

Herron, Nora. March 15, 2017.

Heuchan, Brecht. By Mike Haridopolos. March 16, 2009.

Hillyer, Andrea. November 19, 1990.

Hoffmann, Marion. December 14, 2017.

Huey, Deborah. October 31, 1990.

Isaac, Erin. November 14, 2018.

Jennings, Toni. By Mike Haridopolos. July 15, 2009.

Jogerst, Brian. March 10, 2017.

Johnson, David. November 28, 2018.

Johnson, Jon. February 13, 2017.

Johnson, Marian. September 13, 2018.

Kelly, Kurt. February 9, 2017.

Kiser, S. Curtis. By Mike Haridopolos. January 15, 2009.

———. April 5, 2016; May 3, 2016; August 2, 2016; October 4, 2016; November 1, 2016; November 8, 2016; and February 7, 2017.

Latvala, Jack. September 22, 2016. St Petersburg.

Leary, Phil. September 12, 2018.

Magill, Jim. February 6, 2017.

Mahler, Rick. March 15, 2017.

McGee, Gene. By Mike Haridopolos. January 7, 2009.

———. By P. Dunbar and M. Haridopolos. October 25, 2016. Ocala.

McKinnon, Genean Hawkins. May 18, 2018.

McPherson, Scott. March 14, 2017.

Mears, Kathy. October 4, 2016. Tallahassee.

Messersmith, Frank. October 4, 2016; and November 1, 2016. Tallahassee.

Miller, Mike. August 18, 2016. Orlando.

Mills, Jon. By Mike Haridopolos. 2009.

Mitchell, Emmett. March 27, 2017.

Mitchell, Paul. January 24, 2018.

Morroni, John. May 24, 2016.

Mortham, Sandra. October 4, 2016; and May 7, 2018.

Moya, Chris. January 5, 2017; and October 22, 2018.

Palmer, Andy. December 4, 2017; and November 19, 2018.

Patchett, Dale. March 14, 2017.

Patronis, Jimmy. August 23, 2018.

Pepper, Kirk. November 8, 2018.

Plante, Kenneth. By Mike Haridopolos. January 15, 2009.

Poole, Van. April 5, 2016; and March 14, 2017.

Pruitt, Ken. January 17, 2017.

Quick, Cathy. August 3, 2018.

Reichelderfer, Marc. October 23, 2018.

———. By Mike Haridopolos. October 23, 2018.

Reid, Todd. January 9, 2017.

Richmond, Ronald R. April 5, 2016; May 3, 2016; and October 4, 2016. Tallahassee.

Roberts, Clay. March 20, 2017.

Rojas, Luis. By Mike Haridopolos. January 15, 2009.

Roth, Cari. April 30, 2016.

Russell, Monica. November 14, 2018.

Safley, R. Z. May 3, 2016; and November 26, 2018.

Safley, Robin. October 12, 2016.

Scott, Jim. By Mike Haridopolos. January 7, 2009.

Scott, Rick. By Mike Haridopolos. November 30, 2018

Shiver, Stephen. July 1, 2016.

Sklar, William. October 23, 2018.

Slade, Tom. By Mike Haridopolos. June 4, 2009.

Sprowls, Chris. September 27, 2016; February 27, 2017; and December 20, 2017.

Stargel, John. March 9, 2017.

Stipanovich, Mac. By Mike Haridopolos. August 5, 2009.

———. January 5, 2018.

Stone, Bruce. July 30, 2010. Palm Beach.

Terraferma, Frank. August 17, 2016; and January 25, 2017.

Thorn, Eric. By Mike Haridopolos. November 3, 2009.

———. March 19, 2018.

Thrasher, John. By Mike Haridopolos. January 6, 2009.

Ungru, Jennifer. November 8, 2018; and November 26, 2018.

Webster, Dan. By M. Haridopolos. June 12, 2009.

Whitis, Derek. By M. Haridopolos. October 23, 2018.

Wiles, Lanny. January 9, 2017.

Woodburn, Jeff. March 31, 2017.

Yarbrough, Cameron. November 14, 2018.

Young, Dana. March 20, 2017.

Meetings

Bergstrom, Debbie. Meeting with Peter Dunbar, April 1990. Tallahassee.

DeSantis, Ron. Campaign reception, October 22, 2018.

Dugger, Richard, and Patti Woodworth. Staff conference with Peter Dunbar. January 4, 1989.

Groveland Four Press Conference, April 18, 2018.

Hill, David. Presentation to Martinez staff, May 1990.

Martinez, Bob. Conference with Thomas Pelham and Peter Dunbar, January 6, 1989. Tallahassee.

———. Meeting with President George H. W. Bush, January 6, 1989.

Reed, Donald H., Jr. Meeting with Peter Dunbar, July 1967. Tallahassee.

———. Meeting with Peter Dunbar, June 1968. Tallahassee.

———. Meeting with Peter Dunbar, May 1969. Tallahassee.

———. Staff conference with Peter Dunbar, April 1967; May 1967; and January 1968.

Reno, Janet. Circuit Court Hearing before Judge Clifton Kelly, April 25, 1989.

Rouson, Senator Darryl. Testimony before Senate Rules Committee, April 25, 2017.

Spill Response Task Force meeting, October 16 and 17, 1989.

Templin, Rich. Testimony before House Appropriations Committee, February 23, 1018.

Whitfield, Estus, and David Gluckman. Meeting with Peter Dunbar, March 27, 1989.

Whitfield, Estus, Charles Lee, and David Gluckman. Meeting with Peter Dunbar, April 6, 1989.

Woodworth, Patty. Meeting with Peter Dunbar, January 10, 1989.

Woodworth, Patty, Estus Whitfield, and John Scherer. Meeting with Peter Dunbar. May 1, 1989.

Miscellaneous

"Betty Castor." Bureau of Educational and Cultural Affairs, United States Department of State. https://eca.state.gov.

Biographical Directory of the United States Congress, 1774–Present. http://bioguide.congress.gov.

"Chronology of the Chief Justices of Florida." Public Information Office, State of Florida. https://www.floridasupremecourt.org/content/download/242931/2142417/chiefjustices.pdf.

The Clerk's Manual, 1966–1968, through *2018–2020*. Florida House of Representatives.

Constitution of Florida.

Dunbar, Peter. Personal staff notes, March 16, 1990; and November 7, 1990.

Florida Constitution of 1885.

"Florida Forever." Florida Department of Environmental Protection. http://dep.state.fl.us.

Florida Senate, The, 2012–2014.

Florida Senate, The, 2014–2016.

Florida Statutes.

Florida Tax Watch. "Supporting Sunshine State Shoppers," February 2017.

Journal of the House of Representatives.

Journal of the Senate.

Kirk, Claude R., Jr. White Paper on Conservation and Recreation, 1966.

———. White Paper on Finance and Taxation, 1966.

Laws of Florida.

Phelps, John B. *The People in Lawmaking in Florida 1822–2001.* Florida House of Representatives, 2002.

"Prison Construction." Florida House of Representatives, October 22, 1993.

Reed, Donald H., Jr. Personal Kirk campaign file, 1966.

The Rules, Florida House of Representatives, 1980/1982.

Rules of the House of Representatives.

Senate Handbook 1976–1978 through 2016–2018. Also titled *The Florida Senate.*

Staff Report #1. House Republican Office, July 15, 1971.

Staff Report #2. House Republican Office, October 11, 1971.

2014 Annual Uniform Crime Report. Florida Department of Law Enforcement. http://www.fdle.state.fl.us/Content/FSAC/UCR-Home.aspx.

2016 Florida Tax Handbook. Florida Revenue Estimating Conference.

Speeches and Presentations

Johnson, Marian. Presentation to the Annual Conference of the Florida Outdoor Advertising Association, St. Petersburg, September 22, 2016.

Kirk, Claude, Jr. Address to the Joint Session of the Legislature, April 4, 1967.

———. Budget Address, April 26, 1967.

———. Message on Crime to the Florida Legislature, May 3, 1967.

———. State of the State Address, January 28, 1969.

Lee, Larry. Speech to the House of Representatives, March 8, 2018.

Martinez, Bob. Address to the Joint Session of the Legislature, April 3, 1990.

Patronis, Jimmy. Speech to FOAA, January 24, 2018.

Reagan, Ronald. "Time for Choosing" speech, October 27, 1964.

Secondary Sources

Adkins, Mary E. *Making Modern Florida.* Gainesville: University Press of Florida, 2016.

"Alfred Hoffman, Jr., Ambassador to Portugal." U.S. Department of State Archive, January 20, 2009.

"Ballard Partners, Ft. Lauderdale." *Florida Trend*, May 7, 2018.

Barlow, Margaret. *Our Florida Legacy.* Tallahassee: Legislative Research Center & Museum, 2004.

Bousquet, Steve. "$1 Billion Tax Cuts Top Florida Governor's 2016 Priorities." *Governing*, January 13, 2016.

Bullock, Charles, et al. *The New Politics of the Old South*. 2nd ed. Lanham, MD: Rowman and Littlefield, 2007.

"CAPE Crusade." *Florida Trend*, August 2017.

Colburn, David R. *Florida's Gubernatorial Politics in the Twentieth Century*. Gainesville: University Press of Florida, 1980.

———. *From Yellow Dog Democrats to Red State Republicans: Florida and Its Politics since 1940*. Gainesville: University Press of Florida, 2007.

Corrigan, Matthew T. *Conservative Hurricane: How Jeb Bush Remade Florida*. Gainesville: University Press of Florida, 2014.

Davis, Jack E. *The Gulf: The Making of an American Sea*. New York: Liveright, 2017.

Dunbar, Carl O. *Before They Were the Black Sheep*. Gainesville: University Press of Florida, 2011.

Dyckman, Martin. *Reubin O' D. Askew and the Golden Age of Florida Politics*. Gainesville: University Press of Florida, 2011.

"Florida Conditions Lawsuit Settled after 21 Years." *Prison Legal News*, August 1993.

"Francis Rooney, Ambassador to the Holy See." U.S. Department of State Archive, January 20, 2009.

Garcia, Jason. "Heavy Hitter." *Florida Trend*, March 2017.

———. "Influx." *Florida Trend*, January 2018.

Glines, Carroll V. *The Doolittle Raid*. Atglen, Pa.: Schiffer, 1988.

Green, Amanda. "A Brief History of Air Conditioning." *Popular Mechanics*, January 1, 2015.

Greenblatt, Alan. "Can Andrew Gillum Break Republicans' Winning Streak in Florida?" *Governing*, October 30, 2018.

Guide to the Sunshine Amendment and Code of Ethics for Public Officers and Employees. Tallahassee: State of Florida Commission on Ethics, 2016.

Halberstam, David. "Claude Kirk and the Politics of Promotion." *Harper's*, April 30, 1968.

Hare, Julianne. *Tallahassee: A Capital City History*. Charleston, SC: Acadia, 2002.

Hathorn, Billy B. "Cramer v. Kirk: The Florida Republican Schism of 1970." *Florida Historical Quarterly* 68 no. 4 (1990): 403.

"Hayden Dempsey Rejoins Greenberg Traurig to Lead Florida Governmental Affairs Practice." *Business Wire*, September 13, 2011. http://www.businesswire.com.

Historical Events of the Republican and Democratic Parties, United States Senate Vote. www.govtrack.us.

Howard, Mark A. "Arrows and Wheels." *Florida Trend*, May 2018.

———. "Jeb's Legacy." *Florida Trend*, March 1, 2006.

"John D. Rood, Ambassador to the Bahamas." U.S. Department of State Archive, January 20, 2009.

The John M. McKay Scholarships for Students with Disabilities. https://www.edchoice.org.

Kallina, Edmund F., Jr. *Claude Kirk and the Politics of Confrontation*. Gainesville: University Press of Florida, 1993.

Karl, Frederick B. *The 57 Club: My Four Decades in Florida Politics*. Gainesville: University Press of Florida, 2010.

Kay, Julie. "Saving the School." *ABA Journal*. http://www.abajournal.com.

Key, V. O., Jr. *Southern Politics in State and Nation*. New York: Knopf, 1949.

King, Gilbert. *Devil in the Grove: Thurgood Marshall, the Groveland Boys, and the Dawn of a New America*. New York: Harper Perennial, 2012.

Kirk, Claude, Jr. *A Man and His Words*. N.p.: Executive Press, 1968.

Larrabee, Brandon. "Scott Budget Could Face Legislative Squeeze." *News Service of Florida*, January 31, 2017.

Lemieux, George, and Laura Mize. *Florida Made: The Twenty-Five Most Important Figures Who Shaped the State*. N.p.: History Press, 2018.

MacKay, Buddy. *How Florida Happened: The Political Education of Buddy MacKay*. With Rich Edmonds. Gainesville: University Press of Florida, 2010.

Mayer, Jane. *Dark Money: The Hidden History of the Billionaires behind the Radical Right*. New York: Doubleday, 2016.

Mormino, Gary. "1958: The Dawn of Modern Florida." *Florida Trend*, May 2018.

Morris, Allen. *The Florida Handbook 1967–1968; 1973–1974; 1987–1988*. Tallahassee, FL: Peninsular, 1967, 1973, and 1987.

———. *The Florida Handbook 1995–1996; 1998–2000; 2013–2014*. Tallahassee: Florida House of Representatives, 1995, 1998, and 2014.

———. *Reconsiderations—The Emergence of a Party*. Tallahassee: Florida House of Representatives, 1990.

———. *Reconsiderations—The Speakers: Donald LeGrand Tucker*. Tallahassee: Florida House of Representatives, August 1989.

———. *Reconsiderations—The Speakers: Ralph Harris Haben, Jr.* Tallahassee: Florida House of Representatives, July 1990.

"Nathaniel Reed." *Florida Trend*, September 2018.

Noonan, Peggy. *What I Saw at the Revolution: A Political Life in the Reagan Era*. New York: Random House, 1990.

Padgett, Tim. "Mel Martinez." *Time*, August 22, 2005.

———. "Rick Scott's Tea-Friendly Budget Cuts: Too Deep?" *Time*, February 11, 2011.

Presidential Elections. http://uselectionatlas.org.

Pudlow, Jan. "Sen. Flores Was Raised to 'Love the Constitution' and the Rule of Law." *Florida Bar News*, December 15, 2017.

Scher, Richard K. *Politics in the New South*, 2nd ed. Armonk, NY: M. E. Sharpe, 1997.

Sullivan, Martin. "As Governor, Jeb Bush Catered Tax Cuts to the Wealthy." *Forbes*, April 15, 2015.

Tunnell, Ted. "Creating the Propaganda of History: Southern Editors and the Origins of Carpetbagger and Scalaway." *Journal of Southern History* 72, no. 4 (November 2006): 789–822.

Vogel, Mike. "Florida's Richest 25." *Florida Trend*, April 2017.

Waczewski, Joe. "An Analysis of the Impact of Term Limits on the Legislature." Reubin O'D. Askew School of Public Administration and Policy. December 2006.

Wells, Charley. *Inside "Bush v. Gore."* Gainesville: University Press of Florida, 2013.

"What Florida's Good At." *Florida Trend*, May 2018.

INDEX

Page numbers in *italics* refer to photographs.

PETER DUNBAR is a partner in the law Firm of Dean-Mead and former representative for Pasco and Pinellas Counties. He is a member of the American College of Real Estate Lawyers, was an adjunct professor at Florida State University College of Law, and has recently been selected by his peers as a member of *Florida Trend*'s Florida Legal Elite Hall of Fame. He is the editor of *Before They Were Black Sheep: Marine Fighting Squadron VMF-214 and the Battle for the Solomon Islands* and author of *The Condominium Concept: A Practical Guide for Officers, Owners, Realtors, Attorneys, and Directors.*

MIKE HARIDOPOLOS served in both the Florida House (2000–2003) and Florida Senate (2003–12) and was elected president of the Florida Senate from 2010 to 2012. A college instructor since 1993, he was appointed to the University of Florida Bob Graham Center as an adjunct instructor in political science from 2014 to 2018. He now leads MJH Consulting and also serves as a political analyst for FOX 35 WOFL News. He is the author of *Florida Legislative History and Processes* and coauthor of *10 Big Issues Facing Our Generation.*